MAKING SENSE OF HISTORY

To Ben and Patti Sandars

For their friendship and encouragement

MAKING SENSE OF HISTORY

GEOFFREY PARTINGTON

Rev. date: 07/17/2013

To order additional copies of this book, contact:
Xlibris LLC
1-800-455-039
www.Xlibris.com.au
Orders@Xlibris.com.au
502469

CONTENTS

The Author

Geoffrey Partington was born in 1930 in Middleton, then a town of cotton mills just north of Manchester. His father was a cotton spinner and his mother came from a coal-mining family in Atherton, close to Leigh and Bolton. He attended council schools and in 1941 became the first child from Boarshaw Primary School to win a scholarship place at Queen Elizabeth's School, Middleton. In 1948 he won a bursary to Bristol University to read History. He was a Sunday school teacher in the Temple Street Baptist Church and became a youthful lay preacher.

At Bristol University he gained colours in football and was awarded Upper Second Honours in History. After two years of National Service in the Royal Air Force, he became a history teacher in Glendale Grammar School, Wood Green, and then Twyford Comprehensive School, Acton. He became a senior lecturer in history and history of education in Doncaster and Coventry Colleges of Education, headmaster of Bungay Modern School in Suffolk and an Education Officer in the London Borough of Waltham Forest.

During his classroom years Partington was very active politically. He was elected President of the Middlesex Country Association of the National Union of Teachers, Secretary of its Acton and Ealing branches and National Secretary of the Teachers' Committee for Nuclear Disarmament.

He was an Examiner in History for the Associated Examining Board and the East Anglian Examining Board. He added to his academic qualifications an Honours degree in Sociology and Economics, and the Academic Diploma in Education, of London University and the Master of Education degree of Bristol University. He only returned to serious scholarship as he became disillusioned with political activism. In 1976 his pioneering *Women Teachers in England and Wales in the Twentieth Century,* was published by the National Foundation for Educational Research, which also published in 1980 *The Idea of a Historical Education.*

By that time his Australian-born wife and he had emigrated to Australia with their two children. He taught for nineteen years in the Flinders University of South Australia and then for two years in the University of the South Pacific in Fiji. In Australia he has written ten books, six chapters in books and over a hundred published articles. He was awarded PhD by the University of Adelaide and commissioned to report on teacher education in Britain and New Zealand, and on Social Studies in New Zealand schools. He was a member of the South Australian Experts Consultative Committee on the State Constitution in 1998 and of the Canberra History Summit of 2006.

Introduction

This is an invitation to take a new interest in history or to extend and deepen an existing interest. It tries to help to make decisions about what, apart from purely personal connections we have with events, places, and people, is most important of the valuable and important knowledge available about the past. It examines what some leading intellectuals find most interesting and significant in the past. Then come some short historical sketches, linked loosely by the unexpectedness of events.

Chapter I proposes five Priorities to guide content selection: livelihoods, security from violence, freedoms, relationships, and ideas. With each Priority are some questions and 'Reflections'. They are the sort of questions that I ask myself and my Reflections when starting on a fresh study or revisiting an old one. Each person will have a different range of knowledge and experiences to evoke. Guiding questions help me focus on what I want particularly to find, but do not prevent me from picking up information and ideas I did not have before. Similarly the Reflections suggest which times and places I have found most interesting but do not act as blinkers or a straitjacket for me or restrict your own range of responses.

My own values often show through. I distrust dogmatic claims about lessons from history and see the benefit of historical study as much more like gaining proverbial wisdom than solving quadratic equations or testing Boyle's Law. This does not imply that quantities and numbers are irrelevant. Very often it is only through patient reckoning that we can know whether our first interpretations are valid, but even the deepest insight that history can provide is not an equivalent to Pythagoras' Law. Historical truths are not worse nor better but different. Outside the mind identical actions may cause identical reactions, but the mind acts on reasons, sometimes very bad ones, and well-nigh identical situations are followed very often by highly disparate responses. Human life is underdetermined to a far wider extent than system makers and prophets have maintained.

Prejudice cannot be completely removed from historical study, nor should it, since it is often the residue of painful experiences. It could be said that prejudices are the chief lessons of history! But they can be, should be, and often are under control.[1] One crucial point is whether we recognize bias on 'our' side of an argument as well as the other; fair assessment of evidence and transparency should be expected from all contestants. There should be little difficulty in explaining ideas and actions in a dispassionate way. I have been active in the support of opposed political creeds, but I think that my expositions and explanations have usually been acceptable to those who disagreed with me.

One very difficult problem for me has been and remains the tension between breadth and depth. I fear I may have sacrificed depth for breadth, because my interests changed over the years and my teaching duties changed radically. But I might never have got the balance right, even in my own estimation, let alone that of others. Chapter 2 considers a few of the difficult problems that constantly arise in historical study.

I show in Chapter 3 how the British colonists and their officials tried, although not hard enough, to share with the indigenous peoples what they thought was worth having in their own culture and traditions. Chapter 4 has a double purpose. The course of events is itself of considerable intrinsic interest, but particularly relevant to this book is the ongoing invention of fresh myth. Chapter 5 examines allegations that Australian governments and many Australians have committed genocide against the indigenous peoples, Chapter 6 investigates the reasons for the White Australia Policy and Chapter 7 whether cannibalism has ever been practiced in Australia. Chapter 8 examines the perspectives on the past held by some eminent Australian academics, together with Roger Sandall, Robert Hughes, and A. J. P. Taylor. Chapter 9 examines a campaign in England against R. J. Unstead, who was for many years a highly popular author of history books for primary school children in England. Chapter 10 addresses two groups of women: Old Testament women and Byzantine empresses.

My objections to determinism led me to include as Chapter 11 some short 'tales of the unexpected', ranging from Croesus and Cyrus to Winston Churchill and Margaret Thatcher. Then follows as Chapter 12 a pairing of the Australian diplomat Sir Walter Crocker, and the gifted, if erratic, Londoner Malcolm Muggeridge. Chapter 13 discusses ideas held about the past by the two arguably ablest radical writers of their generation in Australia, Henry Lawson and Joseph Furphy. Chapter 14 considers the prospect of an Australian Republic. The final chapter recalls a few aspects of the 2006 Canberra History Summit convened by the Hon. Julie Bishop, then Minister of Education in the Howard Coalition Government.

In the first appendix some illuminating passages by Merlin Donald, a Canadian Professor of Cognitive Neuropsychology, on the relationship between mind, experience, and human evolution are given. The second appendix is a review of *Is History Fiction?* by Ann Curthoys & John Docker.

Only a minute proportion of events has survived to be recorded. Many events have left their traces, however, and since literacy was mastered documentation of various sorts has increased beyond our capacity to cope. Research by archaeologists, anthropologists, and historians over the last 2,500, but mainly in the last 300, years takes us back about 10,000 years ago to a time when we can first envisage how our ancestors lived. R. G. Collingwood, a great prehistorian as well as a philosopher of history, advised, 'If you can enter the mind of Neolithic man and make his thoughts your own you can then write his history, but not otherwise.'[2] It is a tall order but can be accomplished at least in part. Once writing was invented, however, to supplement oral tradition in songs and stories and as spade work revealed more and more about the past, we began to get a much better chance of getting inside the minds of the long since dead, at least to a similar extent that we understood people in distant countries, alive at the same time as us, but whom we never see. Even that limiting condition has been eroded in the last century and a half with the invention of photography. We should not, of course, believe everything we see, let alone read. In September 1939, the Gestapo provided the German High Command with prisoners, dressed them in Polish uniforms, and shot them as though they had been intercepted crossing the German frontier.

Until, say, 1500, there were people, nearly all men as it happens, who could, if sufficiently determined and capable, find out nearly everything that was recorded about the past of their own society and perhaps somewhat wider. There were more artefacts, parchments, and manuscripts than one person could manage, but many of these were only copies and don't count as extra knowledge. There is no longer any hope of such an accomplishment, What then from the enormous and indigestible amount of information about the past should we study? There are very many different very good selections that may be made, that mandatory national, or global, history syllabuses should be resisted. That said, some selections are unbalanced and inferior. Often the prime weakness is not the choices taken individually, but a disparity, either way round between breadth and depth. Both breadth and depth have good claims, but one contradicts the other so that uneasy compromises are all that are available to us. It would largely negate its value if the study of history were conducted always on the surface of events. That would be like learning the names and basic plots of every play by Shakespeare instead of achieving depth of understanding of even one great play such as *King Lear* or *Hamlet*. At the opposite end requiring avoidance, we have Sir Walter Elliott who, Jane Austen relates, 'never took up any other book than *The Baronage* . . . this was the page in which his favourite volume was always opened: Elliot of Kellynch Hall'. Some explicit principles or criteria of selection seemed to be sorely needed.

I wrote in 1980 a book published in England by the National Foundation for Educational Research: *The Idea of an Historical Education*. I found out only recently by accident that it had become a key text in history methods in some teacher education courses in Britain and was an important component in some GCSE courses. The national Curriculum Authority noted that 'the issue of 'Significance' has received a sizable amount of attention with many articles in the Historical Association's *Teaching History*. One of the first to discuss this issue was Geoffrey Partington's *The Idea of an Historical Education*'. Another unit published by the Curriculum Authority acknowledged that 'a sizeable amount of work has been done on the concept of "significance" much building on the pioneering thoughts of Geoffrey Partington's *The Idea of an Historical Education*'. My ideas on history teaching have also been adopted, or rather adapted, in Canada, particularly by Professor Stephane Levesque of the University of Ottawa, whose *Thinking Historically* will be read with interest and benefit by anyone who has found anything worthwhile in this book.

Which times and places most deserve to be studied? Geoffrey Elton held that 'no argument exists which successfully establishes a hierarchy of worth among historical periods or regions as such',[3] and the great German historian Von Ranke said that 'all ages are equally immediate to God'.[4] In contrast, most people regard their 'own' past as having far more importance than any other. The 'own' may, of course, refer to a family, clan, ideology, religion, area, ethnicity, nationality, or even gender. Yet some periods or generations seem to contain far more significant content than others. Is not The Netherlands more deserving of study in the seventeenth than in the nineteenth century, or the Greek city states during the fifth century BC than Greece two centuries earlier or later? In many ways, the initial choice of topics, periods, or places is even more important than the actual teaching itself in determining whether genuine history or distorted propaganda or special pleading is on offer.

In some other fields of study, problems of bias and distortion in the classroom or lecture theatre are much less acute, because content and sequence are not contestable in the way history is. In mathematics, arithmetic will come before algebra and simple before quadratic equations, and there are stages that cannot be omitted or are omitted only at the price of grave confusion and misunderstandings. In teaching or studying history we often start *in media res*—in the middle of it all.

Von Ranke appreciated that fiction could attract to the study of history some people who would otherwise not have any interest in the past. Von Ranke admired Sir Walter Scott, the true founder of the broad-sweeping historical novel, but Von Ranke was severe on Scott for his errors. For example, Von Ranke wrote: 'Among other things it distressed me that in *Quentin Durward* he treated Charles the Bold and Louis XI in a manner quite contrary to historical evidence'[5] However Veronica Wedgwood, from whom I derived this information, commented that German writers of Scott's time were even more cavalier than Scott with the truth: Schiller had Joan of Arc killed in battle rather than burned at the stake and Goethe made Egmont a young lover at the time of his execution by the Spaniards, whereas he was an elderly married man by then. Shakespeare changed ages for dramatic effect as well. In *Henry IV* Hotspur is made the same age as Prince Hal, the future Henry V, to make their rivalry in the play more realistic. In *King Lear* his characters include the King of France and the Duke of Burgundy, neither political unit then created, any more than in the non-existent England were there Dukes of Gloucester and Kent. But then we do not read *King Lear* for the political history of the Britons, any more than, if we are wise, we view almost any film in the hope of learning 'real' history. Australian films such as *Breaker Morant* and *Gallipoli* are bad historically but not so bad as the typical Western or films of the Stalin and Mao eras. Most historical films leave the teacher with the problem of erasing false history that is more convincing than what we hope are truths in routine classroom explanations.

My 1980 book aimed to show the relevance of critical philosophy of history to the work of history teachers and practicing historians. It examined the claims of 'outlines' against 'studies in depth' and of different balances between them. The first 'criterion of significance' I proposed was 'importance to people in the past': I contended that, since the major purpose of studying history is to transcend parochialism and to understand other people better, we should put what interested or concerned the people we were studying before our own interests. Then followed 'objective criteria': profundity since, even for a tailor or dressmaker, changes in dress are unlikely to seem to have, or in fact did have, as profound an effect on human life as, say, industrialization or conversions to Islam; quantity—the number of people affected; and durability: how long did an event or person exert an important influence? These four criteria were not placed in any order of importance.

It must be conceded that only a few history teachers in the United Kingdom and probably an even smaller proportion in Australia show much interest in philosophy of history, whether that of model makers, such as Plato, Vico, Condorcet, Hegel, Marx, Spengler, and Toynbee, or of 'critical' philosophers of history, such as F. H. Bradley, Collingwood, W. H. Walsh, M. Mandelbaum, P. L. Gardiner, E. H. Carr, and W. Dray. My interest in critical philosophy of history was first aroused during my 'education year': the year in which British graduates were prepared as teachers. Mine was spent in the Institute of Education of London University, and I was fortunate to have as my tutor Hedley Burston, one of the ablest philosophers of history in Britain. Another distinguished historian/philosopher had lectured me in my first year at Bristol University when I was eighteen, but I was too callow to appreciate him, especially since he lectured on ancient history in a thick Italian accent difficult for most of us to interpret accurately. In later years, I cursed myself as one of the ignorant swine before whom Arnoldo Momigliano had cast his pearls in vain.

Arguments that contemporary events should largely determine what history we teach are of two very different types. One demands that contemporary or very recent history itself should be taught as possessing greatest relevance; the other asks for background knowledge to be taught in order to make current events more understandable. Present-day examples include the rise of Islam and the Crusades, although thirty years ago they might have been thought exotic and distant. Some history syllabuses look very much like current affairs programmes: As countries experience new alarms and crises, their history also jumps to the front of the queue. Those countries that avoid the worst of conflicts and upheavals, such as Canada and Sweden, are neglected by this approach, as compared with perpetual trouble spots, such as Israel and the surrounding Arab states. The here and now is not necessarily of greater significance to our lives than the there and then.

Elevation of contemporary history is far from new. The second of the great founding fathers of history, Thucydides, thought there had been nothing before his own time that was worth studying; and even in his own time, he thought that peoples other than Greek speakers had very little of value to offer. Greeks rarely studied languages other than their own, until Roman victories forced their historians and other scholars to learn Latin. Ignoring other languages gave the Greeks much more time for what they thought were the essentials.

By the time I discovered there was renewed interest in the United Kingdom in my work carried out in the 1970s, I had relegated my original criteria of significance: importance to people in the past, profundity, numbers affected, and durability, to second-order priority and had adopted a different approach. I wrote several papers using these five criteria of significance as their framework:

- Changes in safety and security
- Changes in various forms of freedom
- Changes in degrees of inequality
- Changes in ideas about the macrocosm and the microcosm
- Changes in modes of production

Then I had another change of mind. This was the result of a growing feeling that my emphasis on changes and search for Lukacs' 'critical moments' or 'moments of truth' had led me to undervalue the importance of comparatively long stretches of time in which there was virtual changelessness in one or more of the highlighted aspects of life. I moved instead to five Priorities

- Livelihoods/methods of production
- Security and safety: personal, group, and state
- Freedom in its different forms

- Relationships between persons and groups such as generation, gender, social, ethnic
- Changes in ideas about the nature of the world and our place in it

I also became very impressed by the ideas of a colleague in Flinders University. Ken Simpson argued that to be coherent an educational theory must satisfy requirements in respect of needs, authority, and knowledge. I have tried to apply this idea to the teaching and study of history, but shortcomings in this book are mine and not his.[6] Some general questions that go towards meeting Simpson's requirements concerning needs, authority, and knowledge are:

- Are all people capable of acquiring historical understanding, or does one have to be one to understand the history of some groups defined by, say, gender, ethnicity, or other attributes?
- Do some groups 'own' their 'own' history?
- Is historical knowledge analogous to physics-type general laws? Or does it deal with the specific, perhaps the unique, embodied in narratives?
- Is there a coherent identifiable body of historical knowledge?
- Are past changes in, say, postage stamps, horse racing, ceramics, coal mining, and taxation all aspects of a common discipline?
- If there is such a thing as 'general' history, what are its contents and limitations?
- What is the justification for making the study of any historical events compulsory for people of any age? If there are such grounds, which aspects of the past should they include?
- If decisions about the content and/or method of history teaching in schools are to be made at a different level from that of history teachers in each school, in whom should authority for such decisions be vested?

All my sets of criteria are essentially contestable, not as concepts but as conceptions. There is virtually no controversy about the meaning of concepts, but often numerous and lengthy, indeed interminable, disagreements about conceptions. It is perfectly logical for two people to agree completely with each other on a suitable dictionary definition of, say, 'equality', but for each to dismiss the other's conception with 'that's not what I mean by equality'!

Final agreement is unlikely for questions about which forms of equality are the most important, whether 'negative' freedom from control is more or less important than 'positive' freedom of enablement or how individuals and communities can best be secured from danger and harm. As well as disagreements about each major conception, there are also ongoing disputes about the relative importance of each. It is notorious that the balance between freedom and equality is unendingly disputed, as is that between freedom and security. History has witnessed many lurches between a desire for strong rule to prevent anarchy and violence and a desire for greater personal or communal freedom.

Application of both first and second order criteria still leaves us with far more content of interest and value than we could contain in any manageable school history course, but their application will make the task more intelligible and open to rational amendment. The approach should help to dismiss the idea of mandatory national curricula, although provision of specimen syllabuses and questions to be asked in them can only be for the good. Note that the use of these five principles of selection does not entail five separate strands in historical studies.

Chapter 1

Five Priorities

Priority A: Livelihoods

Guiding Questions

- How can people today find out how hunter-gatherers got their food and shelter/
- Why did not more peoples 'cross the ditches' from hunter-gathering to agriculture or animal husbandry and from there to urban life and the formation of states?
- Did any groups lose skills their ancestors had gained and if so why?
- What significance had the existence of over a hundred different languages in Australia before 1788?
- How were boys and girls prepared for their adult roles in hunter-gathering societies?
- Which crafts and trades developed once there were regular food surpluses? Do we have any clues as to how new arts and crafts were mastered?
- How did trade develop between groups with different resources and expertise?
- Which products were most regularly traded and which were regarded as most valuable and precious?
- What effects did slavery have on methods of work?
- How did trade and commerce encourage literacy and then how did literacy stimulate new ideas and products?
- Why are some ancient civilizations described as 'hydraulic'?
- What were the effects of the development of professional priesthoods and professional armies?
- How did ideas of ownership of land or territories arise? Were those ideas very different from those of animals we describe as being territorial?
- Which goods were traded between China and Europe from Roman times to the eighteenth century? On which routes did the merchants travel?

- Which voyages of discovery opened up the rest of the world to Europeans?
- What forms did colonization take?
- What are possible explanations for Britain becoming the first modern industrial state
- Why had China and India not developed similar industries earlier, given the advanced state of their cultures?
- What were the main products exported from the Australian colonies in the nineteenth century that enabled Australians by 1890 to be among the half dozen wealthiest peoples in the world?
- What effects did industrialization have on the cost of clothing and household goods?
- Which groups felt disadvantaged by industrial inventions and development? What responses did they make?
- Which countries at different times lost and gained leadership in different industries and branches of agriculture?
- How did the policies of free trade and protection relate to these changes?
- Why did New South Wales become a free trade state at the end of the nineteenth century, but Victoria a protectionist?
- Why do peoples often object to even non-violent large-scale immigration into what they consider to be 'their' country?
- Do similar 'modes of production' determine the 'general character of the social, political, and spiritual processes of life'? Is this true of peasants, factory workers, merchant bankers, and so on?

Reflections

Advances in technology may bring pains as well as gains, since workers and traders successful in an industry may find transition difficult or lose their livelihoods entirely.

Many skills developed in the ancient world were lost in the centuries following the end of the Roman Empire in the west. After the rising of the seas, the Tasmanian Aborigines lost the ability to catch fish in nets and to make fire, although they could still keep one going once it was alight. The Norsemen had to either abandon Greenland when the climate became colder in the early medieval period or die there of starvation and death at the hands of the Inuit with whom they had been in conflict since the first settlement.

In several great river valleys some 5,000 years ago, mastery of agriculture and animal husbandry made it possible to have surplus wealth, division of labor, life in cities, and literacy. The Egyptians, Sumerians, and Chinese began to calculate present and past time, to list the names of their rulers, and to date notable events of their reigns.

They recorded the rise and fall of dynasties and empires, 'times of troubles', and more prosperous years. However, we know very little of whether any of those peoples thought that life tended over the years to become worse or better. What we do know is that without agriculture and the domestication of animals, there could have been no regular and reliable food surpluses, no division of labor, and no significant advance in arts or sciences. And without the alphabets and reading, there could have been only very limited expansion in the 'external memory' which has made possible the rapid accumulation of human knowledge.

However, after a few generations, stagnation often set in and innovation became rare. Important knowledge may have been restricted by embedding it in religious rituals and magical formulae. History is not unidirectional. There have been many times when life became harsher, freedoms were reduced, and fear and suffering rose to terrible heights. Autocracy was the norm: There were rarely any formal restrictions on the will of the ruler; winners took all after warfare; the property of subjects was in principle open to confiscation; and there were few safeguards against execution at the ruler's pleasure.

Material progress must have been immensely aided by the availability of slave labor, but in nearly every slave society, progress slowed down because manual work became associated with servile status and gaps widened between activities that depended on the use of mind and those that relied on muscle. Almost all of the major inventions that transformed spinning and weaving, iron and steel, canals, and later on, railways were made by artisans who understood the practical problems involved. Then the new industries of the nineteenth and twentieth centuries, such as electrics and chemicals and later still computer technology, required considerable mathematical and scientific knowledge, as well as a grasp of practicalities.

Trade across the Mediterranean with Northern Europe and on the overland routes to China and the East developed during the six centuries or so after the conquests of Alexander of Macedon had increased cultural unity and economic interdependence. The decline of the Roman Empire brought about the almost complete replacement of international trade by subsistence economies. Then, gradually, with monasteries and abbeys often in the lead, arts, crafts, and trades flourished again in many parts of Western Europe. Better ploughs and harnesses put better seeds in the soil. Population rose fairly consistently, take away a few droughts and pestilences, until the Great Plague of the 1340s. Even the Black Death, however, did not cast too long a shadow: It is merriment that is most striking in Chaucer's *Canterbury Tales*. Natural resources are important in helping or hindering the development of different states and peoples, but resources only become available once human minds have discovered how to make use of them. Venice and Genoa had in the past, as Japan and Singapore have today, very limited natural resources, but were highly prosperous. On the other hand, many resource-rich states languish in poverty. It is 'consciousness' that transformed once lonely coasts into thriving ports and harbors and deserts into oil fields.

The expansion of new industries nearly always created unemployment and discontent among sections of the working class and peasantry whose skills and muscle power were made redundant. The result was Luddism, other forms of machine wrecking, and less conspicuously, the development of restrictive practices. The history of trade unionism may well be regarded as part of the wider theme of livelihood. Like most histories, it contains uplifting examples of solidarity and depressing examples of thuggery.

Wheat became a major source of wealth in Australia from the 1820s onwards, but a few good seasons were often followed by drought that ruined many farmers. Novels that looked back on earlier patterns of work were often written by women, but many men also wrote about agriculture and stock raising rather than about mining. The great rural occupations of growing wheat, herding sheep and cattle, and mining were all male dominated and gave outback Australia a serious disproportion between the sexes.

By the 1850s, the expanding woolens industries of Yorkshire were in symbiotic dependence with the squatters and shearers of the outback. By then, more British workers were employed in the manufacture of Australian wool than there were wage-earners throughout Australia. In the British Isles, people washed at night with soap and lit their way to bed with candles made from surplus Australian livestock. By the 1890s, more people in Britain were eating Australian than British meat. In return, iron and steel from Britain provided corrugated roofs over Australian homes, the machinery for Australian manufactures, and the rails and locomotives, or steamers, which enabled Australians to overcome the tyranny of distance. British inventions, first in gas and then in electricity, were soon applied to lighten the southern darkness.

British-born migrants, such as James Harrison in refrigeration and Frederick York Wolseley in steam-powered shearing, were among the first Australians to make powerful contributions to technology and wealth creation. The rapid progress by which a land without solid habitation or a wheeled vehicle became within a century a leader in per capita wealth was aided by the freedom from warfare ensured by British naval supremacy and by massive injections of British capital in Australian agriculture, transport systems, mining, industry, and commerce. The wealth produced by gold, wool, and beef was enough to make possible the rapid growth of cities. Melbourne caught up with Sydney within two decades, despite being settled fifty years later. The problems of distance and sparse population away from the coasts led to the concentration of professions, trades, and crafts in the great cities, in which was conducted the administration of public business for huge territories that became States of the Commonwealth of Australia instead of British colonies at the end of the nineteenth century.

PRIORITY B: PROTECTION FROM VIOLENCE

Charles Dickens, *Pickwick Papers*

'It's always best on these occasion to do what the mob do'. 'But suppose there are two mobs?' suggested Mr Snodgrass. 'Shout with the largest', replied Mr Pickwick.

Mao Tse Tung, 'Problems of War and Strategy' in *Selected Works*, 1938. ii.,6 November.

'Every Communist must grasp the truth, Political power grows out of the barrel of a gun' n

Hilaire Belloc,

Pale Ebenezer thought it wrong to fight,
But Roaring Bill (who killed him) thought it right.

Questions

- Is Homo sapiens by nature a peaceable or a violent species?
- What actions could have been taken and which were implemented in attempts to control and direct human violence?
- What effects had the growth of prosperous cities in river valleys on peoples in less favoured outlying areas, such as grasslands, hills and mountains, and semi deserts?
- What measures did peoples in the towns and cities take to defend themselves against attack?
- How did warfare change with greater wealth and division of labor?
- Along with external conflicts and wars, what internal threats did rulers face?
- Lucretius wrote that 'fear created the gods' (Timor deos fecit). What did he mean?
- How did rulers try to ensure the loyalty of their subjects?
- How did cycles of violence sometimes come to an end?
- What attempts have been made to control the actions of states by international laws, treaties, and membership of world bodies? Why have they had very limited success?
- Have weapons of mass destruction made war less or more likely? How have they influenced patterns of violence?

- Are there examples in the animal kingdom of intimidation by a show of strength or making a big noise?
- Can you think of further examples of states and kingdoms that originated in successful blackmail or conquest but which later gained legitimacy from its subjects and neighbors?

Reflections

A fundamental feature of human history is the pervasiveness of war and violence. Marx and Engels were right in arguing that states are founded on violence, not on social contracts of the Hobbes, Locke or Rousseau kinds. However, Marx and Engels did not recognize adequately the capacity of some robbers and pirates turned heads of state to convince their subjects that their rule was preferable to anarchy or rule by other contenders. In some cases we can trace some of the steps by which leaders of successful armed bands established themselves as rulers of a hostile population but gained the attributes of legitimacy. Examples include Germanic invaders of the Roman Empire in the fifth and sixth centuries and the later Turkish conquerors of Asia Minor and the Balkans. Claims to divine approval or to previously unsuspected ancestors among earlier dynasties often feature in their stories.

One important deficiency in our history teaching, perhaps in our overall national outlook, is the assumption that internal peace and security and comfortable living conditions are the human norm. We assume that the civil society we inherited and consolidated here in Australia will survive without too much effort by us. In political disputes, we stress the issues that divide us and underplay those on which a large majority of us agree.

In hunter-gatherer societies, all fit adult males were warriors and most tribal groups engaged in periodic warfare, but its ferocity was limited, sometimes by exogamy: marrying out of one tribe into another and more generally because slavery was impracticable. Defeated warriors could not be made into enslaved hunters, since they would turn their weapons against their captors; in many cases, the costs of their control exceeded any surplus value produced by their labors. However, our species exterminated rivals, such as Neanderthal and other once far-ranging groups.

Nearly all creation stories are violent. The Assyrians and Babylonians thought that life had been created by Tiamat, the destructive goddess of the sea who murdered her offspring, until one son, Marduk, killed her with an arrow through her belly. In Hesiod's account of the origins of the Greek gods, Earth (Gaea) persuades one of her Titan sons (Cronus) to castrate her husband (Uranus). Cronus swallows his sons, but Zeus escapes and slays his father. Murder, mutilation, and rape are commonplace and do not detract from the sanctity of the gods.

Once rich agricultural lands were farmed in the valleys of the Nile, Tigris, Euphrates, Indus, and the great rivers of China, there was huge temptation for warrior tribes from the mountains and deserts to invade, take control, and become rulers. When they settled down, they often became the targets rather than the assailants.

Although the formation of sovereign states reduced the frequency of warfare, it increased its destructiveness. The availability of guns sharply increased death rates among the Maori in New Zealand and the Amerindians in the nineteenth century, even when fighting only with traditional enemies.

In order to be able to repel invaders and destroyers, a whole society might be involved. Large prosperous states were able to command their own professional armies and/or hire mercenary troops from the groups similar to the attackers. Use of mercenaries was often dangerous: The first Anglo-Saxons to make raids into Roman Britain, Hengist, and Horsa may have arrived as mercenaries, but stayed as invaders. Later, Ethelred tried to get rid of the Danish invaders by paying blackmail called Danegeld. Rudyard Kipling wrote, 'Once you pay the Danegeld, you'll never get rid of the Dane', but there were examples of successful use of mercenaries: Eighteenth-century Britain's armies were largely composed of German mercenaries, whilst the British concentrated on their Royal Navy. The Byzantines, along with hiring Viking mercenaries, sometimes gained by bribing Slavs, Arabs, or Mongols to go away, because after their withdrawal they attacked other areas and sometimes lost the battles.

Buying a breathing space enabled some ransom payers to fight with greater advantage another day, as evident by the tribute paid by princes of Muscovy to Tartars and Mongols. Warriors on horseback needed pasturage and moved on quickly after sacking cities and extracting tribute; some, like the Huns, suffered defeat in other lands or engaged in internal struggles and never returned. Most of the Hurricanes and Spitfires that won the Battle of Britain in 1940 'were built in the eleven months of peace bought by Neville Chamberlain at Munich'.[7]

Citizen armies, even if less skilled in some branches of warfare, were recommended by Machiavelli as more loyal and reliable than mercenaries or professionals, but civilians usually opposed military conscription, as did employers deprived of part of their work force. The Press Gang was an alternative form of conscription for the British Navy from the seventeenth to nineteenth centuries. A high level of support for the way a country is governed seems to have been needed for conscription to be acceptable.

At one level, the histories of Ancient Egypt, Mesopotamia, India, and China consist of cycles of conquering and declining dynasties. After their victories, the conquerors often adopted the superior arts and sciences of the conquered and followed them in decadence.

Rulers were rarely satisfied with their existing territories and feared attack or subversion. Brothers fought with brothers, and sons revolted against fathers. Women in harems plotted against each other to promote the prospects of their children. Vengeance passed down from generation to generation.

The two great Homeric epics portray many acts of great courage, but the characters of the heroes are deeply flawed and violent. The conduct of the gods supporting Hellenes or Trojans is often worse than that of the mortals.

Aeschylus's *Orestes* trilogy is among other things a study in the rights and wrongs of vengeance. Was Agamemnon right in sacrificing his daughter, Iphigenia, to gain the favour of the gods for a wind to take the Greek expedition to Troy? Was Clytemnestra justified in murdering her husband, Agamemnon, in revenge for Iphigenia's sacrifice? Was the son of Clytemnestra and Agamemnon, Orestes, justified in murdering his mother as his religious obligation to his murdered father? In most matrilineal societies, matricide had been the worst of crimes, but in patriarchal societies the slaying of a husband was the most condemned.

Sophocles asks in *Oedipus the King* whether the king is to be blamed for killing his father and marrying his mother: Oedipus had left Corinth precisely to avoid the Delphic Oracle's prophesy that he would commit this crime, supposing his father to be the king of Corinth, not the king of Thebes. The extant plays of Aeschylus, Sophocles, and Euripides indicate that more Greeks felt pity and sympathy for human suffering than we might conclude from accounts of their wars and political conflicts.

The ancient societies most admired are Greek city states and Rome. Yet, despite truces provided by the Olympics and other games, wars between Greek cities and the leagues they formed were endemic and only ended when all were swallowed first by Alexander of Macedon and then by the Romans.

Class struggle was usually bitter, less often between slave owners and slaves than between wealthier landowners who led 'aristocratic' parties and poorer free citizens who, together with rich entrepreneurs, formed 'democratic' parties. Because they often had a good chance of winning power and inflicting atrocities as well as suffering them, Greek factions were usually more eager to wage civil war than were the subjects of oriental despots. Thucydides thought the basic cause of the Peloponnesian War was that 'the Athenians becoming a great force, and provoking fear in the Spartans forced them to fight.'[8] Infinity of names, from street gangs to empires, could be substituted for those of Athenians and Spartans. Thucydides described the killings in the civil war in Corcyra in 427 BCE that led to the Peloponnesian War:

During seven days the Corcyraeans were engaged in butchering those of their fellow-citizens whom they regarded as their enemies; and though the crime imputed was that of attempting to put down the democracy, some were slain for private hatred; others by their debtors because of the monies owed them. Death thus raged in every shape, sons were killed by their fathers, and suppliants dragged from the altar or slain upon it.[9]

As a condition in one of their truces, the Athenians promised Sparta to intervene in their support if there should be a rising of their helots against them. The free citizens of Sparta were warriors who did no manual work, which was carried out by their helots, who were themselves conquered Greeks. Spartans were not noted for their wit, but they were not without cunning. Thucydides described how the Spartans offered freedom to the helots if they would volunteer to fight against Athens and its allies. The Spartans 'thought that the first to claim their freedom would be the most high-spirited and the most apt to rebel'. About 2,000 were chosen from the volunteers. The Spartans 'soon afterwards did away with them, and no one knew how each of them perished'.[10]

Spartans could spy upon, rob, and murder helots without breaking the law. Spartan boys had to endure harsh discipline and punishments in their training as soldiers. They were more likely to be killed by their own comrades if they retreated than by the enemy if they advanced or stood firm. Spartan mothers told their sons to return from battle with their shields or on them.

Jewish scriptures and tribal/national life were also full of violence. Cain slew Abel and brothers were constantly in strife, as evident by Ishmael and Isaac and Esau and Jacob/Israel. The God of Moses was a jealous God who was merciless towards those who break his Commandments. God told Samuel that he would depose Saul as King of Israel because Saul refused to kill every last man, woman, child, and best of all his defeated enemies. The children of Israel engaged constantly in wicked ways, from *Genesis* onwards, although their neighbors were just as bad.

The Roman Republic and Empire expanded and ruled with whatever amount of violence was required. Examples of Roman ruthlessness include the policy of 'Carthago est delenda' (Carthage must be destroyed) advocated by Cato the Elder and enacted after 202 BC, the savage repression of the Spartacus slave revolt, and the destruction of the remnants of the Jewish state and subsequent expulsion of the Jews after AD 70.

In the 'Middle Ages', slavery was replaced in most of Christendom by forms of serfdom which gave the peasant effective rights as well as obligations. Less wealthier than the Roman Empire in the past or industrialized Europe and America in the future, medieval states had to militarize the social order to provide defenders. That was how feudalism arose: Land was distributed on the basis of supply of knights when the overlord was in need of them. The knight became the ideal of manhood. Warrior castes and classes, such as Japanese samurai, Hindu kshatriya, and medieval European knights, endured severe initiation ordeals, privations, and continuous military training.

How did cycles of violence ever end, given the bitterness of so many feuds and the brutality of so many conflicts? Sometimes a merciful policy was successful. At other times brutality succeeded. Under autocracies, winners took all, the property of subjects was open to confiscation, and life itself was at the ruler's pleasure. Yet many peoples preferred a stable despotism to the war of each against all. Many also preferred slavery to sudden death or slow starvation. In many places, people sold themselves and/or their wives and children into slavery as a last resort in distress. Many also preferred a subordinate position in the place in which they were born, under the control of a lord whose family was likely to remain in a permanent relationship to them, rather than be at the mercies of invading strangers.

Some rulers were successful in convincing their subjects, even ones recently conquered or otherwise acquired, that their rule was legitimate and not merely an exercise of naked power. Rulers often tried to persuade their subjects that their rule was blessed by God and made alliances with priesthoods or churches. Descent was sometimes claimed from heroes of the past, such as Heracles, or even from gods, such as Zeus, Jupiter, Wodan, and many others. Subjects were told that only a god-pharaoh or other such divine ruler could secure them an after-life.

The main attraction of primogeniture, including or excluding the female line, was that, apart from uncertainties about paternity and disputes about the legality of marriages, it was usually easy to apply. Its main disadvantages were inheritance by an heir who was physically or mentally weak or by a child. A second method was that the most able of the dead ruler's family should succeed, but there was frequent strife as to who was the most able, and the decision often depended on the outcome of war. A third method was election: Poland, Denmark in Hamlet's time, and the Holy Roman Empire were elective monarchies, but royal authority was often traded for votes, and political weakness usually followed until the state was conquered or changed its succession laws.

New rulers often tried to establish some continuity with their displaced predecessors. William of Normandy, after slaughtering many of his new Anglo-Saxon subjects, asserted that he was the legitimate successor of Edward the Confessor and was applying the established laws of England, not introducing new ways. Claimants to thrones sometimes alleged that they were the children of earlier kings but had escaped from murderous plots of invaders or usurpers. Cyrus, Theseus, and Arthur were examples of lost royal children who reappear to perform heroic deeds

When in *The Pirates of Penzance*, Major-General Stanley kneels before the tombs in his baronial castle to implore their forgiveness for bringing disgrace on the family escutcheon, he is reminded that he has only bought the castle the previous year. His response is: 'With the estate I bought the chapel and its contents. I don't know whose ancestors they were, but I know whose ancestors they are.' Many people have acquired traditions and cultural ancestors in varied ways. Conversions to Christianity or Islam, for example, led to the adoption not only of a set of beliefs about God and the present duty of man but also of extended historical and cultural traditions frequently quite unknown previously to the converts. Communist revolutions led to the study in countries such as China and Vietnam of nineteenth-century European savants such as Hegel and Marx, whose thinking had very few indigenous parallels. Usually, conquerors impose their historical and cultural traditions on the defeated, but there are many examples of the reverse process: Nomadic peoples who conquered the kingdoms of Mesopotamia typically adopted the way of life of the fertile plains within two generations—William the Conqueror claimed to be the legitimate defender of traditional Anglo-Saxon law and custom and the Norman-French medieval English aristocracy adopted the old British Arthurian legends. In open societies like our own, the traditions chosen by many of our fellow citizens include many varieties of Christianity, Judaism, and Islam, the religions of the Book, political ideologies, and ethnic loyalties of many hues, a wide range of Asian religions and philosophies.

Often old enmities were displaced by new ones or merged into them. The early Romans fought for several generations against Latin states of similar character to their own, but most of them, including the Samnites and Etruscans, came to regard themselves as Romans. Final Roman victories over the Cisalpine Gauls, Carthaginians, and the Jews, among others, were followed by mass destruction and genocidal slaughter, but the Transalpine Gauls after the defeat of Vercingetorix and the Britons after the defeat of Boudicca accepted Roman rule and prospered. The small Anglo-Saxon kingdoms: Kent, Essex, Wessex, Mercia, East Anglia, and Northumbria, fought against each other until Danish invaders conquered all of them except Wessex. Scots formed, after the Act of Union of 1707, some of the crack regiments of the new British Army. The Gurkhas fought just as hard for the British as previously against them after their defeat in the 1850s. On the other hand, many Irish Roman Catholics never became reconciled to English, or Scottish, Protestant rule. Yet a high percentage of fit young Irish males who did not emigrate to the United States or to Australia joined the British Army instead.

Periods of civil war and turmoil have often been followed by strong centralized regimes that seemed capable of keeping peace. Examples include the Principiate of

Octavian Caesar, the power of the Tudors under Henry VIII and that of Louis XIV in France after the Wars of Religion and then the Fronde, the Tsardom of Russia under Ivan the Terrible after 'the time of troubles', and a variety of nineteenth and twentieth-century dictatorships.

Cruelty in warfare had been endemic, but some rules were accepted by most belligerents. For example, during sieges the attackers almost always sustained greater casualties than the defenders so that the custom developed that attackers would give defenders two chances to surrender with their lives and most of their property, but that on a third defiance their city, town, castle, or village would be subjected to pillage, arson, rape, and slaughter. Some peoples, such as the Tartars and Mongols, gained a reputation for particular ferocity, but almost all soldiers killed randomly and brutally once they were inflamed by battle and had seen their comrades killed by the enemy.

Attempts were made in the eighteenth century to create a body of international law that could restrain countries from violent policies. After the apparent success in 1815 of the Congress of Vienna in reorganizing Europe after the Revolutionary and Napoleonic Wars, further congresses were held to try to preserve peace. After the First World War, the League of Nations was set up with that aim, and after World War II, the United Nations Organization took its place. It is hard to tell whether any of these initiatives had any effects, but wars continued to take place, despite these organizations.

The thirty-three years between the end of the Napoleonic Wars in 1815 and the revolutions of 1848 were more peaceful than average. There were fewer wars in Europe in the second half of the nineteenth century than in the preceding centuries as well, but those fought were more destructive and led to higher casualties because of more effective weaponry. The death rate in the American Civil War of the 1860s was substantially higher in pitched battles than hitherto. Relative peace in Europe was accompanied by numerous colonial wars in which European forces were able to overwhelm African and Asian peoples. Hilaire Belloc wrote: 'Whatever happens, we have got the Maxim gun and they have not.' In 1914, however, both sides had big guns and the age of optimistic hope in progress came to an end, and the way was prepared for Bolshevik and Nazi regimes.

In the nineteenth and twentieth centuries, treaties such as the Geneva Convention were signed by many states. During World War II, German armies usually observed the conventions regarding 'western' prisoners of war, even when the Holocaust was being perpetrated in concentration camps, although they showed no mercy to Jews, Gypsies, and many Slavs. During the advances of the Soviet armies in 1944–5, many thousands of civilians fled westwards so that they would be captured by British,

American, or other allied troops and not by the Soviets. On the other hand, it was the Allies who dropped the first atom bombs on Japan: a decision that remains controversial

PRIORITY C: FREEDOM(S)

Guiding Questions

- What is the distinction between negative and positive freedom?
- Can freedoms of some sorts be seen as dangerous by some people?
- How have various religions been tolerant of other beliefs at different times?
- Why did some people choose to be slaves?
- Why were the great pyramids, ziggurats, and the massive public works in China, Mexico, and Peru built in about the same phase of development in each civilization?
- Why have some people renounced forms of democracy for various types of dictatorship?
- Many European countries had representative institutions during the Middle Ages. Why did some become weaker and some disappear completely?

Isaiah Berlin made an important distinction between 'negative freedom' and 'positive freedom'.[11] By negative freedom, Berlin meant the absence of obstacles to or restraints upon freedom. This had been the standard view before Jean Jacques Rousseau urged that true positive freedom implied the full realization of a person's or even a group's or a nation's potentialities. Berlin's ideas are presented very clearly by Michael Ignatieff in his *A Life of Isaiah Berlin.*

Human sacrifice was common among the Aztecs and Incas and some of the neighbors of the Children of Israel in Old Testament times. In the Bible, it is inflicted on Jephthah's daughter and nearly on the boy Isaac at the hands of his father Abraham.

The Jewish monarchies in Judah and Israel were usually willing to tolerate the worship of many different gods, but were opposed by prophets of the God of Israel. The books of *Kings* and *Chronicles* are full of examples of 'bad' kings who permitted the worship of idols and were punished by Jehovah for this sin. David was portrayed as beloved of the Lord, but his kingdom was soon divided because Solomon, despite his proverbial wisdom, pursued false gods. Prophets such as Elijah and Elisha demanded the slaughter of all who disobeyed the Lord and worshipped Baal and other gods. Many Jews and Christians admired persecuting rulers such as Josiah of Judah, despite his intolerance and his failed attempt to impose his religion on all his subjects.

However, most peoples were polytheist, and rulers usually permitted their subjects to worship other deities if they so wished, as well as the official gods of the state. An exceptional ruler was Akhenaton, who required all Egyptians to worship only the Sun God, Aton, and to destroy or convert all existing temples to his worship. This was followed by Akhenaton's overthrow or murder in a counter-revolution in which the new worship was overthrown and the old gods restored.

In the assemblies, all full citizens in Athens, Sparta, and many other Greek city states were direct participants, not merely electors or representatives, although the majority of the population remained excluded because they were slaves, helots, foreigners, women, or children. The Greek city states had no objection to worship of an unlimited number of gods from outside as well as within the Olympian system, although fears that 'atheism' might produce political disobedience or moral corruption led to the death of Socrates. Alexander's huge empire and the three large despotic states into which it split after his death all permitted their subjects to worship much as they pleased, within the constraints of political obedience.

Jews were divided. Some were attracted by Greek ways, but the rest revolted under the Hasmoneans and Maccabees and later, when it had become an imperial power, against Rome with disastrous results. The Temple in Jerusalem was destroyed and Jews expelled from Judea . . . Christians were believed at first to be another Jewish sect and of doubtful loyalty to Rome.

Under both Republic and Empire, Rome tolerated those who paid lip service to the emperor and the official deities, but persecuted groups suspected of using religious beliefs as a cloak for political subversion. The Jews, and even more the Christians, incurred prosecution because they refused the political obedience required of all Roman subjects. The ending of all restrictions on Christian worship was soon followed by the adoption of Christianity as the official religion and then to large-scale persecution of 'pagans', those holding the religious beliefs that had prevailed for over a millennium, and of heretics, Christians who disagreed with the complex doctrines of the Trinity authorized in various Church Councils.

Often, the higher the literacy rate, the more heretics and then the greater the intolerance: The illiterate did not argue much about religious doctrine. During the 'Dark Ages', from roughly the seventh to the tenth centuries, there were very few trials for heresy in the new states in the western half of the former Roman empire or any sophisticated apparatus for apprehending heretics. Before and after that period of intellectual torpor, there was persecution in plenty. Augustine of Hippo set the tone. He was for some years a Manichaean and held that the world was a site of eternal struggle between the forces of good and evil. After conversion to Christianity, Augustine came to hold that Christian emperors had the right and duty to persecute heretics. He urged that the Church should show equal severity, since its purposes were far more important than those of the secular authority. Augustine combated all he deemed heretical . . . He died in his bishopric of Carthage during the Vandal siege, but many of his ideas were confirmed by the 451 Council of Chalcedon, which reaffirmed the Nicene Creed . . .

Bitter religious quarrels, especially about the place of icons in worship, weakened the long-surviving Eastern Roman or Byzantine Empire. Neither side could tolerate the other; their only point of agreement was that the issue was a vital one. Finally, after a century of strife, in 843, icon veneration became a permanent part of Greek Orthodox Christianity. There came formal separation in 1054. After the Western crusades began in 1095, relations between Rome and Constantinople were almost as hostile as those of each of them and Muslims.

The medieval concept of freedom was closely linked to that of specific 'liberties'. The craft guilds and merchants' guilds, for example, did not rely on general or abstract theories but on written charters. The Roman Catholic Church, too, associated its freedom from state control with charters and bequests. In opposition, the Gallican movement in seventeenth century France relied on charters that gave protection against papal interference.

Shiaungdi, the first Chinese Emperor, had buried in his massive tomb not only soldiers but also the workmen and architects who had built and planned it. Supreme rulers were often held to be descended from gods and frequently worshipped as gods themselves. Massive amounts of wealth and labor power were lavished on the preparation of pharaohs and their equivalents for an afterlife. Their peasantries were sedentary and disarmed, and many were in bondage.

Law and living reality are often wide apart. Under English medieval law, many peasants were technically unfree and 'tied to the soil': 'A serf owns only his stomach' was a legal maxim. In practice, however, lords and stewards of estates found it very difficult to exact payments over and above customary dues that often stayed unchanged for generations, thus falling in value with steady rates of inflation. If the serf was 'tied to the soil', then almost equally the soil was tied to the serf.

Both manorial rolls and royal charters show that often rulers and the ruled accepted that the law was king, just as much as the king was the law. Even in Tsarist Russia where the sovereign power was able to confiscate property at will, whether of serf or noble, many peasants felt that not only they were tied to the land but also the land was tied to them. It was after emancipation of the serfs that peasant discontent grew sharply and contributed to a revolutionary movement that deprived them of all their rights in land.

The leading Scottish thinkers of the eighteenth century were well aware of the perils facing the rule of law and that it was necessary to exercise vigilance and use force to safeguard constitutionalism or civil society and ensure that contracts were honoured and people protected against fraud or force. Francis Hutcheson was concerned for the vulnerability of prosperous civilians to seizures of power and property by military forces. This fear led Wellington and many others in England to support purchase of commissions. Wellington held that military leaders without a 'stake in the country' would be tempted to use their military power to overthrow the civil order. Although the traditional 'man on a horse' does not literally command states today, his successors have aircraft and tanks to ensure that large populations in Africa, Latin America, and Asia are subdued. The Arab Spring seems (early in 2013) likely to end with only a few constitutional regimes and a large number under military of fanatical rule, as in the previous Arab winter.

A major change took place in much of Europe by the nineteenth century. Great geographical explorations, new scientific discoveries and mechanical inventions, and unprecedented industrial expansion promoted confidence in progress. This confidence was far from universal. It was not obvious to all, not even to all who supported its aims, that the French revolutionary programme had led to greater liberty, equality, and fraternity. Yet it is of world significance, particularly of relevance to Australia and similar states, that our imperial power had developed, although only recently, a form of civil society that enabled governments to be changed peaceably. Without this constitutional system, we would not be able to discuss freely which history should be taught in our schools, let alone to replace governments.

Before the successes of the Dutch and the English in combining military and political power with a considerable amount of freedom, the two were considered almost to exclude each other. Shakespeare wrote that 'uneasy lies the head that wears a crown': It is hard to stay at the top of the slippery pole. The only king of Serbia during the nineteenth century who died peacefully in his bed was mentally ill. Very few military dictators of African and Latin American republics during the last half century have established secure regimes.

Problems that may arise in universal suffrage and representative government include tribalism and voting by ethnicity and lack of a reliable structure of civil order. The willingness of political parties to bid for votes by offering major welfare benefits as bribes to voters may lead to national bankruptcy of the type experienced recently by Greece and Spain. Former totalitarian states, especially Marxist-Leninist states, were left with few functioning organizations apart from the party and state apparatuses so that party hacks could transform themselves into nationalistic autocrats, with the Russian, Serbian Ukrainian, etc. people substituted for the working class or peasantry.

Representative government is a major heritage from the Middle Ages. There was little, if anything, of a general benevolence towards all mankind or zeal for human rights in medieval institutions. The Parliament of England, the Parlements and Etats-Generaux of France, the various Diets and Rats of the Scandinavian and German states, and the estates of the Spanish kingdoms were institutions especially designed to protect and advance group interests. In France, the Parlements became restricted to legal and judicial functions, while the Etats-Generaux was allowed to lapse because the French people as a whole wanted peace and thought that only a strong monarchy, unimpeded by sectional interests, could provide it. Thus the States-General never met between 1614 and 1789, when its summons proved the first step in the overthrow of the monarchy and the destruction of the old France. In Spain, the various Cortes strongly resisted the rising power of the monarchy, especially when the ancient rights and privileges of Catalonia and Aragon were being undermined by Castilian centralization. The Polish Parliament was a major weakening influence on the state. An individual veto existed, and rulers of neighboring states greedy for Polish-ruled territory, or their representatives, sat in the Polish assembly and made sure the monarchy became more and more impotent.

When Western Christendom changed, it changed relatively quickly. Until around 1530 Jews had limited toleration in any Christian state and Christian heretics virtually none at all. Luther did not aim at freedom of faith, but that all Christians should follow the true faith of the Bible, as interpreted by Luther. Just what that truth comprised was never, of course, agreed upon. The first great advance in Western toleration arose from the failure of either side in the sixteenth-century wars of religion and then in the Thirty Years' War to crush the other completely. Attempts to enforce a single doctrine on the whole of Christendom were finally abandoned in 1648 at the Treaties of Westphalia. The new principle was that rulers had the right to enforce their own religious beliefs on their subjects: cuius regio eius religio (whose kingdom, his religion).

England was lucky rather than virtuous in the survival of its medieval Parliament. Magna Carta was later honoured as a major source of English liberty, but in origin, it was a declaration of the rights and privileges of the nobility. But in limiting the right of monarchs to tax at will, or to seize property except by strict application of law, the Great Charter proved a massive step towards a limited or constitutional monarchy and made it very difficult for a despot to emerge in England. Parliaments during the Wars of the Roses and other internal conflicts were the scene of factional fighting, and during Wolsey's period of authority during the 1520s, it seemed likely to fall into disuse, like the French Etats-Generaux, but Henry VIII, in his quarrels with the papacy, realized that the Parliament could also be a powerful force for nationalism.

Most of the laity were anti-clerical and wanted an end to privileges of the priesthood, and the Reformation Parliaments of the 1530s strengthened both monarch and Parliament at the expense of the church and the aristocracy. During the 1630s, Charles I refrained from calling a single Parliament, but was finally forced to do so when the Scots rose in revolt against his religious policies and his army was beaten by them. Only a Parliament could vote him the funds to fight again in Scotland. The House of Commons, led by John Pym, took the initiative and began to strip away royal powers until Charles raised his banner against them and Civil War began in 1642.

David Hume held that at the beginning of the Civil War of the 1640s 'the grievances under which the English labored, when considered in themselves, without regard to the constitution, scarcely deserve the name'.[12] Taxation was historically low during the 'personal rule' of Charles I. It was even lower in Britain's thirteen mainland American colonies before rebellion cum civil war broke out in 1775–6. The hated tea tax was significantly lower than in the past.

England was fortunate also in 1689 when the plans of James II for a Roman Catholic restoration, opposed by what was in law an invasion by William of Orange, James's son-in-law, led to the great Acts of the Glorious Revolution, which gave England a parliamentary monarchy that has lasted well despite its politicians displaying the usual faults of men in office. The convict origins of British Australia made issues of freedom loom large when lived through and in retrospect. Despite harsh punishments that accompanied the difficulty in capturing convict recidivists, the progress of the colonies to a civil society of free people was remarkably swift. That was the case also in Canada and New Zealand.

The Dutch also developed a civil society in which political power coexisted with limits on power and constitutional safeguards. The United Provinces emerged from confusing conflicts in ways as unexpected as the emergence of civil society in England. Wars of religion were as hard fought in the Netherlands as anywhere in Europe, with a patriotic war against Spanish rule an even more potent cause for rebellion than grievances of religious persecution. The patriotic party, led by William of Orange before his assassination by Roman Catholics, offered religious tolerance to Catholics to secure unity against Spain, not out of abstract love of liberty of worship. In the initial stages of long but not unbroken periods of warfare, it were the military factors that decided which provinces became free of Spanish and were ruled with Protestant rule and which remained as the Spanish Netherlands in which Roman Catholicism remained intact. The southern provinces became much more Roman Catholic than a generation earlier, because of flights and expulsions of the sort that later took place between Turks and Greeks in 1920 and between Hindus, Muslims, and Sikhs in Punjab in 1948. Those provinces became known first as the Spanish Netherlands, then as the Austrian Netherlands in 1714, and after 1830 became

Belgium. During the seventeenth century, the (Dutch) United Provinces became the main place of refuge for religious and political exiles, until new European colonies in North America, such as Rhode Island and Georgia, took over that role.

By the late nineteenth century, although Roman Catholicism remained in force in most of the European countries where it had held sway in 1648 and there remained state churches in several Protestant countries, religious persecution rarely threatened and freedom of worship expanded. Several countries, including France and Italy, newly united, had secular regimes, even though their populations were overwhelmingly Roman Catholic in religious faith. Reasonable hopes that this improvement was bound to continue were destroyed with the success of totalitarian regimes in Russia and Germany, but have revived following their overthrow.

PRIORITY D: RELATIONSHIPS

Guiding Questions

- What was the key difference between matrilineal and patrilineal societies? Why did matrilineal systems usually precede patrilineal ones?
- What sorts of rites had young people to endure before they were regarded as adults and full members of a tribe?
- Which different kinds of slavery existed in the classical world and subsequently in Christian and Muslim societies?
- Have conditions for children generally improved over time, got worse, or stayed roughly the same?
- In what ways did many societies try to make sure that membership of a particular class or group was clear to everyone else?
- In what ways did members of the same group or class either compete and clash with each other or present a united front to outsiders?
- In what ways did different societies justify special rights and privileges for some groups in society?

Reflections

Marx saw all history as basically the history of class struggles. We noted the ferocity of class warfare in the Greek cities, and there have been few societies in which conflict between classes has not been important: plebs and patricians, slaves and their masters, lords and peasants, employers and workers, and so on. Nevertheless, class struggle is far from being the only dynamo of historical change or of attitudes towards life. Marx argued that 'it is not the consciousness of men that determines their being, but, on the contrary, their social being determines their consciousness'.[13] However, Engels warned his followers that the 'historical materialism' developed by him and Marx held only that 'the determining element in history is ultimately the production and reproduction of real life. More than this neither Marx nor I ever asserted'.[14] They had done at times, of course.

In tribal hunter-gathering societies, the only important group differentials were those of age and gender. Plato on the other extreme argued in The Republic for a clear distinction between three types of person: those of gold, those of silver, and those of base metals. The key to happiness in Plato's view was that each person in each class should know their places and keep to them, as expounded by Ulysses in Shakespeare's *Troilus and Cressida.*

> The heavens themselves, the planets and this centre
> Observe degree, priority and place
> Insisture, course, proportion, season, form
> Office and custom, in all line of order . . .
> Take but degree away, untune that string,
> And hark! What discord follows; each thing meets/
> In mere oppugnancy.

The medieval structure consisted essentially of three classes: those who fought, those who prayed, and those who performed manual labor. Collective, communal, or family rights in property often constituted obstacles to accumulation of wealth. Ireland and England formed a great contrast for several centuries. Irish tenant farmers had no rights to improvements made during their tenancy, and it was common for land to be divided up between sons or between even more family members. In England, however, as Alan Macfarlane demonstrated in *The Origins of English Individualism,* as early as the thirteenth-century manorial courts recognized individual title, and in many districts in which primogeniture did not operate, owners could will their property to such heirs as they chose. There was an active market in land, and large numbers of children left their own homes when young and worked and married outside their parishes of birth.

In states in which arbitrary seizure of land and chattels was possible through inadequate legal protection, there was little incentive to improve land or invest such surplus wealth that might be accumulated. In early medieval England, however, inheritance of property became normally secure for tenants, serfs, or free, subject to the payment in money, labor, or kind according to the custom of the manor. Lay lords, abbots and bishops, and the kings themselves could not readily interfere with the laws and customs that vested property rights in a large part of the population.

One privilege of priests in the Middle Ages that many lay people disliked was 'benefit of clergy'. This gave priests brought to trial for criminal, including capital, offences the right to be judged by other priests in ecclesiastical courts by other priests, in which sentences were much lighter. The right to claim benefit of clergy expanded to include deacons, summoners, pardoners, monks, and others who had not taken priestly vows. Since most people except priests were illiterate, benefit of clergy was granted if the accused could recite the 'neck verses' from Psalm 51. Combined with rights of sanctuary in churches, a large number of suspected criminals were able to escape justice as meted out on the rest of the population.

Before 1216, trial by ordeal was in force in most Christian countries. Ordeals were mainly of three kinds, which operated in different jurisdictions. In the ordeal by water, the accused was thrust into a pond: If the body came up, that was held to prove guilt, since the water would not accept a guilty person; on the other hand, you could drown before being fished out. Ordeal by fire required the accused to run a set distance holding a red-hot iron: Judgment was delayed until it was obvious whether the wound would heal or not. Ordeal by the cursed pellet required the accused to swallow an object too large to be admitted normally in the gullet. Chokers were found guilty. The assumption in all these ordeals was that human judgment was fallible, but God would speak through the ordeal. The nobility could avoid trial by ordeal by asking for trial by combat fought between the accused and the accuser of a crime. It was often possible to name a substitute: a champion who would fight on your behalf.

The British had a comparable problem in Australia in the nineteenth century. Aborigines knew no courts and had no judges. The state as such did not exist. Consequently, revenge mutilation was the custom if the guilt of an accused party was clear to all. One or more spear thrusts to varying depths would be inflicted by the injured party or, in the case of death, by a male relative. The British were left with what seemed a difficult choice between unequal justice and countenancing barbarous cruelty. The problem has by no means been yet resolved. Some group differentiations remain in most countries, such as age of responsibility and the inability of courts to compel a wife to testify against her husband. If same-sex 'marriages' become legal and polygamy is permitted, it may prove more difficult to find witnesses in criminal trials.

In some ways, class differences became much less conspicuous in the nineteenth and twentieth centuries than in earlier times. Mass production of clothing in particular led to the dress of the rich and not-so-rich becoming much more similar. In extreme cases in earlier centuries, there were sumptuary laws, which imposed strict dress codes according to social class. It was easy then to pick out who was who. Much effort has now to be made by wealthy women and wealthy men, to a much lesser extent, to look much better than the rest. And mass production of food has ensured that the average person has a wider range of good food than what the nobles and even monarchs enjoyed in times past.

Speech codes have become less distinctive as well. A clear indication is provided by listening to Elizabeth II speaking in public at the start of her reign and then comparing it with her delivery during her Diamond Jubilee. Much more marked is the tendency of very wealthy young people to affect a plebeian accent. Domestic arrangements are more similar with the great reduction in the number of people, especially women, in 'service'. This is not to suggest that we live in a classless society but that divisions have become much smaller over the last two centuries.

The position of women underwent a revolution during the twentieth century: During world wars, women entered into roles almost exclusively occupied previously by men; together with the extension of cheap and generally safe contraception, they were among the changes driving these new relationships. The shadow side was perhaps the huge increase in broken families and children with only one parent at home. Overall, the creation of adolescence as an extended period of life was also a very significant change in relationships. Young people were financially dependent on their parents for longer periods as school leaving ages were raised and higher education enrolments increased, yet the disinclination of youth to obey parental direction and the unwillingness of any state or community body to intervene led to considerable tension. That said, in every human generation there have been conflicts between old and young and parents and children about rights, duties, and conduct.

When we consider relationships between groups historically, it is almost inevitable that we also ponder the significance of individuals as against groups. Hegel thought that the lives of 'world-historical individuals' were the key to history, whereas Marx and Engels claimed that individuals were only important in so far as they embodied or represented significant social forces. Yet Lenin's importance in organizing the October Revolution in 1917 is a powerful example of the significance of individuals in history. The 'cult of the individual' subsequently became as pervasive in some communist states as in monarchies, although it was equaled by the 'Fuhrer principle' in fascist regimes.

Mohamed was one of Carlyle's heroes, and it may well be asked whether Islam could have arisen in anything like its actual historical form(s) if the Prophet had been killed in one of his early campaigns. Were the lands of Arabia and the conflicts among its peoples, or with external enemies, much different in the early seventh century than in earlier years in which no significant religious or political initiatives arose in the Arab world? We may ask similar questions about outstanding individuals in almost every major event or movement of which we have knowledge. It is one of the 'what if' games that often prove fascinating, although they rarely lead to reliable conclusions. What if Abraham Lincoln had not been assassinated in 1865? What if the 'generals' plot' against Hitler had succeeded? What if any one of the leaders of the combatant nations of 1914 had insisted on further negotiations before committing his state to war?

PRIORITY E: IDEAS

Guiding Questions

- Which skills and knowledge were most distinctive of Homo Sapiens compared with other primates? How could these have been acquired?
- What sort of questions about the world and their place in it were asked by the first human beings we know of?
- How did religious beliefs relate to family structures and political power?
- What were the powers and intentions attributed to divine beings in various religions?
- What role did animal or human sacrifice play among various peoples?
- How were morality and religious belief associated with each other?
- Why have some people been especially inventive of new ideas either for practical use or for better understanding various aspects of nature?
- What strengths and weaknesses did the Greeks have of the classical age in originating or developing new ideas?
- What changes in the conception of God are shown in the Old Testament?
- What are the possible explanations of double or parallel accounts of events in sources available to us, such as the Old Testament?
- Why were scientists such as Bruno and Galileo or thinkers such as Servetus and Cranmer charged with crimes by religious authorities?
- Why did inventiveness accelerate so swiftly during and after the late seventeenth century?

Reflections

The Old Testament moves quickly from murderous prophets, such as Elijah and Elisha, to ethical thinkers such as Amos and Hosea. Elijah massacred the priests of Baal; and his successor, Elisha, summoned two bears to kill forty-two children who called him 'bald-head'. Sometimes, the later prophets also saw the Lord as a violent warrior, as in *Isaiah* 42: 13: 'The Lord shall go forth as a mighty man, he shall stir up jealousy like a man of war; he shall cry, yea, roar; he shall prevail against his enemies.' The Children of Israel were confident for several generations that if he Tabernacle was carried on to the battlefield victory would be theirs', because the enemy would be filled with fear. That approach may have had some effect on local Canaanite foes or the Philistines, but did not intimidate Babylonian, Assyrian or Egyptian armies.

However, the main themes in *Amos, Hosea, Jeremiah, Ezekiel* and *Isaiah,* for example, are usually very different: In particular, the human race began to be considered as a whole that transcended family, tribe, or nation. Amos challenged the idea that the Lord God thinks only of the welfare of the Israelites. He told them, 'True, I brought Israel up from the land of Egypt, but also the Philistines from Caphor and the Arameans from Kir.' It was not their descent from Abraham or their sacrifices and burnt offerings that would save them, but their conduct: 'Let justice flow like fountains; and righteousness like a mighty stream'. Ezekiel rejected arguments for hereditary guilt such as: 'as is the mother, so is her daughter' and 'the fathers have eaten sour grapes, and the children's teeth are set on edge' as well.

Isaiah went further than Amos in making other nations, including enemies, part of God's concern. The Assyrians, conquerors of the ten northern tribes of Israel, who disappeared from history then, were seen as the instrument of God, as was Cyrus the Persian who centuries later liberated the exiled Jews from Babylon. Isaiah showed concern for the remnants of the old enemy, Moab, and for the usually hated Egypt and Assyria. In his vision of a return to Jerusalem, foreigners and even eunuchs, regarded in Jewish law as unclean, could enter the Temple, in which there would be no more sacrifices of animals, but only prayer and repentance. The passages in the 'second' or Deutero-Isaiah about a messiah and 'suffering servant' formed the basis for Handel's *Messiah* and much other sacred music.

Compared with the monotheist religions that displaced many of them, polytheists were generally more tolerant. Monotheism, however, has usually been seen as an advance, because it conceives that universal laws operate behind the confusing multiplicity of events.

By the fifth century of the Christian era, pagans and Christians alike had to agree that, wherever the responsibility could lie, much of the knowledge accumulated earlier and taught in the schools of classical humanism had been lost, perhaps only temporarily.

Great subtlety in logic, law, and theology was engendered by the medieval universities, but they contributed very little new knowledge in physical sciences, medicine, or practical arts and sciences. Among the few exceptions were the English Franciscans, Robert Grosseteste, Bishop of Lincoln, and Roger Bacon, both of whom made important contributions to optics. The most admired scholars were theologians and philosophers, such as Anselm of Bec, Peter Abelard, Thomas Aquinas, Albertus Magnus, William of Ockham and Bonaventure.

Dividing knowledge between sacred and secular and conceding in advance, as did Peter Abelard, that if any contradiction appeared to exist between theology, scripture, or Decretals of the Church on one side and natural philosophy on the other, then the natural philosophy must be mistaken, gave some space for independent thought, but numerous scholars were persecuted for heresy, including Amury of Bene, David of Dinant, Joachim of Flora, Siger of Brabant, and Boethius of Dacia. Most of the intellectual progress was made in spite of the Church and Christian theology, not because of them.

An important disagreement in medieval thought was between those, such as Anselm of Bec, Thomas Aquinas, and Bonaventura, who believed that philosophy, particularly that of Aristotle, could fortify Christian belief; as against those such as William of Ockham and Duns Scotus (whose name in the form of 'dunce' became used most unfairly to describe stupid people), who denied that any argument from first causes or sense experience could assist in understanding the nature and the attributes of God—they were simply of a different order.

The main transition belts of ancient learning and occasionally sites of improvements on it were Islamic lands, notably Iraq, Sicily, and Andalusia. However, several intellectual movements in the Islamic lands were repressed, some even crushed, by the end of the twelfth century by obscurantists comparable to our current ayatollahs. As a result, the renaissance and the rapid progress of modern science took place in Europe and not in Islamic lands.

The Renaissance of the sixteenth century had two overlapping phases. In the first, there was a revival of interest in such classical knowledge that had survived, especially Aristotle and his modes of classifying knowledge. In the second phase there was greater confidence that new truths were still to be gained of which the ancient world had been ignorant. An ongoing dispute between 'Ancients' and 'Moderns' was presaged. Religious ideas, however, often obstructed scientific understanding more than in medieval times, when churchmen had not felt under threat from unbelief. False beliefs, such as that in witchcraft, shared by great minds such as William Harvey and Sir Thomas Browne, led down many wrong tracks in the understanding of human behaviour. Some of the great scientists and mathematicians of the sixteenth and seventeenth centuries, such as Kepler, Descartes, Boehme, and Newton, had profoundly religious outlooks, but unlike their medieval predecessors, they were generally successful in compartmentalizing their minds. This did not prevent the Roman Catholic Church, however, from identifying as heresies ideas held by men who were otherwise zealous Christian believers or were wrapped in mysticism. With men suspected of scepticism about religious revelation, such as Tycho Brahme, Giordano Bruno, and Galileo, the church was less indulgent, although only Bruno was put to death for his opinions.

The Protestant Reformation made the problem more difficult, because most of the early Protestants followed Martin Luther in insisting on the literal truth of scripture, but in the long run, the division of Christianity into competing churches made it easier for toleration to expand and to include finally not only Unitarians who denied the Trinity but also deists and atheists as well. It was only with the discarding of theological presuppositions entirely, obviating the earlier need to justify what appears to clash with scripture or church tradition, that the dam was burst and the almost incredible flood of new knowledge began to flow.

One major effect of the discovery of the Americas was a reduction in expectations of progress and betterment among many Europeans. The inroads of syphilis, although not so severe as the death rate wreaked by European diseases on the 'Indians', undermined the sybaritic ways of the Renaissance and encouraged puritanical practices. The counter-Reformation Popes put trousers on the nude statues of Michael Angelo, whilst John Calvin, John Knox, and many other Protestants feared that even fewer people of mankind would be saved from damnation than Augustine of Hippo had judged likely.

Some Europeans such as Las Casas concluded from their experiences in the New World that the native populations there were much more virtuous than Europeans. Stacked against that view was the notorious cannibalism and human sacrifice of the Incas and Aztecs. The great voyages of discovery under the flags of Portugal and Spain may have reduced the hold of ancient on modern thought. European voyagers often admired the achievements of Asian peoples, especially the Chinese and Indians, but their experiences of the Americas more often generated sentiments of European racial superiority. Montaigne with respect to the Americas and Rousseau to the Pacific held that that primitive virtue had been destroyed by Europeans in their search for wealth. On the other hand, new worlds, new diseases, and the recovery of much knowledge of the Ancient World than had long been unavailable may well have stimulated creativity in the century of Cervantes and Shakespeare.

The massive reduction in infantile mortality during the eighteenth century required not only the advances in obstetrics and gynaecology made by William and John Hunter and William Smellie but also the abandonment of old wives' tales. Knowledge that ancient superstitions long held had been largely ousted in eighteenth-century Britain helped to convince some British colonists in Australia that Aborigines might similarly embrace modernity.

One outstanding aspect of new ideas in science up to and including the sixteenth century is that they did very little to improve living standards. Copernicus and Isaac Newton were brilliant men, but their major advances in astronomy and physics hardly affected over nine-tenths of the population.

World-changing ideas arose exponentially once empirical investigation and deductive reasoning came together. It is often charged against historical studies that they are

42

excessively concerned with politics and religion to the point of neglect of the arts and sciences. What seems to be true is that political and religious leaders often exert a much more potent short-term influence on the course of events than on long-term ones, whereas discoveries in the natural sciences and most types of invention take a longer time to change ways of life. How large a proportion of available study time should we devote to Isaac Newton, Charles Darwin, Sigmund Freud, Albert Einstein, Madame Curie or to Homer, Virgil, Dante, Cervantes, Shakespeare, Moliere, Goethe or to Michelangelo, Leonardo Da Vinci, Johann Sebastian Bach, Mozart, Beethoven, compared with, say, Martin Luther, Calvin, Ignatius Loyola or with Elizabeth I, Peter I, and other rulers honoured with the title of 'The Great' or with Napoleon Bonaparte, Otto Von Bismarck, Lenin and Hitler, George Washington, and Winston Churchill? The number of acceptable responses is surely so great as to make nonsense of compulsory national syllabuses.

Chapter 2

PERENNIAL PROBLEMS

PROGRESS AND REGRESSION

In *Headlong Hall* in 1817, Thomas Love Peacock created three characters to argue for progress, regress, and changelessness. Mr Foster believed that 'everything we look on attests the progress of mankind in all the arts of life, and demonstrates their gradual advancement towards a state of unlimited perfection'. Mr Escot saw history as 'the great chain of corruption, which will soon fetter the whole human race in irreparable slavery and incurable wretchedness'. Mr Jenkinson held that our 'species, with respect to the sum of good and evil, knowledge and ignorance, happiness and misery, remains exactly and perpetually in status quo'. In the Foster camp was Malcolm Muggeridge, who frequently lamented the glories that were no more. One example runs:

> 'From Augustine to St. Ezra Pound, from Plainsong to the Rolling Stones, from El Greco to Picasso, from Chartres to the Empire State Building, from Benvenuto Cellini to Henry Miller, from Pascal's Pensees to Robinson's Honest to God. A Gadarene descent down which we all must slide, finishing in the same slough'.[15]

Not exactly representative selections to represent the Ancients and Moderns, but that is the way in disputes.

Scripture appears equivocal. In *Genesis* we gather that the Original Sin of Adam and Eve entailed that humanity would never again enjoy the bliss of the Garden of Eden, but whether things would go from bad to worse was not made clear. Ecclesiastes, though, was firmly for Mr Jenkinson: 'The thing that hath been, it is that which shall be; and that which is done is that which shall be done'.[16] A central Christian doctrine is that the Second Adam will secure atonement for the Original Sin of the First Adam, but that time lies in the future. Jesus apparently believed that the 'Day of the Lord' was at hand, and some of those then listening to him would still be alive when this world came to an end. The Second Coming has frequently been foretold since then, but has not yet arrived.

Advances were not always identified as such by later generations. One name well known, thanks to explorer archaeologists such as Rawlinson, is that of Hammurabi of Babylon. His law code has been regarded as backward and barbarous, but in context, its famous injunctions of an eye for an eye and a tooth for a tooth seems to have been intended to reduce blood feuds and ongoing vendettas and also to develop the idea of the king's peace. The principle that acts of violence are not only injurious to victims and their family or clan but also to the public order proved a key requirement for the stability of civilizations.

Edward Gibbon judged that the longest period of prosperous stability in history followed the accession of the Antonines to the Roman Imperial throne. Perhaps some periods in, say, Egyptian or Chinese history compare with the Pax Romana under the Antonines, but later, Western thinkers studied particularly the fall of Rome and tried to apply lessons from it to their own times. Some thought that too many barbarians from beyond the Rhine and Danube had settled within the Empire, while others thought more should have been admitted to counter depopulation. Some thought that the adoption and then enforcement of Christianity hastened decline, while others thought the new faith helped to hold decline at bay. Some thought that the Eastern Byzantine–Western Roman division was ultimately fatal, while others thought that the separation of the Latin and Greek worlds was not only inevitable but should have also been effected earlier so as to preclude the bloody Byzantine invasions of Italy and North Africa. Some thought that truces between Byzantium and Persia would have avoided the triumph of Islam, whereas Muslim scholars considered that triumph both inevitable and glorious.

Gibbon in his *Decline and Fall of the Roman Empire* blamed Christianity in a large part for the decline of Rome and for regression in civilization. Indeed, many Christian fathers such as Tertullian rejected ancient learning and persecuted non-Christians. Tertullian asked:

> What has Athens to do with the Church? What have heretics to do with Christians? . . . Away with all attempts to produce a Stoic, Platonic, and dialectic Christianity!

Pope Gregory I (The Great) warned that 'the same lips could not extol both Jupiter and Christ'. By the seventh century, very little knowledge of the seven liberal arts (grammar, rhetoric, and logic comprising the trivium and arithmetic, music, geometry, and astronomy comprising the quadrivium), medicine, law, or chronology survived in Western Europe. Even less would have survived if other fathers of the Church such as Augustine of Hippo had not hated Christian heretics and schismatics even more than pagans. Augustine permitted the reading of pagan authors such as Virgil, Horace, Quintilian, and Lucan, even obscene ones such as Terence and Juvenal, but banned heretical writings. Bernard of Clairvaux answered the question 'What do the apostles teach us?' with 'Not to read Plato, nor to turn and return to the subtleties of Aristotle, not always to learn in order never to reach knowledge of the truth . . .'[17]

Some Christian rulers such as Philip II of France tolerated Jews after 1282 because they could lend him money, but they were always liable to violence, as at the hands of Philip IV ('the Fair) of France in 1301. Without royal protection Jews were open to sadistic attacks such as those inflicted on them in south Germany in 1350 by the Flagellants. Some church leaders intervened half-heartedly to protect them: Bernard of Clairvaux told a Jew-baiting mob, 'God has punished the Jews by the dispersion; it is not for man to punish them by murder'.

Joinville tells of a disputation between Jews and Christian clergy at the monastery of Cluny. A poor knight was present to whom the abbot had given some bread. The knight asked the Jew, 'I ask you if you believe that the Virgin Mary, who bore God in her body and in her arms, was a virgin mother, and is the mother of God?' The Jew replied that 'of all this he knew nothing. The knight castigated the Jew and 'lifted his crutch and smote the Jew near the ear, and beat him to the earth. Then the Jews turned to flight and bore away their master, sore wounded. And so ended the disputation.'

The abbot told the knight he had acted foolishly, but the knight justified himself by saying, 'there were a great many good Christians there who, before the disputation came to an end, would have gone away misbelievers through not fully understanding the Jews.' The knight was supported by king Louis (St Louis), who said, 'And I tell you that no one, unless he is a very learned clerk, should dispute with them; but a layman, when he hears the Christian law mis-said, should not defend the Christian law, unless it be with the sword, and with that he should pierce the mis-sayer in the midriff, so far as his sword will enter.'

Jews generally sought toleration and avoided provocation outside the ghettoes, but were often harsh in their treatment of dissent within their own ranks. During its expulsion of Baruch Spinoza, the Amsterdam synagogue declared in 1656:

> . . . we excommunicate, cut off, curse, and anathematize Baruch de
> Espinoza . . . with the anathema wherewith Joshua cursed Jericho, with the
> curse which Elisha laid upon the children, and with all the curses which are

written in the law. Cursed be he by day and cursed be he by night . . . The Lord shall not pardon him, the wrath and fury of the Lord shall henceforth be kindled against this man, and shall lay upon him all the curses which are written in the book of the law. The Lord will destroy his name under the sun . . .'

Spinoza's is probably the only name widely known today from the Amsterdam Jewry of his time. The curse of Elisha was:

' . . . there came forth little children out of the city, and mocked him, and said to him, Go up, thou bald head; go up thou bald head. And he turned back and looked on them, and cursed them in the name of the Lord. And there came forth two she bears out of the wood, and tare forty and two children of them.'

The Franciscan preacher Berthold of Regensburg declared:

Had I a sister in a country wherein were only one heretic, yet that one heretic would keep me in fear for her . . . I myself, by God's grace, am as fast rooted in the Christian faith as any Christian man should rightly be; yet, rather than dwell knowingly one brief fortnight in the same house with an heretic, I would dwell a whole year with five hundred devils.[18]

In classical times, secondary schools had been expected to cover the trivium of grammar, rhetoric, and logic, but mediaeval grammar schools concentrated on grammar alone. This represented a 'dumbing-down', but not such a large one as is sometimes supposed. The grammar in both cases was Latin grammar, of course, but Latin had been either the mother tongue or lingua franca in the Roman world and a foreign or second language in medieval times, and so it took a much longer time to master for facility in conversation and translation.

The victory of Christianity may have led to the loss of practical skills and theoretical knowledge. Orders such as the Benedictines accumulated large libraries under the rule of St. Benedict, but no original thinking was envisaged, and works copied were mostly those of the Fathers of the Church, especially Ambrose, Augustine, Jerome, and Gregory I, together with fantastic lives of the saints and documents purporting to validate fake relics and even bodily parts of apostles, saints, and the Holy Family. However, Irish monks such as Columbanus preserved some knowledge of Greek and Latin culture, and their influence spread into the Anglo-Saxon kingdom of Northumbria, in which the Benedictine monasteries of Wearmouth (674) and Jarrow (681) became major centres for preserving and copying manuscripts and, notably with Bede, writing history in the light of Christian providential belief. Some monasteries became major centres for disseminating new ideas and practices about crops and animal husbandry.

Such advances in knowledge as were made in medieval Christendom were made almost entirely by clerics: Arithmetical skill was encouraged even if only to calculate the date of Easter, on which several Christian churches differed very sharply, and scholastic analysis of Aristotle's logic and of doctrinal contentions must have sharpened many clerical wits. By the twelfth century, several scholars had great respect for some of their non-Christian predecessors. Bernard of Chartres, according to John of Salisbury, described his generation in the twelfth century as 'like dwarfs on the shoulders of giants', and the scholarship of the medieval universities was largely directed at recovering and understanding classical Greek thought, especially that of Aristotle.

As a link between this Chapter and the next I would emphasize that, although history is not a simple account of conflicts between right and wrong, we should be concerned with better or worse, with greater and lesser goods or greater or lesser evils. It would be a mistake if we dwelt to excess on human crimes and follies, although we need to be well aware of them. Perhaps even more important though is to fill students and readers with respect for some of the good and great deeds our predecessors carried out. As the prayer has it:' Let us begin the praise of famous men and our fathers that begat us', but let us add famous women and our mothers that begat us as well.

Bias, Prejudice, and Moral Judgment

Can people identify significance in unprejudiced or even-handed ways, or is bias too deep to make that a reasonable expectation? Throughout history, many people have both unconsciously and deliberately misrepresented what happened to themselves and others. So they do today. The reasons for this include material gain, personal prestige, and support for a cause.

All peoples have been ethnocentric to some extent. This, together with changes to them, is shown by chronologies. The Greeks dated years from when they supposed the first Olympic Games to have been held and the Romans from when they fancied their city had first been built. Both these systems were replaced by the Christian system, in which dates were determined by how far they were before and after the supposed birth of Jesus. We have the odd situation at present that Jesus is thought to have been born four years Before Christ. There is an extra complication in that multiculturalism in the West has led to the modification of BC to BCE (before the Christian era), even though those who organized the change do not believe that a Christian era began in our Year One. AD (Anno Domini: in the year of Our Lord) has become CE (Christian era). Muslims date the flight of the Prophet Mahomet from Mecca to Medina in the Christian year AD 622. Traditional usage is followed here.

From hieroglyphics in Egyptian tombs to contemporary media, many stories about the past glorify tribes, nations, religions, or ideologies at the expense of others. Powerful emotions produce sharper conflicts about history syllabuses than about maths and physics. When populations are highly diversified in their values, there are likely to be deeper disagreements about what history to teach and how to teach it than in relatively homogeneous societies. In Australia, during the nineteenth and the first half of the twentieth century, the main educational and religious disputes were between Protestants and Roman Catholics.

The Senior Inspector of the Board of Education of Victoria, A.B. Orlebar, argued in 1864 that, although 'English history is particularly important to our youth', he was 'obliged to report against its introduction into our schools as an infringement of the hours of secular instruction. I have examined school histories of England, and I do not know one to which either the Roman Catholic or the Episcopalian or the Presbyterian parent could not justly object'.[19] Marcus Clarke warned against attempts to avoid controversy in history teaching: 'unless we can invent a New Religion, we must forbear to teach history in our secular schools', since not only 'Henry VIII, Bloody Queen Mary, Mary of Scotland, and the Virgin Elizabeth' aroused controversy, but the discovery of printing and much else besides.[20]

No such reservations troubled Stephen Henry Smith, who later became Director of Education in New South Wales. He held it was important children should know 'how the English-speaking races have gradually come to hold such an important position in the world' and why such people 'are called civilized', in contrast with 'tribes of blacks' living 'a very wretched kind of life', who 'are called uncivilized' and were very different from 'the race to which Australian boys and girls belong!', Smith suggested to his young readers that they, 'read the story and studied it because you felt curious to know something of the great men of our race. As you read on you felt proud, no doubt, to think of the noble progress that the race made.'[21] In his *English History Stories for Fourth Class* Smith suggested, in a section headed 'On the Value of Historical Study', that from learning 'the story of the progress of a great nation', pupils would acquire moral sense too and be prepared for full citizenship 'under the freest form of government the world has yet known'. One fears that Smith would today be barred from class rooms, let alone administering education from on high.

Historians and other intellectuals have not been notably freer of bias and prejudice than the unlearned. Michelet claimed that the French had stayed the same over history: 'la patrie, ma patrie, peut seule sauver le monde'. Mickewicz told the Poles that they alone were 'from first to last faithful to the God of their fathers'; Engels, however, wrote: 'The Poles have never done anything in history except play at brave, quarrelsome stupidity. And one cannot point to a single instance in which Poland represented progress successfully even only in relation to Russia.' Engels drew the lesson that 'the Poles as a nation are done for and can only be made use of as an instrument until Russia herself is swept into an agrarian revolution'.[22]

Within a century, other Europeans changed their stereotype of Germans from impractical idealists to efficient robots. Fichte told the Germans that they 'carry most clearly the germ of human perfection should this perish in you, all hope of humanity for salvation is lost', but Lord Vansittart, Permanent Secretary at the British Foreign Office between 1933 and 1939, described Germany as 'the butcher bird' of Europe. He held that 'this bird of prey is no sudden apparition. It is a species. Hitler is no accident. He is the natural and continuous product of a breed which since the dawn of history has been predatory and bellicose'.[23] Vansittart would have been astonished at the post-1945 history of Germany. Mazzini saw continuity where few others did. He asked, 'Why should not a new Rome, the Rome of the Italian people arise to create a third and still vaster unity; to link together and harmonize earth and heaven, right and duty?'[24]

Milton, James Thomson in 'Rule Britannia', and William Blake in *Jerusalem* and *Milton* thought that history showed that the English had become the new chosen race; Michelet attributed to the English a 'vast and profound vice' of pride, a cruel malady, but one which is nevertheless the principle of their life, the explanation of their contradictions, and the secret of their acts'.[25] As Milton well knew, in the late seventeenth century, the English were notorious for political instability. Thomas Hobbes thought the only hope for civil peace was rule by a state with irresistible power: Charles I had been executed only two years before Leviathan was written; Charles's grandmother, Mary Queen of Scots, had also been executed, as well as two non-regnant queens of Tudor England. Civil wars convulsed England, Scotland, and Ireland. Yet, within less than a century after Hobbes' death, Britain became an exemplar of stable constitutional government, in which changes of leadership could take place without bloodshed. In 'comics' for British children, the typical villain changed within just a few decades from Chinese to Germans, to Japanese, to Russians, and to Chinese again.

We should keep in mind what the late Anthony Flew termed the 'No true Scotsman fallacy'. We start with the proposition: 'No true Scotsman beats a defenceless woman'. When we are told that Sandy McNab is undoubtedly a Scotsman but beats his wife twice daily, we retort that McNab is no true Scotsman.

Poets are as likely to show bias as prose writers. Macaulay's *Battle of Naseby* is a good example. You will have no doubt which side he was on. Charles I was 'the Man of Blood' with 'his long essence hair', and his generals with names regarded as slightly effeminate by Macaulay's day were chosen to represent the Royalists. Prince Rupert, Oliver Cromwell, and John Hampden had similar martial virtues, but Rupert was 'the furious German', whilst the Roundhead troops cheered once they realized that 'brave Oliver is here'. When Macaulay wrote that Hampden 'knew that the essence of war is violence, and that moderation in war is imbecility', we were surely hearing Macaulay's own opinion as well.

Is it really true that 'the cause makes all' degrades or honours valour in its fall? If we are certain which side represented the right cause, should we deny virtue to all on the side we deplore? Would Robert E Lee have been a more admirable man had he offered his services to the Federal Army and not the Confederacy? Can no good be said of Von Rommel because he served an evil leader and a bad cause?

The position is, fortunately, far from hopeless. We could only meaningfully denounce bias if there were some possibility of unbiased, or at any rate less biased, accounts. Most of us concede that some accounts on 'our side' are unfair and that some of our opponents offer fair and logical arguments. And many critics of the possibility of objective knowledge seem confident that their own views are knowledge-based and therefore deserve a place in seats of learning. Although legitimate contestation would remain, even if all bias were overcome, prejudices can be reduced. Holding moral values does not entail bias that merits condemnation.

What sorts of moral judgment can and/or should be applied to the past? One position is the amoral: that anything goes that succeeds and that we should not condemn men who slaughter men, women, and children any more than we blame foxes for killing hens and chickens. Another is moral absolutism: that some deeds and thoughts are intrinsically evil and others good, in any circumstances. A third is unconditional relativism: that right and wrong can only be defined within cultures and that people should not be judged by outsiders. Part of the solution may lie in contingent relativism or, it could also be termed, contingent absolutism. This approach accepts first order or prima facie moral values, but understands that these may conflict with each other: Truth telling and avoiding unnecessary pain is often hard to reconcile. It acknowledges that our choices are often not between good and evil but between lesser and greater evils. Contingent relativism accepts that what is right in one situation may not be right in another. This is not mere casuistry. We should oppose 'an eye for an eye and a tooth for a tooth' as the basis of our own judicial system, but in the laws of Hammurabi of Babylon, the principle was intended to restrict revenge killings. What was significant about the laws of Hammurabi was surely that they limited the legal capacity of families to exact compensation from the guilty. This was a big step towards the idea of 'the King's Peace' later broadened into the Law of the Land. Four thousand years after Hammurabi's time, many peoples had not reached this point and still practiced indiscriminate vengeance against any member of a group held to have injured a member of their own. The courts of Australia today still find it difficult to subject private and group vengeance among indigenous Australians to public law.

We are beset with conflicting emotions, each of which is not only defensible but also part of mature morality: We try to take into account the standards of other peoples and times, but we classify in our minds, even if we do not articulate our sentiments, some acts as good and others bad or at least some as better and others as worse. Examples of these dilemmas abound: the Spaniards in Mexico and Peru were aghast at ritual cannibalism and human dismemberment, but the Aztecs were repelled by Spaniards burning heretics alive. In India, Herodotus related, there was shock and horror that the Greeks would burn or bury their dead, whilst the Greeks abominated the practice of leaving the dead on mountain sides to be eaten as carrion by vultures, a practice still followed by some Parsees.

During the 1970s, MACOS, the American-produced *Man a Course of Study,* devised by Jerome Bruner, was condemned in Queensland because it described neutrally the traditional Inuit custom of casting out to die in the cold and ice the elderly who would wastefully consume scarce resources. Should any moral positions be taken? Should our aim be neutral description of all acts, including massacres and gratuitous infliction of pain and torture?

Dislike of the misuse of moral judgment in history may lead to attempts to exclude it. Herbert Butterfield claimed that 'the dispensing of moral judgments upon people or upon actions in retrospect [is the] most unproductive of all forms of reflection'.[26] Michael Oakeshott warned against entering 'into a field in which we exercise our moral and political opinions like whippets in a field on a meadow on a Sunday afternoon'.[27] Yet, moral and other value judgments are built into our thinking about human action.

Moral dilemmas are little reduced, let alone eliminated, by religious beliefs. Religious believers have to decide first of all whether something is good because God wills it or that God wills it because it is good. They have also to make up their minds about the relative importance of religious injunctions: We should honour our parents, but does that extend to abusive parents? Can scripture always be authoritative? Did the Lord God really take away the throne of Israel from Saul because he refused to kill every man, woman, child, and beast of his defeated foes, as Samuel proclaimed was his command?

A central theological thrust of the Jewish scriptures is that the Children of Israel, the 'chosen people', prospered when they obeyed the commands of the Lord but suffered defeat when they departed from his ways. Yet there is no evidence that the Israelites behaved particularly well in the time of David, later deemed glorious, or much worse when first the Kingdom of Israel and then that of Judah were overthrown.

Is war always the greater evil? Would it have been morally better to allow Hitler to conquer more states and kill more Jews and other persecuted minorities if that number may have proved lower than that of all killed in the 1939–45 War? Should there be tighter controls on the use and distribution of dangerous drugs if further restrictions may raise prices and encourage more smuggling and other criminal activity?

How should we teach about slavery? Slavery was the shadow side of early civilizations. Enslavement only became practicable with agriculture and animal husbandry. Captured hunter-gatherers, if given weapons for hunting, would try to turn the tables on their enslavers. In any case, the costs of their control exceeded any surplus value to be gained from male slaves. Freedom is better than slavery, but enslavement may be the lesser evil compared with being killed or seeing one's children starve. One of the many unpleasant facts of history is that slavery nearly always accompanied the achievement of civilization. Among hunter-gatherers, there was insufficient surplus food to make possible the supervision and control of slaves who, if given the weapons to hunt, would try to turn the tables on their enslavers. In any case, the costs of controlling slaves exceeded any surplus value to be gained from their labors. Agriculture made profitable employment of slaves possible, and mastery of animals, especially of horses, made their capture and control much easier. In many places, enslaving enemies replaced killing them. An intermediate stage was often to kill all the adult men and to enslave the women and young children.

The main slave trading was carried out by Muslim privateers sailing out of the ports of North Africa: the Barbary Coast. They were able to raid deep inland as far as Britain and Ireland, as well as a large part of continental Europe and the whole of its coasts and those as far south as Zanzibar in East Africa and along the Silk Road into Asia. However, enslavement by people who were neither Christians nor Europeans seems to be omitted in Australian school history today. Yet in Britain, France, the Netherlands, and the German states, slavery did not suffuse civil society as it had done in the ancient world. In the sugar and tobacco slave plantations of the Northern European colonizers, slavery did not discourage invention and industry, although a substantial proportion of the nobility of Spain and Portugal associated manual employment with servile status. Spain in the sixteenth and seventeenth century experienced a massive expansion of university expansion, but very few graduates would even consider commerce or industry. The law, the army, the church, and the service of the state were the only honourable callings.

We should also be wary not to associate policies of enslavement almost exclusively with particular races or skin colors. The trans-Atlantic slave trade and associated plantation slavery from Virginia to Brazil came late in the history of slavery. Even at its height, the Atlantic slave traders depended on African rulers to capture and sell the slaves first. Enslavement by Africans, Moors, and Arabs continued to flourish after the leading Western maritime powers abolished the slave trade. The British were leading slavers during the seventeenth and eighteenth centuries, but took the lead in slave emancipation, even though the slave trade was at least as profitable during the campaigns for its abolition as in earlier decades. A moral dilemma about slavery emerged recently in the Sudan, chiefly in what is now South Sudan. Arab raiders had seized numerous Africans from southern villages and sold them as slaves in Khartoum or on the coast. London anti-slavery and missionary societies raised funds to pay as ransom for some of those captured and to return them to their homes. Critics have accused these societies of inadvertently inciting further raids for slaves in order to receive further ransom moneys. Furthermore, some captured slaves were reluctant to be freed, because their home villages had been destroyed and their lives as domestic servants to wealthy Arab families were more comfortable to what they had known before. Should we dismiss or severely discount the achievements of societies based on slavery? Plato defended slavery with what he knew was a lie, although he claimed it a 'noble' one; Aristotle, although he knew that slavery often arose from poverty or captivity, claimed that slaves were so by nature and were only animated machines. The Hellenic and Hellenistic worlds had critics of slavery, including many Stoics and Epicureans, but they never came close to changing public law and policy.

It is rarely long before historical study leads to questions about human nature. Is 'natural' a description of whatever people may do? If so, what can be meant by an unnatural act? If we find enough people who act with the utmost cruelty, will we then judge malignancy to be the natural condition of man? Neo-Darwinians expanded, the power of inherited traits to a point close to determination of the course of a life. Anthropologists such as Franz Boas, Ruth Benedict, and Margaret Mead tried to reduce the importance of inherited characteristics in human behaviour and to emphasize the power of each culture to shape conduct and personality. On the other hand, their cultural relativism deterred them from attempts to change cultural influences so that undesirable habits could be countered and transformed. Behavioral psychologists such as Skinner explained most of human action as determined by experience. However, although much of what we do may be limited by our genes or DNA or by culture and social structure, some capacity for undetermined thought and action is part of being human (and is to some extent shared by other creatures). It would make little sense to study the past if everything we do is predetermined.

We live in an age in which excessive public aversion to the human habit of renewing itself by sexual intercourse has been overtaken by real or pretended loathing of 'racism'. Yet, as the brilliant Australian David Stove argued at some length, dislike of some human groups by others is not only built into our very beings but is also justified on even the strictest construction of the evidence. One does not have to be a believer in the theological doctrine of Original Sin to realize that the Seven Sins are very widespread and that some peoples exhibit particular unlikeable traits more than others. Stove claimed that we know of no peoples that did not have a particular dislike

MAKING SENSE OF HISTORY

for some others' ways and that such dislikes were not held against them, provided that they engaged in no harmful actions against them. Even in highly homogenous populations and in non-vital activities such as ball games, whenever one team regularly wins competitions, the club, its players and supporters attract dislike. Stove was unfortunately right in suspecting that organizations established to combat racial prejudice have many members with more than the average share of prejudice. It is part of what Stove condemned as educationism': a determination through education to rid the human race of all its vices and prejudices.[28]

DEPTH VERSUS BREADTH

Study in depth can only be achieved at the expense of breadth and, of course, vice versa. Would it be better to know all the names and dates of writing of each play by Shakespeare or even to know the basic plot of every play he wrote, rather than to know just one great work well? Georg Lukasz, one of the most able Marxist thinkers of the twentieth century, argued that a key task of the novelist or playwright is to create critical moments that reveal features of a character, relationship, or social structure that normally remain hidden and undisclosed. Such a 'moment of truth' came to Conrad's Jim when he had to decide between jumping to safety and staying on the sinking ship to try and help the pilgrim passengers. It came to Brutus when he decided to join the conspirators, as it came to Julius Caesar when he decided to cross the Rubicon River.

One problem among many is, of course, that one can only pick out such moments of truth if one has already accumulated a great deal of historical knowledge, so that we seem caught in a vicious cycle of regression. A further obstacle is that nearly every historian is a specialist in a kind of history: political, economic, social, ecclesiastical, and so on or in a particular age or period, or in a particular country, people, or region. To become a tenured historian in almost every reputable university, it is necessary to have to have studied, written about, and published work in a very specific subject, usually one that had already considerable scholarly output, which is augmented each year. Historians seem almost compelled to learn more and more about less and less.

Until the seventeenth century it was still possible to aim at, if not to achieve, being Renaissance men, as well versed as Aristotle in more or less every important field of current knowledge. Natural philosophy still encompassed most intellectual inquiries, but was beginning to split into many subjects, each with a growing store of ideas and information. The rival claims of depth and breadth of knowledge became ever more acute, as did contention about which forms of knowledge are of most value.

In over forty years of teaching history, English, sociology, and philosophy of education, I never ended a term or semester without feeling that I had got the balance wrong: Either I had failed to 'cover' the full syllabus I myself had devised or accepted or I had skimmed over it too lightly, instead of stimulating sufficient understanding 'from the inside' of individuals, historical or fictional. I face the same problem even now, whenever I try to write an article.

LESSONS OF HISTORY?

Historical understanding is very much like political understanding, which is not to demean it, because in both spheres honest minds, fully conversant with relevant information, may derive different conclusions from their experiences and studies. They are also alike in that, unlike in laboratory conditions or mathematical calculations, we cannot introduce variables in order to isolate causes. In private life we cannot, say, choose more than one full-time job or spouse at a time and compare the results. There are countless events about which even the best informed historians find it difficult to decide whether it was *propter hoc* as well as *post hoc*.

Subsequent events often influence, perhaps justifiably, our notions of relevance. Just as the history of the British Empire was disappearing from school histories in Britain, mass immigrations from the Caribbean, South Asia, and Africa led to its re-introduction in many schools, although in a very different spirit from that often adopted at the height of imperial pride.

Some events that seemed momentous at the time fade from memory, whereas others that made little impact in their own day have long-lasting effects. Is the Bolshevik Revolution less worth studying now that communism is no more in the former Soviet Union? Would anyone have thought even 200 years after his death that the crucifixion of Jesus would become so important to many peoples that we use it as the baseline for our calendars? Such considerations do not negate the criterion of importance to people at the time, but they cannot be ignored in deciding on curriculum content.

There is not a natural universal interest in the past. The Australian Aborigines were typical of the hunter-gatherers who constituted the human race for over 90 per cent of its existence. They had many myths about a 'Dreamtime' or period of creation, but from that mystical beginning to the moving present, few human figures emerged. One possible explanation for that indifference is that there had been very few changes in the lives and thinking of their ancestors. Before 1788, the human past in Australia, so far as anyone could tell, was very much like the human present and therefore regarded as of no particular interest.

In China too, there was also scant interest before the nineteenth century in life outside 'the Middle Kingdom'. The Japanese, after short periods of interest in other cultures, notably Chinese and subsequently European Christian, turned their backs on the outside world for several centuries. Judaism became the first great monotheistic religion, but for many generations, the Children of Israel assumed that Jehovah was their particular god and not the Almighty God of all the nations. Muslims have shown little interest in events outside the Koran and in subsequent Islamic affairs. Egyptian and Iraqi Muslims ignored the pyramids and ziggurats, respectively, except for loot, until the Western tourist trade began in the early nineteenth century CE. The rage shown by many Iranian clerics at the last Shah's attention to Cyrus and other pre-Islamic heroes of the Medes and Persians helped bring about the 1979 revolution in Teheran.

Despite the claims of the French Annales School of History and some Marxists, human action is rarely, if ever, completely determined, but arises to some degree, however small, from the exercise of free will. If everything that has happened, is happening, and is going to happen were all bound to happen would there be a point in studying history at all? The point of studying history is not to learn general laws that they can readily be applied to new problems. What history does provide are examples of how and why people acted in particular ways in various situations and what resulted from what they did. Historical understanding is a higher form of proverbial wisdom, not a weak imitation of physics.

Often the result of events is something nobody aimed at and often is one regretted by all involved in it, although some unanticipated results may please. When in the eleventh century, Pope Gregory VII (Hildebrand) succeeded in outlawing marriage for Roman Catholic clergy, his motives did not include increasing educational opportunity, but that was one of its effects. Although some clerics had illegitimate offspring, their progeny was quite insufficient to meet the church's need for literate successors, so more schools were needed. A negative result, one that could have been anticipated, was that clerical celibacy deprived countries of those clerical children who after the Reformation made so many important contributions to science, literature, and the arts.

British colonization of Australia had, among other unforeseen results, the creation of a sense of shared Aboriginality among indigenous peoples who previously had little knowledge of each other and could not speak each other's languages. Another was the emergence of constitutional democracies in six colonial states and then in a federal Commonwealth. None in 1788 expected this future for a convict colony, but through historical study, we can understand how and why it came about.

Politicians frequently appeal to posterity to vindicate them and their policies: 'History will show that' . . . whatever it may be was the right/wrong path to take. Many historians, too, have been confident that history provides clear and unambiguous lessons and that the main purpose of teaching history is to impart to students general laws that compare as closely as possible with those of the sciences. H. T. Buckle wrote in the 1850s in his History of Civilization in England that 'in regard to nature, events apparently the most irregular and capricious have been explained and have shown to be in accordance with fixed rules . . . If human events were subjected to a similar treatment, we have every right to expect similar results . . .'[29] Carl Hempel argued that historical explanation ' . . . aims at showing that the event in question was not a "matter of chance", but was to be expected in view of certain antecedents or simultaneous conditions'.[30] Buckle and Hempel were convinced that if we knew all the background circumstances we would then know the outcome. If this were so, there would be no wealthy bookmakers. We usually discover that the results of policies are something of a disappointment to those who commended them and those who opposed them.

Lewis Namier had both fears and hopes: He wrote, 'Possibly there is no more sense in human history than in the changes of the seasons or the movements of the stars; or if sense there be, it escapes our perception. But the historian, when watching strands interlace and entwine and their patterns intersect, seeks for the logic of situations and the rhythm of events which invest them at least with a determinist meaning.'[31]

Yet even the subtle mind of a Namier could hardly have anticipated in 1913 what the political map of Europe would look like in 1919. Nor could the shrewdest minds of, say, 1932, have foretold the frontiers of Europe in 1943 and then in 1947. Experts seem no better at predicting the future through knowledge of the past than the rest of us. Which Kremlinologists forecast the collapse of the Soviet Union and its satellites? Which economists and financial tipsters anticipated the recent global economic crisis? In 1910, Sir Norman Angell wrote The Great Illusion, which explained that a European war was impossible, because the links in commerce, finance, and transport between the possible belligerents ensured they would have to remain at peace. Weather forecasts cannot predict next month's rainfall accurately, but some savants confidently prophesy massive global warming unless we all change our ways and repent. Three decades ago, the danger warned against was a mini ice age.

Sometimes very wrong lessons are learnt from historians, including very able ones. In 1914, most military historians thought that the American Civil War and the Prussian victories over Austria–Hungary and France showed that, whoever won, a new European war would quickly come to a decisive end. In 1939, many military experts deduced from World War I that a new conflict would produce another near-stationary Western Front. During the 1920s, many Bolsheviks thought that they had learnt from past revolutions the danger of the rise of a military dictator, such as Oliver Cromwell or Napoleon Bonaparte, so they were deeply suspicious of Trotsky, who had become 'The Man on the Horseback', but oblivious to the menace of Stalin.

If we take something as apparently simple as the relationship between arms races and major wars, we find that our three main twentieth-century examples differ profoundly. The pre-1914 arms race was engaged in by two opposing camps and was followed by war; the pre-1939 arms race was pursued for several critical years by one side only and was followed by war; the nuclear arms race of the 1950s to the late 1980s was pursued by two opposing camps but did not lead to war. We have already noted exceptions to some supposedly general laws of history:

- Democracies are more peaceable than despotisms or aristocracies.
- All history is the history of class struggles.
- Once you pay him the Danegeld, you'll never get rid of the Dane.
- Successful civilizations develop in moderate climates.
- You can't have too much education.
- National characters remain constant.
- Freedom follows trade.
- The child is father to the man.

Other suggested lessons with instances that refute them include the following:

'History is written by the victors.'

Exceptions to this 'lesson' include the Peloponnesian Wars: The Spartans were the victors, but the history was written by Athenians, such as Thucydides. The Children of Israel lost more battles and wars than they won, but it is their viewpoint we know about through the Bible, not that of their enemies. Most of the Crusades to Palestine were failures, but Crusaders wrote more accounts of them than did the Muslims.

'My enemy's enemy is my friend.'

The enemy of one's enemy is often one's friend, even if only briefly. This sometimes took the form of odds against evens.[32] The 'auld alliance' between France and Scotland was based on a common hostility towards England. Prussian, then German, rulers often cooperated with Russia against Poland and, when no Polish state existed, to suppress Polish nationalism. James II was unfortunate in 1688: Although fighting for the restoration of the Roman Catholic Church in England, he was opposed by Pope Innocent XI, who was in conflict with Louis XIV and supported William of Orange as the enemy of his French enemy. Patterns are not invariable: To date, there have been no alliances between Mexico and Canada against the United States.

Many wars have been three—or four-sided, degenerating at times to Hobbes's war of each against all. Well-known 'triangular wars' include the conflicts between France, Britain, and Indian princes during the eighteenth century and the World War II conflicts between German and Soviet Armies, and nationalist irregulars (South Slavs and Ukrainians among others) opposed to both.

Sometimes it is hard to decide who one's most dangerous enemy is. Many Western statesmen in the late 1930s found it hard to assess the relative dangers presented by Nazi Germany and Stalin's Russia. In the 1980s, Western statesmen were unsure whether Saddam Hussein's Iraq or theocratic Iran posed the greater threat to them. Today western societies may feel that they have good grounds to fear future actions by China, radical Islamists and the surviving North Korean regime, but find it difficult to rank those dangers in order

'Religions cause wars.'

Secularists such as Christopher Hitchens have claimed that conflicting religious beliefs are the root cause of wars, whereas Marx's 'historical materialism' placed religion in a 'superstructure' determined by economic and social relationships. Many wars have arisen almost exclusively from religious differences, but in even more wars, religion played a negligible role and often none at all. Christian heroes such as El Cid fought for both Christian and Muslim rulers. Islam was born in warfare, but Muslims killed more other Muslims than non-Muslims. The Greek cities constantly fought each other, despite sharing the same deities; the Roman Catholic rulers of medieval Europe fought each other more frequently than they fought Muslims and animists.

'Religions and ideologies stay the same.'

There is likely to be some continuity among groups who give themselves, or are given by others, the same name, but changes in meaning and definition are also considerable. What Conservatives (or conservatives) have sought to conserve has varied enormously; today to be a 'Liberal' in the United States is to be radical, whereas in Australia it is to be conservative. 'Right' and 'Left' can only be understood in context. Roman Catholicism today is many ways more like eighteenth-century Anglicanism than eighteenth-century Catholicism. The beliefs of Protestant churches such as Presbyterians and Methodists have shifted massively from biblical fundamentalism to liberal interpretations of scripture and 'progressive' social policies', having said which we are left to define 'progressive' in context. And so it goes on. We cannot dispense with labels but must apply and interpret them with care.

'Arbitrary rule creates sovereign risk.'

Risk of arbitrary seizure or confiscation of property and other wealth reduces incentives to improve land and buildings and deters investment from abroad. Under both tsars and commissars, Russians, nobles as well as serfs, were vulnerable to arbitrary confiscation of all they had. This has been true of many absolutist states, but arbitrary seizures may also be carried out by democracies. However, when Democrats get things wrong in our opinion we call them Populists who are guided by unworthy motives and pressures. That is a variant of the 'no true Scotsman' ploy.

'Power tends to corrupt and absolute power corrupts absolutely.'[33]

In this dictum, Lord Acton followed Pitt the Elder, who told the House of Lords in 1770 that 'unlimited power is apt to corrupt the minds of those who possess it'. But both men included important qualifiers in: 'tends' and 'is apt', and some leaders, such as Solon, Cincinnatus, and George Washington, seem to have resisted corruption by power. Impotence, too, can corrupt and destroy, as Hobbes maintained.

'People act in their own interests.'

This is often the circular argument that any voluntary act, however altruistic it may appear, is what people want to do and they are therefore acting in their own interests. Yet, there are abundant examples of people who consciously acted against what they genuinely believed to be their own interests. There are far more who did not act only in their own interests. Few of us can successfully serve the interests of others unless we know what is in our own interests.

'Historical understanding and proverbial wisdom.'

There are many well-known proverbs that are paired and give contrary and incompatible advice. Sometimes, 'absence makes the heart grow fonder', but at other times it's 'out of sight out of mind'; sometimes 'many hands make light work', but on other times 'too many cooks spoil the broth'. Sometimes it proves to have been right to 'strike whilst the iron is hot' and 'seize the day', but sometimes it might have been wiser to 'let sleeping dogs lie' and 'cross one's bridges when one gets to them'.

This same occurs in historical studies. Faced with the victories of the French revolutionaries in 1794 and of Hitler in 1940, we cry, 'Vive l'audace! Yes! Strike while the iron is hot'. If bold strokes fail, as did Napoleon's in 1812 and Hitler's in 1942, both in invasions of Russia, we note the folly of premature decisions and reflect on the value of letting sleeping dogs lie for longer. Yet different outcomes do not make life irrational or incomprehensible.

My argument is not that we learn nothing or at most very little from history, but that human activity, past, present and future, is not subject to what Sir Karl Popper called 'Inexorable Laws of Historical Destiny'[34]. This in no way precludes us from using past events to infer what the consequences of current aims and policies are likely to be But such inferences are totally different from physical laws that predict, say, given the correct allowance for altitude, what will be the temperatures at which freezing or boiling takes place. Popper's most plausible inference from past experience was that 'You cannot have full employment without inflation', but, as Antony Flew observed, it is quite possible for some agents, particularly governments, to take measures to prevent such a rise in unemployment, although the measures and their outcome might be worse than the threatened inflation. But this is not a law in the sense as that objects heavier than air fall to the ground or are attracted by a superior mass. Flew concluded, 'there neither are nor could be any laws of nature determining the senses of human action'[35].

During recent years historical determinists have placed great confidence in the arguments of E.H. Carr, notably in his *What is History*. Carr's fundamental errors have very recently been repeated by Australian historians Professors Ann Curthoys and John Docker. Carr's clearest formulation was that 'everything that happens has a cause or causes and could not have happened differently unless the cause or causes had also been different'[36]. Carr evidently failed to distinguish between inexorable causes and effects, such as the orbits of planets, and having reasons for actions. Carr's claim was true of the first kind, but not of the second in which, as Flew cites Leibniz, those 'causes' do not 'necessitate' but only 'incline' to a given action. Thus when Luther told the Diet of Worms, 'Here I stand. I can no other. So help me God', everyone who heard him knew that he could do other but had decided not to do, so that each of them must also make the same decision as Luther or a different one.

Difficulties and complexities

All branches of knowledge contain problems of very different levels of difficulty. This may be especially the case with history. At one level a lot of valuable historical knowledge may be acquired through learning by heart or other imitative activities. Swatting takes you further in History than in Algebra! Consequently some critics dismiss history as an easy subject, suitable for those incapable of learning a foreign language or very much of mathematics or physics. Yet to understand the aims and experiences of beings still alive who think and make decisions requires very considerable intellectual ability, and a dose of empathy helps as well. When those beings are of past generations, the demands on the would-be interpreter are even heavier. Collingwood's advice is worth repeating: 'If you can enter the mind of Neolithic man and make his thoughts your own you can then write his history, but not otherwise.'

Good history teachers often begin a new lesson with some consideration of aims and objectives of individuals or organizations or states and governments. Equally important but far less acted upon is the importance in actions and policies of fear and hope to avoid unnecessary danger. A change in the main source of fears may have wide effects

Alliances are often built on the basis of shared fears, so that the removal of an old fear may simply enable another to take its place Once the Persians had been defeated by the combined efforts of Athens and Sparta and other Greek city states, then they began to fear each other. As the Athenian general and historian Thucydides put it, the basic cause of the Peloponnesian Wars was that 'the Athenians becoming a great force and provoking fear in the Spartans, forced them to fight'[1] No untoward act of aggression was required to create that fear. Like the mountain that was climbed because it was there.

Sometimes two basically different antagonisms, say between A and B and another between C and D. blend together temporarily and we may have a war of A and C against B and D, but it might prove to be between A and D against B and C. A classic case is the 'Diplomatic Revolution' between the end of the War of the Australian Succession in 1748 and the outbreak in 1756 of what became known as The Seven Years War. Without cease French and British colonists and soldiers continued to confront each other, because there were real matters at issue between them. Similarly the attempt of Frederick II ('The Great') of Prussia to end the hegemony in Germany of the Austrian House of Habsburg and the resistance of the Queen Empress Marie Teresa was continuous. However partners were changed. English newspapers (those were early days of the power of the press) switched from denouncing Frederick as a ruthless aggressor destroying a nearly defenceless people to praising him as 'Good Old Fritz', an example to all of devotion to his people, once Prussia and not Austria was Britain's main continental ally.

In 1815 the apparent complete collapse of French power prompted two of the victors, Russia and Prussia, to combine to dominate eastern Europe at the expense of the Habsburgs. In response the British foreign Secretary Lord Castlereagh (later Marquis of Londonderry) allied with Metternich, the Austrian Chancellor to prevent them. A fresh war between the recent allies was avoided by the escape of Napoleon from Elba and his early successes in his 'Hundred Days' of Freedom. The Tsar and the King of Prussia were filled with such alarm that they abandoned their plans and entered once more into alliance with Britain and Austria. After peace negotiations resumed after Napoleon's defeat at Waterloo Russian and Prussian diplomacy was more cautious. However, France recovered so quickly that within a few years of Waterloo, French armies were engaged in a new intervention in Spain, where their armies had fought the British so recently in the Peninsula War, and in Belgium, to try to place a French prince as King of the new state.

Within perhaps only weeks of winning the war on the Western Front in 1918 the mood of the German armies turned to doubt that victory was possible and the war came quickly to an end. New figures soon replaced Kaiser Wilhelm II as the bogey man in the thinking of his erstwhile foes. Indeed not very long after the 'Hang the

Kaiser' general election of 1918 in Britain, the deeds of Wilhelm slipped from the consciousness of most peoples as he spent his remaining years in harmless exile in the Netherlands. Many leading French and British statesmen decided that the Soviet Republic was now the greatest danger to their interests. Rid of the main players, Greeks and Turks were able to concentrate their fears and hatreds upon each other.

Naïve thinkers have sometimes suggested that democracy, one person one vote, would reduce, perhaps eliminate, wars. John Stuart Mill argued that to base nationality on race or ethnicity would remove most of the known cases of war. However, like most principles, the democratic creed is open to terrible distortion. The really evil people who seem to be found in every generation and in many countries came to the conclusion that if every man (perhaps even every person) could decide on their ruler by counting heads, the best way to prevail in an election was, not quite literally but not too far from the mark either, to cut off the heads of a significant number of those you hate.

In 1912-3 the former subject peoples of the Balkans, or at any rate the states that then contained them, took advantage of internal strife in Istanbul to band together in a Balkan League to seize and divide among themselves the large amount of territory the Turks still held in the Balkans, with Thrace and the port of Salonika among the prizes. The League won some spectacular victories, partly because the main Turkish forces could not be deployed: they were in Anatolia and their transports had been defeated by the Greek Navy. Each of the allies tried with varying success to break its pre-war agreements and to deceive each other about their intentions Karl Marx would not have been surprised: he had written that the Balkans peoples grudged each other the very air they breathed. They were not the stuff from which international solidarity could easily be made.

The result was a second war in which Bulgaria, which had recently promoted itself to a Tsardom, was defeated by the combined forces of Serbia, Montenegro, Greece and, wait for it, Turkey. Keeping his own Bulgarian government in the dark, Tsar Ferdinand ordered Bulgarian troops to attach Serbs and Greeks immediately. Bulgarian soldiers camped more or less in the next field to their former Serbian allies attacked them at night whilst they were asleep in their tents. This villainy soon became widely known and Greek forces took revenge by destroying dozens of Bulgarian villages and massacring all the population. The Bulgarian government swore revenge after its defeat and was able to act on its threat when Serbia was invaded by Austrian armies in 1914. When German troops carried out similar atrocities against Greek civilians during the Second World War, few Bulgarians, Serbs or Montenegrins wept many tears.

Great miseries were inflicted on each other by Greeks and Turks after 1919. Most of the Greeks who lived in the new Turkey created then had been settled for many generations and many spoke not Greek but Turkish. Their main distinctiveness was their Greek Orthodox Christianity. Similarly many of the Turkish families living in Greece spoke not Turkish but Greek and their distinctive characteristic was Islam. Both uprooted populations endured terrible suffering and, after they reached the places to which aloof bureaucrats had assigned them, they often found, naturally enough, that families not forced to move had occupied all the land and buildings available and there was rarely any authority capable of overturning right of possession.

A spectacular *volte face* was the August 1939 Nazi-Soviet Pact negotiated by Von Ribbentrop and Molotov, but directed by Hitler and Stalin. For about the previous seven years the line of the Soviet government and international organizations under its control such as the Comintern had been that the main danger to 'Progressive Mankind' 'lay in Fascism, most particularly as manifested in Hitler's Germany and Nazi ideology. In speeches at Geneva Maxim Litvinov and other Soviet delegates to the League of Nations pleaded for a United Front against Fascism and War. Recruitment for the International Brigades fighting on the Republican side in the Spanish Civil War was centred on the need to stop fascism and to prevent the spread of Hitler's malign power. In Britain and Australia and other western states communist attacks on the Labor and Social Democrat parties nearly ceased; instead pleas were made to them to understand that they shared a common cause and their differences were merely about timing and tactics, not about aims. No more talk was heard then about 'Social Fascists: Similarly in the German press and radio station a day seldom went by without bitter denunciations of the criminal regime in the Kremlin and its threat to the Aryan peoples of the world. Not only insults were exchanged, but the rival intelligence services engaged in intrigues and sabotage against each other. Just one strand in their relationship suggested that things might become otherwise: both states were, as the saw it, victims of an unjust peace settlement in 1919 and each helped the other with the exchange of arms and strategic materials that the League of Nations imagined it had prohibited.

Then in a single day all was turned upside down. Some party leaders did not believe the news when first they heard it but rejected it as disinformation and provocation. In London the General Secretary of the CPGB himself protested against what he thought was an error on the part of some minor officials in the CPSU(B). Within days Harry Pollitt had recanted as he realized that this alliance with Hitler's Germany could only be the work of Comrade Stalin himself. The western communist parties went into action to denounce the war as an imperialist war in which the working class had no interest in supporting either side. Industrial sabotage and go-slow tactics were carried out in factories and dockyards. Over half of the members in several western countries resigned from the communist party and most of the others were profoundly shaken, even though they somehow managed to try to convince others both that the new line was correct and that its direct opposite had also been right until the day it was jettisoned. It was perhaps just as well for their mental health that western communists did not learn until a further decade of so that as part of the Ribbentrop-Molotov deal the Soviet authorities handed over all the German communists who had taken refuge in the Soviet Union after the Nazi accession to power in 1933.

Many Czechs were expelled in 1938-9 from the predominantly German Sudetenland, whilst after 1945 Germans, both residents of many generations as well as families planted there in 1938-9, were expelled from Sudetenland. The Nazi-Soviet Pact of 1939 and the subsequent partition of Poland between Germany and the Soviet Union, succeeded in 1941 by the German invasion of the Soviet Union, led to the displacement of hundreds of thousands of people, many of them twice and some three times over, as the tide of battle and occupation moved eastwards or westwards. By 1945 'Displaced Persons' added together would have been close to the population of France.

The Soviet and Nazi governments, and those of their satellite states, seemed to vie with each other in ethnic cleansing: hundreds of thousands of Poles, Ukrainians, Latvians, Lithuanians, Finns, Estonians, Byelorussians and Jews, were 'displaced'. In 1946 as part of the Potsdam Treaty historic Poland, which had disappeared once again from the maps altogether in 1939, was once more restored but shifted some two hundred miles westwards: its losses in the East to the Soviet Union were supposedly compensated by the incorporation into Poland of what had been German territories before 1938, most of whose German-speaking populations were expelled.

Move on to June 1941 and another tumultuous change in the thinking of the Left with the German invasion of the Soviet Union. Hitler was once more the font of the worst evils and all must unite to defeat this danger to mankind. Communist shop stewards became ardent advocates of higher production and voluntary overtime and struggled on the factory floor with Trotskyites who continued to regard the war as imperialist and more so, because the motives of the Soviet Union were, they held, even viler than those of Hitler or Mussolini or the Japanese. Once again, one must be cautious in the use of generic terms. The dominant thinking that is accurately depicted as typical of any Right or Left is very likely to be far from universal so that any worthwhile historical judgments have to penetrate below the surface descriptors. Yet, time being always fleeting, we have to make some assumptions about individuals on the basis of the company they keep. Aesop again proves a wise political thinker in proverbs about birds of a feather and the like.

Particularly difficult problems arise for historians when three sided conflicts are waged in which some of the belligerents find it hard to prioritise their fears and hatreds. Several situations of this sort raged in Eastern Europe between 1941 and 1945, most notably in what had been and briefly became once more, Yugoslavia. The three sides were the German invaders and their local allies, such as the Ustashi in Croatia, and two opposed guerrilla movements: Chetniks and Partisans, each fighting to be in a position to take over if and when the German armies were defeated. In Poland and Ukraine and Greece similar highly destructive struggles of this kind took place.

Massive population changes took place in Korea and Vietnam in the second half of the twentieth century. The final frontiers reflected the (mis)fortunes of war, not political loyalties held before the wars began. It was not until the early 1950s that the hundreds of thousands of Europeans who had become 'Displaced Persons' found somewhere or the other a new home. Australia was an early refuge, especially for refugees from the Baltic States of Estonia, Lithuania and Latvia.

The Partition of India of 1947 was largely forced on the Attlee Labor government in Britain by the failure of Indian (Hindu essentially) Congress and the Muslim League to agree on the arrangement that should succeed the British Raj when it withdrew from the Southern Continent in 1947. The final Partition was followed by mass expulsions of Hindus from the new Muslim state of Pakistan and of many Muslims from predominantly Hindu provinces, although several million Muslims remained in the new Republic of India and a few Hindus in Pakistan. India is the fourth largest Muslim country in the world.

The death toll was very high, especially in the two way traffic between West Punjab and provinces awarded to India. One of the greatest British contributions to India, an excellent railway system, was the scene of many of the worst atrocities as trains were ambushed and their passengers slaughtered. East Bengal remained as East Pakistan for less than twenty years: a major revolt against rule from distant Karachi was successful in 1973 after great loss of life. Both India and Pakistan are very difficult to administer because of the great differences in language and customs, although that was rarely acknowledged when the British Raj was accused of neglect, inefficiency and exploitation of its Indian subjects.

The end to British rule in India is also a clear counter example to the glib thought that history will prove who were right and who wrong in past conflicts. If Lord Mountbatten and the British government had known of every word and action of the Indian Congress and the Muslim League at the top and of the Indian masses below, it is unlikely that they could have conceived of a plan that would avoid mass death and suffering. Or that we would do any better! We might conclude that it would have been best to let sleeping dogs lie, but Hindu, Muslim and Sikh hounds were far from somnolent and needed no outsiders to wake them up to the attractions of inflicting severe damage and pain on ancient foes.

It is often useful to be able to identify just what a reaction was caused by. For example, the failure of the Social-Democratic parties in Germany, Britain, France and other European states to act effectively to prevent war in 1914 led many socialists to abandon their previous trust in constitutional methods of social transformation and to adopt instead the harsher organizational structures and revolutionary tactics Lenin had developed. In turn fear and horror at the ferocity of the Bolsheviks spurred many conservative thinkers to abandon parliamentary debate for meeting violence with violence. Fascism and Communism denounced each other but in doing so made recruits for each other. A slogan of the German Communist Party before 1933 was 'First Hitler and then us', but the National Socialists (Nazis) emulated Mussolini's Italian Fascists and got their blow in first. Fascism and Communism each presented itself as the main, indeed the only, safeguard against or alternative to the evils perpetrated by the other. Both were wrong and, despite all the unpleasant features of the world of 2013, there are many more states now with at least democratic pretensions than in the 1930s and fewer totalitarian states. A common defense of political violence is that the other side started it and they must not be allowed to succeed. Some such claims must be right—someone must have struck the first blow or put the first boot in. But rugby players defend themselves with: 'We just got our aggression in first!'. A short film that is a brilliant political lesson was made by Stan Laurel and Oliver Hardy during the 1930s. They have a slight collision with another car and quarrel with him about who was to blame. Then step by step each side destroys a part of the other car until two heaps of junk are all that remains. But both sides felt that honour was satisfied.

Who are 'we' and what in the past is 'ours'?

A great problem for history teachers in many countries, in almost every one of them in fact, is to determine what constitutes 'our' history. There is wide agreement that some priority should be given to the past of one's own country, but what does such an entity consist of historically? Some modern states had come into existence as the end result, so far, of consolidation and incorporation. We often find that the historical title under which they are studied is 'The Unification of Germany/Italy/ France/China and so on. Other countries have been created by revolt, or at least by separation, from another political unit. In what circumstances, to what extents and with what justifications does the history of the state from which your country broke away form part of your history or that of your country as it now exists? That is tricky merely at the political level. Is there an equal moral obligation on the part of the Welsh, the English, the Scots and the Irish to learn about the pre-unity past when they were separate from each other? What difference, if any, does or should it make to that question if subsequently one of those former components has become independent. Similar issues arise across the globe. Is the history of India before the great Mongol invasions a priority for the education of children in Pakistan today; and is the history of the tribes who then swept into India part of the historical past of non-Muslim Indian children. Ought children who live in any part of the Roman Empire, in Italy or in Rome itself, have different historical identities or different courses in school from each other? Clearly a score or more of similarly relevant questions face us.

The problems of ideological discontinuity, whether primarily religious or political or ethnic, are greater than those of pure demography. There was a time when current differences between Serbs and Croats did not exist, any more than Serbia and Croatia. They were generally called Slavs, perhaps South Slavs. A century of so after provisional or final settlement in the north-east Balkans, some of those South Slavs were converted to Roman Catholic Christianity and others to Greek Orthodoxy. The fortunes of war either enlarged or diminished their territories. As a defense of the Austro-German heartland of Christendom, overtures were made to Serbs temporarily free from military crises at home to quit their dwellings and move to the southern borders of what we now think of as Croatia on particularly attractive terms of tenure and protection of culture. Many Serbs did so move and thus the pattern of demography just between those two peoples became increasingly complex. And unfortunately, as we have noted, familiarity does not always lead to harmony and toleration. The question arises at the end of this of what should be regarded as common in the cultural traditions of those two peoples. And that problem can be extended to include ultimately the whole human race. But, as we also know the tyranny of time makes it impossible to study all that deserves to be studied.

.During the time of the former Yugoslavia, which was basically Serbia writ large, Croats who sought independence gave great support to entomologists who claimed that Croatian had been a separate and identifiable language from the earliest times of which we have knowledge. Croatian scholars wrote many pages that listed separate words in Serbian and Croatian and in particular denying that there was such a language as Serbo-Croat, of which modern Serbian and Croatian are merely dialects. Serbian intellectuals on the contrary argued for a foundational and continuing Serbo-Croatian tongue.

Who said History was easy? We return to Europe in the sixteenth and seventeenth centuries of the Reformation and Counter-Reformation (the Roman Catholic fight back), but are unlikely to find its main events much easier to grasp. Let us consider a few states one by one, starting with France.

France remained a Roman Catholic state during the sixteenth century, but at times it seemed a close-run thing and the Huguenots, the French Calvinists, looked likely to take over the whole of France or at least to establish a Calvinist state within France. Calvinism, attracted many converts, especially in the ports of the Atlantic coast and centres of the textile industry. Their leadership included a significant minority of the greatest noble families of France. Some were sincere converts, some sought greater independence from the Monarchy; and some envied the wealth and possessions of the Catholic Church. Many had more than one of these motives, of course. The Huguenots saw the Papacy and the Roman Church as a whole as their main enemy, since they hoped a king of France might convert to Protestantism. They did not envisage that their own leader would become King of France, which he did in 1589 after Henry III was assassinated by a Catholic fanatic.

The main fear of the Catholic League was that heresy might prevail in France. They considered that the long-term interests of France lay in alliance with Spain and the Empire, not in reducing Habsburg power. The main fear of the Monarchists was an anarchic France in which Spanish and German Catholic troops could occupy and plunder the land, but scarcely less and at times more, as the 1572 Massacre in Paris showed, they also feared that the Huguenots would split France permanently into Catholic and Huguenot states.

The Royalist Party was for long periods led by Italians: first by Catherine d'Medici, widow of Francis II, and two generations on by another Italian princess Marie d'Medici, who acted as Regent after the death of her husband, Louis XIII and whose chief adviser, the Italian-born Cardinal Mazarin, widely thought to be her lover as well. Each party was also led for some years by a Henry, so that the French Wars of Religion are also known as the Wars of the Three Henrys: King Henry III, son of Catherine; Henry, Duke of Guise, leader together with his brother Cardinal Guise, led the Catholic League; and the Huguenots were led by Henry of Navarre. Catherine tried to ensure that neither religious party controlled French policy. In her greatest change of heart, or unspeakable treachery, she first arranged the marriage of her daughter to Henry of Navarre in an attempt to conciliate the Huguenots, but then, fearing their recent growth of strength, she planned the massacre of the Huguenot leadership that had come to hostile Paris for the wedding. The bridegroom was lucky to escape with his life. The Massacre of St Bartholomew's Day, 1572, was regarded by many Protestants as final evidence of the wickedness of the Roman Church. One of many things I do not understand is the difference between Paris and London in the religious conflicts of the sixteenth and seventeenth centuries. In England the City of London was a major citadel of Protestantism, usually in its Puritanical and Calvinist forms, whereas Paris was massively for the Mass, if that vile pun can be excused. Henry of Navarre had to convert to Roman Catholicism before Paris would accept him as king of France, as most parts of the country had for five years and more. Paris was worth a Mass, Henry famously declared.

Half a century later tension continued in France between religious allegiance and national interests. Cardinal Richelieu, during the minority of Louis XIII and when he came of age, constantly worked against the Habsburgs to frustrate what he saw as the encirclement of France. He took France in the 1630s into the German war later known as the Thirty Years War against the-Habsburgs and thus against the Catholic side. A Cardinal of the Roman Church was largely responsible for the survival of Protestantism in Germany and the Netherlands.

Because the Popes were secular rulers in Central Italy, they often became involved in or initiated Italian wars. These became international conflicts once Charles VIII of France invaded Milan in 1494 and Ferdinand pursued the claims of the kingdom of Aragon on Naples and Sicily. Sometimes a Pope was on the opposite side from the Catholic League which had been created to support the Papacy and the Roman Church. The Catholic Emperor Charles V frequently clashed with Popes and his mercenary troops, many nominally Lutherans, mutinied in 1527 and sacked Rome because they had not been paid for a considerable time. As late as 1692 when James II of England was defeated at the battle of the Boyne in Ireland, Papal banners were flown by the forces of the Dutch William of Orange, the new king of England and a key Protestant leader. The Papacy thought its disputes with Louis XIV over ecclesiastical appointments in France more important than restoring a deposed Catholic ruler to the Crown of the Three Kingdoms.

The Reformation had two apparently contrary aspects. It was a more religious age in which probably a higher proportion of Europeans took religion seriously and read their Bibles and prayer books than ever before, but there was also more anti-clericalism than before. The two trends were quite compatible, however, since the better read the flock, the more demanding and critical they were of the pastor. Being a Roman Catholic in a Catholic country did not necessarily make one a friend of the clergy. In Spain Ferdinand and Isabella quarreled with Popes over control of the Inquisition; in France Kings were not prepared to lose control over high offices of the Church that affected nearly a third of their territories. The English Parliament during the early fifteenth century passed legislation preventing appeals in law cases from being heard outside the realm. Breaches of the Praemunire Laws finally brought Cardinal Wolsey low in 1529, even though he had broken the statute at Henry VIII's command The main opponents of the Cardinal's influence over Henry were noblemen who remained faithful to the Catholic Church throughout their lives. Priests who rose from humble circumstances and presumed to be the equals or betters of born aristocrats may have been more disliked than younger sons who rapidly become bishops or abbots as a result of family influence. The anti-clericalism of the populace was often directed against "Benefit of Clergy", the legal privileges discussed above in the section on 'Relationships'.

Over a little more than half a century emerged what was in contemporary terms a monster state or aggregation of states under the rule of the Austrian House of Habsburg. The first and apparently remote steps were the marriage in 1469 of Isabella of Castile and Ferdinand of Aragon, the two most powerful Spanish kingdoms that had often been at war with each other; and that of Mary of Burgundy and the Emperor

71

Maximilian which delivered the Low Countries to the Habsburgs. The next more drawn-out step was the creation of a vast Spanish Empire in the Americas, stretching southwards from Mexico, but excluding Brazil which was awarded to Portugal in the 1494 division of newly discovered lands by Pope Alexander VI, himself a Spanish Borgia, at the Treaty of Tordesillas. Spain gained the islands subsequently called the Philippines in the papal distribution that made a hypothetical line of longitude west of the Azores the divider. Next came the marriage of Juana, the eldest daughter of Ferdinand and Isabella, to Philip of Flanders, son of Mary and Philip and Habsburg heir to the Netherlands, Austria and other German lands and parts of Italy. Their son Charles became in 1516 King of Spain and in 1519 was elected Emperor of the Holy Roman Empire of the German people. This was a position with uncertain powers, particularly after several German princes, including the Electors of Brandenburg and Saxony and the Elector Palatine announced their conversion to Lutheranism and ended all allegiance to the Papacy. In 1530 the Confession of Augsburg showed that Lutheranism had taken root in Germany.[37]

Spain was closest to a superpower in sixteenth century Europe, with France in a markedly inferior position until Louis XIV entered into his majority and the Treaty of the Pyrenees ended in 1659 warfare between France and Spain that outlasted by eleven years the German wars in which both had been leading protagonists. As Emperor and an important German Prince in his own hereditary right, together with the possessions of Spain, Charles was the most powerful ruler in the western world.

The problems of the Habsburgs may seem small in comparison with those of other European rulers. However, their extensive territories defied close direction by one person, especially given the slowness of travel, whereas France was compact, although virtually surrounded by Habsburg power, except on the sea and at the feet of the Alps. Harder to surmount than the tyranny of distance were the very different modes of government and customs of the many peoples over whom Charles V ruled. Just in Spain alone it was hard to subdue the quarrels inherited from the feuding medieval Christian kingdoms and their representative bodies, whilst the conquests in America brought not only immense wealth to Spain, but also inflation and a dislocated economy. Spain received an enormous bounty in wealth but squandered most of it.

Also weakening was the disdain of the hidalgo for trade, together with the attraction of careers in the church and the law to the brightest minds. This was compounded by the expulsion of Jews and Muslims, even those who had undertaken conversion to Christianity, since Inquisitors suspected many conversions to be false. It also proved a great help to the Ottoman Empire, then Spain's main naval rival in the Mediterranean, since thousands of exiled Jews and Muslims of high intellectual and/ or entrepreneurial capacity fled to Egypt and other Muslim lands where they became prime creators of wealth for the Turks.

Oblivious to those ill effects on Spain, Louis XIV nearly two centuries later decided in 1685 to revoke the Edict of Nantes which in 1598 had brought peace to France at the expense, so many pious Roman Catholic believed, of countenancing heresy and rewarding heretics. Spain was not a beneficiary of the expulsion of the Huguenots from France. since moving to the other side of the Pyrenees would have seemed a leap from the frying pan into the fire for most Huguenot families. Instead the beneficiaries of the crafts and arts in which many Huguenots were highly proficient were the British and the Dutch, and several of their North American colonies as well, and German states, most notably Brandenburg (Prussia)

For most of the later Middle Ages English rulers were in alliance with one or another of the Spanish ruling families. Originally influenced by the Odds and Evens principle with France in between them, dynastic marriages had made English nobles such as John of Gaunt claimants for a Spanish Crown. The marriages of Henry VIII, and before him his elder brother Prince Arthur, to Catherine of Aragon, and Mary Tudor's marriage to Philip of Spain continued a long tradition.

The main English export in the Middle Ages was wool and its biggest markets were Antwerp and other Flemish cities that were major cloth producers, but colonial rivalries gradually became more important as both English and Dutch tried to break the monopolies of trade with the Americas and East Indies that Spain and Portugal tried to maintain. In 1500 Spain was a valued ally of England, but by 1600 Spain had become the main object of English nationalist fear and hatred. Those feelings were fully reciprocated by Spaniards resentful at attacks by English privateers, little different from pirates or terrorists as the Spaniards saw it, who seized Spanish vessels and/or their cargos in American waters and even the mid-Atlantic. The names of John Hawkins and his cousin Francis Drake were cursed in churches and in taverns.

Elizabeth's England had three informal parties, one of which was centred on her person, as with her father, with the crucial difference that Elizabeth inherited a far weaker position than he had. That was mainly the result of Henry's marriages and the declaration, admittedly subsequently rescinded, of Elizabeth's illegitimacy. The Protestants prevailed under the boy king Edward VI, during whose brief reign Henry's Church of England was changed in a Protestant direction The Catholic party enjoyed power between 1553 and 1558, the five years of the reign of Mary Tudor, eldest legitimate child of Henry VIII and Catherine of Aragon, although Parliament *refused* to restore the monasteries and other religious houses dissolved in the 1530s, Her marriage to Philip of Spain, as well as the martyrdom of leading Anglican churchmen, including Thomas Cranmer, compiler of the Book of Common Prayer, and Bishops Hugh Latimer and Nicolas Ridley, made the Catholic cause much less popular, but still not without chances of future success.

Elizabeth outmaneuvered both Catholics and Puritans in difficult circumstances. It was not until 1570 that Philip gave up hope of marrying her and leading England back to Rome. Elizabeth retained the loyalty of several of the great English Catholic families, so that the Royalist Party (it was not given that name until the civil wars of the 1640s) was relatively stronger than in sixteenth century France, then much weaker during the seventeenth century.

The third party in the English internal triangular struggle was not fully visible in 1558 when Elizabeth came to the throne. Its leaders were Protestants who had escaped to Germany or Switzerland during the Marian persecution. Many of them would gladly have reduced the powers of the monarch and replaced the Royal Supremacy over the Church of England with the equivalent of the Scottish Kirk, but most of them appreciated that a greater peril might face them if Elizabeth were overthrown. They only made their bid forty years after her death They gained their wish but only for a few months in 1644, after which they quarrelled with their Scottish allies, who were defeated by Cromwell's Ironsides at Marston Moor.

Charles I received strong military support from Ireland, but the Irish Catholics were unpopular in England and their unpopularity rubbed off onto their English co-religionists, Protestant antagonism to Irish Catholicism increased sharply and Cromwell had wide approval when he ordered the expulsion of Catholics from their lands in Leinster and replaced them with English families. Thus another step was taken in hatreds still strong today. The Scottish armies were also disliked as foreign invaders when they entered England on the side of Parliament in 1643, so that when Oliver Cromwell and most of the leadership of the Parliamentary armies quarrelled with the Scots and their English Presbyterian allies who wanted a Scottish church system in England, it was dislike of the Scots as much as liking for Cromwell that swung opinion in his favour.

The English supported Dutch independence and religious freedom against Spanish armies, but were also rivals with the Dutch in trade and commerce. There were Anglo-Dutch wars in three successive decades from the 1650s to the 1670s, in one of which a Dutch fleet sailed up the Medway and burned English ships at anchor. The Massacre at Amboyna in 1623 when English merchants were beheaded by the Dutch for infringing what the Dutch claimed as a trading monopoly, caused great bitterness in mercantile circles in England. It was two centuries later that George Canning wrote the squib: 'In matters of commerce the fault of the Dutch/Lay in giving too little and asking too much.' Common Protestantism and formal alliance did not make the two peoples friendly towards each other, but joint fear of France brought them together in emergencies.

'Balance of Power' considerations led English governments sometimes to support Spain against France after years of opposing French power. It was only when after about 1680 that the power of France seemed a far greater danger to the Dutch and to England than either to the other that a long term informal alliance between them became the norm, and France returned to its old place as England's chief enemy. By then Spain and France had become close allies in treaties that created what was often called 'The Family Compact', cemented by marriages of French Bourbons to Spanish Habsburgs that gave Louis XIV strong claims for his grandson to succeed to the Spanish Throne. The result was the War of the Spanish Succession (1702-1714) in which the Duke of Marlborough gained fame.[38]

Scotland, too, had three conflicting parties. Mary Stuart had few of the political skills of her cousin Elizabeth Tudor, whose throne she coveted and for which her hereditary claim was a good one, provided that Elizabeth was regarded as a bastard because the marriage of Henry VIII and her mother Anne Boleyn had been annulled. Mary's failings crippled the hopes of the Scottish Royalists. Mary married as her third husband the Earl of Boswell, the murderer, of her second husband, Darnley. Whether she shared in Boswell's guilt is uncertain, but a rising against her forced her to take refuge in England where she was at the mercy of Elizabeth, the cousin Mary's backers had been trying to depose and to place Mary on the throne of England. Mary's flight into England to escape from her fierce rebellious Covenanting subjects was an embarrassment for Elizabeth, since plots were frequently made to rescue Mary from imprisonment and to depose Elizabeth. Elizabeth did not wish to order the death of a cousin and a queen, but in 1587 she was finally pressed into signed the death warrant.

Disputes about whether regicide could be justified if a ruler was unjust or evil, together with disagreement about the doctrine of 'The Divine Right of Kings', split both Protestants and Catholics. Many leading Calvinists and Roman Catholics advocated regicide, though they preferred to use the term 'tyrannicide', if even the most legitimate of rulers ignored their religious duty and failed to suppress heresy or even encouraged it. Outstanding advocates were the stern Scottish Calvinist John Knox and the Spanish Jesuit Suarez, a learned theologian whose name became loathed in royalist circles. Some argued on purely theological grounds that kings are God's deputies on earth and that only God can depose them. Others argued that a strong hereditary monarchy was the best safeguard against anarchy and civil war. On the continent Lutherans and in England Anglicans embraced the Divine Right theory.

After the execution of Mary Queen of Scots in 1587 and the defeat of the Armada in 1588, militant Calvinist Puritans within the Church of England thought it safe to demand first of Elizabeth and then James far more extensive changes in the Church of England, with at their heart a reduction in the powers of the Bishops or their abolition King James was shrewd when he declared, 'No Bishop, no King', because in the seventeenth century the royal power required consistent support from the pulpit to remain secure. Only prelates appointed by the Crown could provide that and certainly not pastors elected by their congregations, as the 'Congregationalists' urged.

James was given so hard a time as boy and youth by his Scottish guardians that he formed a lifelong hatred for Presbyterian governance of the Kirk, the Church of Scotland, and for Parliamentary control of the king. It is easy to scoff at the Divine Right of Kings, but the amount of human suffering when law and order are absent and Thomas Hobbes' state of nature prevails where each man must fend for himself, we begin to understand the importance of security. Of all the uncertain solutions, hereditary monarchy seemed to many the one most likely to succeed. How to blend freedom and safety is a secret that few peoples have so far discovered.

At the partition in 1556 of Charles V's Empire after his abdication and retreat to a monastery, the Seventeen Provinces of the Netherlands became a possession of the Spanish Crown through Charles' son Philip. Charles brother Ferdinand received the Habsburg lands in Germany and Italy and there began a complex pattern of relationships between, England, France, Spain, the United Provinces and the Austrian House of Habsburg. Each became at some time or the other an enemy of one or the other.

Until about a century ago most historians believed that the modern border between the Netherlands and Belgium was been the result of differences in language and religious inclinations that existed before the Revolt against Spain broke out in 1572. The Dutch historian Pieter Geyl claimed on the contrary that the division owed much more to terrain and the fortunes of war: the north with its lakes, bogs and rivers favored the rebels, whereas the flat but firm plains farther south favored the Spanish infantry. If linguistic factors had prevailed then, or did today, the Flemish-speaking third of Belgium would be in The Netherlands. Furthermore, before open revolt began, the southern provinces, and particularly the city of Antwerp, were rather more Protestant and in favour of independence from Spain than the northern ones. Decades of warfare with their changing battle lines finally ended with the seven northern provinces free of Dutch rule, but the ten southern still subject to it.

During and after the fighting, there was substantial population movement, with Protestants moving north east and the Catholics south west. This increased when the mouth of the River Scheldt was closed to shipping to protect the ports of Amsterdam and Rotterdam from the competition of Antwerp. In the world of art a distinction is made between Dutch and Flemish painters, but the distinction if often an unreal one.

No sage could have forecast at the start of the Revolt against Spain that at the end of the fighting the Seventeen Provinces would be divided as took place. Equally there would be astonishment that, although the names of the units have changed, those frontiers remain largely intact: the Spanish Netherlands (until 1714 at the

76

Treaty of Utrecht), the Australian Netherlands (between 1714 and the Revolutionary and Napoleonic Wars), the unsuccessful reunified Kingdom of the Netherlands (1815-1833) and as Belgium, except during two wartime German occupations. Over the centuries of war the southern provinces lost some areas, small in size but of major strategic value, to France, but the basic division remained intact.

Was Voltaire right when he wrote in 1767 that 'history is nothing more than a tableau of crimes and misfortunes.'? Was Catherine Morland justified in her complaint in Northanger Abbey that history 'tells me nothing that does not either vex or weary me? The quarrels of popes and kings, with wars and pestilences on every page, the men all so good for nothing, and hardly any women at all.' Many, perhaps most, children find current political and religious wrangles far from enthralling and bygone controversies of a similar nature even less inviting. Can we simplify without distorting? I tried hard to condense and simplify some aspects of Reformation and Counter Reformation history, but on a re-reading it is still very demanding: so many names and places!

THE DANGEROUS LURE OF TELEOLOGY

Given all the complexities of human intentions and their often unforeseen results, it is natural for people to seek a key to the doors, a sword that will cut through the Gordian Knot. At the heart of most of these temptations is belief in a *telos*. Teleology takes many forms, but all concur that it tries to provide life with a meaning and purpose that it is unlikely to possess. Millions accept them implicitly and probably nearly as many are conscious advocates or believers. Christianity is, from the viewpoint of the Jews, a teleology that has annexed their history and scriptures to become merely the precursor of Jesus of Nazareth. There is designated 'The Old Testament' with the clear implication that it has been superseded by a New Testament. The finest passages of the greatest of the OT prophets have been put to Christian purposes and by none more successfully than by George Frederik Handel in his Messiah, with Charles Jennens' marvelous transposition of Isaiah and other prophets.

The Jews for their part see history as a drama in which the Children of Israel, the Chosen People of the Lord Almighty, went astray by worshipping false gods and doing evil, for which they have been punished most painfully through the generations, but whose sufferings will end finally in triumphal bliss when the Day of the Lord comes nigh. Muslims are equally confident that the House of Islam will one day in the not too distant future include all peoples.

Most tribes and nations have their historical teleologies, in which a central strand in world history is how step by step, though often with setbacks, their scattered peoples, perhaps under foreign rule, came to form the state destined to be from the beginning.

We noted earlier that rough camps from which rough raiders set forth sometimes became states, and within two or three generations, the forebears of the chief robber were claimed to be gods: Heracles among the Greek deities and Wodan and Thor among the Vikings appeared as the founders of such royal families.

Marx and other secular prophets detected through history a dialectical progress from the equality and unity of the primitive tribe, through painful progressions in which class struggle was the fundamentally decisive force, intertwined with changes in the material modes of production, to the final return of classless society, but one in which there will be wealth and abundance for all, not the restricted productivity of tribal life. Before the proletariat overcomes exploitation and the tyranny of class over class, there may be great suffering. Then will be established the Dictatorship of the Proletariat and the rule of the working class effected through the leadership of the communist parties. Together the thinkers who have read the book of history accurately and the workers who produce the wealth of nations will prepare, perhaps with severity, for the dawn of communism, a classless society in which ultimately the state as an organ of class coercion will fade away, since there will be no more classes and so no more antagonisms for the state to control. Then the human race will return to the equality and solidarity of the primitive tribe, but at vastly higher levels of material and cultural wealth.

Sceptics may scoff that the Day of the Lord, the Second Coming, the Return of the Hidden Imam, and the fading away of the state have the common feature of being guaranteed yet indeterminate events that never take place, but time has passed since prophets first proclaimed their future arrival is short in terms of the life of even our own planet. Karl Popper, an astute critic of the version of teleology he called historicism, rightly argued that there was no predestined end of history, but that human beings had the power, would they but use it, to shape it in many ways. Frederick Engel's words that 'freedom is the recognition of necessity' have been variously interpreted. Those who thought that the worst brutalities of Stalinism were imminent in the theories of Marx and Engels took those words as a defense of tyranny, whereas his admirers considered that he had extended the stoic advice that one should address problems that can be solved, not those impossible to resolve.

Chapter 3

CIVILIZATION IN AUSTRALIA

The very first sentence of the first volume of Manning Clark's *A History of Australia* is: 'Civilization did not begin in Australia until the last quarter of the eighteenth century . . . The early inhabitants of the continent created cultures but not civilizations' [39] Clark added, 'Of the way of life of these peoples before the coming of European civilization, little need or indeed can be said . . . Whatever the reason may have been, the failure of the aborigines to emerge from a state of barbarism deprived them of the material resources with which to resist an invader, and left them without the physical strength to protect their culture.'.[40]

Clark followed the generally accepted view, stated in 1956 by William Howells in his *Man in the Beginning*: 'simply having cities with all it implies, such as food in quantity', transport, trade, artisans, formal government and expanded religions.[41] Not all civilizations are benign and praiseworthy, although it is right to use 'civilized' as a compliment, since so many of our cultural treasures have been created by civilizations during the relatively short time since they emerged.

From the eighteenth century till the 1970s anthropologists, as they came to be called, had contrasted civilization with savagery and barbarism. The latter distinction was defined by the Australian Marxist archaeologist V. Gordon Childe as follows:

Plant cultivation and stock breeding—in a word food production—constituted an epoch making innovation. It is rightly taken to mark in archaeology the beginning of a new age—the Neolithic or new Stone Age—or in socio-economic terms the boundary between Savagery and Barbarism.[42]

Nobody supposed then that all human groups should be called civilized. Indeed, the principal aim of scholars had been to discover how and when some peoples had 'crossed the ditch' from pre-civilized existences to civilized life, together with finding out why other peoples had not made that leap. Childe's politics envisaged a transformation of the dark of capitalism into the light of socialism/communism; this vision, Kenneth Maddock suggested, was applied in Childe's *The Dawn of European Civilisation* to the transcending of savagery by barbarism and of barbarism by civilization.[43] Childe was confident that man's mastery of matter and annihilation of space in the twentieth century is just the consummation of a progressive process initiated by Neolithic tools developed several hundred thousand years ago. Far from celebrating the remnants in hunter-gathering and tribalism, Childe regretted that Australia's Aborigines had not advanced beyond that state. As Professors R. M. and C. M. Berndt put it:

> The impact of the outside world came as a rude shock. Things were happening outside the framework of what the Aborigines conceived to be the established order of life, both physical and social: things which were not provided for within that framework, and could not be pigeon-holed into any known category.[44]

The buccaneer William Dampier in 1697 claimed that the inhabitants of New Holland were 'the miserablest people in the world' who 'setting aside their Human Shape . . . differ but little from Brutes'. Yet James Cook seemed to deliberately rebut Dampier in claiming that despite their wretched appearance the Aborigines were in reality more tranquil and far happier than Europeans.[45] Joseph Banks at one point came close to the 'noble savage' position:

Thus live these I had almost said happy people, content with little, nay, almost nothing. Far enough removed from the anxieties attending riches. From them appear how small are the real wants of human nature.

However, Banks added that they 'seem to have no fixed habitation but move about from place to place like wild beasts in search of food' and 'of cloths they had not the least part but naked as ever our first father was before his fall, they seemed no more conscious of their nakedness than if they had not been the children of Parents who eat the fruit of the tree of knowledge'.[46]

Some of Cook's comments on Aborigines also virtually defined what was thought to constitute savagery: 'Their houses are mean small hovels not much bigger than an oven . . . their canoes are as mean as can be conceived . . . we see this country in the pure State of Nature, the industry of Man has had nothing to do with any part of it.'[47] Cook's claim that along the eastern coast of New Holland 'we never saw one inch of cultivated land' became a common justification for British occupation. Banks and Cook accepted with Locke that 'he that in obedience to this Command of God subdued, tilled and sowed any part of it, thereby annexed to it something that was his Property, which another had no Title to, nor could without injury take from him', but found no evidence, such as signs of habitations, agriculture, or depasturing of herds, by which to recognize Aboriginal property in the soil.[48]

An editorial in *The Sydney Herald* argued:

> The American Indians were divided into nations, having fixed localities—they cultivated the ground, and understood the rights of property. Not so, the natives of New Holland. This vast country was to them a common—they bestowed no labor upon the land—their ownership, their right, was nothing more than that of the Emu or the Kangaroo. They bestowed no labor on the land and that—and that only—it is which gives a right of property in it. Who will assert that this great continent was ever intended by the Creator to remain an unproductive wilderness? Yet what else was it—what would it have remained, but for the labor of civilized man? The British people found a portion of the globe in a state of waste—took possession of it; and they had a perfect right to do so, under the Divine authority, by which man was commanded to go forth and people, and till the land. Herein we find the right to the dominion which the British Crown, or, more properly speaking, the British people exercise over the continent of New Holland.[49]

There is no shame in one's ancestors having been savages, Palaeolithic, or Old Stone Age people, hunter-gatherers, or tribesmen. All human beings share that ancestry. Many ancient superstitions that had survived in England from primitive times were only being eliminated in the late eighteenth century. During centuries in which savants developed new ideas or explored old ones, many ancient superstitions remained virtually intact. Most men and women believed that the earth is flat, that stars and planets direct the course of human events, and that rituals and incantations safeguard against sickness, misery, or sudden and painful death. In England, on the eve of an age of railways and vaccination, beliefs about childbirth included:

- Women of child-bearing age who sat in the chair just occupied by a pregnant woman would soon conceive;
- When a woman was in labor, locks on doors were likely to burst open;
- If a pregnant woman looked upon a corpse, her child would have a very pale complexion.

Missionary Lancelot Threlkeld declared:

> Our mothers danced in a state of nudity danced before the mystic grove besmeared with pipe clay, and would look into the trembling entrail of

81

human sacrifice. If their own invaders had left them 'to languish in this state of primordial brutality, Britons would not now be the colonizers'.[50]

However, superstitious as many of the British were, they found the Indigenous Australians much more so. Some Aborigines believed the first British ships they saw were 'huge winged monsters' or trees growing in the sea. Others thought the British were their dead kinsmen who had 'jumped up' as whites and that they themselves in their turn might return to earth after death as whites with all their powers and goods. Henry Reynolds noted that 'Aborigines clung to their own theory of illness, despite the traumatic impact of introduced disease' and believed smallpox and other epidemics were the work of sorcerers from other Aboriginal groups, who were capable of killing, sometimes from a distance, with bullocks' teeth, sheep's jawbones, and fragments of glass.[51]

Even though they held that their beliefs had remained unchanged since the Dreamtime, and though their way of life has often been regarded as the archetype of the 'closed society', some Aboriginal groups changed their myths over the generations. The dingo was adopted as a totem animal by many Aboriginal groups and has a prominent role in many Dreamtime myths, but dingoes entered Australia long after the first Aborigines.[52] More recently, a clan on the Glynde River in Arnhem Land adopted a square-faced green liquor bottle as a totemic symbol.[53] After a mullock of copper rubble was formed by nineteenth century mining on their traditional lands, the Ngulugwongga people became known as Mulluk Mulluk. By 1852 the Ngarrindjeri story of the Pleiades had seven men smoking tobacco.

Some changes in myth and tradition had obvious political value. The Gunwinggu people became the dominant group at Oenpelli only in the 1950s, but they quickly established Dreamtime links with their new territory.[54] When the Parlamanyin of the Northern Territory died out as a separate group, the Kungarakany quickly laid claim to Parlamanyin territories and myths. When the Maranunngu found that there was rich potential value in lands to the north of their traditional territories, they rapidly made new land claims, backed by the assertion that they were familiar with

The rapidity with which myths can still gain credence was demonstrated by Kenneth Maddock's study of six Aboriginal myths collected during the last forty years about the visit of James Cook to Australia.[55] In the Victoria River myth, in which the first white arrival was Ned Kelly. Ned was kind and gave the Aborigines horses and bullocks, but Cook came along, killed Ned and despoiled the Aborigines. There seems no doubt that the Aboriginal informants considered such manifestly mistaken accounts of relatively recent events to be historically factual. The myth-making at Hindmarsh Island, aided and sometimes instigated by non-Aborigines, is described in the next Chapter.

Initially both James Cook and Joseph Banks were struck by an absence of interest among Aborigines in the skills, techniques, history, and culture of the newcomers, but that did not last long. Later, Aborigines told the anthropologist W. E. H. Stanner that their 'appetites for tobacco and to a lesser extent for tea became so intense that neither man nor woman could bear to be without' and as a result 'individuals, families and parties of friends simply went away to places where the avidly desired things could be obtained'. Professor Stanner considered that 'voluntary movements of this kind occurred widely in Australia' so that 'we must look all over again at what we supposed to have been the conditions of collapse of Aboriginal life'. The reported arrival of Europeans 'was sufficient to unsettle aborigines still long distances away' and 'for every aborigine who, so to speak, had Europeans thrust upon him, at least one other had sought them out'. Marcia Langton has claimed that it was 'terrifying' to be an Aboriginal woman on the frontier, but large numbers of Aboriginal women sought out white men, partly because they thought they would be better fed, but also partly because they would not get beaten up as frequently.

Henry Reynolds agreed:

> European goods like steel axes and knives; pieces of iron, tins, cloth and glass were all eagerly sought and used by Aboriginal tribes even before contact had been made with settlers on the advancing frontier. Western food, tobacco and alcohol also exerted a tremendous attraction.[56]

Stanner concluded that 'disintegration following on a voluntary and banded migration is a very different kind of problem from the kind we usually picture—that of the ruin of a helpless people, overwhelmed by circumstances' and that 'nowhere, as far as I am aware, does one encounter aborigines who want to return to the bush, even if their new circumstances are very miserable'. One idea Stanner thought needed 'drastic revision' was that 'to part an aboriginal from his clan country is to wrest his soul from his body'. Even though 'there is a real and an intense bond between an aboriginal and the ancestral estate he shares with other clansmen', so that he is delighted to see it again after absence, 'he has been away voluntarily; and he was soon to go away again voluntarily'.[57]

Yet, whether the Aborigines advanced to meet the colonists or the colonists penetrated irrespective of the will of the Aborigines, the population loss soon proved to be the same, as diseases to which Aborigines had never developed immunity struck many down. Pitt-Rivers suspected 'a law which consigns to destruction all savage races when brought in contact with a civilization'. In the words of Charles Darwin, 'Wherever the European has trod, death seems to pursue the aboriginal.' This was far from favoring genocide but acceptance, fortunately mistaken, of forces beyond control. The forces Darwin listed were intertribal warfare, a wandering way of life, high infant mortality, and exposure to European disease, together with the 'difficulty in procuring food' brought about by the killing of native animals by introduced predators.[58]

Controlling convicts, not civilizing new Aboriginal compatriots, was the prime objective of London officials and their representatives in New South Wales and Van Diemen's Land. Soon, however, some thought was given to law and education: two main instruments for civilizing. Problems in criminal law included the ancient tradition of group vengeance for insults and injuries and the apparent impossibility of Aborigines taking an acceptable oath in court.

English case law distinguished between conquered or ceded and settled colonies. Conquered and ceded colonies, such as Bengal, continued to be ruled under their own laws, whereas in settled colonies, English law was assumed to follow immediately on possession. This distinction was also often used to differentiate civilized peoples from barbarous ones, such as Maori in New Zealand, and from savage ones, such as Australian Aborigines.

In the Gove Land Rights Case in 1971, Mr Justice Blackburn's opinion, overturned by the high court of Australia in the Mabo Case in 1992, was that Blackstone's words 'desert and uncultivated' had 'always been taken to include territory in which live uncivilized inhabitants in a primitive state of society', not only or mainly territory which is unoccupied. The British did not claim sovereignty over New South Wales on the false assumption that it was uninhabited *terra nullius*. Governor Phillip and all who sailed with him were well aware that it had Aboriginal inhabitants who made various uses of land.

Two policies were in contention. After reading about them, try to decide which was the better one: It seems to me a good example of history not revealing what ought to have been done. The first policy recommended the 'strict application' of English law as the best means of eventual assimilation and civilizing of indigenous people. Its advocates regarded inactivity in combatting indigenous practices as tolerating 'barbarity' and 'savagery'. Governor of South Australia George Grey rejected the idea that Aboriginal customary law should be tolerated even in the short term. He insisted that it was such toleration that had defeated previous attempts to civilize Aborigines. Grey argued that the 'anomalous state' of Australian Aborigines was due to their traditional laws, which prevented any race 'however highly endowed' from being civilized: Those forced to continue living under them would simply 'remain hopelessly immersed in their present state of barbarism'.

George Grey claimed that enforcing English law in internal Aboriginal relationships and disputes would make it easier for younger Aborigines to emancipate themselves from ancient superstitions and from control by the older traditionalist men. Grey rejected the idea that Aborigines were incapable of being civilized, insisting that they simply had not had genuine opportunities. He was confident that steady work, education, and the enforcement of English law would lead them to civilization.[59] He was adamant that Aborigines would 'remain hopelessly immersed in their present state of barbarism' unless they were made 'from the very commencement amenable to the British laws, both as regards themselves and Europeans'. In 1848, Colonial Secretary Earl Grey endorsed the South Australian governor's view that 'civilized' law and order required the strictest possible application of English law to Aborigines.[60]

The opposing approach was that it was impracticable and unfair to expect Aborigines to obey laws that they did not understand. Governor of Western Australian, William Hutt, argued that Aborigines were not in a position to be treated in all points as British subjects and that the authorities had not the means to superintend and control the 'bush and the wild districts'.[61] Hutt held that enforcing English law would produce 'singular anomalies' such as interference in violent Aboriginal marriage customs. Support from London came from James Stephen, under-secretary for the colonies and thus the senior civil servant in that department. Stephen considered it a great error to set aside native customs, 'excepting only so far as might be necessary for the prevention of War and of inhuman practices' that breached 'universal laws of humanity', such as cannibalism, human sacrifice, and infanticide. Stephen argued that merely because customs seemed 'absurd or impolitic' or even 'pernicious in themselves' was inadequate justification for British intervention.[62] The 1837 'Buxton Report' of a House of Commons select committee on indigenous peoples showed perhaps undue confidence when it recommended for New South Wales 'short and simple rules as may form a temporary and provisional code for the regulation of the Aborigines, until advancing knowledge and civilization shall have superseded the necessity for any such special laws'.

Despite all his efforts to inflate the legal implications for land rights of the struggles of humanitarians to protect Aboriginal interests, Reynolds has never suggested that their efforts had much effect on the law. He argued that in the 1840s 'Colonial Office officials were clear about what they wanted to achieve', namely, 'the reservation in Leases of Pastoral Land of the rights of the Natives'.[63] He thus seemed to concede that the Aboriginal native title had not been accepted practice or legal doctrine before the 1840s, since there would then have been no need to try to introduce it during the 1840s. Furthermore, he complained frequently and at length that it was not accepted after the 1840s.

Since the Aboriginal native title did not exist before the 1840s or after the 1840s, where did it exist during the 1840s? The absence of legislation establishing or recognizing the communal native title forced Reynolds to claim that it existed 'less in the Order-in-Council, which was a public document published in the *New South Wales Government Gazette*, and more in the dispatch [from the Colonial Office] which was only for official eyes' and in the correspondence of Earl Grey and others.[64] Yet, it is a well-known principle of law that preparatory papers are inadmissible on the question of the interpretation of a statute. In any case, the preparatory papers cited do not substantiate Reynolds' contentions.

A strictly historical view was taken in the Gove Lands Case by Justice Blackburn, whose judgment was described by Judge Dawson as based on 'a full and scholarly examination'[65] and was taken in every other case before 1992 before an Australian court. Dawson J. noted that 'the policy which lay behind the legal regime', so much detested by the other members of the high court, 'was determined politically and, however insensitive the politics may now seem to have been, a change in view does not of itself mean a change in the law'.[66] His Honour argued that 'it requires the implementation of a new policy to do that and that is a matter for government rather than the courts. In the meantime it would be wrong to attempt to revise history or to fail to recognize its legal impact, however unpalatable it may now seem. To do so would be to impugn the foundations of the very legal system under which this case must be decided'. The majority of the high court decided that historical revision and policy-making were within its competence, irrespective of whether the legal foundations of Australia were impugned or not.

The High Court in *Mabo v Queensland* adopted Reynolds' view of what land law ought to have been and ought to be, not what it had been and was. It decided that when the Crown gained the radical title over the territory it did not become the beneficial owner of the land, which remained in the possession of the indigenous people and was protected by common law. The court held that the Crown extinguished the native title in a piecemeal fashion over many years as the wave of settlement washed over the continent, but that native title had survived on the Murray Islands. Since it would be unjust to deny the Aborigines what had been conceded to the Torres Strait Islanders, this previously unknown 'native title' was extended to mainland Australia, despite differences manifested in their ways of life at the times of acquisition.

Manning Clark alleged that in London before the First Fleet sailed in 1788 'no one paused to ponder the effect on the aborigine; no one questioned the wisdom or pondered the effects of transplanting European civilization to the vast south land . . .' and that all the colonial officials 'bore the taint of supercilious intolerance towards all other forms of civilization . . . They bore too that other taint of European civilization—its destructive effect on all primitive cultures with which it came into contact'.[67]

86

It is hard to credit that Clark had ever read any of the numerous papers that showed that many British officials had a deep and genuine concern about the interests of primitive peoples. For example, Lord Stanley, later fourteenth Earl of Derby and Prime Minister, described Aborigines as 'broken into small, nomadic tribes . . . did not herd animals, or grow crops, and had little if any religion and no principles of civil government, or recognition of private property'.[68] Maori, in the words of Lord John Russell, then Whig spokesman on the colonies, were, unlike the Aborigines, 'not mere wanderers over an extended surface, in search of a precarious subsistence; . . . but a people among whom the arts of government have made some progress; who have established by their own customs a division and appropriation of the soil; who are not without some measure of agricultural skill, and a certain subordination of ranks; with usages having the character and authority of law'.[69] Not really superficial or supercilious comments! . . . Clark seemed to have thought that the impact of modernity on the Aborigines could only have been destructive, irrespective of intentions: He wrote, 'When those aboriginal women uttered their horrid howl on first seeing the white man at Botany Bay in April 1770, that howl contained in it a prophecy of doom . . .'[70] Yet, if their intentions did not matter, on what basis did he condemn particular policies adopted by the colonists?

The British colonists had three conceivable choices about education: They could scrap their own ways and adopt those of the natives, leave native people as they were, but maintain their own ways, or try to share their culture with the natives. In New South Wales, officials and missionaries often started with feelings of optimism, sometimes fuelled by the facility many Aborigines showed in acquiring the English language and in translating one Aboriginal language into another. Governor Macquarie believed that, if 'cultivated and encouraged', Aborigines would quit their 'wild wandering and unsettled habits' and 'live in a state of perfect peace, friendliness and sociality'.[71] He supported a settlement at Blacktown 'for the purpose of civilizing the aboriginal natives of Australia' and financed William and Elizabeth Shelley's school for Aborigines at Parramatta. Between 1814 and 1820, thirty-seven Aboriginal children studied there, and in 1819, a girl from the institution reportedly won first prize in a public examination.

Early optimism usually faded rapidly. At Parramatta, Elizabeth Shelley, by then a widow, bemoaned that Aboriginal girls who had been trained at the Institution, instead of civilizing their menfolk, returned to the bush and lived as if they had never been to school.[72] Matthew Moorhouse, Protector of Aborigines in South Australia in the 1840s, gave up hope of educating young Aborigines after seventeen years in the post, because they were threatened by elders with death by sorcery if they adopted white ways, which few wished to do anyway. Aboriginal Protector in Port Phillip District (later Victoria), E. S. Parker, stated in 1854 that Loddon River Aborigines bitterly opposed white schooling for their children. Parker was told that he 'was stealing their children by taking them away to live in huts, and work, and "read in books" like white fellows'.[73].

Some officials, such as the Police Magistrate of Port Macquarie, W. N. Gray, and some missionaries, such as William Watson of the Church Missionary Society, decided the best chances of success would arise if Aboriginal children were 'caught early' and urged, 'taking the children from them very young, and bringing them up in an establishment where they would have no opportunity of seeing any but Europeans'. This attitude, whether admirable or deplorable, was entirely 'non-racist', since it was based on the view that Aborigines did not lack genetic potential for intellectual development, but that their 'closed societies' failed to provide experiences necessary for such development. Such official efforts, however, were very fitful and were replaced in the 1860s by policies of protection of the apparently declining Aboriginal population.

One of the most cogent explanations of the cognitive obstacles to becoming capable of coping with civilization has been provided by Canadian Professor of Psychology Merlin Donald (see the appendix on Donald). Australian academics became more fastidious and demanding over the years. For example, Professor Mulvaney held that 'in earlier contact times, much confusion and some fatal disputes might have been avoided if Europeans had attempted to adapt to customary behaviour'. He castigated the typical colonist because 'he automatically imposed his social rules, rather than deferring to his host . . . Take the custom of offering wives to overnight visitors as a token of friendship. Refusal by a European of such hospitality also would signal animosity'. Mulvaney did not indicate which choice he himself made in those circumstances. If Philip and other British officials had accepted the sexual favours offered to them, we can be sure that they would be blamed for that as well or even more, on grounds of exploiting Aboriginal women. Professor Marilyn Lake could write the indictment there.

If only Governor Philip had taken a course in anthropology before landing at Botany Bay or, better still, visited a few pre-1788 Aboriginal housing estates, he might then have met Mulvaney's requirements. Mulvaney wrote that Philip had ordered convicts to build houses for Aborigines, but 'foreshadowing the failure of so many government Aboriginal housing projects, the design was unsuited to Aboriginal needs'.[74]

Largely without government officials realizing that it was taking place, towards the turn of the nineteenth century, there was a significant increase in the number of Australians of Aboriginal descent. Clearly, some immunity had been built up against the ravages that measles, smallpox, and other diseases had inflicted during the first century of colonization. In addition, Donald's demythologization was taking place on a considerable scale. Movement away from ancestral lands weakened traditional beliefs, as did acquaintance with Western technologies, Christianity, and ways of life practiced by the colonists. This process most likely took place among individuals and families who had 'passed over' to some extent into the general population, but took place in many situations of cultural contact. In a sense, it was the very opposite of gaining immunity from diseases: It was an opening up to new ideas and influences previously blocked or rejected.

Many prominent Aborigines, almost all of them part-Aborigines, welcomed this process and wanted to accelerate it. In 1928, a deputation to the Premier of Western Australia was led by William Harris, a part Aboriginal. Harris complained that 'educated natives' were treated as though they were 'wild blackfellows' and argued that all natives educated up to the standard of white men should be exempted from the Aborigines Act.[75] William Cooper, a leading spokesman for Victorian Aborigines and initiator in 1938 of the Aboriginal 'Day of Mourning', argued that 'the British were once as we are now. The conquering power of Rome, whatever else it did, lifted the British to culture and civilization. We want that same uplift'. Cooper asserted:

> We want the right to full education, academic, cultural and industrial, and to be able to take our place beside the white race in full equality and responsibility. We ask the right to be fully British.[76]

It was that aspiration that Paul Hasluck sought to fulfil after the Second World War. As Professor Russell McGregor commented, 'The Aboriginal political leaders of the 1930s based their demands for human rights not on any concept of Aboriginality, but on an ideal of civilization'.[77]

Chapter 4

HINDMARSH ISLAND AND THE FABRICATION OF MYTH

In 1984, the Binalong Pty Ltd, controlled by Tom and Wendy Chapman, began work on what they hoped would become a major marina complex on Hindmarsh Island. Their preparation seemed meticulous and environmentally friendly. The chairman of the Conservation Council of South Australia asserted that the Hindmarsh Island development was a model of how to proceed. The ALP government of John Bannon supported the project enthusiastically but made it a condition for building the marina and that a bridge be built to connect Hindmarsh Island to the mainland at Goolwa so as to prevent interminable delays on the existing ferry if and when the marina and other developments were completed.

The first opponents of the marina and then the bridge included retired persons and people with holiday homes on the island and environmentalists concerned about nesting grounds for birds, migration of feral animals, rabbit infestation, and pollution effects on the Coorong and Lower Murray. Their ranks came to include prominent SA Liberals, such as Ian McLachlan, Dean Brown, Michael Armitage, Leigh Davis, and Diana Laidlaw, as well as Greenpeace, Australian Democrats, and union militants such as Davey Thomason of the Construction, Forestry, Mining and Energy Union.

Aborigines were absent from the early ranks of the opponents. The Chapmans were anxious that all known Aborigines in the area should be consulted, but this was by no means easy, since none had lived on Hindmarsh Island for many years. The Chapmans commissioned Dr Rod Lucas to investigate possible Aboriginal sites of significance. Dr Lucas reported in 1990 that there were no recorded mythological sites specific to Hindmarsh Island. This statement proved later to be an embarrassment to Dr Lucas, when his wife, Dr Deane Fergie, became a central figure in Hindmarsh Island disputes.

Dr Lucas advised the Chapmans in 1990 that, like Norman Tindale in the 1930s and Catherine and Ronald Berndt during the 1940s and 1950s, he had found it difficult to construct genealogies and thus to know who should be regarded as traditional custodians of any Aboriginal sites there might be. His report recommended the Chapmans to 'consult directly with the relevant Aboriginal representative bodies identified herein, and with any other Aboriginal persons chosen by these bodies'. The Chapmans consulted Henry Rankine and George Trevorrow, leading figures of the Raukkan (formerly Port McLeay) Community Council, the Coorong Consultative Committee, and the Ngarrindjeri Lands and Progress Association. George Trevorrow and Henry Rankine both knew considerable Ngurunderi lore. When controversies about the marina and bridge first arose, they made no objections on grounds of traditional beliefs or practices, nor did Jean Rankine, Henry's wife, described later by Professor Cheryl Saunders as a 'senior Ngarrindjeri woman', nor did any members of the Campbell clan who claimed to be the traditional owners or custodians.

Commissioned by the South Australian Department of Environment and Planning, Dr Vanessa Edmonds reported no evidence of any Ngarrindjeri or other Aboriginal beliefs about Hindmarsh Island, although she identified middens, burial places, which the Chapmans were very willing to protect, even though no Aboriginal interest had been shown in them in living memory. Dr Neale Draper, a senior archaeologist in the SA Department of Aboriginal Affairs, also found no Aboriginal burial sites or other cultural associations of sufficient importance to warrant a ban on a bridge rather than the barrages. His department gave the go-ahead to the contractors for the bridge.

Frustrated by the apparent progress of the marina and plans for a bridge, one local opponent, Bill Longworth, suggested to Davey Thomason, 'Let's see if we can get some Aboriginals down from Murray Bridge to help us with our cause.' During 1993, Sally Francis, an ardent conservationist with a weekend shack on Hindmarsh Island, persuaded George Trevorrow and Henry Rankine to join the coalition. Subsequently, both men denied that they had been consulted by the Chapmans about their plans, and George Trevorrow spread false rumors that the Chapmans had carted away 'truckloads of Aboriginal bones' and that a Goolwa taxi driver had boasted of having a 'boot load of boong bones'. A newly formed Lower Murray Aboriginal Heritage Committee (LMAHC), with George Trevorrow as Chairman and Doug Milera as Secretary, now declared that Hindmarsh Island had a sacred shape and a 'spiritual character' that would suffer fatally if it were joined to the mainland. Next, they decided that the proposed bridge could interfere with the 'meeting of the waters', salt seawater and fresh Murray water. As yet, however, they made no reference to 'women's business' in or near Hindmarsh Island.

The distinctively male Ngurunderi was the central figure in traditional Ngarrindjeri lore. Among other feats, Ngurunderi had pursued and killed a gigantic Murray Cod with a spear, which could have been his phallus, and he created the Murray from his own urine, possibly supplemented by that of his wives. In another story, his wives were disobedient and ate some bream, a fish forbidden to women. Ngurunderi was obliged to take revenge on his wives: They were drowned and became islands. These stories may not have seemed a promising basis for 'women's business'.

Ronald and Catherine Berndts were told by the Ngarrindjeri that the River Murray was to them 'like a lifeline, an immense artery of a living "body". The body was "symbolic of Ngurunderi himself"'.[78] However, one index entry proved a disappointment to feminist anthropologists: 'secret-sacred issues, absence of'. As recently as in 1989, Allen and Unwin published Women, Rites and Sites: Aboriginal Women's Cultural Knowledge. It contained contributions by leading female anthropologists. They named several sites in South Australia as having special significance for Aboriginal women, but none in or around Hindmarsh Island or Goolwa.

The Liberal government formed after the 1993 state elections was keen to scrap the bridge, but previous ALP governments had entered into contractual obligations, disregard of which would cost more than the bridge itself. Samuel Jacobs QC, a retired judge of the Supreme Court of South Australia, was commissioned to make an inquiry. He confirmed the new government's worst financial fears so that the decision was made to proceed with building the bridge. Samuel Jacobs wondered why Trevorrow and Milera had not raised their concerns about the shape of Hindmarsh Island earlier and why it would suffer more if joined to the mainland by a bridge rather than by a ferry. Judge Jacobs was unimpressed by Dr Neale Draper, who criticized the shortcomings of earlier investigations, several of which he had himself conducted, and who raised totally new concerns about the spiritual character of Hindmarsh Island. Dr Draper had received a personal research grant for further investigations on Aboriginal artefacts and cultural associations in Hindmarsh Island, but governments were rarely sufficiently generous and the money ran out before he could make a further report.

As Cheryl Professor Saunders noted of events up till 1993, 'the Aboriginal women still had not been involved at this stage'.[79] The first women to enter the drama were Sarah Milera, wife of Doug, and Linda Warrell. The Mileras were brought up from Murray Bridge to help the anti-bridge campaign. They were recruited by union officials and offered a house on Hindmarsh Island by anti-bridge campaigner Ann Lucas. Sarah Milera knew little about Hindmarsh Island to start with, but began to remedy that deficiency by reading the Berndts' A World That Was in 1993. 'Women's business' of various sorts was, of course, very common among several Aboriginal groups, and some in the north of South Australia had been studied by archaeologist Linda Warrell. She visited the bridge campaigners on 26 March 1994. Lindy Warrell said to Aborigines Tom and Ellen Trevorrow, 'It would be nice if there were some women's business.'[80]

In 1992, following disputes about building a marina at Sellicks Beach, Lewis O'Brien, a Kaurna Aborigine, and G. Williams claimed that the mouth of the Onkaparinga River was an Aboriginal women's site. They suggested that a phrase used by German scholars Teichelmann and Schurmann in their 1840 dictionary of the Kaurna language was evidence that 'the Kaurna people talked about body parts'. They concluded that Aborigines could identify the internal sexual organs of women and had noted their similarity to the Onkaparinga estuary.[81] The Kaurna (Adelaide Plains) Aborigines are an entirely separate group from the Ngarrindjeri, but this was probably the start of women's business at Hindmarsh Island. At a gathering of leading men in the LMAHC, Chairman Victor Wilson showed Secretary Doug Milera an aerial photograph of Hindmarsh Island and said, 'This is a woman, it's a creation of the Ngarrindjeri people and I'm going to Doreen Kartinyeri to explain it and to find out about it.'[82] Wilson and Milera had been involved in the Onkaparinga dispute and were able to apply the vagina/river mouth analogy to the Murray mouth and Hindmarsh Island.

The article was in one important respect, however, damaging to later claims about 'women's business' at Hindmarsh Island, since the beliefs asserted about the Onkaparinga were not regarded as secret. The maps of the Onkaparinga estuary and mouth, provided by courtesy of the Adelaide Street Directory and the South Australian Education Department, were of the very same kind which opponents of the bridge claimed later would be a sacrilege to display in public, as well as threatening to Ngarrindjeri women, physically and spiritually. Furthermore, any such belief associated with Hindmarsh Island would have been used openly by opponents of the Bridge long before June 1994, just as Mr O'Brien did during the Onkaparinga dispute.

Doreen Kartinyeri was born in Raukkan in 1935 but at ten went away to school in Adelaide. Then she lived at Point Pearce and there married a non-Ngarrindjeri man with whom she had six children before moving to the north of South Australia with a Western desert man. She became interested and skilled in genealogies. However, before she realized what the future held for her, she admitted in a Rigney family history she wrote in 1983, 'I didn't know much about the culture, customs and language but I do know the identities of the Point Pearce and Point McLeay people.' She obtained a modest position in the Family History Unit of the South Australian Museum, but soon her powerful personality enabled her to exert influence over her nominal superiors.

One remarkable feature of the whole affair is the absence of Doreen Kartinyeri from Hindmarsh Island controversies until April 1994. Even Professor Saunders admitted that the issue of 'the secret knowledge of women' only 'emerged in late March or early April 1994'.[83] Since Doreen Kartinyeri did not live near Hindmarsh Island or Goolwa, she may not have known before April 1994 that proposals for first a marina and then a bridge development on Hindmarsh Island had been sharply contested since 1984. However, this supposition undermines any claim that she had a deep interest in Hindmarsh Island, let alone that she feared that a bridge there would imperil Ngarrindjeri fertility. Working as she was in Adelaide in the South Australian Museum and given that she had participated in the Sellicks Beach campaign, it seems incredible that she had never heard that a bridge was proposed to Hindmarsh Island or, if she was well aware of the situation there, that she should have suppressed for so long information deemed in 1994 to be sufficient to ban its construction. Dr Fergie alleged later in 1994 that Doreen Kartinyeri 'was in hospital in Adelaide in early January of this year when she heard about the proposed construction for the first time', but she did not claim that Doreen Kartinyeri had been in hospital, presumably in an isolation ward, for the previous ten years as well.

Between 12 and 15 April 1994, Doreen Kartinyeri visited the museum with Sarah Milera. According to some senior colleagues, she 'appeared to be desperately seeking information on Hindmarsh Island and its environs'.[84] She asked Dr Philip Clarke and Dr Steve Hemming, a man fervently committed to Aboriginal causes, to go through the collection with some urgency to locate material related to Hindmarsh Island and the Coorong/Goolwa region.[85] Dr Philip Jones, Director of the Museum's Anthropology Division, testified that as late as 22 June she was looking for any archival or collection material to allow for an interpretation of Hindmarsh Island as a special place.[86]

Steve Hemming did not fail Doreen Kartinyeri. He told her that the lakes and Murray Mouth were evocative, from the mythological point of view, of a woman's internal organs and that the authority for this was Catherine Berndt. Hemming also claimed in late August 1994 in the presence of Philip Jones and Philip Clarke that Ronald Berndt had said the Lower Murray region bore some resemblance in Ngarrindjeri mythology to a woman's body. However, the only relevant passage in the Berndts' works is to a male body. Within a short time, the Berndts were disparaged rather than cited. Dr Rod Lucas led the attack on delinquent women anthropologists, including Catherine Berndt. He asserted that Alison Brookman, an anthropologist who testified before the Royal Commission, was only 'young and inexperienced' when she spent time with 'the renowned song-woman, midwife and Berndt informant, Pinkie Mack'; she 'had not established a relationship of trust with Pinkie Mack and would not be surprised if culturally sensitive information had not been imparted to her'.[87] He doubted whether Dorothy Tindale 'was in a position of trust to have had restricted or esoteric knowledge revealed to her'. He claimed that 'at the time of her fieldwork amongst the Ngarrindjeri, Catherine Berndt was young, childless and inexperienced'. Dr Lucas doubted, too, 'that Fay Gale knew as much as she thought she did, precisely she had not "mingled or lived amongst" Aboriginal people'.[88]

On 9 May 1994, Victor Wilson convened a meeting of fifteen Ngarrindjeri women, most of whom were his relatives, on Hindmarsh Island at 'The Pines' camp, kindly made available by the University of Adelaide. Doreen Kartinyeri declared, 'I'm here to tell you women why the island is sacred to us.' She explained that Victor Wilson had asked her to tell them about 'women's business' on the island and had told her that 'the men could not stop the bridge so was up to us women to stop it'. She admitted that there was insufficient written evidence to make a case to the minister for a section 10 declaration, but that did not dismay her. She said the island was sacred because during the nineteenth century Ngarrindjeri women had gone there to abort foetuses if they thought the fathers could be white. The preferred method was to place rocks on their stomachs to procure miscarriages. She also asserted that 'women's business' began 40,000 years ago, although for much of that period there were no white men around to father mixed race children and Hindmarsh island was not an island. 'Women's business' about Hindmarsh Island, Doreen Kartinyeri proclaimed, had been passed down to women, from mother to daughter, throughout the generation, but somehow she was now the only person who possessed the knowledge. She did not claim to have received the secret knowledge from her own mother, but named two other women as her informants: her grandmother, Sally Kartinyeri, and her aunt, Rose Kropinyeri. Later, in a letter to Robert Tinker of 12 May 1994, Doreen Kartinyeri made a poor move and claimed as a further source her aunt, Laura Kartinyeri. 'Nanna Laura' was the daughter of Pinkie Mack, a midwife of the interwar years looked upon with veneration by many Ngarrindjeri women. Although the other two supposed informants had died many years earlier, Laura Kartinyeri was still alive and could be questioned.

None of the other women present had previously heard these stories, but they agreed to send a joint letter to Robert Tickner, Commonwealth Minister for Aboriginal Affairs, telling him the island was sacred to Ngarrindjeri women.[89] As yet unaware of the dangers posed by exposure of such information to males, especially non-Aboriginal men, Doreen Kartinyeri asked Sarah Milera to show the draft letter to radical lawyer Tim Wooley, who said it would be better if Mr Tickner were provided with more information. Two sentences were added, one claiming that the traditional name of Hindmarsh Island was Kumarangk and that 'kuman' meant pregnant in Ngarrindjeri, although Philip Clarke believed the word meant 'The Points' and referred to a feature of the landscape. By then, Victor Wilson and Doug Milera had joined the women. Wilson pointed to an aerial photograph, and Doug Milera told the women that Hindmarsh Island and the waters around it were sacred to Ngarrindjeri women. While they were looking at the map, Doug Milera said, 'Look, it's in the shape of woman's privates.' Doreen Kartinyeri said, 'Yes, I can see it now. I can see it.'[90]

The next section of the letter came courtesy of Tim Wooley and nearly replicated a part of Neale Draper's most recent report, in which he had concluded:

> This area represents a crucial part of Ngarrindjeri cultural beliefs about the creation and constant renewal of life along the Lower Murray lakes and the Murray mouth and the Coorong. The most serious cultural heritage dilemma concerns the Goolwa channel and its vital cultural significance as part of the Meeting of the Waters.

The final version signed by Doreen Kartinyeri and sent to Mr Tickner on 12 May was very different from the rough draft that the women had originally signed and about three times as long. Judge Stevens found that Steve Hemming and Francesca Cubillo-Alberts, another Museum employee, helped to write it and that it was typed and faxed by Steve Hemming. In it, Doreen Kartinyeri claimed she had always known about the stories, but until recently had not known the exact place to which they referred. Judge Stevens commented that 'if Doreen Kartinyeri did not know the exact place to which her stories related, she could not have known of the "women's business". By its nature, the place was an inextricable component of the "women's business".'[91]

Under section 10 of the Aboriginal and Torres Strait Islander Heritage Protection Act of 1984, Robert Tickner hastened to stop further development. Before enforcing a permanent ban, he made an emergency declaration on 12 May, banning development for an initial period of thirty days, which was subsequently extended to sixty days and finally on 10 July to twenty-five years. He also appointed Professor Cheryl Saunders of the Centre for Comparative Constitutional Studies, University of Melbourne, to prepare a report for him. Professor Saunders was not an anthropologist, but an expert on the Australian constitution. Her approach was guided by Menham, who wrote in his report to the federal government on the Old Swan Brewery Area in Perth:

> It is in my view sufficient to report to the Minister on whether the area is of significance to Aboriginal people in accordance with their traditions and to report on the evidence that touches upon the degree and intensity of belief and feeling that exists in relation to the area under discussion.[92]

She also considered relevant the remarks of Justice Brennan in Commonwealth v Tasmania, the 'Tasmanian Dams' case:

> The phrase 'particular significance' in section 8 cannot be precisely defined. All that can be said is that the site must be of a significance which is neither minimal nor ephemeral, and that the significance may be found by the Aboriginal people in their history, in their religion or their spiritual beliefs or in their culture. A group of whatever size who, having a common

Aboriginal biological history, find the site to be of that significance are the relevant people of the Aboriginal race for whom the law is made.

Professor Saunders cited the Hon. J. H. Wootton's section 10 (4) report on the proposed Junction Waterhole dam in Alice Springs:

The Act does not specify that any degree of antiquity must attach to be observances, customs and beliefs, which may obviously change over time, although the word 'tradition' in its ordinary meaning carried the notion of being handed down from generation to generation.[93]

All Professor Saunders evidently needed to find was a 'degree of intensity of belief', which was rapidly generated, and some significance, even if not very 'particular'. The 'ordinary meaning' of 'tradition' could safely be disregarded and the term extended to cover claims never made until very recently. Two or three sincere believers, of an approved type, would be enough to determine state or federal legislation. When Justice John Van Doussa looked into the issue of fabrication, he advised that one sincere believer might be enough to confirm or establish the authenticity of an Aboriginal tradition. He also concluded that there was no evidence that Doreen Kartinyeri and her supporters had fabricated their stories, although he did not declare that there was evidence they had not done so.

Professor Saunders boldly declared that it was unnecessary for her to identify the 'traditional owners' of the relevant area, despite the emphasis usually made in land rights or sacred sites cases on establishing which Aborigines have claims to be 'traditional owners'. Rod Lucas noted that the so-called Ngarrindjeri Tendi, allegedly a revival of a traditional representative body and then controlled by Tom and George Trevorrow, saw 'no value' in 'identifying, through genealogical mapping, the traditional owners.'[94] The traditional owners would very likely prove to be the Campbells, who could not be trusted to keep to the party line.

The Aboriginal Legal Rights Movement (ALRM) retained feminist anthropologist, Dr Deane Fergie, a lecturer in the University of Adelaide and a friend and colleague of Doreen Kartinyeri, to act as a 'facilitator' to support and advise the Aboriginal women objectors in their dealings with Professor Saunders.[95] Dr Fergie was an ideal choice. She had submitted her doctoral thesis with the injunction that it was never to fall into the hands of men and had become well known as a champion of gender exclusivity, which by the 1990s was a most desirable attribute in an anthropologist. She had no special knowledge of the Ngarrindjeri, and like Sarah Milera, she began to read the works of the Berndts. Dr Fergie was accepted by Professor Saunders as an authoritative interpreter of Ngarrindjeri culture and traditions, but Judge Stevens found:

> Without any prior knowledge of historical or contemporary Ngarrindjeri culture, or of the significance ascribed by Doreen Kartinyeri to the area, Dr Fergie was at a serious disadvantage in making any assessment of the group of women present at Graham's Castle on 19 June 1994. Any inferences or conclusions drawn from her observations of the women and their interaction are necessarily unreliable.[96]

On 18 June 1994, just before the first meeting between Doreen Kartinyeri's women and Professor Saunders, a letter appeared in the Adelaide Advertiser from Rocky Marshall, a non-Aboriginal activist. Marshall claimed he had been told by his grandmother, born at the Goolwa Police Station in 1861, that when she was a girl 'the black women came to have their babies in the bushes behind the police station'. In Marshall's story, Hindmarsh Island was a maternity home, rather than an abortion clinic. Marshall alleged that his grandmother told him of an Aboriginal legend in which the Murray Mouth was the vagina, Hindmarsh Island the womb, Mundoo Island as the egg, and the river, surrounding lakes, and mainland a connected part of the whole. Few grandmothers regale their infant grandsons with such stories, but similar tales had been circulating in activist circles for several days. Parts of the contents of the secret envelopes written down by Dr Deane Fergie were probably a paraphrase of his letter. Doreen Kartinyeri and her friends were not pleased with Rocky Marshall, perhaps because realization was dawning that the internal anatomy of women's sexual organs was unknown in traditional Aboriginal society, as were aerial views of the Murray Mouth. 'Women's business' of this kind was highly vulnerable to ridicule, so total secrecy was required. Ironically, the next key gathering took place at Marshall's home on 19 June 1994. Various witnesses described his treatment as a 'berating' and a 'haranguing'. Dr Fergie said it looked to her 'like a ritual shaming'.[97] Alan Campbell and his sisters Amelia and Merva, who claimed to be the traditional owners, had not been invited but turned up just the same. They denied the authenticity of the new 'women's business' and were therefore thrust out of the meeting by Doreen Kartinyeri.

Professor Saunders met thirty-five Aboriginal women at Graham's Castle Convention Centre, Goolwa, on 20 June 1994. She and most of the Ngarrindjeri women were in a high state of excitement. Doreen Kartinyeri recited a poem, claimed by her to be traditional: 'To all the mothers that was, to all the mothers that is, to all the mothers than will be.' Doreen Kartinyeri explained that most of the women had only heard the day before about the 'women's business' she also claimed had been passed for thousands of years from mothers to daughters. The women were quick learners, and when one of the younger ones exclaimed that she had always 'had a feeling about Hindmarsh Island and now I know why', several agreed, including some who had never been on the island before. The women all held hands and several followed Doreen Kartinyeri in shedding tears.

Sarah Milera tried to impress Professor Saunders and Dr Fergie with her knowledge and status. Sarah Milera related that, since arriving in Goolwa and Hindmarsh Island, she had experienced some 'behaviour of her Ngatchi (totem bird)', made 'unexpected finds of cockleshells and an ancestral spear', and had visions of a 'traditional Ngarrindjeri man'. An ancestral spear would have been an archaeological discovery of great importance and a piece of remarkable serendipity given her short stay on Hindmarsh Island and the failure of archaeologists to make such discoveries. To preserve its sacred secrecy, Sarah Milera buried the spear. Dr Fergie interpreted these experiences as an indication that Sarah Milera 'had established a significant spiritual relationship with her ancestral past which provided her with compelling visions of this area's significance in Ngarrindjeri tradition'.[98] Even though Sarah admitted she 'did not learn the women's secret tradition until recently', she was described by Professor Saunders as 'a significant informant in the preparation of [the Fergie] report.'

Doreen Kartinyeri repeated George Trevorrow's allegations about the Chapmans, the Goolwa taxi driver, and Aboriginal bones. She then elaborated, although with some significant alterations, her story of Hindmarsh Island as an abortion site, the river mouth as symbolic of the womb, and the whole area as the centre of a mystic 'meeting of the waters'. Again she warned that a bridge would imperil fertility and the land would become sterile. She told Professor Saunders:

> The Ngarrindjeri women regard the Murray mouth in general and Hindmarsh and Mundoo islands and the surrounding and separating waters in particular as crucial for the reproduction of the Ngarrindjeri people and their continued existence.

Professor Saunders's comment was:

> This tradition is not mythological but spiritual and an actual reflection of traditional practice, handed down from mother to daughter, drawn out of the landscape itself: In the words of Doreen Kartinyeri, 'This is not just a dreaming; it's a reality.'[99]

Thirty-one of the thirty-five Aboriginal women who met Professor Saunders had never heard of the purported spiritual significance of Hindmarsh Island until the day before this gathering, but they declared their trust in Sally Kartinyeri, Rose Kropinyeri, and Laura Kartinyeri, Doreen Kartinyeri's purported informants. One woman, Dorothy Wilson, a Ngarrindjeri woman who married into the family of Nanna Sally and Aunty Rose and who was Programme Director of the Nungas Club at Murray Bridge, wondered why Doreen Kartinyeri alone should have been entrusted with such knowledge.

Soon after she returned to Adelaide, Dean Fergie was commissioned by the Aboriginal Law Reform to advise Professor Saunders and Mr Tickner. On 11 July 1994, Dr Fergie spoke with Philip Clarke at the SA Museum. According to Clarke's evidence to the Royal Commission, Dr Fergie claimed that 'as long as thirty-five Aboriginal women believed in secret sacred business now, it had a reality that she could not ignore'. Clarke urged her to consult more broadly within the Aboriginal community, especially with elderly women regarded as authorities on Ngarrindjeri culture. In response she claimed that since none of them had worked within the feminist anthropological tradition, they were not crucial to the issue of whether 'women's business' as described by Doreen Kartinyeri existed in the Lower Murray. Among the names provided by Dr Clarke were those of Ngarrindjeri women who later gave evidence to the Royal Commission, as well as that of Laura Kartinyeri. Dr Fergie never contacted any of those women.[100]

Dr Fergie's report was sent in draft to Professor Saunders on 1 July 1994 and the final form on 4 July 1994. Whilst typing the final version on her word processor, Dr Fergie was in frequent phone contact with Doreen Kartinyeri. Changes from the version at Graham's Castle seemed to have included an expansion of the dire consequences of a bridge from female Ngarrindjeri sterility to cosmic barrenness, together with a new claim that joining Mundoo and Hindmarsh Islands would destroy the Ngarrindjeri. Dr Fergie divided her precious freight into two envelopes. One envelope contained the revelations of Doreen Kartinyeri, as transcribed by Deane Fergie. The other held Dr Fergie's anthropological assessment of these revelations. Both were labelled 'To be read by women only'. Not, of course, by all women, not even by all Ngarrindjeri women. Trusted supporters of Doreen Kartinyeri, including non-Aborigines such as Mr Tickner's adviser, Suzanne Kee, and Professor Saunders' assistant, Ann Mullins, were allowed access, but not Diana Laidlaw, one of the responsible South Australian ministers, and developer Wendy Chapman. Among Ngarrindjeri women who were refused access were Dorothy Wilson, Dulcie Wilson, and Bertha Gollan. Ms R. Layton, counsel for Doreen Kartinyeri, advised the Royal Commission on 27 July 1995 that 'there had been a decision' that these Ngarrindjeri women and others could not read the content of these envelopes.

Dr Fergie's open report gave only a vague idea of what the women's business consisted of, but sought to endorse its authenticity and importance. The open report was sufficient to convince Mr Tickner, who placed a twenty-five-year ban on any bridge to Hindmarsh Island on 10 July 1994. On 15 February 1995, Mr Justice O'Loughlin announced in the Federal Court that he had quashed both the Saunders' Report and Mr Tickner's twenty-five-year ban. Justice O'Loughlin held that it was not a proper exercise of power on the part of the minister to rely so heavily on the subject of 'women's business', yet deny himself access to the contents of the secret envelopes. The sealed envelopes had an eventful history. On 10 March 1995, Ian

McLachlan resigned as shadow Minister of Aboriginal Affairs after it became known that their contents, sent inadvertently to the opposition, so Mr Tickner's Canberra office claimed, had been photocopied within Mr McLachlan's office.

After they had time to reflect on the new supposed 'women's business' at Hindmarsh Island, a group of Ngarrindjeri women broke ranks and alleged that the story was fabricated to stop the bridge. The group included Dorothy Wilson, Dulcie Wilson, Audrey Dix, Bertha Gollan, and Rita Wilson. Several testified at the Royal Commission that as girls they never heard of Hindmarsh Island being special for any reason. Nobody they knew had ever been there for special rites at puberty or any other time. None had heard earlier the supposedly traditional verse recited by Doreen Kartinyeri: To all the mothers that was, to all the mothers that is, to all the mothers that will be.

Dorothy Wilson at first believed Doreen Kartinyeri's claim that Grandma Sally, Aunt Rose, and Aunt Laura had told her of secret 'women's business', but she had then checked with numerous older Ngarrindjeri women who had never heard of the 'women's business'. After Laura Kartinyeri, the sole survivor of the three women Doreen named as his informants, told her that she had never known anything about 'women's business' at Hindmarsh Island and had not passed anything on to Doreen, Dorothy Wilson began to doubt Doreen's claims about the dead Grandma Sally and Aunt Rose as well.

When John Campbell visited Laura Kartinyeri in Murray Bridge, she denied to him that she had ever been told by her mother about any 'women's business' at Hindmarsh Island. John and Alan Campbell asked to inform Mr Tickner, and this the eighty-nine-year-old Laura did this on 17 March 1995. On 8 April 1995, Sue Laurie, whose father had been born at Point McLeay and whose grandfather had been the schoolmaster of the Aborigines there, visited Laura Kartinyeri. Laurie was told by the old lady that she had been threatened by women from the Aboriginal Land Rights Movement that she would be sent to gaol if she said anything more about Hindmarsh Island.[101] Allan Campbell complained to the South Australian Museum that Doreen Kartinyeri had threatened to destroy papers relating to his family tree 'if you don't side with me on the "women's business".'

At a 'reconciliation meeting' at Graham's Castle, Goolwa, on 22–23 April 1995, Doreen Kartinyeri demanded that all non-indigenous people, including the guest speaker, leave the room. When Dorothy Wilson asked what was in the secret envelopes and why some white women knew when she and other Ngarrindjeri women did not, Doreen Kartinyeri replied that no one in the room except her knew what was in the envelopes and that no one would know until after the court case was finished. When Dorothy Wilson asked why other Ngarrindjeri women from Murray Bridge and

Millicent, particularly Dulcie Wilson, had not been invited to the meeting, since they were authorities on Ngarrindjeri culture, Sandra Saunders of the Aboriginal Legal Rights Movement (ALRM) replied, 'We are not talking about our culture . . . we are talking about the stopping of the bridge . . . and that's why the other women weren't invited because it's not for all Ngarrindjeri women, it's only for the Ngarrindjeri who want to stop the bridge.'[102] Sandra Saunders claimed that 'these outcasts' had been 'divorced from the cultural and spiritual beliefs of their ancestors'. Doreen Kartinyeri, Val Power, and Margaret Jacobs claimed the dissident women had 'gone against their own people instead of coming and asking the rest of the Ngarrindjeri women to explain the stories to them'. Stand-over tactics were soon employed. Bertha Gollan received threats that she would be sung to death if she gave evidence to the Royal Commission. Her reply was 'If I die tomorrow, I die with a clear conscience'.

Intimidation was not confined to Aborigines. After being interviewed on 30 May 1995 by Chris Kenny on Channel Ten Adelaide, Philip Jones of the South Australian Museum was 'harangued' by Doreen Kartinyeri, who accused him of betraying her. Next day, a deputation from the Aboriginal Land Rights Movement demanded of the Director of the Museum that Dr Jones be dismissed. Otherwise, he was told, 'the Museum's collection of Ngarrindjeri objects would probably be demanded back by the Ngarrindjeri people'. On 19 June 1995, two staff members of the Anthropology Division of the Museum complained that Doreen Kartinyeri had threatened them with a subpoena concerning information supplied by the Family History Unit to a person she thought antagonistic to her.[103] Since Aboriginal organizations had already successfully pressured Westpac to withdraw the Chapmans' borrowing facilities and had thus driven them into bankruptcy, these were not idle threats.

Ten Ngarrindjeri women at the Royal Commission attested that Laura Kartinyeri had never mentioned any 'women's business' connected with the Lower Murray to them over the years and that she had repeatedly denied she had ever passed on any 'women's business' to Doreen Kartinyeri.[104] Doreen Kartinyeri's claims about the two dead women she nominated were denied in sworn evidence by seventy-five-year-old Bertha Gollan, seventy-one-year-old Betty Tatt, fifty-four-year-old Rita Wilson, sixty-four-year-old Phyllis Byrnes, and several other senior Ngarrindjeri women who were relatives of one or the other of the two and had lived close to them. Doreen Kartinyeri's sister, Connie, was raised by Nanna Sally, whereas Doreen went away to the Fullarton Girls' Home in Adelaide, yet Connie testified she had never heard anything about 'women's business' from her grandmother. In any case, if 'women's business' had been passed from mother to daughter, there would have been no need for Doreen Kartinyeri or anyone else to be chosen as its special custodian.

Judge Stevens decided that 'notwithstanding the lack of direct evidence relating to the more particular description of the "women's business" contained in the Confidential

Appendices, there has been a body of evidence out of which it has been possible to infer their contents'.[105] As far as I know, no one has ever challenged that the 'women's business' in the envelopes included claims as given below:

1.   Hindmarsh Island had been used during the nineteenth century by Ngarrindjeri women as a place for aborting foetuses.
2.   The Ngarrindjeri over many generations believed that the Lower Murray was shaped like a woman's internal sexual organs and had thus regarded it as sacred to women.
3.   Building a bridge, as distinct from barrages or ferry ramps, between Goolwa and Hindmarsh Island would interrupt the 'meeting of the waters' and destroy the fertility and perhaps the entire existence of the Ngarrindjeri people.

Judge Stevens found 'no suggestion' of 'women's business' at Hindmarsh Island before or during 1993 and decided that these beliefs had been concocted during the 1990s and mainly in 1994 in order to persuade the federal government to ban the Hindmarsh Island Bridge.[106]

Dr Deane Fergie launched vituperative attacks on the Royal Commission. She agreed that there had been 'a fabricated account of the "women's business" 'but that the fabrication had been '*in and by* the commission itself' (emphasis as in original).[107] She was very angry about the use in the Royal Commission report of the phrase 'secret sacred women's business', whereas, she claimed, the phrases she used were 'women's secret knowledge' and 'oral tradition'. Her implication seems to have been that Doreen Kartinyeri never thought that anything sacred was involved in her claims.[108] In 1996, Dr Fergie argued that earlier she had only suggested that the 'restricted knowledge related to a specialist domain in Ngarrindjeri culture—the domain of the female putari or midwife'. This move partly solved one problem for Deane Fergie and Doreen Kartinyeri: Why was it that so few Ngarrindjeri women knew anything about women's business, knowledge, or oral tradition, secret or open, sacred or profane, relating to Hindmarsh Island, especially if, as Doreen Kartinyeri claimed at first, this information had been routinely passed on from mother to daughter? A problem with the new account was that Doreen Kartinyeri and Deane Fergie were not midwives. Deane Fergie might have been wiser had she placed all her writings into sealed envelopes.

One reason advanced by Doreen Kartinyeri why other women had not been included in the handing down of 'women's business' from mother to daughter was that they were Christians. One difficulty with this claim was that the three women she named as her informants were all Christians. Furthermore, if the knowledge was passed from mother to daughter at puberty, as she also claimed on several occasions, its transmission would be little affected by any religious views the girls came to hold later in life.

If there were an ancient Ngarrindjeri belief that the building of a bridge between Hindmarsh Island and Goolwa would destroy Aboriginal fertility, it might be thought that Christian churches would seek to dispel such a superstition. Instead, the moderator of the Uniting Church in South Australia wrote to one of the 'dissident women' that 'missionaries, particularly in the Southern areas of Australia, did teach that conversion required relinquishing of Aboriginal spirituality. But we, or the missionary societies involved, were wrong'.[109] Dulcie Wilson, a sixty-three-year-old Ngarrindjeri woman who had been for many years a prominent member of the Salvation Army, commented in a letter in New Times in August 1995: 'It was my understanding that the Christian missionaries' main purpose was to bring the gospel message of Christ's love and salvation to the Aborigines. I am therefore bewildered as to why some churches have come out in favour of so-called Aboriginal spirituality.'[110] Since the 'dissident' women at the Royal Commission were Christian and were subjected to threats of sorcery even in the courtroom, it might be supposed that Australia's Christian churches might be sympathetic to them, but their harassment never received a word of public censure from the churches of South Australia.

Rev. B. A. Clarke and Rev. Ken Sumner of the Uniting Church of South Australia and the Uniting Aboriginal and Islander Christian Congress were among the critics of the Royal Commission who attacked it on the grounds that the evidence of the 'proponent women' was not available They bemoaned that 'without the Ngarrindjeri witnesses from the community', that is Doreen Kartinyeri and friends, 'the Commissioners' choices were very limited indeed'.[111] Since Doreen Kartinyeri and her supporters, with the exception of Veronica Brady, refused to appear before the Royal Commission, one is reminded of the man who killed his parents and then complained he was an orphan.

The Royal Commission was also attacked by the South Australian Council of Churches because 'using such legal machinery may risk undermining religious belief'. At a meeting in Maughan Church in July, 1995, sponsored by the Uniting Aboriginal Christian Congress and its Synod's Social Justice Unit, Vi Deuschle, an ally of Doreen Kartinyeri, claimed:

> We're calling this Brown's Inquisition . . . These judges won't have full knowledge of the beliefs across cultural boundaries. They have no knowledge of the Aboriginal world view, so how can they make judgment about our beliefs?[112]

These commentators seemed incapable of distinguishing between a right to hold and express belief and power to determine public law on the basis of undisclosed private beliefs.

In 1860, Dr Wyatt testified to a Select Committee of the South Australian Legislative Council that infanticide, particularly female infanticide, sometimes took place among the Ngarrindjeri, most often if the mother was still suckling another child. The missionary George Taplin told the Select Committee that, although the men 'do not like the idea of allowing their wives to prostitute themselves to white men', many of the men and women 'like to have white children . . . because they excite more compassion among white women and can obtain larger gifts of food and clothes'. To lessen family discord, the fiction of claiming that the women with pale-faced babies had eaten too much white flour was developed. There was no indication that Ngarrindjeri babies of mixed descent were more likely to be killed than were other babies, but if anything it was the reverse. By 1913, the next time a Royal Commission was appointed in South Australia to investigate Aboriginal issues, the decisive majority of the Ngarrindjeri people was of mixed descent. No evidence before 1994 links Ngarrindjeri infanticide or abortion with Hindmarsh Island.

Doreen Kartinyeri's claim that there was such a link was indignantly rejected by the dissident Ngarrindjeri women. Dulcie Wilson, when told by Doreen Kartinyeri that white men took the Aboriginal women to Hindmarsh Island to destroy their half-caste babies, replied, 'If that's the case, why are we the color we are today?'[113] Pinkie Mack, whom Doreen Kartinyeri claimed as the authentic source of the 'women's business' at Hindmarsh Island, was the daughter of a white Australian, the Sub-Protector George Mason, and was named because of her coloring.

In 1994, it was never claimed that dire consequences to the health and fertility of Ngarrindjeri women resulted from building barrages, although these had changed the landscape considerably and sometimes prevented any 'meeting of the waters'. The foundations of the Goolwa barrage alone required 4,770 timber piles of up to ten metres in length to be driven into the riverbed. A central line of interlocked steel sheet piled 10–12 metres in depth acted as a cut off. The building of the ferry approaches required pylons to be driven into the riverbed, 30–40 metres from each side, to a depth of up to eighteen metres. Many Aborigines helped build these barrages; John McHughes, the sole remaining Aboriginal resident in the Goolwa area by the 1990s, took a leading part in that work. He never heard of any objections or of 'women's business' relating to Hindmarsh Island.

At first, Doreen Kartinyeri and Deane Fergie praised the barrages, whilst condemning bridges. Doreen Kartinyeri even suggested that 'in a sense, the barrages aid the proper functioning of the Lower Murray waters in modern conditions and drew an analogy with a "pace-maker".'[114] Some Aboriginal women told Dr Fergie that any bridge would 'make the system sterile', because a bridge 'goes above the water' and 'is a shore to shore, direct and permanent link'.[115] However, Hindmarsh Island and Mundoo Island were already joined together by a bridge. If the key point had been to ensure continued 'meetings of the waters', bridges were surely preferable to barrages, which are built to restrict the free flow of tidal water in order to preserve fresh water upstream. Judge Stevens concluded that 'there is no foundation for any distinction between the construction of a bridge, a second ferry or the Goolwa barrage in the context of the "women's business".'[116]

Dr Lucas was appalled that the Royal Commission used 'various empirical "facts" in order to discredit Ngarrindjeri belief'. These empirical 'facts' included changes in the sea level and the course of the Murray, which among other things ensured that there was for a very long time no Hindmarsh Island at all, of any shape. Dr Lucas noted correctly that 'the use of an obscure and remote geological history to refute Aboriginal heritage claims is not new'.[117] And there were many other heritage claims as well. Indeed the intellectual climate of the nineteenth century was transformed by empirical 'facts' that made it very unlikely that the world had been created in 4004 BC or that the whole world had been inundated by Noah's flood.

Since 1994, Doreen Kartinyeri and her supporters have turned against barrages as well as bridges. Doreen Kartinyeri told feminist anthropologist Diane Bell in 1996 that the construction of the barrages 'stopped the flow of water with the tides' and thus 'destroyed the rushes the people used for weaving'.[118] Maggie Jacobs claimed that the Ngarrindjeri had suffered 'because 'the rising water' had covered the fish traps. In contrast, Eileen McHughes was concerned that the water level had fallen, which indeed it has since white settlement began and is now too low.[119] Diane Bell did not seem to notice that Maggie Jacobs and Eileen McHughes had opposite complaints about the water level or that no Aborigines have been on Hindmarsh Island to set fish traps for many years.[120]

Although, of course, she could not 'go into the details because of the sacredness of it', in 1996 Doreen Kartinyeri revealed to Diane Bell that Auntie Rose, no longer around to contradict her niece, had once told her that when the jetty was built at Raukkan 'the women were in a lot of pain, young babies were dying and women were having miscarriages . . . There was crying. There was moaning. And the older women were rolling around just like they'd had a stake driven into their side'. Diane Bell looked up the diary of George Taplin and found a reference to the building of the jetty but none to the agonies of the women. Bell asked, 'Could we expect him to have recorded it had he noticed?' It would be, she suggested, like asking 'for evidence of the hell to which sinners go in order to acknowledge that following the Ten Commandments is a central Christian doctrine'.

Late in 1995, a further appeal was made by Aborigines to stop the bridge. Two additional grounds were advanced for a new ban: that a six kilometre strip along the Goolwa foreshore and the Sir Richard Peninsula contains what was once 'a large Aboriginal township' and that a one kilometre stretch of land on Hindmarsh Island opposite Goolwa contains 'a traditional Aboriginal residential place known as Rowaldorong'. The only surviving part of the earlier claims was that there is sacred mythology concerned with 'the mixing of the waters'.

With the passing of time, past sufferings are recalled more clearly and felt even more keenly. Doreen Kartinyeri's recall became ever more powerful. By 1996, she had remembered that in 1954, when her first child was born, she looked at a map on the back of a door. She realized in 1996: 'I was looking at Mundoo and between Hindmarsh Island, and I could see the inside of a woman, like it represented the shape of the womb and the ovaries.'[121] Her insight was remarkable, since it was apparently a small-scale map 'from Port Augusta down'. Eileen McHughes revealed to Diane Bell that when in 1994 at Hindmarsh Island a toilet was taken from a truck 'it sort of moved, made a dent in the earth . . . it was just like we'd been stabbed in the heart'. Sarah Milera told Bell, 'It's not just a feeling. The injury can put you in hospital. When they drove the pegs into the ground I felt a spiritual wounding . . . they rushed me to the hospital. They didn't know what to do with me, because I was wounded with pegs going into the ground where children were born. I was really hurt.'[122] Sarah Milera also told Bell, 'I was directed to Goolwa through my dreams', not by Davey Thomason as was thought earlier.[123]

Wonderful beliefs flourished among the affirmative Ngarrindjeri. Eileen McHughes remembered learning from her grandfather, Michael Gollan, that dead bodies were 'smoked' on Mundoo Island. When his family would go home from Raukkan, they would hear a baby crying, until one day they found the baby on the ground and put it up in a tree. They never heard those sounds again.[124] Maggie Jacobs related that in 1967, when David Unaipon died in hospital, the bird he used to talk with began to sing and flap his wings to tell his niece some miles away that he had died and in Tailem Bend, because the bird looked straight in that direction.[125] Sheila Goldsmith had a bird that told her when a letter was coming from her fiancé.[126] Veronica Brodie told Diane Bell that as a result of women's traditional ceremonies coming to an end the whales had left the Ngarrindjeri shores, but would return if and when those ceremonies resumed.[127] Veronica Brady's grandfather, Dan 'Killer' Wilson, had many magical powers, so it is not surprising that Veronica had much of interest to reveal. Old Dan could sing people to death or just whack them down with his waddy. Daisy Rankine claimed that two of her great-grandmothers, Louisa Karpeny and Pinkie Mack, were sorcerers and could brew a muldarpi, a spell that for maximum effectiveness needed ingredients such as hair, bones, and a bit of rag or pair of pants.[128]

Daisy Rankine told of a child that was taken by a shark because her parents were lazy and negligent. In their search for the child, the parents entered the land of a hostile clan and were in danger. To save themselves, they transformed their shapes and swam away to the Big Hill at Raukkan. The mother, transformed into a sea-monster, sucked in the sea and opened the Murray so that salt water and fresh water were mixed. That was one important reason why the Murray was sacred. Daisy Rankine claimed recent sightings of the sea-monster and of people who had heard her wailing close to where the shark took her child.[129] However, to explain the opening of the Murray to the sea, George Trevorrow went for Ngurunderi rather than the parents of the child lost to the shark.

Some young South Australians have had the benefit of a Ngarrindjeri Aboriginal Studies course to counter scepticism about traditional beliefs. The handbook explains that those who obey traditional law get knowledge and may even gain the status of elders, but that anyone who disobey will be punished and remain unimportant as well as ignorant.[130] 'Aboriginal Studies' in our universities are controlled by a peculiar ideology that combines postmodernism and primitive superstition. In a special 1996 number of the Journal of Australian Studies, published by the University of Queensland, on 'Secret Women's Business: Hindmarsh Island Affair', the seven contributors were Deane Fergie, Rod Lucas, Steve Hemming, Betty Fisher, Lyndall Ryan, whose work on Tasmanian history Keith Windschuttle has recently demolished, Christine Nicholls, and Kathie Muir. Although they are great advocates of 'Aboriginal autonomy', the editors of the Journal of Australian Studies evidently could not produce a single Aboriginal contributor. Dulcie Wilson or Dorothy Wilson would have obliged if asked, but such politically incorrect Aboriginal women are beyond the pale of our current university establishments. Australia is likely to witness many more follies similar to that of the 'women's business' at Hindmarsh Island. In the end, however, the spirit of Dulcie Wilson, Dorothy Wilson, and Bertha Gollan will triumph over fabrications. *Magna veritas et praevalebit.*

Chapter 5

GENOCIDAL AUSTRALIA?

Before the 1980s there was no hint of planned murders warranting the description of genocide occurring in Australia, except that there were sometimes Rumours, some of which might be true, that Aborigines' water holes had been poisoned by colonists, but given the shortage of water at most times and places in the continent, it would be an unlikely act for any branch of government to take. And we may reasonably assume that they did nothing of the sort.

Serious claims that the crews of the First Fleet and its successors or the soldiers or the convicts had been instructed by Pitt the Younger, Lord Sydney, Governor Phillip, or persons unknown, to murder Aborigines by infecting them with smallpox do not seem to have been made until after the Second World War, when Noel Butlin, a statistician and professor of economic history in the Research Schools of Social Sciences, ANU, made several such accusations. Such a charge from such a source could not be ignored, but Charles Wilson, Hugh Morgan, Judith Campbell, and others soon showed the Butlin accusations to be dependent on unreliable hearsay. Butlin was forced to argue that it was at least not impossible that, despite the lack of any evidence whatsoever, the wicked British had done it.

Professor Butlin set the tone of much of the subsequent debate with unpleasant personal references to those unconvinced by his arguments. On just four *Quadrant* pages, he accused the unbelievers of being 'grotesquely misleading', alleged his book was 'beyond the level of [Morgan's] understanding', and described Wilson as a mere 'business historian' who had been 'promoted in his role of reviewer' of the Butlin book 'far beyond the level of his understanding'. It was time, but perhaps too late, that both Morgan and Wilson 'grew up'. Imputations of venality against Hugh Morgan included the revelation that he was a 'senior mining executive' and 'preoccupied with Aboriginal land claims'.[131]

Butlin's critics noted that the deadly smallpox of 1788–9 had been spreading slowly from the north for over a decade and was not the result of any 'variolus matter' that could have been put on ship in England, since the toxicity would have faded during the long ocean voyage, during which there were no smallpox infections on board ship. New information provided by Butlin himself included that 'no known group of humans' were 'ever able, on first encounter, to resist smallpox' and that smallpox left pockmarks on the survivors. Butlin noted correctly that population statistics for New South Wales and other parts of Australia may well have been too low and that there had been 'potential white triggers at or near the spot where and when smallpox was sighted by whites'. That must be true: If no whites had been there, they certainly could not have sighted anything at all.

To show how fair minded he was, Butlin explained that smallpox transmission might have been 'by some authority', 'deliberately by convicts', unintentionally by convicts, or 'unwillingly by blacks'. He claimed that nobody 'can possibly rule out any of these', but he never offered, or even tried to offer, any evidence whatsoever for his dreadful allegation of genocide against the first founders of the New Australia that had been so generous to him. A few on the outer edges used Professor Butlin to bolster their accusations of genocide: Gary Foley told *The Bulletin* that 'asking Aborigines to celebrate Australia Day was like asking Jews to celebrate the advent of the third Reich', and Clive Holding referred to the arrival of the First Fleet as the prelude to a 'holocaust', but the cautious remained silent for a little while. Indeed, the unpleasantness had almost been forgotten when the charges were revived in 1999 by ex-South African Colin Tatz who asserted that 'almost all historians of the Aboriginal experience—black and white –avoid the word genocide'.[132]

However, as though reacting in shame, the use of the word could hardly have expanded more rapidly. The 1990s witnessed a new wave internationally of anti-genocide campaigns. Tatz made many clearly baseless allegations. He conceded that 'the letters patent and instructions to governors in the eighteenth and nineteenth centuries' were 'benign utterances of far-away governments', but he contended that settler violence against Aborigines was not controlled. He accused the British and subsequent Australian authorities of 'a litany of deprivation' of Aborigines. He even claimed that 'to date, no one has refuted the hypothesis of the late Professor Noel Butlin, an eminent economic historian, of introduced disease as an intentional weapon of extermination'. Tatz added the Native (Aboriginal) Police to smallpox as the British scourge of Aborigines. He did not discuss the effect of higher fire power in the settlement of quarrels that preceded the British arrival by many generations. The British could exert even less control on off-duty Native Police than on white settlers. If the British had refused to create a Native Police Force, there would have been accusations of racial prejudice, but once armed, some indigenous constables did use their firearms to settle old tribal grievances. Although not on the scale of the

Maori Wars, tribal conflicts produced many more causalities after the arrival of the British and gunpowder.

Tatz did not mention any of the amenities introduced by the colonists, including medical treatments that had dramatically reversed the fall in Aboriginal populations. Yet he blamed recent governments for the fact that Aborigines topped the medical statistics for diseases they didn't exhibit even thirty years ago, had much greater rates of unemployment, much lower home ownership, and considerably lower annual per capita income, but much higher arrest and imprisonment rates and institutionalization, with crimes prevalent which were rare as recently as the 1960s, namely, homicide, rape, child molestation, burglary, physical assaults, drug-peddling and drug-taking, and, sadly, youth suicide, no longer a criminal act, at a rate among the highest on this planet. Tatz even tried to use the successes of assimilation against wicked Australia. Because of 129 men and women in the Aboriginal and Islander Sports Hall of Fame, twelve had been removed from their homes as children, another six, possibly seven, had been adopted by white families, while another twenty-two had grown up in institutions, Tatz argued that the numbers removed from their homes were much higher than governments had admitted, but he apparently did not consider that it children in that group, members of the "Stolen Generation", were stronger and fitter than the average of not only the indigenous population but also of Australians as a whole.

Tatz surpassed Butlin in personal abuse of opponents. He described them as 'a small coterie of journalists', some in concert with one renegade anthropologist, all lacking any academic or practical credentials in the field of Aboriginal affairs, contrive to claim, inter alia, that the charge of genocide is either pedantry or mischief. Very quickly, the renegades increased to two (named this time): Dr Ron Brunton and Professor Kenneth Maddock. Tatz, once a critic of McCarthyism, then indicted:

> An array of conservative critics who refute genocide and/or the gloom and mourning pervading Aboriginal colonial history. Few are reputable academics like historian Geoffrey Blainey, political scientist Ken Minogue and anthropologist Ken Maddock. Ron Brunton is an expert on kava, the alcoholic beverage made from roots in the South Pacific. There are senior politicians, like John Howard, John Herron and former premiers Wayne Goss and Ray Groom . . . There is a journalistic group vehement about the Bringing Them Home Report. That group included Michael Duffy, Frank Devine, Christopher Pearson and Padraic McGuinness. There is also a netherworld of radio talkback 'philosophers', Alan Jones, John Laws, Stan Zemanek, and Howard Sattler. What many of these men have in common—apart from a seeming antipathy to Aborigines generally and to the whole Aboriginal 'thing'—is that they do neither fieldwork nor

homework . . . There is a mining and financial group, spearheaded by Henry Bosch and Hugh Morgan.

No examples were offered of errors of which these ignorant fellows were guilty, but the dismal failure of Butlin and Tatz to indict Australia successfully with genocide seems to have stimulated other academics to enter the lists Among these was Robert Manne who had not shown much interest in Aboriginal affairs before his ideological volte face of the late 1990s, but, cast adrift from *Quadrant,* he seems to have looked round for good causes: His flirtation with Santamaria-type protectionism and attacks on 'economic rationalism', in which he showed considerable economic irrationalism, were soon followed by new passions for Aboriginal land rights and against climate change.

Manne claims that his Damascus moment came when 'watching a documentary called Frontier': He came across words spoken by A. O. Neville, Protector of Aborigines in Western Australia about the 'breeding out' of 'half-caste' and perhaps all other Aborigines. The fact that this policy was never adopted either by the Commonwealth or any state government did not deter Manne from claiming that Australia began a new form of genocide in 1939, the same year World War II broke out. However, in contrast to the Nazi prohibition of sexual intercourse between Jews and non-Jews, Neville and his colleague Cook in the Northern territory encouraged sexual relations between part-Aborigines and whites.

Manne ignored the pre-1939 Australian 'new deal' for Aborigines. This was based, as Charles Rowley put it, on 'a common citizenship, without postulating genetic changes' and expressing 'a long-term objective for policy that was other than some kind of social engineering for the disappearance of the race into the white majority, taking the emphasis off miscegenation'. Russell McGregor commented that 'at the first post-war Conference of Commonwealth and State Aboriginal Welfare Authorities in 19.46 the need for reproductive management to control color . . . received not a mention'. Why then Manne's relentless emphasis on the wicked intentions of Cook and Neville, without fair examination of the policies, opposed by Cook and Neville, that were adopted? Professor Inga Clendinnen noted that Manne seemed convinced Neville and Cook won broad acceptance for their eugenicist policies and were able to implement them, but that a close reading of the historical record of actions does not support this claim.[133]

The alarm expressed by Professor Clendinnen and some other academics who could normally have been relied upon to support the 'progressive' side in the History Wars seemed to galvanise several of the leading prosecutors of Australia as a genocidal state into a controlled withdrawal from part of the contested field, without, however, confessing any previous error. A popular way of reducing risk in controversy has long been to use words in very different ways from their normally understood usage. This deception has been practised with success in disputes about sexual abuse, in which 'incest', for example' was stretched in statistical tables issued by the tax-supported Adelaide Rape Crisis Centre to include 'any explicit sexual behaviour that an adult imposes on a child under the age of 17'. On genocide a leading exponent of this tactic has been Professor Bain Attwood. At least four times in one book Attwood accused his opponents of not realizing that the term 'genocide' includes not only the mass killing of a people but mass deaths. He boldly denied that he, Lyndall Ryan, and other combatants had ever accused any Australian government of planning to get rid of their Aboriginal population. They had merely pointed out what was quite true, and had been confirmed by Charles Darwin himself, that mass deaths had followed in the wake of British colonization. When words are used in ways likely to deceive, even if that is not the intent of the user, they may be called 'weasel' words, because of their slippery nature, or concertina words, because they can be stretched or compressed, according to the player's wish.

In one example, Attwood tells Windschuttle with condescension that he has 'come to his take on Aboriginal history largely through popular historical discourses'. It derives from the way the term has been used in these rather than in any academic writing . . . Particularly in popular usage, it tends to carry two meanings, though these are often so intertwined that they cannot always be distinguished from each other. On the one hand, 'genocide' is a symbol of mass killing It is used to draw attention to the killers. On the other hand, 'genocide' is a symbol of mass death. In this case, the focus of those deploying the term is obviously upon an outcome and the victims.[134] As is so common, the weaker the case, the more pompous and obscure the language. One wonders what school students in, say, year 7, the top primary year in most Australian states, think are the accusations about genocide in connection with Aborigines? Or the parents of those children? In my experience, they believe that the charge made by scholars such as Ryan and Attwood is of genocide in its plain unvarnished sense of deliberate obliteration of a population, not your cultural genocide resulting from their living in houses and going to school. Not all children or their parents believed the accusations to be true, but they certainly did not realize that an attempt was being made to include in the meaning of 'genocide' the disappearance of a language, separation from traditional lands, etc.

Similarly, tactics had been used about child sexual abuse. Fantastically inflated figures were first of all circulated, creating widespread distress among people who had never guessed that so many rapes and acts of incest had been taking place in Australia throughout their lifetimes. When the deceptive change of definition had been exposed, we were told that we must surely have realized that most of the talk about rape and incest had included unwanted sexual approaches by persons over sixteen to persons under that age. Including trivial acts among very serious ones is not only dishonest but harmful to children who are really being abused, since attention is distracted from their plights. Similarly, exaggerations sure to be exposed and repudiated can only weaken concern about real suffering experienced by indigenous people in the wake of colonisation.

Manne claimed that Australians were being 'invited by newspaper articles and right-wing magazines once again to discuss Aboriginal policy in the absence of Aboriginal people'. He named no names, but two principal objects of his vituperation, *The Australian* and *Quadrant*, gave ample space to Aboriginal contributors. Manne initially accepted without question the finding of the 'Bringing Them Home Report'—that Aboriginal child removal policies of the Commonwealth and state governments before 1970 made them guilty of genocide.

Frequently used against Neville has been his rhetorical question at a 1939 Commonwealth conference: 'Are we going to have a population of 1,000,000 blacks in the Commonwealth, or are we going to merge them into our white community and eventually forget that there were any Aborigines in Australia?'[135] Further evidence offered of Australian genocide is a resolution passed by that 1939 conference.

> This conference believes that the destiny of the natives of Aboriginal origin, but not of the full blood, lies in their ultimate absorption by the people of the Commonwealth, and it therefore recommends that all efforts be directed to that end. Nobody who knows about these groups could deny that their members are socially and culturally deprived. We must improve their lot so that they can take their place economically and socially in the general community. Once this is done, the breakup of such groups will be rapid.[136]

The statement most often cited against Cecil Cook is given below:

> In the Territory the mating of aboriginals with any person other than an aboriginal is prohibited. The mating of colored aliens with any female of part-aboriginal blood is also prohibited. Every endeavour is being made to breed out the color by elevating female half-castes to white standard with a view to their absorption by mating into the white population. The adoption of a similar policy throughout the Commonwealth is, in my opinion, a matter of vital importance.[137]

Whatever Neville and Cook may have hoped for, the governments of Australia did not have the resources or conviction to try to control all Aboriginal sexual activities. In fact, their policy, to the small extent to which it was ever applied, helped to increase the number of part-Aborigines, not to 'breed out the color'.

Despite a well-made film featuring Kenneth Branagh as Neville, latter-day exposure of the protectors' dastardly scheme failed to mobilize public opinion, which seemed more concerned about forced marriages of underage girls in some indigenous and other cultural milieus.

The obvious solution, and the one adopted, was to change the meaning of the word 'genocide'. This was not an Australian first, since some Americans and Europeans had hit on the idea already. The numerous accusations that genocidal racism is inherent in Western civilization included academic denunciations of 'Neo-Darwinism' or 'social Darwinism'. Prominent among those condemned were Charles Darwin's cousin, Francis Galton, and Herbert Spencer. Other British scientists singled out included Pitt-Rivers, Myres, Sir John Lubbock; Australians, mainly immigrants from Britain, included C. S. Wake, Baldwin Spencer, Alfred Howitt, and Lorimer Fison. Conspicuously omitted from the charge sheets were V. Gordon Childe and Frederick Engels, extenuated by virtue of their Marxism.

These attacks on Neo-Darwinism and in Australia on protectors Neville and Cook followed accusations in the United States that Christopher Columbus had initiated the genocidal extermination of Central Americans and Caribbean Islanders. Claude Levi-Strauss alleged that millions of Indians died 'of horror and disgust at European civilization'.[138] Tzvetan Todorov described the conquest of America as the cause of 'the greatest genocide in human history'.[139] The death toll was indeed tragic, but the Spaniards did not deliberately infect the peoples they conquered with diseases. Disease spread both ways: Large numbers of Spaniards and other Europeans died of syphilis and other diseases contracted in the Americas to which they had no immunity. And the critics of Europeans have had little to say about the Black Death of the 1340s and other attacks of plague that were introduced unwittingly by Mongols and other conquering horsemen from Central Asia.

In his 1967 *Race and Racism* South African Pierre van den Berghe coined the term 'Herrenvolk (Master Race) democracies' to describe societies such as Australia which, he claimed, extend 'full rights to the master class but deny rights to subordinate classes on account of their assumed inferiority'. George Fredrickson, then a professor of history at Stanford University, conceded in his 2002 *Racism: A Short History* that hatred by some human groups for others has been widely displayed throughout history, but he and his colleagues seemed to be looking for a way to pick out the United States and other Western societies as the most guilty of peoples and states. He differentiated between xenophobia—virtually universal but limited to hatred of alien beliefs and cultures, which could be changed, and racism—directed at the indelible and inheritable nature of victim peoples. The victims of xenophobia can change their cultures or religions, but the victims of racism cannot change the colour of their skins.[140]

In Frederickson's account, modern racism has its roots in egalitarian ideas that emerged first in the eighteenth century with the mingling, despite the obvious differences in their world outlooks, of evangelical Christianity and the rationalism of the Enlightenment. Although many eighteenth-century Christians and freethinkers had been widely regarded as responsible for major advances in civilization, such as the abolition of the slave trade and then slavery itself, and for more humane treatment of criminals, the sick, the elderly, and children, Frederickson and Van den Berghe took them to task. Their argument was that elsewhere and previously racial inequality was taken for granted. However, in states that gave formal recognition to equality before the law, actual inequality of treatment needed special arguments to justify exclusion of some groups from the benefits of law. If all men were born equal but some men were slaves, then one solution might be that slaves were not fully human. The argument concluded that xenophobia only became full-blown racism when the scientific revolution of the eighteenth century undermined *Genesis* but also for the first time, made it possible to classify human beings in the same way as animals and plants.

Many critics of Western racism largely ignore non-Western racism. The Chinese geographer Xu Jiyu, for example, wrote that black Africans 'appear as if they were living in the most ancient times . . . They were unable to develop a civilization by themselves'.[141]

A plausible explanation for the Frederickson and Van den Berghe theses is that the West advanced very rapidly materially and intellectually during the seventeenth and eighteenth centuries, whilst non-Western civilizations such as China and Mughal India lay largely dormant, as did almost all the hunter-gathers. Yet, the developmental theories devised by the Scottish enlightenment philosophers and by Buffon and Montesquieu, later taken up by Marx, led to savagery being regarded as elongated backwardness that had socio-economic explanations. They did not suppose that hunter-gatherers were less capable of reason than peoples whose own ancestors had 'crossed the ditch', or ditches, to civilization only a few generations earlier: a length of time increasingly seen to be a paltry fraction of human existence.

Several Australian scholars, however, could find only xenophobia and racism in the expansion of Western civilization. Professor Dirk Moses claimed that the two narratives, settlement and genocide, 'cannot be split off'.[142] Moses considered that 'Australia had many genocides, perhaps more than any other country'.[143] Professor Moses is not fastidious in controversy. He suggested that some statements by Ron Brunton, Hugh Morgan and Keith Windschuttle raised concern as to "whether such figures experience castration anxiety, that is a fantasized danger to their genitals".[144] That seemed dangerous ground for one with the name of the only leader of his people who was not circumcised until after his marriage.

Professors Ann Curthoys and John Docker have made many charges of genocide against Australia. One major influence on their thinking is the jurist Raphael Lemkin who died in the late 1940s, but whose reputation in progressive circles has steadily risen. Curthoys and Docker contend that Australia was 'not only potentially but inherently genocidal' and that 'Australian child removal practices fall within the definition of genocide used in the 1948 UN Genocide convention'. They consider that 'the English were the most "overtly genocidal" of European empire-builders', who 'pioneered a trail for the Nazis in Germany' by 'displacement of indigenous populations and their replacement by incoming peoples held to be racially superior'.[145]

In a recorded conversation with Lorenzo Veracini, Docker insisted that 'any debate on genocide and its relation to Australian history had to involve the question of settler-colonialism'. Docker related that Ann Curthoys and he had been studying, in a 'post secularist' way, the historical importance of biblical stories like *Exodus* for European and Western settler-colonial history. They found especially inspirational "Edward Said's wonderful essay '*Michael Walzer's Exodus and Revolution: a Canaanite Reading*'". Yet, bloodthirsty as the Children of Israel often were, should we condemn their genocidal acts but ignore comparable atrocities their foes committed? The cities of Canaan, like those of the Philistines and the Phoenicians, had been built on the basis of successful aggression, and nearly every one of those peoples claimed as did the Israelites that their God had allotted to them a Promised Land on which others happened to dwell at that particular time but which they had divine authority to conquer.

Ann Curthoys explained to Lorenzo Veracini that she was engaged in 'finding a way to understand Australian settlement history in a way that places it carefully within a larger history of colonization and genocidal desire and practice'. She stated that 'very slowly, all migrants and their descendants, including those of non-Anglo-Celtic background, came to be recognized as colonizers, as part of and benefiting from colonization with its history of indigenous dispossession'. Curthoys elaborated:

> I think confronting the question of genocide in some ways returns us to a full recognition of the murderous desires that underlie colonization, the taking of someone else's land. It may not have been genocidal to decide on a penal settlement at Botany Bay; there was at that point still a hope that the settlers and the Indigenous peoples could live in peace and harmony. But the same cannot be said of the decision to continue with settlement. Once it was known that Indigenous people lived in the interior, wanted the settlers to leave, and died in great numbers wherever the settlers went to such an extent that their survival seemed unlikely, then the decision to continue the colonizing process has a genocidal component to it. In

continuing the colonizing project the British government, and the British and local-born settlers in the Australian colonies, knew what they were doing. Everyone knew that their presence meant death and destruction for the original occupiers of the land. Putting all this in the context of world history, of British imperial and colonizing history, and of genocidal desires and practices throughout history, helps us see ourselves as part of a broader tragedy in human history.[146]

Docker often cited the late Palestine-born Christian Edward Said. Said classified most writing by Westerners about Arabs and Islam as 'Orientalism' which, he holds, was and continues to be 'inextricably tied to the imperialist societies that produced it, making much of the work inherently politicized and servile to power'. Said argued that a long Western tradition of false and romanticized images of Asia and the Middle East had served as, and was intended to serve as, an implicit justification for Western colonial ambitions. He claimed that Western stereotypes emerged as early as *The Persians* of Aeschylus.

In modern times, Said claimed, European scholars monopolized the study of oriental languages, history, so as to infer that Eastern scholars were incapable of doing so satisfactorily. Yet many languages and archaeological remains recovered by Western scholars such as William Jones, Henry Rawlinson, Edward Mitford, Austen Henry Layard, and George Smith had been totally neglected during centuries in which they had come close to being lost forever. The problem was not only indifference but also sharp hostility, especially among Muslims, to any praise of pre-Islamic times. In Iran, Islamic reaction against the last Shah's plans to reconstruct monuments of the Medes and Persians helped to bring about his overthrow. Egyptian interest in the Pyramids was largely confined before the French expedition of 1799 to grave robbery and re-use of stone.

Said's contention that the West oppressed the East for more than 2,000 years is unsupportable: The Arabs penetrated across the Pyrenees and by the Mediterranean coast deeply into France, and then the Turks conquered most of North Africa and the Balkans. Said rarely condemned the extension of Russian or Chinese power into Central Asia because he wished to concentrate his venom on the West, especially the dreaded 'Anglo-Saxons'.

Said claimed that Western writers cannot be objective or fair-minded, because all authors 'are embedded first in the language and then in the culture, institutions and political ambience' of their own societies. However, Said himself was apparently able to escape from limitations of time and place. In a farewell tribute in 2003, Tariq Ali had the honesty to say of Said's orientalism that 'like all great polemics, it eschews balance'.

In his discussions of both genocide and slavery, Docker followed Lemkin in selective choice and omission, often seemingly on the basis of colour and race. White slaves, of whom there were millions in the classical Mediterranean states and in the hands of Arabs, Turks or Mongols get little mention. Even the slaves and sacrificial victims of Aztecs and Incas received sparse mention; and one would imagine the Chinese, Arabs, and myriad African peoples to have been close to being innocent of slavery and slave trading. In his *The Origins of Violence* Tibet does not even appear in the Index but genocidal acts he alleges Israel has committed against Palestinians appear on at least nine pages.

Included in Lemkin's types of cultural genocide is prohibition of cultural activities or codes of behaviour and demoralization. Surely Docker can list a hundred 'cultural activities' that should be prohibited: Witch burning, suttee, and child marriage immediately spring to mind. And just how would placing limits on 'demoralization' be hard to fathom? One has a perfect recipe for ongoing hatred and persecution.

Docker, and behind him, Lemkin is fundamentally ambiguous. Docker wrote

> In Lemkin's view, genocide signifies a coordinated plan of different actions aiming at the destruction of a group. Such actions involve considerations that are cultural, political, social, legal, intellectual, spiritual, economic, biological, physiological, religious psychological and moral. Such actions involve considerations of health, food and nourishment, of family life and care of children, and of birth as well as of death.

What if there is no coordinated plan? No genocide in that case? Has each category listed from cultural to moral to be undermined before we call it genocide? Or just one of them or any number in between? These are 'accordion' definitions: they can be expanded or contracted at will. Docker writes of victims of genocide going on to commit genocide themselves, but if they can still do that, the genocide applied to them must have been inefficient.

In the Second World War in Yugoslavia, the three main warring parties simply killed when they could, without there being a fixed oppressor–oppressed relationship. Sri Lanka and numerous African states, especially Rwanda, are more recent examples. The killings after 1946 of each other by Muslims, Hindus, and Sikhs far exceeded all the deaths inflicted over two centuries by British 'oppressors'.

Docker's The *Origins of Violence* is based on two incompatible lines of argument. The first is the universality of human violence, including genocide as defined by Raphael Lemkin and Jared Diamond. And they did not confine genocide to human beings. From Africa, Jane Goodall was forced to concede that chimpanzees, our closest primate relatives, are highly aggressive and genocidal within Lemkin's definitions. Thus, according to Docker, genocide was universal and ubiquitous, yet he wrote of the atrocities he attributed to 'Western Civilization', with special attention to the Jewish scriptures and the myths and history of Ancient Greece, as though they were uniquely guilty.

In *The Rise and Fall of the Third Chimpanzee* Jared Diamond argued that genocide amongst human groups probably began millions of years ago, when a 'militarily stronger people attempt to occupy the land of a weaker people, who resist'. Diamond noted that genocide is quite common among animal groups—especially in social carnivorous species such as lions, wolves, hyenas, and ants, but he was most impressed by Jane Goodall's observations of inter-chimpanzee aggression and killing. On this line of argument, we are all genocidal, given the opportunity and incentive.

Diamond suggested that at the end of the Ice Age some hunter-gatherer groups adopted agriculture and unwittingly created a new global force for destruction. The sedentary farmers outbred and then drove off the bands that had chosen to remain hunter-gatherers, because 'ten malnourished farmers can still outfight one healthy hunter'. Hugh Brody's *The Other Side of Eden: Hunter-Gatherers, Farmers, and the Shaping of the World* added the idea that the so-called nomads had been the stationary ones, whereas the 'settled' farmers crossed land and sea as genocidal invaders

Yet hunter-gatherers were more likely to kill adult males they defeated, because they could not set them to profitable work without restoring their weapons which would then be turned against their captors. On the other hand, defeated populations in agrarian states could be set to labor at considerable profit so that serfdom and slavery rapidly followed agriculture, but genocide fell, except when resisting cities were finally captured.

A very strange comment from Docker on the chimpanzee research was about 'the curious prominence of Western white women like Goodall and Dian Fossey in the conduct and shaping of primate research in Africa amidst pressing contexts of imperialism and colonialism and, from the early 1960s, decolonization'[147]. What was curious about their prominence I do not know: Would Japanese men or Fijian women been less curious?

In Africa, the main group picked out by Docker as genocidal was the British in Kenya, who he depicts as exceptionally cruel to the long-suffering Kikuyu. On the basis of a footnote to Caroline Elkins, Docker asserted that 'throughout the 1950s British colonial officials had been brutally repressing the Mau Mau movement and in effect imprisoning the entire Kikuyu population, accompanied by the torture, mutilation and death of many thousands of Kenyan people'. Indeed, Docker claimed,

British colonialism was 'not too dissimilar from that of the Gombe chimpanzees, though on a vastly greater and worldwide scale'. Docker failed to mention any of the criticisms of Elkins's work: James Mitchel wrote, 'I shudder for those of her students who expect academic rigeur: Elkins doesn't let facts stand in the way of a good rant.' David Elstein contended that her casualty figures were 'derived from an idiosyncratic reading of census figures and a tendentious interpretation of the fortified village scheme'; Elkins' Harvard colleague Niall Ferguson described her book as a highly 'sensationalist account of the rebellion'. In 2007, the demographer John Blacker demonstrated in detail that her figures were grossly overestimated. The Kenyan historian Bethwell Ogot, from Moi University, argued that Elkins was blind to atrocities on the part of Mau Mau. Docker seemed to conclude in Orwellian fashion that all *homo sapiens* are equally genocidal but that Europeans, especially the British, are more equally genocidal than others.

Support came from other sectors of academia. Richard White held that 'the Australian national character' projected by the outback pastoral worker and the sun-bronzed lifesaver was 'uncomfortably close to Nazi ideas about the Aryan master race'. White sneered at the concept of progress, perhaps so as not to offend peoples who manifestly had made very little: There are derisive references to 'sparkling symbols of Anglo-Saxon progress', to Macaulay presenting the 'educated English gentleman' with 'history as the story of progress in which civilization had progressed to its highest point in England'. Why did Marx and Engels choose England as their refuge? Where would Professor White, with the aid of Dr Who, choose as his abode if flown through time to the second half of the nineteenth century? White alleged that *The Origin of Species* 'seemed to give a scientific—and therefore moral—sanction to despotic social relationships'. When did Darwin befriend despotism?

For the new anti-racism to have maximum effect, non-white Australians had to be absolved from blame. Professor Henry Reynolds played down racial tension between non-Europeans and held that 'places like Cairns and Broome and Darwin were remarkably peaceful', even though the 1920 race riots in Broome, 'incontestably the worst in Australian history', were fought by Japanese against Timorese and Koepangersr, whilst white Australians tried to restore peace.

Professor Stuart Macintyre rebuked the colonists for regarding themselves as settlers, when they were invaders who ignored the destruction of 'a civilization more ancient than their own'. Macintyre attacked George Higinbotham, the Australian Liberal Parliamentarian, for making 'no admission of the deliberate genocide that had marked the initial pastoral occupation'.[148] However, since there was no such deliberate genocide, Higinbotham was hardly remiss. Macintyre, like so many other progressives of our time, pours ridicule on every policy open to Australian governments a century ago. For Macintyre, it was evil not only when Aborigines were placed in Reserves but also when Reserves were closed and Aborigines driven out of 'a place of refuge'. It was apparently infamous of Deakin to propose a 'Half-Caste Act' in 1886, but Macintyre does not state whether he would have had all 'Half-Castes' treated in the same way as 'full-blooded' Aborigines or all 'half-castes', 'full-blooded Aborigines', and all other Australians treated uniformly in social and educational legislation.

In many places it is believed that if there was one part of Australia that was most certainly guilty of genocide against the Aborigines, it was Tasmania. And some Australian historians have agreed. Professor Lyndall Ryan claimed that they were 'victims of a conscious policy of Genocide.'[149] In 2002 Cassandra Pybus told Channel Nine News that:

> The Aboriginal people of Tasmania were all but wiped out. I mean it was one of the clearest cases of genocide that we know of and recognized as such at the time.

A year later, perhaps after a prudent friend had bade her caution, Pybus said, 'I don't want to call it genocide, but I'm not going to tidy it up either'[150]. That should have settled the matter.

The basic attitude of the progressive mind to race changed rapidly towards the end of the century. Take the following statements of prominent Americans:

Henry Louis Gates: 'Race as a meaningful criterion has long been recognized to be a fiction.'

Tzvetan Todorov: 'Whereas racism is a well-attested phenomenon, race itself does not exist.'

Naomi Zack: 'The concept of race does not have an adequate scientific foundation.'

Joel Williamson: 'Scientific scholars generally agree that there is actually no such thing as race.'

Eugenia Shanklin: 'Race is a concept that exists in our minds, not in our bodies . . . I have grown weary of explaining to my students that there is no such thing as race.'

Martin Luther King, Jr: 'I have a dream that my four little children will one day live in a nation where they will not be judged by the colour of their skin, but by the content of their character.'[151]

Those sentiments were first cheered in Australia, but soon the cheer-leaders began to insist that race was crucial to each individual, group, and entire society. In Australia, the first priority in Aboriginal education became to strengthen 'Aboriginal identity'. To cast doubt on a person's race, at least if that person is Aboriginal, can lead to the courts of law. Left-wing parties began to engage in 'identity politics' as the best way to gain office.

In reality, many European explorers and other travellers abroad, often missionaries such as Bartoleme de Las Casas, Francis Xavier, and Bougainville, formed favourable opinions of new peoples they met and tried to protect them from exploitation. So did many influential thinkers in their home countries, such as Baron de Lahonton, and the Jesuit Joseph-Francois Lafitau. Montaigne denounced the French wars of religion as far more savage than any of the atrocities alleged against genuine savages,

Chinese civilization was much admired in England in the age of Jonathan Swift and his patron Sir William Temple, although it fell sharply in esteem after the 1793 mission to Peking of Lord McCartney. Peoples of West Africa were described with sympathy by Francis Moore, William Smith, Anna Marcia Mackenzie, and Thomas Salmon, together with the leasers and mass membership of the anti-slavery movement. Early accounts of Pacific Islanders were filled with praise of their 'soft primitivism'. James Cook's artist Sydney Parkinson wrote that 'ambition, and the love of luxurious banquets, and other superfluities, are but little known' there.[152] Joseph Banks was at first impressed by the military bearing of Maori warriors, and after refusing to believe that any species should prey upon itself or that the New Zealanders ate human flesh 'as a dainty or even look upon it as part of common food', he refused to make the obvious conclusions from human bones he observed.[153]

There is almost complete silence in our classrooms and lecture theatres about the best of the West, but this is surpassed by the even greater silence about the worst of the rest, such as massive human sacrifice among the Aztecs and Incas (except when some of Inga Clendinnen's graduates are teaching in the school), extensive long-term Arab slavery in Africa and the Barbary Coast, and enslavement of black Africans by other black Africans. Yet nearly every African state encountered by Western sailors and traders from the fifteenth century onwards was based on slavery. Our scholars seemed blind to the abolition of, first, the slave trade and then slavery itself in the British Empire, when it still flourished elsewhere in lands many educators are too selectively tender-minded to name.

Chapter 6

SHOULD WE SAY 'SORRY' TO THE CHINESE?

Demands for apologies for past misdeeds allegedly committed by one's ancestors, or even non-ancestral predecessors, have multiplied in recent years. Some Chinese Australians now demand a national apology for their ancestors' experiences under the White Australia Policy. At least a glance at the historical record is obviously needed before we make up our minds.

BRITISH ATTITUDES TO CHINA BEFORE 1788

The British colonists brought to Australia diverse conceptions about different peoples. For many centuries, the few Europeans who travelled to China considered its civilisation as more advanced in most ways than their own. The Chinese government was seen as stable and admirable, and Europeans were anxious to acquire its products such as silk and spices, whereas the Chinese wanted nothing European. However, the Chinese made virtually no improvements on their great inventions, and by the late eighteenth century, China was regarded by many Europeans as despotic and corrupt and the mass of the population subservient and devoid of rights. The Chinese held that foreigners should obey their emperor, holder of 'the mandate from heaven', and kowtow at his feet. In John Powelson's words, 'The main purpose of Chinese law was to preserve the power of the state, not the rights of the individual.'[154] It would also be fair to claim that the general level of xenophobia or racism, however these may be defined, was as high among the Chinese in China as among the Australians.

THE ENTRY OF THE CHINESE

Chinese miners entered the Australian gold fields in large numbers in the 1850s, and by 1861, Chinese formed 11 per cent of the adult male population of Victoria. Many complaints against Chinese arose from gender imbalance: Frequently, there were over a hundred Chinese men to one woman. Prostitution and homosexuality inevitably flourished. Contradictory accusations were hurled against Chinese immigrants: rampantly homosexual, but constantly preying on European girls; birds of passage, but staying and building up their numbers; indolent, but working sweated hours. The Chinese were accused of being anti-union, but when in 1893, Chinese cabinet makers in Melbourne formed a trade union and sought to affiliate with the Trades Hall Council, their overture was rejected.

AUSTRALIAN RESPONSES

In current debates about the White Australia Policy, a central issue is whether hostile Australian attitudes towards Chinese were based on biological or neo-Darwinian racism or, more restrictedly, on adverse perceptions of their ways of life. Workers and their unions were frequently anti-Chinese. In 1858, Rocky River miners petitioned the New South Wales Legislative Assembly to remove the Chinese, because they were 'not peaceably disposed' and 'their general filthy habits' were 'repulsive to the Christian population'.[155] An Intercolonial Trade Union Congress voted that 'the importation of Chinese is injurious, morally, socially, and politically, to the best interests of this colony'. Delegates declared that they had 'never allowed their families to trade with Chinese', that 'Chinese and Kanakas could not be compared to Europeans, no matter how low the latter are',[156] and 'that the Chinese quarters of Sydney were hot-beds of opium, debauchery and degradation'.[157] A motion was moved that it should be 'compulsory upon the Chinese to denationalize themselves by cutting off their pigtails and adopting European clothes and customs', but an amendment deleted the 'pigtail clause' because it 'would savour of religious persecution'.

Many Australians thought that the Chinese here lived in squalor and were willing to work for what were in Australian terms very low wages. Few Australians seemed overly concerned whether defects they attributed to the Chinese were inherited or acquired characteristics: 'Nature versus nurture' controversies seem to have been rare.

The NSW Premier, Charles Cooper, sought to protect the Chinese from the violence of the miners at Lambing Flat and at the same time persuade the miners to continue to vote for his Liberal Party (then the main radical force in Australian politics). His task was made harder by the reluctance of the police to intervene to protect the Chinese. And nearly all of the diggers arrested and clearly guilty of assault and battery were acquitted.

What peasants and workers in China thought about state policies did not matter to their rulers, but the arrival of Chinese in large numbers coincided with the grant by Britain of virtual internal self-government to several Australian colonies. Australian politicians had to listen closely to the opinions of the masses after manhood suffrage was introduced in Victoria, South Australia, and New South Wales in 1850s.

Some newspapers contained virulently anti-Chinese material, such as *The Australian Banner:* Chinese faces are 'indexes of minds low, animal-like and licentious', and *The Bathurst Free Press*: 'Their bodies of 'puny stature and fragile build', containing a 'festering mess of animal existence'.[158] Edward John Hawkesley's *Republican People's Advocate and New South Wales Vindicator* attacked the colony's leaders for 'their endeavours to import among us Coolies, Chinamen, and cannibals'. *The Empire,* owned by Henry Parkes, described the Chinese as 'a race known to be given to every abomination and the practice of the most infamous vices', such as infanticide, perjury, and drug addiction.[159] Politicians such as the radical demagogue John Lucas followed as much as led popular opinion, when he denounced the Chinese in the NSW Legislative Assembly as 'immoral, filthy and treacherous'.

Some intellectuals were extremely hostile to Chinese immigration. Daniel Deniehy, Irish-Catholic politician and publicist, described the arrival of Chinese gold miners as 'an overwhelming influx of barbarians, men of low social development, and given to the indulgence of vices unfit to be named by a decent man';[160] Dr Rev. John Lang, Presbyterian cleric and republican, dismissed 'Chinese labourers' in 1852 as 'a miserable looking people, many of them, it is believed, have been convicts in their own country. They are an inferior and abject race'.[161] Henry Lawson thought that 'a time is coming when the Chinaman will have to be either killed or cured – probably the former – I think the European nations should have left the Chinaman alone in the first place'.[162] A.G. Stephens, Literary Editor of *The Bulletin,* held that 'it is certain that the establishment of Asiatic settlements, or of a Eurasian breed, will tend to degrade and destroy the white breed and the white Commonwealth'.[163] Charles Henry Pearson, educationist and politician, wrote, 'Coloured and white labour cannot exist side by side . . . China can swamp us with a year's surplus of population . . . We are guarding the last part of the world, in which the higher races can live and increase freely, for the higher civilization.'[164]

It would have been hard to be more equivocal than Baldwin Spenser, the leading Australian anthropologist of his day:

> I would like to deport the whole lot of them because with their opium and spirits they ruin the blacks and are doing no good to the country. If only the white men here were half as industrious as the Chinese, this would be a great country . . . [165]

There were also defenders of the Chinese. Inspector of Police Charles Nicholson told the 1857 Select Committee of the Victorian Legislative Council on Chinese immigration:

I have seen the Chinese on the goldfields and also in the towns and I have always observed that they are a remarkably quiet people . . . they give less trouble to the police in the colony than any other portion of the population.[166]

The Congregationalist minister the Reverend J. West was perhaps the most active and eloquent defender in the 1860s of the Chinese against racial abuse, as was another of his cloth, James Jefferis in South Australia and Victoria at the end of the century. Jefferis condemned 'absolute exclusion', 'temporary exclusion', and 'exclusion within territorial limits', but approved of 'restriction – rigid if they liked – but restriction fair and honorable'.[167] Jefferis believed Chinese and other Asian people could be assimilated into Anglo-Australia, once its foundations were firmly laid, provided they tried to adopt British ways of life. Jefferis, who attracted large congregations and influenced Protestant opinion throughout south-eastern Australia, was doubtless ethnocentric but clearly non-racist in his thinking.

Australian Historians before the 1970s

Before the 1970s, scholarly opinion was that the white population during the nineteenth century contained a significant but not exceptional amount of racism. Several historians of Australia such as Ray Markey believed that fears of large-scale non-white immigration had been justified and that low wage rates and poor conditions of work acceptable to some Chinese, Indian, and Melanesian immigrant workers would have undermined working-class standards.[168] Vance Palmer believed that the anti-Chinese violence of Spence's shearers and miners arose from 'fear of being forced down to the economic level of the Chinese'.[169] Kylie Tennant acknowledged the 'Chinese virtues of living contentedly in awful conditions and working for a small wage' and praised them for sending their money home 'to redeem their relatives'. Yet she argued that the White Australia Policy was 'not a racial or national discrimination, but an economic necessity', and 'its aim was 'to maintain the standard of living and the degree of civilization existing in Australia'.[170] Russel Ward deplored that 'wholesale assault, robbery and arson were committed on the defenceless Chinamen and on their property' and that several were 'either murdered outright or died as a result of ill-treatment and exposure'. However, Ward considered that 'their completely alien culture aroused distrust . . . in the minds of the white majority', who 'did not fear them, but feared that more and more would come to live in Australia'.[171] Ann Curthoys, later to complete a volte-face, seemed sympathetic to the fear that 'as a large inassimilable non-British group' the Chinese would 'refuse to accept free British institutions, merely using them for their own end to achieve political dominance'.[172]

Manning Clark went further than most historians in defending racist sentiment. William Lane, a founder of the Australian Labour Federation in 1889 and editor of its newspapers, *The Worker,* and later *Boomerang,* held:

'We must be White first, or nothing else can matter', that 'In Australia, Anglo-Saxon, Teuton and Latin are coming together as one homogeneous whole . . . They demand that all undesirable races be immediately and absolutely excluded' and that 'Words cannot express our contempt and hatred for those whites who are fighting against their own kith and kin in this racial struggle. They deserve no consideration. The Chinese must go and their friends, those white traitors had better be flung out with them'.[173]

Manning Clark praised William Lane because he had 'declared boldly that the worker was entitled to the wealth he produced' and 'denounced bourgeois governments and bloody minded capitalists for the harsh, brutal, and cowardly treatment of the embattled bush workers week after week'.

The 'Platform' of *The Bulletin* included 'Australia for the Australians – the cheap Chinaman, the cheap Nigger, and the cheap European pauper to be absolutely excluded'. A typical article ran as follows:

Disease, defilement, depravity, misery, and crime . . . are the indispensable adjuncts which make Chinese camps and quarters loathsome to the senses and faculties of civilized nations. Whatever neighbourhood the Chinese choose for the curse of their presence forthwith begins to reek with the abominations which are ever associated with their vile habitations.

William Guthrie Spence was the most powerful trade unionist of his time: the father of militant unionism, first among miners and then shearers. His Australian Workers' Union barred from membership 'Chinese, Japanese, Kanakas, or Afghans or coloured aliens other than Maoris, American negroes, and children of mixed parentage born in Australia'. Spence described the anti-Chinese race riots at Lambing Flat as 'one of the early developments of democratic feeling in Australia. So strong was it that . . . the diggers . . . drove the Chinese off the field, some of the pig-tailed heathens losing their lives'.

Manning Clark related that, after joining colonist John Rawson in singing a hymn, 'blacks came back to his tent bringing quantities of human flesh and began to eat it with much pleasure, and seemed hurt when Rawson refused to eat it, because they had joined as best they could in the white man's strange corroboree'. Clark's account of Aboriginal cannibalism of Chinese miners will be found in the chapter on cannibalism.

AUSTRALIANS AS GENOCIDAL RACISTS

The balance of opinion changed very quickly. As late as 1988, John Hirst made perhaps the only error in his *The Strange Death of Colonial Democracy* when he optimistically opined that 'no one will quarrel with a people who wish to avoid the

MAKING SENSE OF HISTORY

disruption or total transformation of their society by unrestricted immigration'.[174] By then, people who expressed such sentiments were already being branded as racists or white supremacists. Students were told in schools and universities that the Right is racist and the Left the standard bearer of human rights and equality of peoples; many have never discovered that conservatives were the main defenders of Chinese from slanders about their morality and conduct. Students now rarely know that the police were reluctant to charge the miners and did not act as a reliable and ferocious instrument of the ruling classes.

Condemnation of the White Australia Policy as a national blot only gained force after the policy had been step by step abandoned. Why the major change especially in Left thinking? There was loss of faith in the 'historic role' of the worker class, who were increasingly 'consumerists' and wanted better houses, cars, and television sets rather than major social change, violent or peaceful. Outback workers, once described by Henry Lawson as planters of the 'Green Tree New', were outed as dispossessors of the Aborigines and enemies of international solidarity.

Humphrey McQueen launched 'New Left' history in his 1970 *A New Britannia,* a sustained attack on post-1788 Australia in general. McQueen argued that colonial Australians did not constitute a true working class, because they had petty bourgeois ideas, including racist ones. This was another example of the 'no true Scotsman fallacy'.

Professor Verity Burgmann denounced the 'Anglo-Celtic industrial chauvinism' of the founders of the Australian Labour Party, only slightly extenuated because it was 'encouraged by British imperialist racism' and 'the all-pervasive influence of ruling class ideology'.[175] Professor Raymond Evans compared anti-Chinese rioting in Brisbane in 1888 with the Nazi Kristallnacht of 1938, when ninety-one Jews were murdered, even though no Chinese was killed in Brisbane.[176]

The influence of overseas accusers of genocide, such as South African Pierre Van den Berghe, American George Frederickson, the Polish Jew Raphael Lemkin, and the Palestinian Edward Said, was and remains important in the thinking of several leading Australian historians. For the new anti-racism to have maximum effect, non-White Australians had to be absolved from blame. Professor Henry Reynolds played down racial tension between non-Europeans and held that 'places like Cairns and Broome and Darwin were remarkably peaceful', even though the 1920 race riots in Broome, 'incontestably the worst in Australian history', were fought by Japanese against Timorese and Koepangersr, whilst white Australians tried to restore peace.[177]

129

THE ARGUMENTS OF KEITH WINDSCHUTTLE

In 2004, Keith Windschuttle sought to vindicate the position first stated by Myra Willard, who closely followed the line adopted by Alfred Deakin. Deakin was usually careful to speak in respectful terms about other races and to describe the White Australia Policy as an instrument for unity and progress, not a reflection of racism or assumed superiority. Willard had written:

> In the formation of their policy the leaders of the people were not actuated by any idea of the inferiority of the mentality or physique of the excluded peoples. 'It seemed to them that the dissimilarity of their development, and consequently of their outlook and training, would cause a body of resident Asiatics to be fateful to progress along the lines that seemed best to Australians.'[178]

Windschuttle denied that many, let alone most, Australians had been thoroughly racist. He dismissed writers in *The Bulletin, The Republican*, and *The Boomerang,* relied upon by the Herrenvolk historians as evidence of that racism as unrepresentative: 'a minority group' whose 'socialist, republican and racial theories were publicly rejected by the electorate'.[179] He claimed that William Lane's 'political constituency was confined to a comparatively small group of radicals' and that 'he did not speak for the whole of Australia, let alone for the whole of the labour movement', although nobody had ever thought he had . . .

Windschuttle found that racist novels such as Lane's *White or Yellow?* Kenneth Mackay's *The Yellow Wave,* and C.H. Kirmess's *The Australian Crisis* had few readers, compared with novels by Mary Grant Bruce, Ethel Turner, Mary and Elizabeth Durack, and Mrs Aeneas Gunn. However, some popular authors, such as Rosa Praed, Thomas Roydhouse, John Hay, Erie Cox, Brunton Stephens, Edward Dyson, Campbell McKellar, A.G. Hales, and Francis Adams contained considerable popular prejudice. Dyson wrote gruesome stories about Chinese brothel keepers who recruited white girls and also about violence to Chinese: One such story was chosen among the 'best of the period' by Cecil Hadgraft. According to Richard Nile and David Walker, 'Dyson was perhaps the best-paid free-lance writer in the country'.[180]

Windschuttle denied that Henry Parkes' claims about a people's 'inferior nature and character' indicated 'any support for, or indeed any familiarity with, either Darwinian theory or "eugenics" programs of selective breeding', but such familiarity was not needed to be a racist, then or now.[181] Windschuttle claimed unconvincingly that since Parkes' unsuccessful attempt to restrict immigration during the Afghan crisis was 'confined to Chinese and did not affect other Asians', it 'cannot be plausibly described as racist legislation'.[182]

THE 1901 DEBATES

White Australia Policy was not a principal issue in the debates about the federation in the 1890s, because each major political grouping (protectionist, free trade, and labour) had agreed on it a settled national principle at the 1888 Intercolonial Conference. In a three-party situation that marked the parliamentary politics of the early post-federation period, the Labour Party was the most zealous for a White Australia, with the Protectionist Party and some of the Free Trader Party's leaders, such as George Reid, not far behind. To show Labour he was reliable on White Australia, Reid suggested that there was unanimity that 'the current of Australian blood shall not assume the darker hues'. However, Reid tried to avoid absolute exclusion and opposed the dictation test, which, he claimed, 'will reflect ignominy and discredit upon Australian legislation'.[183]

Professor Neville Meaney claimed that in the 1901 debates 'there was not one voice raised against the principle of racial discrimination',[184] and Professor David Walker said that 'Bruce Smith's was 'the only sustained critique of the White Australia Policy brought before the Australian Parliament'.[185] Professor Henry Reynolds held that the debates were 'pervaded with ideas of race and blood' and Professor Gavin Jones held that 'most speeches demonstrated 'racial pride and arrogance'. Windschuttle counter-claimed that these historians had plucked 'a few lines out of Hansard' to produce 'cavalier generalizations'.[186]

Professor Geoffrey Sherington was right that in the federation 'a "White Australia" was the one policy which almost all Australians accepted',[187] but were most of them motivated by fear of racial pollution, fear that cheap labour would undercut wages and undermine working conditions, fear that a large underclass composed mainly of non-whites would undermine democracy and create a system of block-voting by race, or fear that demagogic white politicians would 'play the race card' for narrow partisan ends? Many Australians, of course, were influenced by more than one of these motives. Windschuttle claimed:

> Rather than being pervaded with ideas of race and blood, the majority of parliamentary opinion wanted to exclude Asian immigrants because they would potentially undermine the standard of living of Australian working people. Of almost equal concern was the politicians' fear that the creation of a racially-based political underclass would inhibit Australia's attempt to create an egalitarian democracy. Far from being fixed on 'racial contamination', most politicians supported the Bill for economic and political reasons.[188]

There was certainly a wide range of opinion. At the extreme racist end were mainly Labour members, such as King O'Malley: 'We have more to fear from the educated coloured people than from the ignorant coloured people, because the latter will not attempt to mingle or associate with the white race.'[189] Labour leader Christian Watson said:

> The objection I have to the mixing of these coloured people with the white people of Australia . . . lies in the main with the possibility and probability of racial contamination . . . The question is whether we would desire that our sisters or our brothers should be married into any of these races to which we object. If these people are not such as we can meet upon an equality, and not such that we can feel that it is no disgrace to intermarry with, and not such as we can expect to give us an infusion of blood that will tend to the raising of our standard of life, and to the improvement of the race, we should be foolish in the extreme if we did not exhaust every means of preventing them from coming to this land, which we have made our own.[190]

Jeremy Sammut has suggested that Watson and some other Labour leaders used pseudo-scientific phrases to add respectability to their basic concern for higher wages and their dislike of Chinese ways of life as they observed them.[191]
Samuel Mauger of the Protectionist Party held:

> We have something like 800,000,000 Chinese and Japanese, within easy distance of Australia, from whom we have to fear contamination . . . If you bring the white man into contact with the black you too often suspend the very process of natural selection on which the evolution of the higher type depends. You get superior and inferior races living on the same soil and that co-existence is demoralizing to both. They naturally sink into the position of master and servant, if not admittedly into that of slave-owner and slave.[192]

Senator Staniforth Smith of the Free Trade Party argued, 'All anthropologists agree that the Caucasian races cannot mingle with the Mongolian, the Hindoo, or the negro.' 'Mulattos are the shortest lived of any of the Branch races, and are very unprolific . . .' 'The half-caste of India comes to a premature end without reproduction, and if there are any offspring they are always wretched and miserable.'[193]

Non-racist arguments were made mainly by members of the Free Trade Party. Donald Cameron said that 'no race on the face of this earth has been treated in a more shameful manner than have the Chinese . . . they were forced at the point of the bayonet to admit Englishmen and other Europeans into China . . . we should, in a spirit of fair play, allow the Chinese to come into Australia in reasonable numbers'. '[194] Cameron surmised that two-thirds of the members 'really object to the Chinese, not so much on the ground of the possible contamination of the white race, as because they fear that if they are allowed to come into Australia the rate of wages will go down'. That accorded with Windschuttle's reckoning and negated the claims made by Meaney, Reynolds, Walker, and G. Jones.

Bruce Smith declared, 'The foundation of the bill is racial . . . the whole thing is a bogy, a scarecrow. I venture to say that a large part of the scare is founded upon a desire to make political capital by appealing to some of the worst instincts of the more credulous of the people . . . The public have been told over and over again that the purity and whiteness of the Australian Commonwealth is being endangered by the incursion of these hordes of Asiatics. I say that it is a fable; that it is altogether a fairy story.'[195] Sir John Downer of the Protectionist Party did not 'anticipate or fear any intermixture of races from any Asiatics who may come here'.[196]

There were non-racist Labour voices. James Fowler said of Indians, 'Many of these peoples are at least our equal in all that goes to make up morality, or even intellectual or physical qualities. We should not, therefore, argue this question upon such grounds.'[197] William Higgs declared, 'No one who has paid any attention to the question of the coloured races will attempt for one moment to despise either the Japanese or the Chinese.'[198]

Two politicians of particular relevance are Alfred Deakin and William Hughes. Deakin claimed that he respected 'the general conceptions of equality that have been the guiding principle of British rule throughout the Empire'.[199] However, he also spoke of the threat to the 'national manhood': 'We here find ourselves touching the profoundest instinct of individual or nation – the instinct of self-preservation – for it is nothing less than the national manhood, the national character and the national future that are at stake'. 'That end, put in plain and unequivocal terms, as the House and the country are entitled to have it put, means the prohibition of all alien coloured immigration, and more, it means at the earliest time, by reasonable and just means, the deportation or reduction of the number of aliens now in our midst.' The two things go hand in hand, and are the necessary complement of a single policy – the policy of securing a 'White Australia'. In his secret role of 'Australian Correspondent' for London's *The Morning Post* Deakin condemned 'unreasoning hostility to strangers and foreigners for which no justification can be offered' among his countrymen, but also stated that 'Australia and New Zealand are determined to keep their place in the first class and in order to secure that pride of place agree to putting racial pride before economic gain'. Deakin wrote as if to confound Windschuttle:

> Mr Chamberlain long ago laid down the principle that no discriminations could be authorized if they applied by name to particular peoples or complexions. It is for this reason that our Immigration Act sanctions in

133

unlimited phrases the exclusion of all comers, although designed and only
used to exclude the coloured races . . . In fact and in effect our colourless
laws are administered so as to draw a deep colour line of demarcation
between Caucasians and all other races. [200]

In 1854, well before Chamberlain's time, the Colonial Office discussed 'whether
the Imperial Government should retain the power of disallowing any Act which
is palpably immoral, especially in relation to the unrepresented Aborigines or
immigrants of colour'.[201] Sammut suggests that Deakin built on popular prejudice
that considered non-whites as incapable of exercising the political rights and duties of
Australians. Sammut regards this as 'racial prejudice', but not 'biological racism'.[202]
Deakin never suggested that this incapacity was an innate flaw, but the practical
implication was that here and now those peoples could not fit in.

Hughes, another future Prime Minister, stated before 1901 that the Chinese in
Queensland were a 'leprous curse' and that the United States presented a warning to
Australia with its 'terrible blot'. Hughes feared that Asians 'will multiply and pass
over the border in a mighty Niagara, sowing seeds of diseases which will never be
eradicated, and which will permanently undermine the constitutional vigor of which
the Anglo-Saxon race is so proud'.[203]

Hughes knew that the White Australia Policy might stimulate hatred of Australians
among excluded nations. He did not conceal this belief from the Australian people
but used it later as a major argument for military training, an independent navy, and
conscription. He argued that a White Australia was worth fighting for if it was worth
living in. Hughes supported an expansion of Commonwealth power on the same
argument. He asked, 'Is the establishment of a White Australia a small matter? Is it
nothing that we are keeping the fountain of our race pure?'[204] He conceded in the
Imperial War Cabinet in 1918: 'We were going to say to thousands of millions of
people that no one else should come to Australia which we had no moral right to
do.'[205] The White Australia Policy meant a lot more to Hughes than protection of
wages and working conditions, as it did to most Australians of his time.

RESPONSES TO WINDSCHUTTLE

A counter-attack was launched by Dirk Moses, then Associate Professor of History
in the University of Sydney: 'Like other history warriors – think of columnists
such as Christopher Pearson, Andrew Bolt, Paul Sheehan, and Miranda Devine –
he [Windschuttle] does not engage in serious research or reading. Given the tight
deadlines, their practice is to trawl the web in search of hot topics for hastily-written
opinion pieces.' Moses added:

Windschuttle ferreted around a few libraries . . . but it should not be passed off as serious history; in Windschuttle s hands, it is a debased version of investigative journalism.

The history wars in Australia are characterized by a striking division: ill-informed journalists and creatures of the media (like Windschuttle) versus historians.[206]

Professor Tony Taylor dismissed all with anything to say in favour of Windschuttle as 'anti-Indigenous Australian bigots and racists', who embody 'diehard right-wing opinion' and 'scarcely concealed ultra-conservative, bourgeois bigotry'. He depicted 'Windschuttle's friends' as 'mainly Sydney-based conservative commentators, some with their vanity websites, their newspaper columns, their litigious and their humourless denunciations of any insult, imagined or otherwise'. Windschuttle had alleged that 'no graduate student seeking to write a dissenting thesis should waste his time applying to any of our academic schools of history'. Taylor made it very clear that he would not even admit Windschuttle as a doctoral candidate. Taylor had been chosen by the Howard Government to head a national survey of history teaching in schools.

Timothy Kendall argued that the policy was 'mediated by a pervasive and incontrovertible racism which had at its heart the assertion of white biological and cultural superiority' and that 'whiteness operated as a cultural ideal which was critical to the formation and establishment of an Australian national identity'.[207] Gwenda Tavan's *Long, Slow Death of White Australia* held that racism remains in the 'hearts and minds of everyday people' to this day.

Jeremy Sammut contested Windschuttle's claims that the White Australia Policy was 'largely economic, political and cultural in origin rather than racist' and that 'despite the ethos that emerged within sections of the labour movement and among nineteenth century radical intellectuals, Australia has never had a mainstream culture that can properly be described as racist'. Windschuttle responded that 'Sammut fails to provide any good evidence for the psychological assumptions of visceral and latent racism on which his account depends'. Windschuttle must set a high standard for 'good' evidence.

Sammut and Windschuttle drew very different conclusions from the slowness of, and lack of major public controversy about, the dismantling of the White Australia Policy. Sammut argued that it was 'proof of the racial prejudice this policy entailed' and that between 1939 and 1972 the Liberal government relaxed the immigration regulations step by step 'while not appearing to be changing the White Australia Policy at all'.[208] Windschuttle agreed that the ending of the policy 'was accomplished with a minimum of fuss', but concluded that this was because White Australia sentiments were weak. He claimed, 'Had the policy been based on the racist version of nationalism claimed by most academic historians, this could never have happened.'[209]

Professor Marilyn Lake claimed, 'Windschuttle's argument, that Australian nationalism was not race-based, is not just perverse; it sets up false dichotomies.' However, in an attempt to resolve the 'apparent contradiction between John Curtin's international socialism and his commitment to White Australia', Lake scored an own goal. She accepted that being a 'white man' was central to Curtin's identity' and that he 'saw the White Australia Policy as necessary to uphold the white worker's standard of living' on which his status as a man depended.[210] She agreed that the ALP 'had written the preservation of racial purity into its platform'. She acknowledged that Curtin opposed the entry of Italian migrants in the 1920s and that he condemned the Bruce government for allowing migrants from southern Europe 'to dilute our racial homogeneity'.

Yet Lake insisted that 'these facts' about Curtin did not make him 'a racist', because he 'was an advocate of self-determination for colonized peoples and he was at pains to condemn racial prejudice'. He thought the Chinese and Japanese were 'different', but wanted them treated with respect.[211] Lake succeeded in showing that an 'international socialist' could support the White Australia Policy, but also demonstrated that thousands of other people who supported the policy were not partisans of a Herrenvolk regime.

CONCLUSIONS

As Professor Russell McGregor noted, a racial hierarchy existed in north Queensland, with whites at the apex, 'certain Asians (often Japanese, sometimes Chinese) on the next rung down; other Asian such as Malays and Javanese below them; Pacific Islanders next, the Torres Strait Islanders, followed by Aborigines at the bottom of the scale'.[212] If all white Australians had emigrated or been slaughtered in 1880, a new racial hierarchy with comparable inequalities would soon have emerged.

Throughout the nineteenth century, successive British governments were much more racially tolerant than the Australian colonial governments that already enjoyed considerable self-determination in internal affairs. An unforeseen result of non-white immigration was to strengthen feelings of Britishness among Australians and to weaken independence and republican movements. Had it not been for the fear of antagonising the British government, the 1901 legislators could well have imposed an explicit colour bar on immigrants, but instead they resorted to the ludicrous dictation test.

James Jefferis suggested in 1888 that 'if the Chinese came in great numbers while Australian society was still in its "formative stage" the results would be most unhappy for our future' so that it was necessary 'to limit and regulate their coming, in the interests of humanity, in the interests of Englishmen, and the Chinese themselves who are to be hereafter incorporated with us'.[213] After that 'formative stage' had been completed, he thought controlled immigration from China and the rest of the world was feasible for Australia.

Jefferis' view has been confirmed by forty years of peaceful non-discriminatory immigration, of which large numbers of Chinese have taken advantage. Australian governments ought not to apologise to Chinese-Australians or to the government of China for restrictive immigration policies. Although the language tests were profoundly misconceived, restriction then helped to consolidate the new unified Australian Commonwealth and later enabled many Chinese and many other peoples to integrate successfully in an Australia which millions of them wished to make their new homeland, even without gold to be found.

Close inspection of past evils committed by Chinese people, without taking due note of historical contexts, would rightly be condemned for stirring up racial hatred and reinforcing negative stereotype. Yet vicious attacks on Herrenvolk Australia are very acceptable in our universities.

Australians as a whole and the 1901 Parliament in particular were less racist/ xenophobic than our 'Herrenvolk' historians alleged, but more prejudiced than Windschuttle allowed. Windschuttle deserves praise for rebutting calumnies against Australian parliamentarians and people, but he attributed to them greater virtue than they, or most peoples at most times, including the Chinese and Japanese, possessed.

There seems little doubt that several leading combatants in our 'history wars' had firm and impenetrable conclusions before they undertook their research. An apparent determination to play down or even ignore evidence embarrassing because of one perspective or the other, combined with frequent personal abuse of their academic opponents, can hardly have strengthened public confidence in the integrity and intrinsic value of historical study. One might have hoped that tenured academics would show some courtesy to other contestants in essentially contestable issues, but instead, as the examples of the language of Dr Taylor and Professor Moses illustrate, a concerted effort seems to have been made to apply *ad terrorem* tactics against the outsiders. They were unfortunate in choosing to revile Keith Windschuttle, one of the most meticulous researchers among Australian historians.

The generally positive progress of Australia as a country under the rule of law, wide freedoms, and representative government would have been unlikely to have been sustained, or the Chinese and other Asian and Islander immigrants would have been absorbed had there been no White Australia Policy. By the time, during the 1960s, that the policy was discontinued, Australia's civil order was strong enough to accommodate a large, although not an infinite, flow of immigration, and by then most of the Chinese seeking to migrate to Australia were largely experienced in Western ways, via Hong Kong, Singapore, and the coastal ports of China. It would be hard to find other Australians who contribute more to the prosperity of this country than they do.

Chapter 7

CANNIBALISM IN AUSTRALIA?

For many centuries it was generally accepted in many parts of the world that many peoples had once practiced cannibalism and that several still did so. Most Australian colonists believed that some Australian Aboriginal peoples were among that number, although Watkin Tench of the First Fleet dissented and wrote that, 'From their manner of disposing of those who die [as well as from other observations,] there seems no reason to suppose these people cannibals'. However, despite Tench's doubts, no Australian scholars seem to have denied that some Aborigines had practiced cannibalism before 1979, but many began to do so in the wake of American William Arens's 1979 *The Man-eating Myth: Anthropology & Anthropophagy*. Arens claimed that allegations of cannibalism among indigenous peoples had been concocted by colonizers to justify their aggressions. In Australia progressive academics began to express fears that claims of Aboriginal cannibalism, true or false, caused distress to the Indigenous and strengthened white racism.

Richard Buchhorn, a former priest and then Assistant Secretary to the Catholic Commission for Justice and Peace, and interviewed in such ABC programs as Ockham's Razor, alleged that the evidence provided for cannibalism among Aborigines was 'on a par with that for alien abductions' and that claims that 'these people are cannibals' could 'usually be translated' as 'we want their land'. In 1998 Richard Hall's *Black Armband Days* stated that Aboriginal cannibalism was largely a product of the fevered imagination of Daisy Bates.

Law lecturer Katherine Biber, claimed that 'cannibal discourse is the product of colonial anxiety, what Obeyesesake terms a "dark fantasy" and a "paranoid ethos"'[214]. Obeyesesake, a Sri Lankan anthropologist, believed that '"cannibalism" was a British discourse and its practice was introduced to the natives [Polynesians] by the British'.

Biber wrote that 'historians and anthropologists rejected allegations of Aboriginal cannibalism when they were re-articulated in 1997, when *The Truth*, a book attributed to (although not written by Pauline Hanson) alleged that Aborigines practiced cannibalism and, especially, baby-eating'. Biber claimed that 'these cannibal claims were derived from works by Hector Holthouse, Henry Mayhew, various travellers and explorers and, especially, Daisy Bates.'

Biber evidently knew 'from the outset of her research that there is no credible historical evidence to support allegations that indigenous Australians practiced the forms of cannibalism sought by the colonists.' One wonders why in that case she felt it necessary to conduct research into the question. According to Biber, literary scholars such as Peter Hulme and Frank Lestringant had 'located cannibal discourse within a particular genre of colonial fantasy.' Biber conceded that 'Aborigines and Torres Strait Islanders—in some areas, in rare circumstances, and in the conduct of rituals—practiced some forms of anthropophagy, notably mortuary cannibalism', but that 'From an anthropological perspective, these practices had meanings to their practitioners that are not easily translated in colonial categories'. Anthropologists such as Biber apparently 'resist reading anthropophagous practices through the squeamish lens of Western cannibal myths . . .' Lestringant argued in 1997 that 'anthropophagy (the practice of eating human flesh) does not equal cannibalism', but he failed to explain what the distinction might be.[215]

Jan Wegner of James Cook University, who taught 'Aborigines and cannibalism' as 'a topic for a third-year course', described Hector Holthouse's River of Gold, first published in 1967, as a 'turgid potboiler' which, however, 'still seems to be first port of call for accounts of Aborigines and cannibalism.' Wegner believed that Arens had shown that 'there is no solid evidence for the type of cannibalistic practice as proposed by Pauline Hanson'. Paul Turnbull, also of James Cook University, agreed that 'Hansonesque history is largely confined to Holthouse'. Turnbull claimed that miners and police in North Queensland mutilated corpses and then tried to 'blame it on the Aboriginal people trying to defend their country'.

Bryce Moore of Fremantle Arts Centre Press found 'any discussion of cannibalism among Aborigines obnoxious, simply because those who seek to draw attention to it implicitly tender cannibalism and other perceived forms of "savagery" as a justification for the dispossession and genocide practiced against Aborigines during the course of the white invasion'. Moore added that he did not 'think that there is any solid evidence that Aboriginal people were "cannibals" and that 'on balance the charge is more appropriately leveled against Britons.' Professor Laura Behrendt claimed that 'narratives of native savagery became particularly important at moments on the frontier when tensions arose between colonisers and colonized. At these points, the narratives supplied the justification for force, violence,'

In *The Encyclopaedia of Aboriginal Australia*, 'generously sponsored' by the Department of School Education, the Disadvantaged Schools Program, The Aboriginal Education Unit and the Council for Aboriginal Reconciliation', Dr Ian Howie-Willis claimed of cannibalism among Aborigines that 'evidence of its actual practice is fragmentary, inconsistent and inconclusive' and that the allegation was used as a 'rationalization for denying indigenous Australians their rights, occupying their land and destroying their culture', and 'so-called witnesses of cannibalism often put forward as their personal experience the unverified experience of someone else'.[216]

The success of the opposition to include some nasty activities of some of our species has encouraged obscurantism of that which readily expands further beyond the original denial to support censorship of almost any knowledge that some people will find disturbing. At the same time, frustration at the suppression of truth may lead to recklessness in argument and acceptance of conspiracy theories on a grandiose scale. This may have been the case with Mr James Cooke, RN, whose self-published *Anthropophagitism in the Antipodes or Cannibalism in Australia* is a mixture of information difficult to find elsewhere and reckless abuse of opponents who fail to accept his claims as valid evidence, although many of them are also far from polite in controversy.

G. Horne and G. Aiston, members of the Australian Mounted Police, recounted the following in 1924 in *Savage Life in Central Australia*:

The first case was at Apawandinna, halfway from Cowarie. A very fat Blackfellow chased an emu and became overheated in the chase, and died. The other Blackfellows were very worried over the death. They examined the man, but could not find anything to show as a cause of his death. He was a good-natured man, very popular with the tribe, so that it was unlikely that he had been 'boned'—a form of magic widely practiced among the Wonkonguru tribe.

Finally, the old men of the tribe decided to cook the body. They cut it up and distributed it right round the camps of the tribe, which at that time extended from Killalpaninna to Birdsville in Queensland. The idea of the old men was that if the dead man had been 'boned,' his flesh would poison the man who had 'boned' him, and anyone who was innocent would be protected from such a death by eating a piece of him. I talked it over with one old man who had eaten it in order that the rest would not think him guilty of 'boning' the dead man. He put it to me this way: 'Spose 'em me no eat 'em. 'Nother fella say, Him kill 'em. Me eat 'em, then all right.'

E. O James wrote in *Origins of Sacrifice:*

> Among the native tribes of Australia, the bodies of those who fall in battle, honoured chiefs, and new-born infants, are frequently consumed to obtain their qualities, just as in the Torres Straits (which separate the northernmost territory of Australia from the southernmost part of New Guinea) the tongue and sweat of a slain enemy are imbibed to get his bravery.

S. Kyle-Little, a Patrol Officer in the Native Affairs Branch, wrote in *Whispering Wind*: *Adventures in Arnhem Land* in 1937 that'

> It appeared that a white man by himself on such a mission as mine might easily find himself wrapped in pandanum-leaves and roasting quietly on the ashes of an Arnhem-Land fire. 'From well corroborated evidence, a form of cannibalism is still practiced by three groups between the Blyth and Liverpool Rivers,' Gordon Sweeney, a Patrol Officer in the Native Affairs Branch, one of my predecessors, wrote. 'The bodies of all except the children, old people, and the diseased are cut up after death, the bones taken out and the flesh cooked and eaten. There appears to be no special ceremony at the time, or ceremonial significance attached to this practice, at least among two groups, the Manbuloi and the Gumauwurrk. A third group, the Rauwarang, do not allow the children to eat. The bones are shortly afterwards handed to the relative who is to carry them at the usual Buguburrt corroboree, which under this name is practiced throughout the social area. The reason given for the cannibal practice in all three groups is that the people think that eating human flesh will make them clever at hunting, at spearing kangaroos, finding wild honey, getting yams, etc.'

> I wondered about Sweeney's warnings of Cannibalism. I had known the Australian aborigine for too long to believe that he was a blood-thirsty, man-eating savage. Provoked, he was savage. But I did not mean to be provocative. As for man-eating, I discovered later that this was only partly true. The Liverpool River natives did not kill men for food. The ate human flesh largely from superstitious beliefs. If they killed a worthy man in battle, they ate his heart, believing that they would inherit his valour and power. They ate his brain because they knew it represented the seat of his knowledge. If they killed a fast runner, they ate part of his legs, hoping thereby to acquire his speed.

Colin Simpson wrote in 1938 in his *Adam in Ochre:*

'In 1933 I was able to talk to old men who had eaten human flesh. The chief of Yam Island described to me how he had eaten finely-chopped man-meat mixed with crocodile-meat, at his initiation. He added that it had made him sick. The purpose, as he put it, was 'to make heart come strong inside. 'In the Wotjobaluk tribe, a couple who already had a child might kill their new-born and feed its muscle-flesh to the other one to make it strong. The baby was killed ritually, by striking its head against the shoulder of its elder brother or sister . . . Human flesh-eating among many tribes was a sign of respect for the dead. At a Dieri burial, relatives received, in strict order of precedence, small portions of the body-fat to eat. 'We eat him,' a tribesman said, 'because we knew him and were fond of him.' But revenge cannibalism is typified in the custom of the Ngarigo tribe, who ate the flesh of the hands and feet of slain enemies, and accompanied the eating with loud expressions of contempt for the people killed.

Those people were not university lecturers and possessed no degrees in anthropology, but the opinions of other non-experts are regularly accepted as authentic oral history, provided, that is, that the stories they tell suit the intentions of the interviewers. However, many scholars have testified to cannibalism among Aborigines.

Walter Edmund Roth gave in 1897 detailed accounts of a custom among the Pennefather River Aborigines, of cutting off, baking and then eating the soles of the feet and fleshy front part of the thighs of dead young men.[217] Roth held that those Aborigines believed the ritual would reveal the identity of the sorcerer responsible for the men's deaths. Roth also described dismemberment, cooking and eating of the dead among the Brisbane people[218]. Alfred Howitt described in 1904 some of their rituals for eating enemies killed in battle. Some Aboriginal groups ate their enemies but not their own kin, whereas other groups ate their own kin but not their enemies.[219] Ripping out the kidneys of a defeated enemy and eating them before his eyes as he died was a custom among some Aborigines that fascinated or terrified some colonists. Joseph Furphy ('Tom Collins') wrote in 'A Vignette of Port Phillip', based on the death of an Aboriginal friend of his boyhood, that 'it was deemed the prerogative of any victor in mortal combat to take as a trophy the kidneys of the vanquished'.

Baldwin Spencer held in 1928 that among the Aranda cannibalism had been confined to weakly elder siblings, who would gain thereby strength to survive by eating children who died young.[220] Ursula McConnel provided information in 1937 on burial cannibalism among peoples on the Daintree and Mossman Rivers on the eastern coast of Cape Yorke Peninsula.[221] Professor A.P. Elkin claimed in 1937 that burial cannibalism, practiced across parts of Queensland, the Gulf of Carpentaria, the northern Kimberley and north-eastern South Australia, had a sacred function: parts of the corpse were often available only for specific kindred. Elkin held that in parts of Central Australia and East Kimberley a mother would sometimes consume the flesh of a child stillborn or dead very soon after birth, so that its spirit might soon be born again within her. Elkin added in 1938 in *The Australian Aborigines* that cannibalism 'was, incidentally, a quick method of preparing the 'mummy,' the flesh being eaten instead of merely being dried in the sun or over a fire.[222]

Several examples of Aboriginal cannibalism were cited by Ronald and Catherine Berndt in 1999. The Berndts suggested that colonists may have formed an exaggerated idea of the extent of Aboriginal cannibalism, because groups frequently falsely accused their neighbors of it, but they had no doubt that 'burial cannibalism was fairly widespread'.[223]

Manning Clark began his *History of Australia* before denial of Aboriginal cannibalism became politically correct on the Australian Left. Even his third volume, covering 1824-1851 was subtitled 'The Beginning of an Australian Civilization.' In it he described how 'on the Monoro some white men watched with horror the massacre of some Mega blacks by a party of Monoro blacks, who then skinned and ate them'.[224]

Clark frequently referred to cannibalism, sometimes with that mixture of the facetious and the oracular which irritated some readers so much, but which evidently captivated many others. He related that a week after joining colonist John Rawson in singing a hymn, 'blacks came back to his tent bringing quantities of human flesh and began to eat it with much pleasure, and seemed hurt when Rawson refused to eat it, because they had joined as best they could in the white man's strange corroboree'.[225] In his volume four Clark wrote that in 1875 'Black men lay in ambush' for Chinese who 'thronged the roads from Cooktown to the gold-fields on the Palmer River'. The Aborigines 'surrounded them, and massacred those who did not run quickly enough to escape, and threw their bodies onto the coals and ate them'. He noted, too, how 'Rumours flew around Cooktown and on the fields that the aborigines had converted a cave just off the track to the Palmer into a Devil's Kitchen where they hung the bodies of Chinese by the pigtails until they were ripe for roasting on the coals'. Clark claimed that some Aborigines boasted that '"roasted Chinkie" had been added to their menu'.

What should be done about academics who deny obvious incontrovertible truths within the areas of their teaching? Should we pardon them if they plead that they genuinely wished to spare Aborigines pain and embarrassment? If so, why should they be so selective in their compassion? Confrontation with modernity has often been painful, even when it penetrated gradually, but greater suffering is inflicted when it is experienced suddenly and without preparation. Yet it is only by 'crossing the ditch' that full human potentialities can be realized. Australia's Aboriginal hunter-gatherers failed to cross the ditch in their own time and so were pitched across it with many bruises, but how many want to return to the old life?

Chapter 8

SOME PERSPECTIVES ON HISTORY

The academics considered here do not all have History as their main discipline, but each has strong historical interests.

- Inga Clendinnen
- Clive Hamilton
- Robert Hughes
- Marilyn Lake
- Stuart Macintyre
- Robert Manne
- Noel Pearson
- Henry Reynolds
- Margaret Simons
- A. J. P. Taylor

INGA CLENDINNEN

Professor Clendinnen was born in Geelong to parents she found extremely dull and unexciting. Perhaps that is why she chose very exciting topics as a teacher, lecturer, and author. She graduated from Melbourne University in 1955 and remained there as Senior Tutor in History when she was not raising a family. In her forties, she contracted hepatitis and was close to death. During her illness, she tried hard to remember events in her own life and after recovery devoted herself to authorship. She might, of course, have changed the balance of her life even without her near-death experience, but illness triggered a reappraisal of her life.

Her first book was the biographical *Tiger's* Eye, but then she concentrated in turn on the Aztecs, the Holocaust, and early contacts between Australian Aborigines and colonists. In 1999, she presented the fortieth annual Boyer Lectures. Awards she has received include Officer of the Order of Australia. She has won prizes for several of her books.

Clendinnen chose first to specialize in a field rarely entered by Australian historians: the Aztecs and related peoples of Central America. Clendinnen visited Mexico on several occasions and was delighted that 'people love children in Mexico. They're very indulgent to children, they like them and like the people who've got children and who are treating them right, you know'. Yet this feeling was often combined with an admiration for the ferocious Aztec, Maya, or Inca past with its forbidding record of infant sacrifice, among other aspects of life and death . . .

Inga Clendinnen was 'happy to say, of Aztec society. The rules of social organizations are different. It's very difficult to apply any ready-made theory to them. They can't be easily dealt with in conventional political terms, and I think that eased relationships within the class [the students she was teaching] vastly'.

Her special interest was in ritual actions which she considered possessed 'revelatory potential'. Her admiration for the grace of the mature warrior and the exuberance of the novices seems strangely detached from the torments and killings so artistically represented. She may have stretched empathy beyond its proper limits in her efforts to understand the mind-set of young Aztec warriors. Their virtues of courage and loyalty seemed to win her forgiveness for their cruelty and blood thirstiness. She described very vividly the tortures that befell the defeated in ritual conflict or, for that matter, were endured by the large number of other people needed to propitiate the Gods by the sacrifice of their lives and of their hearts and other organs. She admitted to having been attracted by the Aztecs through their taste for one-to-one combat with sacrificial death as the penalty for the loser. She explained:

> It's a very slow motion form of combat and the identification between the two warriors is intense and dramatized ritually at every point . . . . They fight obviously according to protocols . . . . One of them is finally brought down. He is then kept like a fighting cock, displayed, celebrated, jeered at, and then on the appointed day, he's stripped of his warrior's regalia, daubed with the white of the sacrificial victim and white feathers, and is taken to the gladiatorial stone, as we've dubbed it, which is an elevated stone about a metre high and about so wide, rather less than two metres wide, and he's tethered to that by one ankle to a ring in the centre. And he is given a club, which is a standard combat weapon, but this club instead of being studded with obsidian blades, is covered in white feather down, so it doesn't have the sharpness of the razor sharp blades . . . And then against him come in sequence four Aztec warriors, not the one who beat

him, four others, leading warriors from either one of the two great warrior orders, the eagles and the jaguars. And they strike at him and their aim is to cut him delicately, clearly around the legs, because that's the only bit they could get to, so that he will slowly lose blood, bleed a lot, until he collapses on the stone, and then he has his heart excised and offered to the sun god . . . There are people crowded and screaming and, you know, elevated by this . . . his skin is then taken off, and I can give you details of how that's done if you want i.'

After human sacrifices and blood-letting, Professor Clendinnen taught about the Salem witch trials. She confessed, 'I taught Salem witchcraft—I do go to extremes.' Then on to the Holocaust, Clendinnen admitted that initially she found it difficult to comprehend the scale of evil perpetrated, but she was determined to penetrate into the minds of victims and torturers, including Jews who served German designs in the camps and usually survived.

She followed Primo Levi in insistence on the banality of evil, but was prepared to probe more deeply into Nazi motives and concepts of society than Levi whose revulsion from the Holocaust made the idea of justification of Hitler's policies impossible to contemplate.

Clendinnen admitted:

One of my early difficulties in grasping what the Nazis thought they were up to was that I could not take their professed racist ideology seriously. Instead of listening hard to what they were saying, I assumed the violence of the language to be largely rhetorical. In western democracies politicians frequently do not mean what they say, so that any threats they make may be discounted, but most of the leading Nazis did not conceal their intentions and were zealous in implementing them.

When Professor Clendinnen came to study Australian contact history, she had thus already delved deeply into sympathetic interpretation of behaviour that her own dull relatives in Geelong would have found appalling, but she found it hard to extend her sympathy to the British colonists. Clendinnen criticized her younger self for being 'like most ignorant liberals' vaguely aware' of 'violence and expropriation', but that was about the end of her knowledge. That sounds confessional, but in effect she placed herself above those ignorant liberals who had not been liberated like her from unreasonable prejudices. In her Boyle lectures, she alleged that different attempts by indigenous peoples to come to terms with the intruding dominant white culture came to nothing because their 'gallant, creative attempts had been obliterated by ignorance or malice'. That is very different from the picture drawn by Cook and Banks among others: They were astonished at the lack of interest in their devices and customs shown by Australian Aborigines, whereas other peoples throughout the Pacific had shown great curiosity in them.

Professor Clendinnen has been an innovative teacher. Perhaps the violence of Aztec life and the ever-moving colonial frontiers of nineteenth century Australia need to be studied in with some mobility? Clendinnen told interviewer Robin Hughes in 2000, 'I mean you couldn't possibly do Mexican history without seeing Marlon Brando in *Viva Zapata'*. One wonders how Prescott and the historians of old functioned at all.

Clendinnen's initiatives were apparently a great success. The La Trobe University students, less academically credentialed than those at Melbourne University, were paired randomly and played the Name Game, in which each participant interviewed the other about childhood memories She thought the Aztecs a highly suitable subject, since virtually none of the students had studied them before and so all were on equal ground. The migrant, the mainstream, and the indigenous, if any, started the course with an equal lack of information. She thought it an advantage that there were no 'entrenched positions' and that it was 'very hard to do a class analysis,' although Marx and Engels might have disagreed.

Clendinnen shares many core beliefs of her contemporaries. She is an extreme relativist who wrote that where we 'draw the line about conduct' is a 'matter of personal decision'. That in itself was defensible, but Clendinnen seemed also to believe that it was only a matter of personal decision: not merely that individuals ought to work out their values free from coercion.

Inga Clendinnen has been widely praised as an author, but has attracted some severe criticism as well. Unexpected was the harsh treatment given by Julie Myerson of *The Guardian*, whose sympathies might reasonably have been anticipated to be very much with her. However, Myerson wrote of Tiger's Eye that 'this disjointed and unsnagging volume' could not be justified by its author's 'ordeal and brave recovery . . . This ragbag of incidents and observations never amounts to a well-crafted whole' and was to be judged as an 'emotional scrapbook' that failed to come off. Myerson asserted that 'the book hopscotches from illness memoir to childhood reminiscence to short fiction and research notes. Then there are the pages of Clendinnen's post-operative hallucinations; dreams are dull to all but the dreamer'. You just cannot please them all.

Professor Clendinnen is no admirer of mass culture 'and made the familiar claim that contemporary society (of the Western type)' brought about the 'commodification' of the individual. She believes it is a 'sorry state we seem to be heading towards'. However, among her peers, Clendinnen is moderate ideologically. Her refusal to go all the way with genocide-obsessed colleagues had been complemented by her public criticism of systematic attacks on the ANZAC tradition made from within many university history departments. She was stirred into action by assertions that the tradition and the annual ceremonies were divisive and backward-looking and should be curtailed if not abolished.

Clendinnen was especially dismayed by *What's Wrong With Anzac? The Militarization of Australian History*, co-authored by Mark McKenna, in which she perceived an insulting scarcity of reference to the scholarly work of Ken Inglis on Gallipoli and other military campaigns of the Australian armed forces. Inglis had been her tutor at Melbourne University, and he has made notable contributions to military history. She was reported as protesting:

> I was shocked actually. I shot down to the bookshop to pick up a copy when I heard about it. Historians have standards and I couldn't believe it. Ken is the major scholar in this area but he hasn't been properly referenced.

Prominent 'history warriors' Marilyn Lake and Henry Reynolds were also rebuked by Clendinnen for their dismissal of Australian participation in war as a continuation of colonial obsequiousness to imperial rule. Clendinnen was fully prepared to criticize her country, both past and present, but not to accept every charge made against it.

ROGER SANDALL

Here are some passages from the late anthropologist, the New Zealand-born Roger Sandall. The contrast between his view with that of Inga Clendinnen is remarkable.

COLLAPSING THE MAYA

But I don't care if the Maya civilization did collapse. I don't think we should shed a single retrospective tear. It might be interesting to know how or why it fell—whether from war or drought or disease or soil exhaustion—but I don't much care about that either. Because quite frankly, as civilizations go, the Mayan civilization in Mexico didn't amount to much.

Now I know this is a shocking thing to say. Gallery owners in New York and elsewhere will cry out indignantly about the glories of Maya art. They will show you terra cotta figurines and fine reliefs and paintings and tell splendid tales of 'kings' and 'nobles' and such. In deference to this view, we shall gladly concede that Maya art is not uninteresting. But it is sheer romantic fantasy to mourn the passing, around AD 900, of an aristocracy of hypersensitive native aesthetes—though anthropologists and art critics have written reams of such stuff.

Glamorous talk of 'kings' and 'lords' and 'nobles' always sounds better than a realistic description of murderous and predatory chieftains with little but power, conquest, self-glorification, enslavement, and killing and torture on their minds. Yes, they wore spectacular feather head-dresses. Yes, they built sky-high piles of masonry. But their hands dripped blood—incessantly.

They were doing what bellicose tribal populations have always done—straining the carrying capacity of the land, warring with neighbors, and trying in grisly ways to appease their gods. Who has not felt the pathos of ruins? Is it surprising that when the American John Stephens stumbled upon the ruins of Maya temples in Yucatan he got carried away?

> Here were the remains of a cultivated, polished, and peculiar people, who had passed through all the stages incident to the rise and fall of nations; reached their golden age, and perished . . . We went up to their desolate temples and fallen altars; and wherever we moved we saw the evidence of their taste, their skill in arts . . . We called back into life the strange people who gazed in sadness from the wall; pictured them, in fanciful costumes and adorned with plumes of feather.

> Captives were tortured in unpleasant ways depicted clearly on the monuments and murals (such as yanking fingers out of sockets, pulling out teeth, cutting off the lower jaw, trimming of the lips and fingertips, pulling out the fingernails, and driving a pin through the lips), culminating, sometimes years later, in the sacrifice of the captive in other equally unpleasant ways such as tying the captive up into a ball by binding the arms and legs together, then rolling the balled-up captive down the steep stone staircase of a temple.

I suppose it all depends on what you expect a civilization to offer. The Mayans, and the Aztecs too, offered barbarism plus pyramids. Personally I don't think that's enough. What we expect of any civilization worth the name is something that lifts us up, something elevating if not ennobling—something that looks beyond the endless cyclical violence of the barbaric past, however interesting its art may be . . .

What I look for in a civilization is mind at work. That's what we find in ancient Greece when Heraclitus maintained that everything changes and Parmenides retorted that nothing changes. A serious religion with a seriously uplifting ethic is also welcome: Failing that, as among the Greeks, let's have a serious freethinker like Xenophanes, who wondered why the faithful always imagined that their gods looked like themselves. As for maths, one Pythagoras is worth a million Mayan astrologers, while a single calculation by Eratosthenes is worth a wilderness of numerologists.

Then there's drama. A serious civilization has to get beyond ritual, beyond charades and dressing up and sacred mumbo jumbo and human sacrifice. You have to see mind at work. And that is what the Greeks gave us too in Aeschylus, Sophocles and Euripides. But over and above philosophy, science, and the arts, there must be an attempt to move politics beyond the turmoil of barbarian chiefs everlastingly contesting blood-soaked patches of ground. The civilization of the Maya never got past that in Yucatan. But in Greece, 1,000 years before the Maya (and eons before the Maya in terms of cultural development), an alternative and enlightened tradition of political thought and action, long in gestation, had already received its quintessential expression under Pericles. His oft-quoted speech in defense of Athens can never be quoted enough.

Clive Hamilton

Clive Hamilton has a very impressive academic record: BA in history, psychology, and pure mathematics from the ANU, Bachelor of Economics with a first from University of Sydney, and PhD from the University of Sussex. He must have been a university student for about ten years before he became a postdoctoral fellow at the ANU for another four. He then became director of a graduate programme in ANU for another four years. He remained at the ANU for another ten years as a senior lecturer in Public Policy and a Visiting Fellow at the National Centre for Epidemiology and Population Health and a Senior Research Economist in the Commonwealth Department of Industry, Science and Resources. He then founded what he called The Australia Institute, of which he was Executive Director. He was appointed to overseas posts at Oxford, Cambridge, and Yale. It is doubtful if anybody else in Australia has clocked up more time in prestigious academic institutions. He is currently Professor of Public Ethics at the Centre for Applied Philosophy and Public Ethics, a joint centre of the Australian National University, Charles Sturt University, and the University of Melbourne. Hamilton has written a dozen or more books, including his 2010 *Requiem for a Species*, which expands his thoughts on the politics of climate change and was received by his admirers like another *Origin of Species* combined with *War and Peace*. Another work widely discussed was his *The Freedom Paradox*.

The first problem here is that Hamilton failed to explain clearly what is meant by the classical paradox of freedom; the accepted view is that each of us wishes the maximum freedom to do what we want, but each of us fears what others might do to us if they had unlimited freedom. That seems simple enough but Professor left its meaning in greater confusion than when he began that book.

Many claims he has made are very dubious. He asserted that 'we were told our wealth and freedom' would produce 'autonomous, fulfilled individuals', but did not say who told us this. Certainly not Adam Smith, David Hume, or John Stuart

Mill. Those advocates of free markets were well aware that wealth and happiness are plain different things. What they did believe was that it was better for people to be richer than poorer. It is unfortunate that Hamilton does not agree with this. Hamilton expressed regret that 'many of us settle for a life of conformity marked by the pursuit of substitute gratifications such as wealth, the perfect body, celebrity and status,' but in moderation, these are all defensible objectives that Aristotle himself thought compatible with the good life. And then Professor Hamilton seems to have pursued celebrity and status more than most of us.

Hamilton feared that 'we live in an age of over-consumption, intemperance, and moral confusion', but every age has contained many intemperate and confused people and many people, too, who overindulged themselves on the admittedly fewer occasions they had the opportunity to do so, compared with our own time. Hamilton told Australians they must 'look to metaphysics—ideas about knowing and being that are beyond the psychological and social structures that condition everyday experience—to discover what unites us all in our humanity'. Hamilton proved, however, to have below average feelings of unity with the whole human race. Hamilton believed that 'it was Kant who had the blinding insight that a free will and a will under moral law are one and the same', although he was anticipated by a French (Swiss actually) philosopher, Jean Jacques Rousseau, who wrote that the 'mere impulse of appetite is slavery, whilst obedience to the law which prescribes to ourselves is liberty'. Unfortunately, the 'free will' of many is at times far from moral, as with Rousseau's disciples during the 1794 Reign of Terror in France.

Hamilton also advised us to read the Hindu classics, because his "entire thesis hangs on a single insight, the simple but profound realization, common to so much philosophy and religious thought, that each of us is united with all things, an idea expressed most purely in the words of the Hindu classics—thou art that". Just as muddle-headed as Julia Gillard's, 'we are us', Hamilton fears that 'rationality may have become an obstacle to further progress'. Not the most confidence building utterance in a university professor.

Hamilton was distressed that 'the real incomes of most people rose to three or four times the levels enjoyed by their parents and grandparents in the 1950s, but people are no happier'. Hamilton exaggerated the improvements in living standards, but they had been indeed very substantial and made nonsense of other claims made by Hamilton that 'capitalism' had failed. You need to live in a non-capitalist society to understand the difference. That is why so many people from such states try to get to countries such as Australia. On nearly every count, peoples in non-capitalist states are far less happy than we are. Of course, we are not fully happy: We are human beings whose infinite capacity for dissatisfaction has been the driving force which led us out of the caves to watch colour TV in heated and lighted homes. Hamilton added, 'If affluence—the object of so much determined effort—has failed to improve our well-being, why have we tried so hard to become rich?' But there is no evidence that our greater affluence has failed to improve our well-being. It has certainly extended our life spans. I am eighty-two and look forward to lots of arguments and debates in the future.

Professor Hamilton asked, 'Which is morally worse: Holocaust denial or climate change scepticism?' His own answer was that although 'it sounds like a no-brainer, the real life consequences of climate sceptics may far outweigh those of Holocaust deniers'.[226] It not only sounds a no-brainer, but it is one. My objection is not to his position on the contribution of human activity to global warming, but his refusal to credit his opponents with any respectable motives, although he accuses them of attributing unworthy motives to him. Hamilton frequently makes statements such as that 'it now seems certain that without urgent and more stringent emission cuts within the next few years, humans will be powerless to stop the shift to a new climate on earth', but there is nothing certain at all about the matter.[227] His charge that his opponents are engaged in a 'denialist campaign of harassment and intimidation' fits his own attitude in debate better. Furthermore, there was substantive evidence that statistics had deliberately been manipulated.

Hamilton frequently castigated the Howard government for inaction. He wrote that 'the Australian delegation in Copenhagen should not be surprised if the rest of the world takes a jaundiced view of any argument for the treatment of land-based emissions, based on our past Kyoto behaviour'. But he does not speak for the rest of the world, which is largely indifferent to our policies. At least, the Howard government did not make promises it had little or no intention of keeping. Hamilton lamented that 'the spirit of the Copenhagen summit was marked by a degree of fractiousness, pig-headedness, selfishness and deviousness not seen at previous UN conferences'.[2] Most UN Conferences since 1946 (and of those in the League of Nations before UN) have been like that. Hamilton pitied Queensland because it 'is being sacrificed to Australia's and the world's unwillingness to take global warming seriously', but droughts have not devastated Queensland so far and its voters have now elected a coalition government with a huge majority. The Victorian government also came under Hamilton's censure, because it continued 'to engage with scientists on climate manipulation, despite vehement criticism that it funded a conference looking at last resort geo-engineering methods'.[228] How wicked to talk with the wrong scientists and to encourage research into less draconian measures than those supported by Hamilton!

Even an ALP government has proved a disappointment: 'Julia Gillard doesn't get climate change', Hamilton fears. He noted that 'the science, economics and politics of climate change have been discussed and argued endlessly' without reaching the consensus he demands should be achieved.[229] Worse than stalemate, Hamilton has been forced to acknowledge that the last two years have 'witnessed a steady loss in public belief in the catastrophic dangers of global warming and increased opposition to the proposed carbon tax'. His explanation is that Australians have 'transformed themselves from a citizenry worried about global warming, and asking for something to be done, into an outraged mob indignant to discover that their noble desire to protect the future means they must pay a bit more for petrol and power' and that the 'public's penny-pinching has been exploited by a handful of ranting shock jocks'. Although a reputed expert on the media, Hamilton is not sure whether these ranting shock jocks seek to attract the support of elites who 'fulminate, before turning off their spittle-flecked microphones to return to their harbor-side penthouses' or to the lowest of the proles.

Hamilton's *Scorcher* is a conspiracy theory novel written in pretentious language that claims to expose the evil motives of international corporations and semi-fascist hit squads. Hamilton seemed obsessed with 'cui bono and hidden agendas'. Seemingly unaware that he is insulting a significant slice of the population, Hamilton claimed that 'like those whose opinions they value—shock jocks and television demagogues—climate deniers are disproportionately older, white, male and conservative—those who feel their cultural identity most threatened by the implications of climate change'.

In the November 2009 *Quadrant,* Mervyn Bendle asked whether Hamilton should be considered an eco-fascist. Bendle pointed out that totalitarian parties in Plato's Athens and Hitler's Germany were committed environmentalists, as are several extreme Right as well as Left extremists today. In order to avoid the dangers the global warmists fear, the state must acquire massive increases in power. Bendle quoted Hamilton's advice that the future will otherwise be 'so horrible that we [must] look to any possible scenario to head it off, including the canvassing of "emergency" responses such as the suspension of democratic processes'. Hamilton, like Robert Manne, demands that non-experts stay out of debates on global warming and the like, with just a few exceptions, such as Al Gore and themselves, whose purity of soul grants them exemption.

During the Reformation and Counter-Reformation years there were many three-sided wars and even a few with four different simultaneous conflicts. These frequently arose from different divisions in religion from politics, but we should also try to differentiate between conflicts likely to be long and destructive, because all the parties have, or think they have, substantial interests at stake, and those which are incidental and may be settled or even may undergo a change of partners. "Balance of Power" considerations may be important here.

Professor Hamilton rightly distinguished between 'normal' criminal acts and breaches of the law carried out in supposed support of a cause. Then, quite wrongly, he castigated all who acted illegally in pursuit of causes of which he disapproved, but exonerated those who broke the law for causes he favoured. He wrote that 'the protesters who expect to be arrested this weekend in the campaign to close down Hazelwood power station may break the law, but they will have justice on their side'. Although he opposed punishment for trespass and wilful damage by his followers, he demanded legal action against people who committed no crime but merely dissented from his views. Hamilton condemned the 'leaking of police information detailing the victim statements of two women accusing Julian Assange of rape' as 'a serious denial of justice'. The professor of ethics advised that 'no one ever achieved radical social change by being respectable', but one can think of many such people.

Hamilton's *What's Left: The Death of Social Democracy,* written in the *Quarterly Essay*, is based on a speech Hamilton made at the 2002 ALP National Conference. It starts off with a rant about the 'Howard government's penchant for penalizing the most vulnerable', an allegation far from fact, and with a sneer about 'the neo-liberal story of the wonders of free markets: the soaring demand for private schooling and the comfortable suburbs filled to bursting with DVDs, swimming pools and 4WDs'. Apparently a few delegates told him how wise and inspirational he was, but the large majority set to thinking how to convince voters that Labor state governments and the unions were responsible for this surge in the standard of living of the masses. Hamilton was right to draw attention to widening gaps in income levels, but the explanation for this is that although many people increased their real incomes, a few remained as they were or worse off. By and large the aged, the sick, and children shared in increased prosperity, if only modestly, but drugs, alcohol, and gambling ensured that some stayed where they were or improved their lot only slightly. Part of the increased wealth was created by an increase in the numbers of women in paid employment, which has had adverse as well as beneficial effects, but that was not extensively considered by Hamilton.

Hamilton suggested that Bob Hawke's *Accords* were part of a plot to reduce proletarian militancy and to weaken the unions. Others identified as renegades of the Hawke type were Tony Blair in Britain and Gerhard Schroder, who in Germany prolonged office by promoting 'Thatcherism' with a smiling face. Hamilton also bemoaned that 'the people had lost interest in politics and that this apathy posed a threat to democracy'. It is true that protests in the streets and illegal occupation of properties have become increasingly confined to tertiary students, but this loss of enthusiasm about party politics or fanaticism may be evidence of the maturity that Hamilton elsewhere seeks to encourage. In examining the local picture in the decline of social democratic parties, it is surprising that Hamilton makes no mention of the 'Michels Thesis' that all political parties that enjoy electoral success become more concerned with retaining the spoils of office than in implementing their original policies. With radio and TV, the trend has become much more powerful than in Michels' pre-1914 Germany He may well, too, underestimate the number of Australians who engage in voluntary work and the energy displayed when issues of local development and environmental changes are at stake.

Although he could not claim it had already taken place, Hamilton asserted that 'the Howard government's changes to industrial relations will see wages at the bottom falling', but no such process took place. The whole tone of many of his writings is an appeal to resentment and a sense of grievance. Hamilton is banal and predictable in his references to the plight of indigenous Australians as 'a matter of national shame', and makes no notable suggestions about how to change the situation.

One sentence epitomizes what is wrong with Hamilton's thinking: 'I don't believe that such a society [such as Australia's] could provide the conditions of existence for citizens to lead contented and fulfilling lives'. It is absurd to suppose that any society or state can do any such thing. Only when false hopes have been aroused that a government might transform the human condition does extremism erupt in dismay that no such prospect has been attained. And what contempt it shows for ordinary people who he implies can only fulfil themselves if some government or the other acts in a given way. Like some other prominent public intellectuals, Hamilton was thrilled by the emergence of Mark Latham to the ALP leadership and later by the ascendancy of Kevin Rudd: these men represented to Hamilton a highly desirable alternative to 'the reactionary politics embodied in the figure of Kim Beazley'. Whatever his shortcomings, Australia would surely have been better governed had Beazley been Prime Minister rather than Kevin Rudd or Julia Gillard.

In *Silencing Dissent,* which Hamilton edited jointly with Sarah Maddison, they argued that 'the Howard government is pervaded by an intolerant and anti-democratic sentiment', but they could not produce any instances of dismissal or demotion on ideological grounds. The worst torment specifically alleged is 'character assassination'. In one of the two unconvincing cases Hamilton cited, Professor Barbara Pococck alleged that Senator Abetz attempted to malign her reputation, because she had 'represented with others, the shared grave concerns of 151 Australian academic experts about the Government's Work Choices Bill'. I would not have guessed that so many such persons were employed in Australian universities on that subject. In a Chapter on non-government organizations written by Hamilton and Maddison, the only specific example of harassment cited is that the finances of The Wilderness Society were audited three times over two years. Yet, he has also demanded that Australia's security services should monitor the activities of denialist activists, most of whom are respectable, elderly people, as Hamilton often points out in derision.

Clearly, however, many intelligent people consider Hamilton is on the correct path. In a 2010 Federal by-Election, Hamilton was the Australian Greens' candidate for the affluent Melbourne constituency of Higgins. He came a respectable second out of ten candidates. He gained about a third of the votes cast, but the ALP did not run a candidate. This was at the zenith so far from the political appeal of the Greens. It does not appear as yet that Canberra has lost much by Hamilton's failure to be elected or that Charles Sturt University has retained too much, but there is time yet to prove me wrong.

Hamilton has been a favourite with the Australian Broadcasting Corporation, especially in *The Drum*. Unscripted, he displays very clearly many of the faults he imputes to his opponents: neglect of evidence, *ad hominem* attacks, and pejorative language. Clive Hamilton is one of the more reckless of our public intellectuals. He seems unable to resist the exhilaration of diatribe. In the United States, too, he puts part of the blame for the attempted murder of Arizona Congresswoman Gabrielle Giffords and the killing of six bystanders on 'the rise of violent anti-government rhetoric and imagery'. He accuses the Republican Party, infiltrated by the Tea Party, of plotting charges of criminal activity against scientists who argue in favour of the global warming theories. Hamilton concedes that Tony Abbott is not foolish enough to attack scientists directly, but he asserts that 'his dog-whistling can be heard by all but the deafest . . . Short of an outright endorsement Abbott could have sent no clearer signal than by his decision, alone among political leaders, to meet with Christopher Monckton when he toured last year.' There seems to be no way that a person in Abbott's position can meet that type of insinuation. He is condemned for doing X, but if he fails to do X, he is accused of sly suppression of his intentions and desires. The danger for Hamilton is that people like Abbott may take my advice, speak out, and be willing to be hanged for a sheep rather than for a lamb.

Hamilton called Lord Monckton 'surely the craziest and most outrageous of all prominent climate deniers'. Hamilton asserted that 'Monckton believes that climate science is a communist plot, promoted by the Hitler Youth', and that 'he also fantasies about his own history, claiming to be a member of the House of Lords and a Nobel Laureate, to have single-handedly won the Falklands War (he persuaded the British Army to use germ warfare on the "Argies"), and to have invented a cure for Graves' disease, multiple sclerosis, influenza, food poisoning, and HIV'. Hamilton also called Lord Monckton a 'notorious climate change Sceptic who engages in "media manipulation"'. The cunning Englishman evidently suborned even the normally reliable 'Fran Kelly and the ABC, so that she did not "question her controversial guest and his preposterous claims"'. Hamilton summed up, 'While the debate is superficially about the science, in truth it is about deep-rooted feelings of cultural identity. This makes deniers immune to argument. Their influence will wane only as they grow old and die.'[230]

Hamilton's personal attacks on Gina Reinhart seemed to arise from her not only being rich but also determined to become richer and because her father, like thousands of other Queenslanders at the time, was friendly towards Joh Bjelke Peterson. She herself had contributed to the funds of the Institute of Public Affairs, but that hardly seemed to deserve public vituperation from a university professor. Hamilton did not join the protests when Andrew Bolt was charged in court and found guilty of racism for doubting the aboriginality of persons with white skins who live in similar ways to affluent non-Aborigines.

Some of Hamilton's books are worth reading. *His Women at War is the Final Surrender* deals fairly and accurately with the divisive subject of women in the armed forces The book has its flaws, such as the sneer against Anzac Day that is now almost obligatory for Australian radicals. In general, however, he marshaled almost all the considerations relevant to women as combatants and discussed them cogently. Yet much of what he has said or written in the public record is wild and irrational.

Hamilton spent almost as many years in tertiary studies as Plato recommended for his chosen few who were to be the guardians of the state, but as with them, it seems unlikely that the direction of any major policy will be in his hands. Since there are several years of productive labor left in Professor Hamilton, we must hope that he is more often imbued with the open-mindedness of his *Women at War* rather than the tunnel vision of his *Requiem for a Species, Death of Social Democracy*, his contributions to *Silencing Dissent,* and then the muddle of his *The Freedom Paradox*. In particular, he would set a better example to young people who may look up to him as a public intellectual and senior academic if he confined himself to relevant arguments about matters such as climate change and did not attribute hidden disreputable motives to those who come to different conclusions from his own. Hamilton undoubtedly wishes to be of service to humanity, but he ought to think longer before he commits himself to intemperate speech and pen. A resolution to assume that his opponents are roughly as sincere as himself and not hired by big business to dim the light would be an excellent start.

ROBERT HUGHES

Among the praise paid to Robert Hughes after his death were tributes to the sparkle, insight, and historical accuracy of his account of convictism in nineteenth-century Australia that he entitled The Fatal Shore. 'The Rocky Horror Shore' would have been a better title for a book that derives all its merits from the most famous Australian convict novel: Marcus Clarke's *For the Term of His Natural Life*. Hughes adds insult to injury to the research by his habit of declaring that he intends to explode a major historical myth, then to make vague reference to historians who have already exploded the myth, and finally he attempts to revive the myth. This he does in respect of the condition of Britain, the case histories of the convicts, their treatment in Australia, and the status of women in colonial society. He met with a success so

159

remarkable as to raise doubts about not only the scholarship of many reviewers but also their common sense.

The demolition of the myth that a significant proportion of the convicts were decent honest folk who stole or maimed because of grinding poverty had been carried out effectively by Manning Clark, with detailed confirmation by L. L. Robson. Few convicts were political offenders, although the 'Scottish Martyrs' of 1795 the Irish defeated at Vinegar Hill in 1798 and the leaders of the 1830 Laborers' Rising in the southern countries of England were among those who were. Few men or women were transported for first offences, and the overwhelming majority were professional criminals. They were old and strong enough to have made an honest living had they so chosen, as was proved by the success in Australia of so many of them who decided to become law-abiding emancipated citizens after serving their sentences.

Hughes acknowledged this, but within a few pages began to resurrect the exploded myth by assuring us that 'poverty begets theft' and telling in detail such sad stories as that of a clerk transported for seven years for stealing 'a quantity of plated goods' from his employer, whom he had previously served faithfully, to pay for medicine for his sick wife.

Hughes depicted two totally separate Georgian Londons, with 'an absolute gulf between the new West End and the old rotting East End'. This rotting East End, including much of the present cities of London and Westminster, is presented as a solid mass of squalid slums and rookeries. Hughes offered the worst cases brought by the promoters of the 1833 factory legislation as if they were typical. He wrote that 'occupational diseases ran rampant. Sawyers went blind . . . metal founders died paralyzed with lead poisoning and glassblowers' lungs collapsed from silicosis', etc., etc. After 1815, England went from bad to worse: Evidently, 'England began to pay the full price of its recent defeat in war (sic)'. Few of us had realized that Napoleon Bonaparte won the Battle of Waterloo; was it in Paris that a railway station was named after the battle?

In Hughes's account, England during decade after decade was 'struck by a series of internal crises', in which 'workers were pincered between falling wages and rising prices, the mechanization of hand trades created runaway unemployment, and the inexorable spread of enclosure, was driving people from the country to the slum'. Apparently 'hopelessness, poverty and resentment were endemic to post-war Britain'.

Even the briefest reference to such easily accessible authorities as I. R. Christie, T. S. Ashton, W. O. Henderson, W. H. Chaloner, J. D. Marshall, Dorothy Marshall, Dorothy George, G. E. Mingay, E. L. Jones, Asa Briggs, M. W. Flynn, J. D. Chambers, Phyllis Deane, or R. M. Hartwell would have forced Hughes to tear up many purple passages and amend his gross and misleading generalizations. No reader could guess from The Fatal Shore that during the years with which it is concerned Britain achieved an unprecedented increase in wealth, that massive reductions in mortality rates led to population explosions in both Britain and Ireland, and that employment increased in each decade on the land as well as in the towns and cities.

Hughes wrote as though the urban poor in England were all demoralized lumpen-proletarians and as though criminals formed a distinctive social class. He alleged that the 'tendency of propertied Englishmen . . . to invest the struggling and the poor with an aura of criminality was sometimes amplified by Evangelical Methodism'. Methodism, especially primitive Methodism, was embraced by many of the struggling and poor, and many Methodists were well able to distinguish between the undeserving and the deserving poor.

Hughes noted quite correctly that 'there is no doubt that many Britons made their living, wholly or in part, from crime'. He failed to understand, however, that most of the deported became criminals not because they were starving or even particularly poor or because most of them were ferocious psychopaths, although some of them were. Most thieves stole on the basis of rational calculation: The chances of being caught were small, and judicial procedures favoured the accused. During the course of the eighteenth century, it is true that the number of crimes carrying the death penalty vastly increased, but the number of executions did not, even though the population was rising rapidly.

The second myth exploded and then reconstituted by Hughes was of the horrific and brutalizing nature of convict society in the Australian colonies. Hughes wrote sensibly enough in his introduction.

> Denied its voice as history, convict experience became the province of journalists and novelists—a vivid, trashy Grand Guignol, long on rum, sodomy and the lash but decidedly short on the more prosaic facts. This folklore of the System kept its memory alive. But it was one-sided, and especially in its treatment of Port Arthur, sometimes luridly exaggerated.

Unfortunately, this is a fair description of The Fatal Shore.

Hughes justly described John Hirst's Convict Society and its Enemies as 'a landmark in recent studies'. Hughes conceded:

> Colonial Australia was a more 'normal', place than one might imagine from the folkloric picture of a society governed by the lash and the triangle, composed of groaning white slaves tyrannized by ruthless masters.

He also admitted:

> For all its flaws the assignment system, in Australia was by far the most successful form of penal rehabilitation that had ever been tried in English, American or European experience.

These historically accurate judgments could have been written by Hirst himself. Even before the end of the Napoleonic Wars, convicts transported to Australia were writing to relatives and friends in Britain, urging them to come out too. The Bigge Commission was set up as early as 1819 to find ways in which transportation to the Australian colonies could be made the deterrent to crime in England it had been intended to be. Yet *The Fatal Shore* resurrects the lash and the triangle as the typical features of convict life.

Very few political prisoners or criminal first offenders transgressed against the law once they were in New South Wales. Most of the habitual thieves also decided that it was more sensible to make an honest and fairly comfortable living on assignment to free settlers or to former convicts (emancipists) than to resort to villainy again. Most convicts were unchained and indistinguishable to the naked eye from free settlers. There were not too many people to rob with much profit. The Aborigines had nothing for the professional thief, whilst most of the white population were convicts and ex-convicts (emancipists), who were not easy to relieve of their possessions.

On the other hand, there were even fewer police there than in Britain, and most of the police were emancipated convicts. Only the very worst criminals therefore thought a return to crime a risk worth taking. As a result, the punishment for recidivists was harsh and brutal. Deterrence is always a balance between the chances of being caught and the severity of punishment if you are caught. The odds on arresting and taking highway robbers and burglars to prison were very low, so the treatment of those who were caught was rough. Life in the secondary penal colonies, such as Norfolk Island and Port Macquarie, was highly unpleasant, but. Hughes's unrelenting emphasis on the lashings of the minority of recidivists seriously distorted the entire system.

The third myth which Hughes claimed to dispel, but re-created, concerned convict women. Early commentators, such as the Reverend Samuel Marsden, dismissed the convict women as a pack of incorrigible whores and thieves. The feminist historian Anne Summers argued that 'the whore stereotype was devised as a calculated sexist means of social control'. Since then much scholarly work has been devoted to the study of women in convict New South Wales. Hughes made only one brief reference to the work of Portia Robinson, whose *The Hatch and Brood of Time* (1985) demonstrated very powerfully that many convict women made successful common law marriages and lived in ways very different from that of whoredom. Many women who made their living in England on their backs, together with some thieving, teamed up with men who had also decided that honesty was the best policy in New South Wales. Hughes virtually ignored Robinson's decisive evidence.

Hughes was very well treated as an expat both in Britain and the United States, but he rarely lost an opportunity to deride them. He had ever greater contempt for those Australians he described as 'local imperialists, who believed that Australia could only survive as a vassal of Great Britain'. He identified with those who alleged that having been shipped out of Britain as criminals Australians were shipped back as cannon fodder; so 'that when peace came, the survivors could return to their real mission as Australians growing cheap wool and wheat for England'.

To Hughes, England was the mother of evil: 'England drew the sketch for our own century's vaster and more terrible fresco of repression, the Gulag'. Hughes added:

> A young country does not serve as the pad on which England drew its sketches for the immense Gulags of the twentieth century without acquiring a few marks and scars . . . The final aim of the transportation system then, was less to punish individual crimes than to uproot a class enemy from the British social fabric. Here lay its peculiar modernity; its prediction of the vaster, more efficient techniques of class destruction that would be perfected, a century later, in Russia.

Let us hope that Australians never have to experience at first hand the Gulags with which Hughes so glibly compared their colonial past.

MARILYN LAKE

Tasmanian-born Professor Marilyn Lake, after several years in a Personal Chair in the School of History at La Trobe University, where she was appointed Founding Director of Women's Studies, has now been appointed to a Chair in the University of Melbourne. She has also held a number of Visiting Professorial Fellowships, including Stockholm University, the University of Sydney, the University of Western Australia, and the Australian National University.

Professor Lake was awarded an ARC Professorial Research Fellowship in 2004 and an Australian Prime Minister's Centre Research Fellowship in 2007. She has been awarded a second Australian Research Council Professorial Research Fellowship that began in 2011 to investigate the international history of Australian democracy. She has published thirteen books and numerous articles and book Chapters in Australian and international publications. Recent books include What's Wrong with Anzac? written with Henry Reynolds, Mark McKenna, and Joy Damousi and Drawing the

163

Global Colour Line: White Men's Countries and The Question of Racial Equality, co-authored with Henry Reynolds. It was awarded the Queensland Premier's Prize, the Ernest Scott Prize, and the Prime Minister's Prize for Non-Fiction.

Marilyn Lake had named Foucault's *Discipline and Punish* as her 'theoretical framework', but she had been influenced by many feminist intellectuals as well. Lake holds that 'historians are implicated in contemporary politics, particularly Australian historians, whether they like it or not'. Liberals and Nationals however do not count in this dispensation. Lake practiced what she preached. Her principal themes included the evils of war, the oppression of women, and the sufferings of Australia's indigenous peoples.

Lake held that Aboriginal people were warriors, patriots, resistance fighters, and indispensable guides to the European explorers and settlers. In addition, they were 'efficient resource managers in an inhospitable continent and as proponents of religious beliefs which also worked to maintain the country'. She held that Aboriginal women enjoyed high status in traditional society: They were 'the chief breadwinners and significant custodians of their country'. They were 'not oppressed by a body of man-made "laws" that issued forth from legislatures embodied—as in British and Australian parliaments—in male form'. Aboriginal women used to possess a 'strong subjective sense of equality'.

According to Lake, in contrast to the felicities of life enjoyed by Aboriginal women in their traditional groups, all women, Aborigine and colonist, suffered under colonization. Unmarried male 'wandering members of the British race were dangerous predators, whilst women's situation was one of isolation, vulnerability and defencelessness'. Lake depicted that a typical married woman's life in the outback was made miserable by their husbands' drinking, gambling, and predatory sexuality. In an attitude that some might consider slightly racist, Lake seemed, like the white wives, especially affronted by husbands' sexual use of Aboriginal women under the marital roof. She held that it was the spectacle of white men's systematic sexual abuse of Aboriginal women and 'unprotected' white women and girls that confirmed twentieth-century Australian feminists in their view of sexuality as inherently degrading for women. As a result, she believed, women were even more fervent advocates of a 'white Australia' than the men. Lake made no references to the evidence compiled by Helen Hughes, Jenness Warin and Stephanie Jarrett of the misery and exploitation to which so many Aboriginal women and girls are subjected, but she may take account of Jarrett's recent book on violence against Aboriginal people. [231]

Yet Lake also asserted that 'in the context of a British colonial settlement white women assumed a special authority as the agents of civilization and custodians of the race'. This would have been difficult had women been as helpless as she had previously argued. Lake claimed sensibly enough that drinking and sexual promiscuity were regarded as especially heinous offences in and by colonial women. She added that 'this tyrannical double standard was enshrined in law'. Since this was so mainly because of pressure by women, that fact undermined much of Lake's lamentations about women's helplessness. She herself was adept at using double standards. She depicted the gender balance in both Britain and Australia as unfairly disadvantageous to women: In Britain, many surplus women were, she maintained, forced into spinsterhood or extra-marital immorality; in Australia, they were weak because they were outnumbered. Lake usually told only one side of a story, but could justify her partiality as a necessary balance to even worse misrepresentations on the other side in the past. She reminded us that 'Aboriginal workers were not given adult wages, often no wages at all', but ignored the 'rations' given to the extended families of Aborigines working on sheep stations.

Crude sexism entered Lake's discourse when she referred to men's 'casual sex with animals, other men, indigenous and other "unprotected" women and girls, as well as the dissolute practices of gambling and drinking'. What evidence had she about the habits in the outback of men compared with women? How do we evaluate their comparative immorality, especially once differences in opportunity are taken into consideration? We may hope that not too many a Pasiphae assaulted the virtue of the native fauna of Australia, but research may reveal surprises.

Lake went beyond most of the Australian feminist Left in her hatred and scorn for the colonial male. She explicitly contrasted the pictures painted by Russel Ward and that 'Old Left' with those of 'New Left' in which she and Henry Reynolds became so prominent. She wrote that for Russel Ward the Bushman was to be admired as 'the practical man, rough and ready, independent and anti-authoritarian, a man given to few words, but resourceful and supportive of his mates'. However, for 'historians of Aboriginal dispossession, such as Henry Reynolds', it was the Bushman who embodied 'the criminality, brutality and violence that characterized the settlement of Australia'. In contrast, Lake rejoiced, Reynolds had revealed Aborigines to be political subjects around whom the history of Australia should be centred.

Lake took her messages into classrooms and lecture theatres. She stated:

> I teach general courses in Australian gender relations, which I have done for about ten years, and I always have quite a bit on the policy of taking the children away. When I first started teaching that, the general community were not aware of this history. The students were shocked about what they were learning about their countries past . . . I think we have to proceed to write and teach about racism.

The campaigns during the recent and ongoing 'history wars' by Lake and her colleagues have surely succeeded beyond their wildest hopes, in her words, in inculcating 'heightened consciousness about the place of massacres on the frontier, dispossession of Aboriginal people'. Yet in September 2011, Lake expressed concern that 'the numbers of students enrolling in humanities subjects, in particular humanities subjects, is declining'. She added that 'there has been particularly talk of a crisis in enrolments in Australian history and in Australian studies . . . it seems to be the case that students perceive Australian history to be boring or that they assume that they know it already, that they've done it at school and that they don't need to do it again'. Her interviewer reminded her that 'a lot of academics complain that students arrive at university with no rudimentary knowledge of Australian history'.

Lake rejected any suggestion that 'black-band' interpretations of Australian history might alienate many students. She attributed the unpopularity of Australian history to John Howard and his supporters. Evidently, they 'racialized asylum seekers and those who come in boats', and this meant that 'they're not seen to be people like us but people of another race'.

Reflecting on her own career, Lake considered that she began as a fiery polemicist, but with the passage of years, her work became underpinned by humanist empathy. As a result, she had become more sympathetic to the 'maternal feminists' whose restricted views, as she saw them, held sway in women's movements then. Some of her admirers feared this may indicate backsliding in her denunciations of recognition of conservatism, paternalism, and racism, but there seems no danger that this will happen, although it is to be desired devoutly.

Lake is appalled by 'the obscenity of war', which must have often made her work as a historian very painful. She feared that Australian history was close to being taught:

> As if it's all one long war. So it doesn't quite matter whether you know when Australians were fighting World War I or World War II or Korea or Vietnam or Iraq, they displayed the same values. Courage, mateship . . . They display the spirit of Anzac . . . So during the last fifteen years or so, school children have been inundated with lessons about military history and they've been going on the pilgrimages to Gallipoli and stuff. Anna Clark had said more money has been spent on educating children in military history than any other field of history in Australia.

And Anna Clark should know, because she is a granddaughter of Manning Clark. I am assuming that, where there is no suggestion of disagreement, Professors Lake and Reynolds concurred in their arguments. They began by asserting that a 'relentless militarization of our history' has recently taken place and that money lavished on military history and commemorations by the Howard government has fostered an ultra-patriotic, rather militaristic viewpoint in children. Evidently, federal money was intentionally allocated to Anzac themes in particular 'to divert attention from the history of Aboriginal dispossession and frontier massacres by opening up a new front'. Yet the Howard government generously financed expositions of Aboriginal history as well, most of them highly critical of colonialism and Empire.

The professors alleged that the educational militarists were led by John Howard, but that shameful support was provided by gutless Labor politicians as well, including Bob Hawke, Paul Keating, and Kevin Rudd, not to mention the mass media, publishers and authors, schools across the nation, the RSL, and parts of the public service.

Howard and company are not entirely to blame, however, since the rot had set in long ago. Sending Australian troops to the Sudan and South Africa is seen by Henry Reynolds as disgraceful cultural cringing. No suggestion is offered that some Australians felt an interest in those conflicts independently of their loyalty to Britain, where many of the volunteers had been born. The Uitlanders in Transvaal were very much the sort of men whom Lake and Reynolds praised at the Eureka Stockade. No discussion was offered of fears of German power in New Guinea, much closer than the Japanese. Despite frequent references to the Holocaust and genocide, Professors Lake and Reynolds did not seem to worry too much about the possible fate of Australians under German or Japanese rule.

Lake believed that 'the Anzac lessons were a national curriculum. Anzac lessons and materials and stuff were sent out from Canberra. That was, in effect, a national curriculum'. Books about ANZAC are, according to Lake, 'heavily subsidized and supported and they do focus on military battles'. Howard history, Lake claimed, neglected 'the impact of war on the home front, the divisions on the home front, the fight against conscription, divisions between men and women'.

Her argument on enrolments in history seems self-contradictory. On the one hand, she alleged that numbers in history courses were falling because wars dominated them, but also complained that almost only history courses that had attracted higher numbers were in military history.

Lake and Reynolds believed that 'with few now in our society who can bear direct witness to the obscenity of war, our schoolchildren are charged with the onerous responsibility of keeping the legend alive, wrapped in the Australian flag'. The 'Anzac myth' especially distressed them.

It taunted and troubled us. It loomed larger than ever in Australian historical memory—with the generous help of the Australian War

167

Memorial and the Department of Veterans Affairs. The myth will remain our creation story until the nation is reborn, until we have the courage to detach ourselves from the mother country, declare our independence, inaugurate a republic, and draw up a constitution that recognizes the first wars of dispossession fought against indigenous peoples. Thus we can truly make history in Australia.

The 'Anzac Tradition' is, she urged, 'the vehicle by which the ideas of the Edwardian militarists are preserved and passed on to a new generation', which then may emulate the 'white supremacists, representatives of the White Australia Policy, which promoted racial purity'. Lake condemned the 'Cronulla mob' for attacking Lebanese youths whom they accused of assaulting slightly dressed Australian women on beaches. She alleged that assaulting women is part of the white Australian male tradition and implied that accusations against the Lebanese were racist inventions.

Lake did not oppose war as such; she wished there had been a war of independence against the British yoke: 'Unlike the American colonies—whose example of independence was implanted in historical memory and always before the constitution makers of the 1890s—the Australian federal fathers failed to achieve the heroic goal of manly independence.' Lake had high hopes of the new history curriculum 'that is being designed and thought about for implementation in all Australian schools. And from what I've seen of it, it looks very progressive and very exciting to me: for example, there's a suggestion that we should be more conscious of locating Australian history in its Asian context. Chinese colonists in Australia in the 1880s were amongst the first in the world to talk about notions of common human rights'.

Given that the direction of the national curriculum for history has been in the safe hands of progressive scholars such as Professor Stuart Macintyre of Melbourne University, it should prove generally satisfactory to Professor Lake. However, whilst alienating many other students, the new history curriculum is unlikely to attract many students of Chinese origin, even, or especially, if their land of origin is celebrated as the home of human rights, liberty, equality, and fraternity.

Professor Lake's attempt to exclude John Curtin from the charges of racism she sometimes makes rather freely is discussed in the chapter on White Australia.

Lake would like the Gillard government to ensure that students know that Australia 'was once a quite racist, xenophobic country under the policy of the White Australia Policy'. It is unlikely that Lake's wish will be fulfilled: A Gillard government is not likely to last long; the teaching lacks conviction, and most students will resist brainwashing. Yet, if they ever read Curtin's speech when war with Japan began in 1941, they may want to know what were the 'imperishable traditions' of which Professor Lake has left them largely ignorant.

Although one has no reason to suppose that Lake would relish a woman's life in traditional Aboriginal societies, she frequently praises its supposed advantages for women as compared with their subservience in the sexist post-colonial west. She is a fervent opponent of wars, but almost exclusively of those fought by Western societies, including her own country.

Like many other feminists, Professor Lake purports to be a disadvantaged battler and outsider, even though they hold a large number of top academic posts in history, social sciences, and English in our universities. Manning Clark in his old age praised the historians who had ensured that 'the descendants of the British have discovered the evil in their past' so that 'the horrors are being faced'. As a result, Clark said accurately, 'In all the history departments of the universities and colleges of advanced education, teachers and students are burrowing away in libraries to find more examples of white barbarism and cruelty against the Aborigines'. He did not seem to comprehend that the 'New Tree Green' whose sprouting he had once celebrated had been chopped down and set on fire in the process.

MARCIA LANGTON

In January 1997, I was invited to take part in the ABC Radio's *Peter Thompson's Breakfast Programme*. One of the other participants was Marcia Langton, then a professor in the University of the Northern Territory, a member of the National Aboriginal Council for Reconciliation, and a member of the Order of Australia. She became a Fellow of the Academy of Social Sciences in Australia in 2001 and was awarded the inaugural Neville Bonner Award for Indigenous Teacher of the Year in 2002. She subsequently became Inaugural Chair of Australian Indigenous Studies at the University of Melbourne and Chair of the Cape York Institute for Leadership and Policy. The then Federal Minister for Education, Dr Brendan Nelson, appointed her as Chair of a new Higher Education Council.

I had recently published a book entitled *Hasluck versus Coombs: White Politics and Australia's Aborigines*. Langton told listeners:

> Hitler had Goebbels, John Howard's got Geoffrey Partington . . . This is the most outrageous interpretation that I've heard in a long time. Geoffrey Partington's book was so appalling and the footnotes were so shonky that serious people didn't bother to review it . . . it is entirely irresponsible, but, you know, I urge historians in the Academy to take this man's work to task because it is entirely irresponsible. This is the treason of the clerks

that Dr Coombs was talking about that we let people like this assume the mantle of historian when the unmitigated garbage that comes from his pen and his mouth.

The only time I had met John Howard had been for about two minutes in Parliament House when Dr John Herron, then Minister for Aboriginal Affairs, launched my Hasluck versus Coombs in 1996. None of its reviewers found any significant errors in its referencing. And at least I did not attribute 'the treason of the clerks' to Dr Coombs. And did those few words we exchanged transform John Howard's thinking?

My view on self-determination was expressed in that book as follows:

> If asked, however, the overwhelming majority of the Australian people as a whole, and very likely a majority of Aborigines, would agree with Hasluck that the future of Aborigines ought not to be a matter for Aborigines alone to determine, any more than it would be right to exclude Aborigines from participating in the determination of the future of non-Aboriginal Australians. It is ironical that, together with declarations about the unity of humanity and the global village, we should find such an emphasis on the exclusive right of self-determination of a minority group, or rather of a set of related minority groups, most of whose members live intermingled with non-members. The real challenge that faces us all is to ensure that the living standards and opportunities in life of Aborigines should be broadly comparable to those of non-Aborigines, while at the same time respecting that some Aborigines may wish to exercise different choices from those made by most other Australians. Different choices lead to different outcomes, some of which may be unpleasant, but that is the nature of choice.

In *Treaty* Professor Langton argued:

> The calls for a treaty go to the heart of the juridical denial in Australian case law of the existence of Aboriginal nations in Australia prior to the seizure of the land and consequent dispossession of Indigenous people by the British Crown. In Australia, the denial at law of Indigenous sovereignty and, indeed, the very existence of Aboriginal polities has a peculiar history. Here, the doctrine of terra nullius—or empty land belonging to no-one—was applied to justify colonization.

> It is this attachment with a place through ancestors and tradition that enables those of us who can claim a kind of sovereignty that predates the colonists to have a sense of place that is deeply emotional and also social and political at the same time. It is this attachment of blood and spirit that

makes the sacrifices worthwhile and makes it possible for one to believe in one's own humanity.

The Australian state has consistently failed to understand and to accept the right of its indigenous peoples to be allowed the fullest rights of self-determination. It is little wonder that calls for a separate nation find ready adherents in the Aboriginal community.'

Who would form this 'separate nation'? Langton herself pointed out that in pre-contact Australia 'there was no such thing as an 'Aboriginal', but rather Bundgelung, Wiradgeri, Eora, and hundreds of other groupings. At that time, she did not approve of the way in which the term 'Aboriginal' homogenizes (sic) all those people into 'a single group to whom a wide range of negative stereotypes and functions can be applied by the dominant culture'.

With which people who have descended from pre-contact Australia should or could treaties be made now? Should persons of mixed ancestry, by far the majority of Australians currently identified as indigenous, apologize to themselves? Would not such a 'treaty' imply that Aborigines are not part of the Australian nation as it now exists? And does Langton really believe that 'blood and spirit' permanently define or constrain one's own humanity? During the 1990s, when the Aboriginality of Mudrooroo, Archie Weller, Roberta Sykes, and other claimants to Aboriginal status faced challenges, Aboriginal woman author 'Wanda Koolmartrie' proved to be a white man and 'Eddie Burrup' a well-known white woman, Elizabeth Durak. More recent disagreements as to what constitutes Aboriginality have become increasingly acrimonious

Pauline Hanson and all who consorted with her were, of course, prime objects of Langton's censure, but most of the rest of us were also condemned. In 1998, Langton told a conference in Britain on racial reconciliation that the forthcoming Australian elections could have 'a catastrophic impact on Australian race relations, since there was a stark choice. Voting for more racism or not'. She claimed that a victory for the coalition government would 'heighten racial tension and bring Australia into international disrepute as the next South Africa, entrenching racism and deliberately choosing not to make peace with its Aboriginal Peoples'. She alleged that the Howard government had flouted international law in order to pursue its controversial anti-Aboriginal agenda and had implemented the final dispossession of Australia's Aboriginal peoples by depriving us of our property rights.

Professor Langton claimed that it was 'terrifying' to be an Aboriginal woman on the frontier, yet there was considerable evidence that large numbers of Aboriginal sought out white men, partly because they thought they would be better fed, but also partly because they would not get beaten up as often.

171

Langton once alleged that the Lutheran missionaries' purposes constituted a 'mad vision', partly because they gave the Western Aranda 'endless sermons in German'. In fact, as Peter Valee pointed out in 'Dreamtime and Nightmares', posted on *Quadrant Online,* 'their policy was to learn the local language, and they translated into it and taught in it for several years before English was taught'.

Professor Langton attacked 'the continuing maltreatment of the exponents of Aboriginal women's business and the continuing denial of a fair hearing to Ngarrindjeri women who sought protection of places of great mythological significance [on Hindmarsh Island, in South Australia]'. Yet, overall, Australian governments give greater consideration to Aboriginal beliefs, ancient or modern, than to any other religious beliefs. In the Hindmarsh Bridge controversies, the only obstacle to the fullest and fairest of hearings was the refusal of some Aboriginal women to testify before men, including male Ministers for Aboriginal Affairs. About the Hindmarsh Island Bridge disputes, Langton admitted disarmingly, 'I personally do not know much about the facts of the case, and it is not proper that I should know.'

Langton, however, is often sensible. She accepted that traditional beliefs were by no means changeless. She disagreed with claims that 'the Altjira (the pre-contact cosmology of the Western Aranda) leads them in their life and is their law. apparently referring to all Aranda people today.' She commented, 'Such a conclusion is neither historically accurate nor adequate as description of the current state of Aranda culture.'

Langton realized early on that land rights, welcome as they might be, were unlikely to be the solution to the main problems that beset Aboriginal societies. She supported Peter Sutton's view that 'recent emphasis on land rights had been accompanied by "the loss of opportunities to develop economically and modernize Aboriginal institutions that were no longer effective"'.

Langton told Luke Slattery in *The Australian* (11 February 2008): 'Of course some Aboriginal land is sacred, but not all of it. There are degrees of sacredness in any case. Some places are sacred for a time and then not for a long time, like ceremonial grounds.' Langton generalized, 'White people don't understand these subtleties. The idea that Aboriginal land can't be desecrated is just a green slogan.' In a more realistic vein she noted that '60 per cent of mining operations are co-located on Aboriginal lands. In exchange, Aboriginal people want protection of actual sacred sites, and fair compensation'.

Her comments about 'The Stolen Generation' were for many years unrelated to evidence. She declared:

[Children] were taken from their families by the Commonwealth and other Australian governments with no reason other than to deny them their Aboriginal legacy and hence the future of Aboriginal society.

[The Equal Opportunity Commission Inquiry revealed that] unknown numbers, perhaps tens of thousands, were removed, and that the direct evidence of the survivors, who number about 13,000, revealed that there was sometimes extreme physical and sexual abuse at the hands of adoptive and foster families and employers (to whom some were indentured or enslaved).

The 'Apology' was a national acknowledgment of the wrong and harm done by previous governments to an entire race on the grounds of race-hate. The Commissioners [of the Human Rights and Equal Opportunity Commission] found that the race-based child-removal policies were a special instance of genocide under the definition in the convention. This is crystal clear, for instance in Western Australia, where the instructions and justifications were aimed at eliminating the entire race.

Langton held that is the failure of all within the Australian governments that is at least partly responsible along with history for this terrible situation. Her emphasis was that 'Really to blame was the terrible violence inflicted on Aboriginal people by colonial officers, police, missionaries, and the general citizenry in an orgy of race-hatred.' But, although all Australian governments had for many decades been evil, none had been so vile in Professor Langton's eyes as that of John Howard. She stated:

Howard's regime 'debilitated our (the Indigenous) social and economic capital and the political structures that might have enabled us to participate more effectively'.

The victims of the child-removal policies of earlier Australian governments had suffered 'years of abuse and humiliation, first as a result of being taken from their families and second as the targets of Howard's cheer-squad for White Australia'.

However, the worst Langton could report from personal experience was that as a girl she had a two-mile walk from home to school and was frequently late for school. In one school, she was excluded from religious education classes. She did not mention that this was part of the 'conscience clause' available to parents for their children. Many students would have been pleased to miss RE, but Langton's explanation was that the principal hated her 'because she wasn't Anglican or Presbyterian or

Methodist, you see'. That principal made her sit on a bench in the school hall during RE as a 'form of humiliation and exclusion'. Something made her bitter and full of hatred, but surely it was something of a more painful order than that?

Langton believes that 'persisting in a high school like that in 1960s Queensland makes you pretty tough. It also makes you smart'. In her own judgment, she needed to be tough as a university teacher. Some unnamed people were hateful to her. She called them 'the Ku Klux Klan academic Chapter who try to make my life hell . . .' She bemoaned, 'Even though I had first-class honours degree and a PhD nobody would address me by my correct title. You know, I'm always Ms Langton not Dr Langton or Professor Langton.' Can this really have been so? Not a single academic willing to call her Professor?

Langton considered that the best way to increase Aboriginal capacity was through education. Unfortunately, she clung to the policy she expressed in 2000 at an Aboriginal festival to effect the 'incorporation of Aboriginal knowledge systems into the curriculum of Australian universities, colleges and schools. We don't want our intellectual traditions to be ignored any longer—and we want them to be treated with respect in educational institutions'.[232] She did not specify just which Aboriginal knowledge systems and intellectual traditions she had in mind. Her recent Boyer Lecture left the content of his knowledge system vague and ill defined.

Langton understood that 'poor attendance, especially in remote communities, continues to thwart teachers and principals. Aboriginal kids perform poorly on national benchmark tests for literacy and numeracy. Often trailing four years behind white kids, they rarely catch up'. Langton alleged that 'there aren't enough classrooms or chairs or desks or paper', but many new and well equipped schools have failed to produce significantly better results. If inadequate financial support was the key problem, great leaps forward would already have taken place. There are often many more chairs than bottoms to sit on them.

Langton added that 'the kids come to school and they can't speak English but they have to teach in English, and the kids can't understand anything that's said to them because they have a degree of deafness, or come from a sick home situation, or are just bored out of their brains'. She is better at restating problems than in solving them. Success in the world as it is cannot be gained through greater fluency in a mother tongue spoken by only a thousand people.

Like herself, many of Australia's leading indigenous activists, such as Patrick and Michael Dodson and Noel Pearson, attended 'elite private schools'. Langton praised the 'very high standard' of education they provided. As its foundations, Langton identified, first, 'learning formal English to a high standard and learning in the

174

formal mainstream Western tradition, the history of ideas', and, second, avoidance of racism: 'I just don't want to have to defend my daughter every day against racism'. Many non-government schools may well be less racist than some government schools, but Langton provided no evidence for her claim that government schools, faulty as they are in several ways, are notably racist . . . Neither did she explain just how curricula can be permeated with both traditional Aboriginal beliefs and practices and the 'formal mainstream western tradition'.

Langton's pride in the educational and professional achievements of many indigenous Australians is admirable, but it undercut her attacks on the integration/assimilation policies that made those achievements possible.

Professor Langton has changed her mind on many important issues, usually for the good. She has criticized the welfare dependence that, she believed, had entrenched Aboriginal communities in poverty. Calling for a radical overhaul to the Aboriginal work-for-the-dole programme, Langton said that Aborigines had been 'enmeshed' in poverty since they were caught up in the safety net and that the one-dimensional social-worker, welfarist (sic) approach to the Aboriginal situation had made things worse.

Langton has been consistent in her concern about drunkenness among Aborigines. She urged (30 November 2007) in the *Sydney Morning Herald:*

> It's time for both the federal and the Territory government to stop playing politics with the lives of the vulnerable and shut down the alcohol take-away outlets, establish children's commissions and shelters in each community—as Noel Pearson has suggested—and treat grog runners and drug dealers as the criminals that they are. Otherwise, they will all have the blood on their hands.

Langton conceded in *Too Much Sorry Business,* a report of the Aboriginal Issues Unit of the Northern Territory, that 'many Aboriginal societies in the Northern Territory have never been dispossessed and yet the grog problem is crippling these same Aboriginal people . . . Once Aboriginal people are in the grip of alcohol they find it difficult or impossible to escape'[233].

Langton praised the Aboriginal leaders in Cape York and other areas for their self-imposed restrictions on alcohol and drugs for having reduced domestic violence to the extent that there were no longer women staying in the women's shelters.

Some leading Aborigines were by no means ideal role models. Langton wrote:

'Big bunga ("big men" or "big penises" according to Sutton) politics brought the Aboriginal and Torres Strait Islander Commission (ATSIC) into disrepute and finally led to its disestablishment in 2004. The 'big men' had failed to show leadership on the most pressing issues in those communities: housing, health, and education'.[234]

Langton found some cunning ways to circumvent the machinations of Big Bunga men. In *Too Much Sorry Business,* she revealed that when she chaired the National Indigenous Working Group on Native Title in 1997 and 1998 she would do the following:

> Schedule difficult agenda items for times in the afternoon when she knew that troublesome ATSIC commissioners would be at the TAB betting on horse races. If they were binge drinkers or false statistics users, the tactic was to start the meetings at the earliest possible hour of the day, or even worse, cut into their social time by reconvening meetings after dinner with an announcement that it would be a drafting session. Assured that copies would be available in the morning, the 'big men' and their flying wedges of advisers and minders would retire and leave the detail to mere lawyers and policy advisers . . . In winter, we could pretend that the heating—set too high—did not work, and in summer that the air conditioning—set too low—could not be changed. These were the tactics that women used to ensure positive and achievable outcomes and to avoid being bullied into enforced compromises and silence.

In 1988, Langton wrote in *Medicine Square, Being Black: Aboriginal Cultures in Settled Australia,* 'My aim is to demonstrate that swearing and fighting in contemporary Aboriginal society constitute dispute processing and social ordering derived from traditional Aboriginal cultural patterns.' She added that 'swearing and fighting' in 'settled' Australia should not be seen as drunken anarchy and anti-social behaviour but as two aspects of evolving indigenous law. Yet, she also claimed that 'domestic violence is not tolerated by Aboriginal peoples, it is not considered to be acceptable and is certainly not a part of traditional law, nor has it ever been'. Two incompatible statements and both wrong.

Langton condemned compulsory sentencing in the Northern Territory and Western Australia for offenders with three previous convictions as a 'dumbing down' of Australian politics and policy. She alleged, in *Too Much Sorry Business,* that those who supported mandatory sentencing had been 'fed a diet of sensationalist, terrifying, but false statistics about crime, criminals, punishment and imprisonment and the threat to their personal safety, homes and property'.

She stated that Aboriginal people who spoke to her during consultations took the view that young people, especially minors, should not be jailed, and that jail converted the young with a propensity for youthful misdemeanours into recidivist criminals. Langton's informants wanted, she claimed, 'minor offenders brought to book under customary law mechanisms, a course of action that had proved far more successful than imprisonment of young males in faraway towns'.

Then, with a massive and rapid change of mind, Langton began to claim that the criminal justice systems of Queensland, and of other states to a lesser extent, were not too punitive, but too lenient. They 'rewarded rapists and murderers: Instead of jail sentences that would apply to anyone else, they are freed, often after a laughable lecture, or sent to a prison where living conditions are often better than in the communities from which they come. They are released into the communities where their crimes were committed, and recidivism takes on a special meaning: the younger sisters or cousins of their original victims are the next in line to be raped'.

In 2007, she expressed her disgust that the rape of a ten-year-old Wik girl in Aurukun by three adults and six juvenile Wik males was treated by the Queensland criminal justice system, she claimed, as barely a cause for concern. District Court Judge Sarah Bradley imposed twelve-month probation orders and failed to record a conviction against any of the nine who had pleaded guilty . . . Langton concluded that an 'apartheid regime had been created wherever Aboriginal communities are quarantined by remoteness, welfare dependence, a racist criminal justice system and government officials who entrench this expensive social pathology with dysfunctional policies'.

Despite these flashes of good sense, Professor Langton continued to denounce many who seek Aboriginal betterment just as much as herself. She claimed in *A Heartland of Instability: Dancing on Our Graves* that it was 'global knowledge that Australia treats its Indigenous people barbarously'. She alleged that it was not only in the past but also in the present that Australia was starkly divided, as exemplified by 'the treatment of asylum seekers and by the gap between privileged Australia and the underclass'.

She distinguished between the racism of the Right: 'They think we're all coons. It's nasty', and the racism of the white Left: 'They think we have some kind of higher spirituality through our relationship with the land. In the end we become spiritual people who can't ever be competent citizens'.

Faced with the failure of the Cubillo and Gunner cases, Langton was 'disgusted that a judge could reason that a young frightened illiterate mother's thumbprint taken by a government officer could necessarily (sic) be voluntary'. Langton ought to have asked herself whether that 'young frightened illiterate mother' had been capable of taking adequate care of her child.

But, as with her views on punishment, Langton changed direction on child removal. She began to urge that too few, not too many, Aboriginal children were being taken away from dysfunctional families. She even accepted that the Howard government acted in good faith in the Intervention.

Langton described the 2007 *Little Children are Sacred* **report as** the 'tipping point'. It revealed that 'since the ending of child removal many Aboriginal women and children were suffering more neglect, abuse and violence than before, because of ongoing problems associated with alcohol and pornography, sexual abuse, illicit drug use, poverty, illness, homelessness, unemployment and gambling'. She described the Intervention as 'the greatest opportunity we have had to overcome the systemic levels of disadvantage among Aboriginal Australians'. She noted that most of the factors contributing to the 'astonishing rates of rape and violence against women and children –rivers of grog, easy access to pornography, a lackadaisical approach in the court system with a callous disregard for victims were of long standing . . . and were undeniable, yet denied repeatedly by some Aboriginal men and women who ignored these issues in favour of pursuing theoretical definitions of rights'. However, the deniers had at times included Langton herself.

Langton began to direct more of her vitriol on to the Australian Left. She claimed that the Left had 'minimal impact' on the problems of Aboriginal people, because its members rarely strayed beyond the comfort of the cities. She even suggested that Aboriginal people living in rural Australia could have more points of connection with Pauline Hanson's supporters than with 'city-based leftists'.

'Left-wingers who see themselves as the defenders of Aborigines often do not know what they are talking about, and that their attitudes are not supported by the facts,' she said. She had 'abandoned any hope that the left could provide Aboriginal people with useful support . . . The left has a romantic set of universal values, such as solidarity and brotherhood, but outside the urban Western cafe society, where ideas have few consequences, these concepts disappoint: They let people down'.

She ridiculed 'SBS's house version of that compound of victimocracy, anti-Westernism and weird genetic theory that makes up ethnic identity politics'. No wonder Peter Sutton wrote, 'Marcia Langton's support for the Intervention was described to me by a liberal colleague as Marcia having "gone over to the other side"'. However, Langton continued to attack her earlier as well as her new targets as virulently as ever. She may have learnt something from Bob Hawke and Paul Keating, who, when they pursued policies detested by many on the ALP Left, would launch especially vitriolic attacks on the coalition, as an assurance to the Left that they were still loyal to socialist principles.

Typical of Langton's venom is a Chapter entitled 'Indigenous Affairs' in *Dear Mr Rudd: Ideas for a Better Australia,* edited by Robert Manne. Examples from its fourteen pages include the following:

> Bandied about by the unsavory characters who inhabit the murky purgatory between amateur history and fascism that is Australia's own denialist history school, there can be no doubt that some Australian governments deliberately and knowingly set out to eliminate the 'Aboriginal race'. Informed by proto-Nazi eugenicist thought, or put more simply, fruitcake ideas about racial purity and the duty of the white man to destroy the lesser races for the good of the nation, some governments set up breeding programmes to ensure that no so-called 'full bloods' ever 'mated' with 'half' or 'quarter' castes, and that 'part Aboriginal' people 'mated' only with lesser 'castes'.

> The denialists will not stop terrorizing the victims, nor does perverting the nation's history, but Rudd's leadership have the potential to relegate their falsehoods to the margins of the debate about our past.

> The nation would be healed if we could consign this history to our past by admitting that it was wrong to take children from their families in order to prevent Aboriginal ways of life and traditions from continuing.

Langton mocked Warren Snowden because he had:' apparently recently discovered after living there [The Northern Territory] for 30 years that there are no high schools for Aboriginal children to attend except in the mining towns and the highway towns. There are no schools. The little schools that exist in the remote communities are basically a one or two room affair'. (Sic) She described Dr Gary Johns as 'another opinion columnist' who 'thought he had the right to write about Aborigines.' Johns had been ALP Member of the House of Representatives between 1987 and 1996 and served as Special Minister of State, Assistant Minister for Industrial Relations, Parliamentary Secretary to the Treasurer, and Parliamentary Secretary to the Deputy Prime Minister.

Langton alleged that former chief ministers of the Northern Territory, Tuxworth and Stone,' contributed more than their fair share of race hate to the community.' She slighted 'The man who signed so many of the orders to remove children, the late Harry Giese . . . I once stared at Giese from across a room wondering how he could have been so cruel and why he was a kind of demi-god to the Country Liberal Party hard men.'

She wrote of 'the race-hatred wielded with callous deliberation and deviousness by Howard's regime. She alleged that. the terrible situation' faced by Aborigines was caused by the "terrible violence inflicted on Aboriginal people by colonial officers, police, missionaries and the general citizenry in an orgy of race-hatred."' Langton referred to

> 'The heart-breaking pain of the past 10 years, knowing that there has been a just acknowledgment of the crimes against them. There are no words that could heal the wounds of those people who were taken from their families by the Commonwealth and other Australian governments with no reason other than to deny them their Aboriginal legacy and hence the future of Aboriginal society.'

She did not reveal when and where this heart-breaking pain was inflicted during the 1990s and early 2000s which were by then 'the last ten years that "part Aboriginal" people "mated" only with lesser "castes"'

This was a total distortion of the historians she sees as her enemies and of Australian governmental policies; her comparison with Nazi racial policy is both ludicrous and offensive. The Nazi leadership aimed at a drastic reduction, if not the total physical destruction, of groups they hated, whereas for the last century and more there have been significant increases in the number of Australians identified as Aborigines

Langton had, initially at least, high hopes of John Howard's successors. She wrote in *New Matilda* that.

> With Howard and his class of haters now on the side-lines, it is finally possible to . . . rationally and calmly consider the potential benefits that might flow from shortening the funeral 'sorry camp' periods of confinement or limiting the impact of traditions such as 'house-cursing . . . and both respect traditions and provide a path to a safe and secure life.'

None of the numerous occasions for Aboriginal absence from work or school resulted from government policies, so it was unclear how they might be affected by changes in government in Canberra.

Langton called upon Kevin Rudd to set up a new federal watchdog to prevent misuse of commonwealth funding, particularly in the Northern Territory. She condemned the 'consultancy class' that was profiting hugely from their rides on the current 'hopeless gravy train' with 'six-figure salaries derived from commonwealth grants'. 'Labor mates' and members of the NT bureaucracy were, in her view, very prominent beneficiaries. She estimated that at least $50m was being creamed off the SHIP funding as administrative costs. However, persons likely to be appointed as Rudd's watchdogs were already members of, or affiliated to, that 'consultancy class'. Langton also called on the Commonwealth to grant contracts for Aboriginal housing and school building to 'well-run, highly accountable Aboriginal bodies such as local housing associations.' Unfortunately, few such associations exist.

In 2011 Langton denounced 'Larissa Behrendt's foul Twitter message about Bess Price's comments on the absence of rights for Aboriginal women in her community on ABC Television's Q&A program'. She described Behrendt's words as 'an exemplar of the wide cultural, moral and increasingly political rift between urban, left-wing, activist Aboriginal women and the bush women who witness the horrors of life in their communities, much of which is arrogantly denied by the former'.

Langton added:

> Whereas Bess, a grandmother who resides in Yuendumu, is a first-hand witness of terrifying violence against women, lives in one of Australia's poorest communities, and campaigns for the needs of women and children, especially their safety and everyday physical needs, professor and lawyer Larissa Behrendt lives in Sydney in relative luxury as compared with Bess's situation, has no children, has a PhD from Harvard and is the principal litigant in a case against conservative columnist Andrew Bolt, who published several columns accusing the 'fair-skinned' Behrendt and others of falsely claiming to be Aboriginal to get the perks. Australians, whether they support reconciliation or not, must be astonished at the viciousness of the twittering sepia-toned Sydney activists. Andrew Bolt should be rubbing his hands with glee—Behrendt has delivered on all of his stereotypes, and this time I have to wonder if he is not right after all . . . What indigenous or human rights, or for that matter civil rights, are Behrendt and her Twitter followers defending in this extraordinary exchange?

Larissa Behrendt had tweeted: 'I watched a show where a guy had sex with a horse and I'm sure it was less offensive than Bess Price.'

Langton stated:

> I have never in my life witnessed such extreme disrespect shown by a younger Aboriginal woman for an older Aboriginal woman, except where the perpetrator was severely intoxicated on drugs or alcohol. Nor have I witnessed, except once or twice, such snide dismissal by a younger Aboriginal woman of an older Aboriginal woman's right to express her

views. Those of us who were brought up in the Aboriginal way were taught from a young age to show respect for our elders and not to speak while they are speaking. This is a fundamental and universal law in Aboriginal societies.

Langton caused some anger among groups who once praised her. Her 2012 Boyle Lectures were overall sensible and constructive. She recalled that when her old friend and mentor W. E. H. Stanner delivered the Boyer Lectures in 1968, *After the Dreaming: Black And White Australians—An Anthropologist's View*, he implied that Aboriginal life was incompatible with modern economic life. Today, Langton argued, the expectation is quite the reverse. She drew attention to the hundreds of Aboriginal businesses and Aboriginal not-for-profit corporations that are succeeding in competitive conditions.

In 2012 Langton was unfairly criticized by *Crikey*, a journal that had been among her admirers before she supported the Howard 'Intervention'. Crikey claimed that Langton had failed to disclose that some research she had carried out was partly funded by three mining companies—Rio, Woodside, and Santos. Yet Langton was funded not only by mining companies but also by governments and universities. Her proposal for partnerships between indigenous schools and high performing interstate schools to enable more children to go to boarding schools is eminently sensible but has been condemned by some on the Left as the basis of creating a new Stolen Generation. She should have known that any deviation from political correctness was likely to be met with malice and distortion.

Marcia Langton has become a prominent role model for indigenous Australians, particularly students and women, who wish to engage in academic or political debate. She has shown great energy over the years and there is, in itself, no disgrace in changing one's mind, but at first sight it seems bizarre that she should be seen as a champion of 'reconciliation'. Civility in controversy is a virtue she has displayed only rarely. Yet recent actions such as her defense of Bess Price against the insult directed at her by Professor Larissa Behrendt show that Professor Langton may yet become a major unifying figure in Australian public life rather than a promoter of discord.

STUART MACINTYRE

Professor Stuart Macintyre is an active and influential author and teacher and has been for some three decades a leading figure in the interface between education and politics . . . With Henry Reynolds, he has probably been the most influential of the leaders of the 'black armband' school of historians who feel considerable shame at Australia's record in its treatment of immigrants and indigenous peoples.

Macintyre graduated from the University of Melbourne before completing a Master of Arts at Monash and a Doctorate of Philosophy at Cambridge University. He has held academic appointments at Melbourne, Cambridge, Murdoch, and the Australian National University. In 1990, he was appointed Ernest Scott Professor of History at the University of Melbourne and a Laureate Professor of that university in 2002. From 1999 to 2006, he was Dean of the Faculty of Arts. He has also held the Chair of Australian Studies at Harvard University. He has been President of the Academy of the Social Sciences in Australia, the Australian Historical Association, and the Humanities and Creative Arts panel of the Australian Research Council.

Towards the end of his *Concise History of Australia*, Macintyre compared his approach to history to that of Ernest Scott, in whose honour the chair Macintyre then held was named. According to Macintyre, 'The idea of the historian as an observer of events has since fallen into disrepute.' Macintyre added, 'The historian is now inside the history. Inextricably caught up in a continuous making and remaking of the past.' That assumption is open to challenge. Many of us would prefer it if he sought, as R. G. Collingwood advised, to get into the inside of the minds of others or, as I advise, to apply a form of contingent moral absolutism: to hold principles consistently, but to take fully into account the historical contexts that handicap or facilitate the formation and execution of moral action. It may seem strange that a former Marxist should have travelled theoretically so far from the objectivity claimed for Marx's 'historical materialism'. Perhaps it is a consequence of dismay that history has not worked out as expected. It is not advanced capitalism that collapsed, but backward communism. Nearly every prophesy Macintyre once made, as I did in England just a little before his time, has been totally discredited.

Professor Samantha Young claimed that 'studies of Australian history' can be said to fit in one of two boats: the left and the right. This distinction could also be framed as the republican versus the monarchist or the nationalist and the British loyalist. One objection to this is that many Australians have successfully combined, as many still do, loyalty to Australia and to its monarchy. Another objection concerns the fluidity of terms such as Right and Left. It is not just that people change their positions, but that positions also change: Doctrines once thought constitutive of one camp are replaced by other policies, sometimes of a completely different character. The White Australia policy was an obvious twentieth-century example of the change of heart of most Australian Left historians during the 1970s.

Macintyre may also have failed to examine with sufficient care the meaning of 'self-determination' of indigenous Australians that he claimed to support. Do non-Aborigines enjoy self-determination and, more importantly, do they enjoy more of it than the indigenous? Does it mean equal rights of citizenship or exclusion or separation of some kind? Are Aborigines to become more like other Australians or remain permanently very different, with much less desirable conditions of life? And who are the indigenous and non-indigenous, when some 80 per cent of Australians classified as indigenous are of mixed descent, often with a preponderance of non-indigenous genes? Despite his disputes with Andrew Bolt, I hope that Macintyre would agree that any linkage of citizenship status to genes would be deplorable. My hopes are strengthened when I recall the report of the Civics Expert Group over which he presided in 1994.

> As we approach the centenary of the Commonwealth, Australians are able to look back on a remarkably successful record of democratic self-government. The public institutions created in the closing years of the last century have proved flexible and resilient. The outcomes of the democratic process enjoy popular acceptance—in contrast to the experience of most other countries, we seldom experienced a challenge to the legitimacy of our civil order or resorted to violence. The political process has operated peaceably. A broad measure of freedoms has been maintained and extended. The rule of law operates. There is a high level of tolerance and acceptance.

In *A Historian's Conscience*, edited by Macintyre in 2004, he castigated John Howard for asserting that for him the balance sheet of Australian history is 'overwhelmingly a positive one'. This, Macintyre held, was to turn a blind eye to Australia's greatest shame, the many injustices and indignities inflicted on its indigenous people' and 'attacked the ethics and principles of the country's historians, those at least whose work raised uncomfortable questions about the past'. I expect that Professor Macintyre has made league tables with states taking the place of teams: I wonder which countries he would place above Australia as having a developed civil society, high living standards, and, despite the beat-ups about frontier wars, a remarkable record of internal peace. Does he not notice on his travels to conferences that most of the cities he visits have far more men in uniform on the streets than is the case with cities in the Anglosphere?

Stuart Macintyre is among the most influential writers on communism in Australia. He has been attacked as much by factional rivals such as the late Bob Gould, who described it as an 'essentially Stalinist company history of Australian Communism' as by anti-Communists, but his account is often insightful. Macintyre's *The Reds,* published in 1998 well after the collapse of the Soviet system in Europe, takes the Communist Party of Australia from its foundation to the German invasion of the Soviet Union in 1941. To outsiders, that may seem an odd date at which to end, but the fortunes and policies of the Australian Party were very dependent on Soviet directives. Between 1939 and 1941, they had denounced the war against Germany as an imperialist struggle in which the working class had no interest. This anti-war line had itself been a sudden departure from the anti-fascist/popular front line of the 1930s and had led to many resignations and lapses. After June 1941, the courage of the population and the strong resistance of the Red Army created admiration among many people in the Western states at war with Hitler: In consequence, the Australian Party reached its highest numbers ever by 1945 when Hitler was finally defeated.

Macintyre became convinced that it had become 'apparent to all but those most impervious to reason that the communist project itself was deeply flawed, that it nurtured tyranny within its emancipatory scheme'. Other ex-Communists blamed evil individuals or factions who had been allowed to gain control of the party apparatus. Macintyre gave valuable insights into why people joined the party and why they left it. Most joined because they believed that capitalism was the cause of unnecessary wars and unemployment and inequality. They were prepared for some unpleasantness on the road to socialism or communism, since omelettes could not be cooked without breaking a few eggs and because the casualties of the prolonged revolution were bound to be fewer than those of imperialist wars that the coming of communism would bring to an end.

They left because Soviet policies, such as the Moscow Trials, the 1939 Treaty with Hitler, and the revelations by Krushchev of accusations of mass brutality and murder, so long denied by the faithful, were in fact true. There were also strong disagreements on internal matters: Some comrades thought the leadership too opportunistic, others too sectarian. Some wanted to work in the wider labor movement, but others wished to concentrate on the special needs of the party. Many must have shared with me the growing conviction that it was not the foul means we had so often tried to justify that was the problem, but the end itself. The Soviet Union and the states under its tutelage seemed as far distant as ever from what we had conceived as socialism or communism that we were no longer prepared to sacrifice much of our lives to its eventual achievement. The more optimistic accused us of possessing too limited a view of historical change.

Macintyre showed how different was the Communist Party from other Australian political organizations. Almost all of a party member's life was related to the fight for socialism and the class struggle; political lessons were to be drawn from every experience. To be a party member was to subject oneself to 'democratic centralism': There could be discussion before the party line was established, but then absolute discipline was required in its pursuit. Thanks to the Moscow Gold long denied to exist, the British and Australian Communist Parties could appoint full-time officials, and many comrades gained leading paid positions in trade unions and were expected to contribute to party funds from their salaries. By 1939 in Australia, 'there were communist headquarters in every city, hundreds of suburban branches conducted their regular "cottage meetings" AND the party published a four-page newspaper.

Soon it sustained a whole spectrum of alternative cultural activity', including choirs and dances. Unlike the early 1950s, just before the Krushchev revelations, when the party boasted numerous intellectuals and university teachers, the pre-war party was essentially proletarian. It was dominant in several powerful trade unions and at trade halls. Macintyre portrayed the strong sense of comradeship generated by party membership, which often turned to bitter hatred after a defection or failure to carry out the party policy. Concentration on party work could also isolate profoundly.

Life as a communist teacher must have been quite similar in England and Australia. I met an Australian couple at the Moscow World Youth Festival in 1957. I was elected to speak on behalf of young British teachers when, after the festival, party comrades and a few others on whom we checked as diligently as we could were invited to visit Leningrad and Kiev. We visited a few schools, all of which were exemplary. That could have been made easier by the festival taking place during the long school holiday, so that the pupils occupying the desks were either keen volunteers or specially roped in because they gave a good impression. My then wife, who later became National President of the National Union of Teachers of England and Wales, and I had a chance to compare notes with the Australian couple. Macintyre's account of party life in Australia seemed authentic enough to me. What I would have appreciated was more on the effect of living what were almost double lives: not in the sense of spying for the Soviet Union and the like, but because the belief system within party circles was so different from that outside it.

In my experience, particularly when the going was bad, usually because Soviet or Chinese policy had aroused rancour and criticism, some comrades became secretive and embittered: They felt they had given up a lot in terms of friendships and careers, but with little to show for it. Within small groups, the contrast was often sharp between the haters (not only of the capitalist system but also of most of the people within it as well) and the ardent lovers of the human race who were usually confident that the situation was ripening for a critical advance of the progressive forces. In England, their favourite author was Palme Dutt, from whose editorials in *Labor Monthly* reassurances that a critical change was about to take place in capitalism societies nearly always came.

Then there were the few who managed to deal easily with tensions and complications and were our stars in the 'broad movement', although not always regarded as the deepest thinkers on industrial tactics or Marxist dialectics. Macintyre seemed to have been able to keep friendships even at times of bitter political disputation and to provide leadership to a group that would contain more than the average proportion of the prickly and eccentric. I should not be too critical of Macintyre here: He provided more insights into party life than did most ex-communists in their memoires.

Macintyre exaggerated the oppressiveness of the Australian security agencies, but who on the Left does not? He let pass hypocrisy in arguments in favour of civil liberties in Australia by defenders of real 'police states'. He called Evatt's opposition to the Anti-Communist Bill of 1951–2 his 'finest hour' and condemned the Royal Commission into the Petrov allegations as 'partial'. Macintyre conceded that Evatt's response was 'intemperate', but overall he was very lenient on 'The Doc', whom he probably regarded as a not very useful idiot. Macintyre was highly critical of the Roman Catholic politicians who formed the Democratic Labor Party (DLP) after the 'split' and kept Menzies and his successors in the coalition leadership in office for nearly a generation . . . A more balanced picture is given in Robert Murray's The Split, but Macintyre's own assessments are well within the range of scholarly acceptability . . .

Bob Carr, the former Premier of New South Wales and currently Foreign Secretary, scoffed at Manning Clark's 'over-reliance, in describing Australia in the 1920s, on the newspapers of the Marxist Left. It would be like writing a history of Australia in the 1970s from yellowing copies of *Tribune* and *Direct Action*'. Carr found Macintyre even less balanced than Clark. Carr wrote:

> An even more extreme example, Stuart Macintyre *in A Concise History of Australia* has no index listing for McKell [Sir William—Premier of New South Wales and only the second Governor-General of Australian birth]. Yet he devotes more than twenty pages to the Communist Party. This shows an exasperating neglect of the real life of the country, reflected much of the time in the reformist politics championed by the democratic Left—the ALP and non-communist union leaders—and so often achieved at State level.

Macintyre shares a trait possessed by many Australian intellectuals. They claim that all education is necessarily political, but then object like naive choirboys if any challenge is made to their political grip. In 2006, the usually tolerant and naive Brendon Nelson was the objective of Macintyre's concern for academic rectitude, because as education minister he actually intervened to veto a few grants. Macintyre described the sufferers as 'victims of a form of political interference in the system of national competitive grants that is unique to this country'. One does not need to be a conspiracy theorist to suspect that extraneous conditions play a major part in research grants in this country (and in many others of course).

Macintyre has often called for greater popular participation in education and government more widely, but apparently he saw no role for cabinet ministers and other elected politicians to comment on the supposed relevance of research proposals. I would reckon outsiders like Nelson and even Gillard to be more objective than the 'peer group' of old chums who currently subsidize each other.

It is difficult to reach a satisfactory balance between the various contenders for political and administrative power, but we often find that when X are in office, the cry is for them to exercise democratic control, but when non-X have power, then the call is for impartial professionals and experts to make the decisions. Apparent victims of Brendon Nelson included Mark McKenna, described by Macintyre as an 'outstanding historian', who had his application for a fellowship to write a biography of Manning Clark rejected. There has been no shortage of biographers of Manning Clark, who did not receive fellowships for the purpose, but Macintyre was proved right that money spent on McKenna would be fully justified.

The 'History Wars' took shape in that name in May 1984 when a letter appeared in the Melbourne *Age* and other national newspapers signed by twenty-four staff members, including Macintyre, of the Department of History at the University of Melbourne. The letter dissociated its authors from public views expressed about immigrant numbers and composition by Geoffrey Blainey, then Ernest Scott Professor of History and Dean of the Faculty of Arts. The correspondents alleged that Blainey's claim that any Australians feared that Asian immigration was too large and too rapid in several cities was racist and incendiary. Picketing, mainly by Melbourne University students but with considerable outside support and other organized action, made it well-nigh impossible for Blainey to lecture on campus. His speeches and lectures at the university for the rest of the year had to be cancelled at the request of the university authorities. Blainey resigned from the university at the end of 1988. Several years later, Stuart Macintyre, by then himself Ernest Scott Professor of History, wrote belatedly:

> Blainey is not a racist and he was understandably indignant when accused of racial prejudice. Nor was he prejudiced against Asians. He had a long-standing interest in East Asia and a particular respect for its peoples. He had welcomed the abandonment of the White Australia Policy and he supported immigration from Asia, only in reduced numbers and altered expectations. He did not propose exclusion on grounds of race but, rather, was concerned with the incorporation of immigrants into the host society.

Macintyre has alleged personal suffering from 'the technique of vilification'. One example is given below:

> On the morning of the launch of my book the Australian ran a feature article that presented me as a godfather who controlled and intimidated other historians, and implied that I have acted corruptly within the Australian Research Council . . . Some days later a paragraph appeared in a column of the *Daily Telegraph*, alleging that more than ten years ago, when the *Melbourne Herald-Sun* was campaigning against the Victorian

Labor government and I was involved in a protest campaign against press bias, I had used the stationery of the University of Melbourne until I was dissuaded. Such are the tactics of the History Warriors. It is a tactic of personal denigration that is designed to discredit an opponent.

Our old Soviet comrades would not have known whether to laugh or cry at this extremity in the annals of political persecution. The big problem in Australia today is not that research grants are distributed unfairly, or that, as with Blainey, extraneous matters may prevent the proper execution of academic duties, but that in humanities and social sciences it seems virtually impossible for the politically suspect to get any academic appointments. Even the best of the politically incorrect are unlikely to make it to the short list.

Macintyre, in common with many history professors and in lesser light, made a point of disparaging the amateur and journalistic ways of their opponents with their own meticulous adherence to detail. Macintyre wrote: 'History is also a profession, which teaches and conducts research; and here the most powerful force is the principle of peer assessment. Peer assessment, by examination of research theses, refereeing of books and articles, and appraisal of applications for research grants both enforces standards and shapes the topics.' However, Macintyre himself has frequently conflated references at the end of long paragraphs, thus making it very difficult for the reader to check a reference. This practice was even more marked in the writings of Manning Clark. Although many who praise Clark's work publicly deride it in private, his iconic stature as the chief prophet and intellectual produced by the Australian Left still finds him many public defenders. Macintyre has been among the most zealous. One has to concede further that average history graduates do not possess many special skills that would separate them clearly from interested amateurs, few have archival or statistical skills, and many do not speak or read a language other than their mother tongue.

When Peter Ryan, formerly publisher at Melbourne University Press of Clark's six-volume *History of Australia,* wrote a few months after Clark's death that the work was mediocre and a reproach to the press—and to Ryan, personally, he had become convinced that he should have spoken out earlier—Macintyre accused Ryan of personal cowardice for publishing his criticism only after Clark had died. Robert Manne, then editor of *Quadrant,* in which Ryan's critique appeared, testified that Macintyre's accusation was false, even 'almost self-evidently'. Ryan had discussed such an article with Manne whilst Manning Clark was still alive. The accusation of cowardice was particularly bizarre, since Macintyre, like Clark, probably never touched a toy gun, whereas Ryan served with conspicuous gallantry in New Guinea in the jungle and mountains. It seems very unlikely that Clark was ever a Soviet spy, since he was too volatile and unreliable to be trusted in such a role. It must have come as a shock to Macintyre and many others likeminded when Mark McKenna's biography of Clark was even more damning of Clark than Ryan's memoir had been. His relationship with young female academics and his invention of being an eyewitness in 1938 of the Krystallnacht, although he was not even in Germany then, undermined confidence in many of his other tales.

Macintyre sometimes erected straw men in order to knock them down and admitted to minor faults on the Left in order to demonstrate his impartiality when defending them against more serious charges. For example, he conceded that an official of the Communist Party had made recruits for Soviet intelligence who passed on information, but Macintyre claimed that this was a patriotic act, based on the belief that the Soviet Union as an ally of Australia should not be excluded from knowledge available to other members of the alliance. However, Australian communists who spied for the Soviet Union were rarely recruited when Australia was in alliance with the Soviet Union after 1941. Soviet intelligence was suspicious of using people who had not been tested when the communist cause was at its most unpopular.

Macintyre has also been energetic in the promotion of the study of history, particularly of Australian history in both schools and universities. In the University of Melbourne, he, by no means solely, gained significant early successes that included the establishment of an 'Australian centre', seeped in radical ideology and taught mainly by academics who shared his opinions. Largely under Macintyre's leadership, the Left also won almost complete control of the history and other humanities departments. However, the mass of students were less captivated than their radical lecturers. According to Professor Mark Considine, successor to Macintyre as Dean of Arts, the total number of student at the Australia Centre had fallen to 38 per cent to ninety-six students in 2010, and the fall in undergraduate numbers had been steeper at 44 per cent to just sixty-eight students. The total full-time student load for history fell to 17 per cent from 2007 to 533 students in 2010.

Professor Considine decided the situation was bad enough to commission a formal investigation. The inquiry recommended complete extinction of teaching in the Australian Centre, although research already commissioned could be completed, and the undergraduate major in Australian studies was no longer a high enough priority to warrant the amount of resources that it was using. Professor Considine rejected claims that the decline in student enrolment in Australian history courses reflected a general lack of interest in Australian history, but rather a demand for that history to be taught in the context of global issues. However, belief was widespread that accusations of excessive radicalism had reduced the scholarly standing of the Australian Centre and of University of Melbourne humanities courses as a whole. Macintyre led a doughty rear-guard battle but with little success. It was a blow, since he had championed radical courses and anticipated they would attract larger student numbers, but by the turn of the century, thousands of Australian students were satiated with denunciations of their sinful national past. The official report claimed that the curriculum did not 'appeal as much as it should'. A few students became militant enthusiasts, but the majority were determined to get well away from any more such courses. Permanent staff in history fell from about thirty-five in 2002 to twenty-three in 2010.

Macintyre had mixed fortune, too, in his work on school history. He was appointed by the Keating Labor government in 1994 to chair its Civics Experts Group; its report was overall sensible and defensible. He remained a member of the Civics Education Group under John Howard's government, whose then Minister for Education, David Kemp, appointed him in 1999–2000 to chair an inquiry into school history. Macintyre did not bring much Marxist doctrine into his curriculum proposals, but he is a centralizer who is attached, like many other scholars and politicians unfortunately, to a mandatory national curriculum in history, indeed in every major curriculum area. There is no case for such a national curriculum in history.

The 'History Summit' summoned by the then Education Minister Julie Bishop in 2007 took place after the history wars had been waged for several years. The strange response of Julie Bishop was to exclude the leading figures on both sides from the 'summit' in order to avoid extremism! If not Hamlet without the Prince of Denmark, the absence of Macintyre and Henry Reynolds on one side and Keith Windschuttle and Patrick McGuinness on the other made it like Julius Caesar without Brutus, Mark Anthony, and Cassius, as well as Caesar himself. Even my own presence did not make up for their absence. Macintyre expressed disappointment at the failure of all those consulted at the summit and later by the Rudd ALP government to agree on the content of a national history syllabus and how to teach it. It would have been a much bigger worry if there had been consensus. Better to have a few unsatisfactory school syllabuses rather than centrally directed uniformity.

ROBERT MANNE

Robert Manne's parents were Jewish refugees from Europe. He encountered no anti-Semitism during a happy childhood in the Melbourne suburbs. He never met any Aborigines, and the first he heard of them, he claimed, was 'William Dampier's description of them as "The most miserable people in the world"'. The adult Manne commented, 'I would like to think that intuitively I grasped their [the words'] racism, but I doubt whether that was so.' Apparently Manne never considered that Dampier may have been entirely objective and that those Aborigines were 'more wretched in condition' than any of the other numerous peoples he had met. After all, some people had to occupy that place if you put that question to yourself.

Manne's parents voted for ALP, and his first political hero was Gough Whitlam and his first cause multiculturalism. Manne's last political act at Melbourne

University was to carry a banner that read 'Neither Washington or Hanoi'. Why then did Manne associate with Liberals, Australian conservatives, and send his essays to the conservative magazine *Quadrant* for publication? Manne attributed his political direction then to the influence of Frank Knopfelmacher and Vincent Buckley, as well as his growing knowledge of the Holocaust, during which one of his grandparents was murdered. But many social-democrats and socialists as well as conservatives were anti-communist; that number included several important figures in the organizations that published *Quadrant* in Australia and journals like Encounter elsewhere. A reasonable speculation is that Manne looked at the large number of bright young men and women in the Socialist and Labor clubs and also at the small number of such young people at Liberal or other conservative meetings and saw where the main chance lay for rapid advancement. Manne got it right: The student and post-graduate would-be intellectuals continued to be thick on the ground among left-wingers, but were precious rarities on the right.

So when I first wrote in *Quadrant* in 1980, Robert Manne was not only an established contributor but also a rising star in the liberal-conservative political skies. During the 1980s, Manne wrote an excellent book on the Petrov Affair and good articles in *Quadrant* on Wilfred Burchett, David Combe, and others, whose activities deserved close scrutiny. His possible limitations were exposed in a book he edited called New Conservatism in Australia: It left readers little the wiser as to what might constitute 'new Conservatism' in Australia or even who these 'new Conservatives' might be. Lacking, too, was any consideration of the economic basis of Australian society or of fiscal and economic policy. Manne disarmingly admitted to 'having no competence in economics whatever'. This did not appear to concern him or to prevent him from pontificating on tricky issues in economic theory.

Manne and I were involved in a peculiar situation in Sydney sometime in the mid-1980s. He, Frank Knopfelmacher, and I were all invited to speak at a conference which even Blind Freddy must have understood was organized by a front organizations for the Unification Church, better known as the Moonies from the name assumed by its Lady President, wife of Reverend Sun. Knopfelmacher and I gave our papers on the first morning of the conference. Rob Manne was programmed to speak in the afternoon. During the lunch break, he rushed up to Knopfelmacher and me to inform us who the organizers of the event were. We nodded and agreed that was so, but we both believed in preaching to the unbelievers as well as to the saved (the reverse from the Moony standpoint, of course). Manne seemed in dire distress and exclaimed that it would be disastrous for his political career were it to be known publicly that he had addressed such a gathering. And off he went. Knopfelmacher and I had no political careers to wreck, and I doubt whether anybody would have bothered much had it become known what company Manne kept. It showed me that he was capable of changes of mind and did not always do his homework thoroughly.

Manne either had a Damascus road type of experience after appointment as Editor of *Quadrant* or envisaged from the start a coup which would deprive people he already detested of a useful weapon in their armoury. If the *Quadrant* Board had anticipated that Manne's main themes as editor would be denunciation of economic rationalism and free trade, agitation to combat climate change, and allegations of Australia's past oppression of, and even genocide against, Aborigines, he would never have been appointed editor.

Once Editor of *Quadrant,* Manne alleged that 'adherents of the doctrine of laissez-faire are almost as devoted to Adam Smith as the left once was to Karl Marx'. He claimed that the Order of Lenin, supposed by some to have been awarded to Manning Clark for major services to the Soviet Union, had been confused with an inferior award, but if a prominent Australian, say John Howard, had been awarded any medal, high or low, by say General Pinochet, Manne would not have dismissed the incident so lightly

Many were surprised when, after years in which he had been polite in controversy, even mannerly, Manne lapsed into crude invective. He accused P. P. McGuinness of 'atrocity denialism in the David Irving mode' and described Pauline Hanson as a 'painfully inarticulate woman of sullen resentment and stubborn defiance'. Nobody else, in Manne's view, could have 'put the case for the rule of an enlightened elite against the prejudices of the benighted mass so unselfconsciously'. Manne seemed unable to write down the names of Andrew Bolt or Keith Windschuttle without adding an insult.

Manne's attacks on Helen Demidenko became paranoid. He moved from reasonable criticism of her mixing fact with fiction to denial that there had ever been such a thing as 'Jewish-Bolshevism'. Yet he knew that virtually the entire communist apparatus in Ukraine had been Jews and that they were killed in the purge of 1937, together with several of Lenin's closest Jewish comrades—Zinoviev, Kamenev, Radek, and thousands of their supporters in the party. Stalin tried to make them the scapegoats for the Ukrainian famine and associated disaster. The earlier unjust sufferings of Jews at the hands of Russian Tsars and Ukrainian nationalists did not reduce the pain of the later sufferings of Ukrainians under Soviet rule, nor did the murder of the Jewish old Bolsheviks by Stalin made their role in Ukraine any better in retrospect.

Perhaps more worrying still was Manne's comment about the arguments of Demidenko's critics. 'It does not matter here whether some of these arguments were wholly or partly true. All that matters is that such views were held sincerely by a number of those who had read The Hand with attentiveness and care.' Several priests who led pogroms against Jews during the Black Death of the 1340s and on other such occasions sincerely believed that Jews had deliberately spread the plague. Would their sincerity have been sufficient for Manne to defend those priests?

On the domestic front, Manne noted the high correlation between, on the one hand, opposition to an Australian republic and mass immigration with 'low levels of education and wealth' on the other. 'Ministers of religion, artists, academics journalists, welfare agencies, virtually every association of doctors and psychiatrists were for the great Australian republic, but were outvoted by an ignorant mob. Like many intellectuals before him, Robert Manne loves the people but does not trust them to identify their own best interests. He places the vulgar 'will of each' well below the 'good of all' that is determined by the general will, itself to be interpreted by public intellectuals such as himself and Raimond Gaita.

There were few continuities that one could perceive in Manne's ideas, but one concerned his own profession, a concern that most people treat in a responsible way. His support for the increase in higher education places was tempered by concern about its student quality. As late as 2002, Manne admitted that, although every new university year he encountered groups of first-year students of whom a sizeable minority were satisfactory, the majority were not. The unsatisfactory fell into two types: 'One group soon drop out of their studies . . . Another group of students pursue their studies to the end', but 'they are not really curious about what they are studying . . . Their essays are genuinely distressing to read. I am always puzzled about what has happened to these students during their twelve long years at school'. Not long afterwards, however Manne was denouncing the Howard government for university 'cuts', even though student numbers continued to increase under the coalition.

Manne accused *The Australian* of 'protracted character assassination' of Aboriginal lawyer and activist Larissa Behrendt because it reported how Behrendt tweeted that watching a show 'where a guy had sex with a horse' was less offensive than Bess Price. Manne dismissed Behrendt's words as only a 'sour joke'. He suggested that the tweet was done 'forgetting it would go public. No offence was intended. The apology should have settled the issue'. Yet Manne was unwilling to excuse Andrew Bolt's queries about the Aboriginality of people who do not look or act like the large majority of Aborigines.

Manne has been notably inconsistent on expertise and authority. He has demanded that all 'non-scientists' should accept the 'consensus among scientists' about global warming and its human cause. He has denounced non-experts such as Cardinal Pell for intervening in a matter about which he has no special knowledge, although Manne does not apply that limitation to himself or, say, former Vice-president Gore. Manne argued that there is a genuine consensus among scientists so that debate between unqualified people is foolish and might have disastrous consequences.

Manne once feared that the Geoffrey Blainey case implied that 'academics in Australia, by and large, will not tolerate arguments concerning the ethnic composition of our migrant intake' and that researchers would not 'publicize research that took the view that institutional day-care for babies did them significant harm. And so on.' Yet he joined the ranks of the would-be censors.

Manne posed as a Dreyfus of his time, persecuted by, not the army or gendarmerie, but the Murdoch Press. Throughout his disputes with *The Australian,* Manne enjoyed the security of professorial tenure, but he seemed to feel it an affront that his every message should not appear in its pages.

Manne claimed *The Australian* was damaging the country and undermining true journalism by publishing material he believed should be repressed, such as stories critical of the Rudd government. Many other people would have felt some shame after the plotters of Rudd's overthrow attacked him in even more vigorous terms than had *The Australian.* Manne also condemned that newspaper for giving space to Keith Windschuttle to deny the 'almost uncontested common wisdom' that Australia was founded on genocide.

In 1990, Manne denounced 'the unprovoked aggression by Iraq against a weak, peaceable and stable neighbour, Kuwait', together with the 'crimes of Saddam Hussein: his gassings of Kurdish villages . . . and his horrid and futile war against Iran, which cost the lives of perhaps half a million of his own people'. By 2000, Manne was stating confidently that 'Iraq possessed no WMD' and that '11 September was exclusively the work of al-Qaeda'.

Manne attempted in *Bad News* to show that the bar *The Australian* set for Iraq was unfairly high. In 2004 he wrote, 'Under Howard, Australia had been involved in an unprovoked invasion of Iraq without a UN mandate to disarm a country of weapons it did not possess.' Yet in 2003, Manne had accepted the verdict of the Australian with most experience on the matter, Richard Butler, a man of long-term left-wing beliefs.

Butler had stated bluntly:

> Iraq does have weapons of mass destruction. There's no question of it, and that is serious. And Iraq's current stance with respect to this final opportunity they've been given to be disarmed is actually to cheat. The declaration of their weapons is not honest and the conduct of some 400 inspectors that have stayed on the case in recent times has been superficial and inconsequential. So there is a problem, a serious problem, that needs to be addressed, not only because of the problem of weapons of mass destruction but because . . . the Security Council of the United Nations has endangered its own credibility and future.

Butler bemoaned the 'absence of a mechanism' to ensure that international treaties are observed, but even as he called for a new world council 'to enforce the law', Saddam Hussein was successfully organizing wholesale evasion of the Food for Arms arrangements made by the UN. Leading figures in the UN were profiting from these evasions. As each week went by, Saddam became more confident that he could defy with impunity the terms of the armistice and interim peace treaty he had signed.

The weapons of mass destruction that Butler and other authorities expected to be found in Iraq were not found. Whether Saddam Hussein was carrying out a game of double bluff or whether weapons were moved to safe hiding inside or outside Iraq remains uncertain. The West, including Australia, had to choose between two evils: war on Saddam or his retention of absolute power and continued support for terrorist activity. Despite all the setbacks since his overthrow, the attempt to establish civil society in Iraq and to reduce terrorist threats was the better course of action. Had a defiant Saddam continued in power, Gaddafi would not have modified his anti-Western policies, and no Arab Spring would have begun, even though it may would reach summer in any Arab state.

In addition to planning to eliminate Aborigines from Australia, Australian governments, or at least that of John Howard, were in Manne's imagination also plotting to get rid of a large number of the rest of us by failing to prevent massive increases in temperature caused by human activity. The population level might have been partially maintained by mass immigration, but the Howard government tried to stop that as well. Australians who voted for Howard did so for the similar reasons that many of them voted earlier for Pauline Hanson. Manne wondered how Australians could countenance the Howard government 'behaving in regard to asylum seekers with a level of cruelty and indifference they had once assumed no Australian government ever would'. How could the ALP have elected as leader a man who, just like John Howard, 'barely wanted to think about the idea of multiculturalism'? How could Mark Latham, in whom Manne had once placed his hopes, decide that 'Philip Adams, the emblematic figurehead of the pro-Labor left intelligentsia, had no place inside the ALP'? Most of all, however, why had John Howard been sent to terrorize the Australian people.

In the November 2008 issue of *The Monthly*, Manne declared that he had 'become a Ruddite'. In *The Weekend Australian* on 26–27 June 2010—just after Julia Gillard became prime minister—he ridiculed Rudd's 'hyperactive, controlling, hectoring and interfering' temperament. Manne claimed then that Rudd lacked a 'native political instinct', exhibited a 'manic work ethic', and lacked 'political touch'. In less than two years, Manne had gone from being a Ruddite to depicting the former prime minister as a hectoring, manic, control freak devoid of political skills.

PAT O'SHANE

However hard I tried, I doubt whether I could ever review any book as savagely as some of my own have been. There are some subjects dangerous even for the informed insider to pontificate about, let alone the naive outsider. This I realized rather too late in the day was the case with writing about the past or present of indigenous Australians. I had some warnings, since some comments on my 1986 *The Australian Nation: Its British and Irish Roots* showed that it did not thrill all who read it, but it was a book on 'Nugget' Coombs, Paul Hasluck, and Aboriginal policies that really incensed some readers. I say readers, since it was almost impossible for some of the critics to have read any of the book at all. However, the two most hostile reviews were by indigenous women who had certainly opened its pages, even if they had not forced themselves to read it from cover to cover.

Nobody is entitled to demand that others should read what they write, let alone praise it. If you don't like the heat, don't go into the kitchen. In later years, one may sometimes come round to the viewpoint of even the most ferocious critics. I did within a few years of ceasing to be a communist and a Marxist. I felt some sympathy with Pat O'Shane when I came across today (13 November 2012) her very hostile review in 1996 of a book I wrote then called *Hasluck Versus Coombs: White Politics and Australia's Aborigines.*

Although she was supposedly reviewing my book, Pat did not mention it by name in the first half of the review. Instead she gave a graphic account of methods employed in 'protection' system in most of the Australian colonies in the nineteenth century (and in the states that they became in the twentieth) They made every Aborigine, man, woman, and child, a ward of the state and subject to the orders of a protector and his assistants or those of Christian missionaries in the case of Aborigines on mission stations.

It struck me that Pat had not bothered to read much of my book, because I went to some trouble to show that Paul Hasluck entered Aboriginal politics with the intention of ending the protection system. I quoted fairly lengthy passages in which Hasluck objected in terms not very different from those of Pat that the system in place treated every indigenous Australian as little better than an imbecile and that this situation should end. His aim was to exclude 'race' from the statute book. If a person needed protection, as some did, that was an individual matter and could not justly be based on any racial classification. In fact, if Pat were to read again what she wrote in 1996, she would find that she was arguing the case in which Andrew Bolt was recently sentenced as a criminal for maintaining in 2012: that no Australian citizen should have fewer or more rights and privileges in law than any other on the basis of racial identity.

Pat retold some nasty crimes committed against Aborigines. She then sternly admonished me on the grounds that 'he does not once mention those incidents'. Now that is true, since neither Coombs nor Hasluck had any part whatsoever in outrages against Aboriginal people, as Pat, I am sure, would concede.

She added that my references were 'narrow and mostly by Paul Hasluck and H. C. Coombs'. She listed many types of document that I did not cite. I can only plead that my task in that book, clearly indicated in its title, was to compare the policies advocated by those two men, not to write an account of Aboriginal policy from 1788 to the 1990s.

Pat O'Shane may have been more pertinent when she claimed that my 'arguments, to the extent that they might be so called, are fatuous, cheap and shallow'. That they may have been, but it seems a pity that Pat did not provide a single example of their fatuity. Pat had some suspicions about my motives in writing the book. She suggested that 'in the present climate of social disharmony and divisiveness being fostered by our incumbent political masters, there are those who will eagerly grasp what Partington has written and wave it like a rallying standard'. I did not observe anyone doing that, but I did receive a fair number of compliments for the book, modest as it was in its intentions and execution. I received not a cent for writing it and actually completed it in Fiji, where I went to teach after Flinders University made me an offer I could not refuse to take early retirement at the age of sixty-four. The University of the South Pacific in Suva had its merits, but access to Australian government documents was not among them and, as I admitted at the time, I was forced to rely on secondary sources, except in Aboriginal Education, which I had studied in some depth.

Pat expressed the hope that the Australian people 'are not prepared to let this rubbish become the received wisdom in this society'. I have to admit that my writing on Aboriginal education has not become received wisdom. Indeed, attitudes very much like that expressed by Pat dominate Aboriginal policies today. On the other hand the book influenced several people to support a unified Australia rather than one divided by race and culture

My main concern after rereading Pat's savage criticism is that any young scholars trying to make their way in the world would think twice about writing anything at all about Aboriginal policies. I am too old to be affected by praise or censure, but many young and insecure scholars may well be intimidated by fear of legal action and administrative sanctions in their own institutions if they were to write only one careless sentence from which closet racism may be imputed.

HENRY REYNOLDS

Tasmanian-born Henry Reynolds was educated in state schools and the University of Tasmania where he gained BA and MA degrees. He taught in secondary schools in Australia and England. After returning to Australia in 1964, he became a lecturer and then professor in James Cook University, where he received his doctorate in history. He then took up Australian Research Council positions at the University of Tasmania in Launceston.

Reynolds has received many awards and honours, including: the Ernest Scott Historical Prize, the Harold White Fellowship at National Library of Australia, the Human Rights and Equal Opportunity Commission Arts Award, the Australian Book Council and Banjo Awards for non-fiction, the Queensland Premier's Literary Awards, and the Harry Williams Award for *Why Weren't We Told?* and with Professor Marilyn Lake for Drawing the Global Colour Line. Many of Reynolds's books have been used extensively in history courses across the country and have regularly reached the Top Ten bestseller lists.

Reynolds made a baseless attack on Geoffrey Blainey during the 1984 Affair. He declared:

> Literary panache and reputation as a gadfly have disguised just how conservative and conventional much of [Blainey's] writing is. He tells the story of European pioneering—of settlers fighting forest and flood, drought and distance; of thrusting entrepreneurs; of material progress. It is primarily a struggle against nature. It is heroic and apolitical. Conflict of class, race and gender are largely ignored. Throughout there is a boyish enthusiasm for outdoor adventure. Rattling good yarns proliferate, and while the prose is modern, the enthusiasms are Edwardian.

Reynolds said that Blainey 'had lost the respect of practically the whole profession' through his intervention in the immigration debate. Hence, a whole team got together with the jackhammers . . . What you've got to expect if you engage in that sort of public controversy is that you are going to be shot at . . . If you are going to get down there and engage in the crossfire you have got to expect to be clobbered and people will really jump on you, and you can't have it both ways.

Yet Reynolds was comparatively moderate. He accused Blainey of providing ammunition for a 'right-wing counter attack on the land rights movements', but conceded 'it is not possible to prove that they were committed with intent to destroy the Aboriginal people'. He commented on claims that the Tasmanian Aborigines

199

were destroyed through genocide that 'there were of course many people who were of Aboriginal descent living on the Bass Strait islands, and this was known at the time but they were seen as being something different. They were seen as half castes. So that there was that view that she was the last of the tribe'. Alan Atkinson noted that Reynolds found that 'an examination of Arthur's public and private writing proves that he was desperately anxious to ensure that the island's indigenous people survived British occupation', although many of the colonists were 'extirpationists at heart'.

Reynolds observed that Tasmanians who have been rejected in their claim to identify as Aborigines are 'most outspoken and who use the term genocide and ethnic cleansing'. He argued that 'the onus still must be on people to establish their indigenaity (sic) if they want to make a public claim now, not if they simply want to feel themselves as Aboriginal—that's their business'. Reynolds added illogically (perhaps inadvertently) that claimants to Aboriginal identity must be able to 'establish beyond reasonable doubt that [they] are descended from non-Europeans'. It seems odd that descendants of Afro-American whalers or Afghan camel-drivers should be able to claim Aboriginal identity more easily than descendants of Greeks or Italians.

Reynolds also pointed out that child removal in Tasmania was done 'under the rubric of the normal social welfare legislation—under which white children were taken as well' . . . There was no special legislation which gave to the government unique powers over Aboriginal communities. Children were clearly taken away and brought up by foster parents or brought up in institutions—as was so all over Australia.

In *Indelible Stain,* Reynolds resisted pressures to condemn Australia as a genocidal state. He thought it possible, though not certain, that the 1798 smallpox epidemic in NSW was deliberately introduced, that 'there is no available evidence to suggest that it was the intention of the colonial government to effect the extinction of the Tasmanians', that killings of Aboriginal people by squatters were on the whole small in scale, personal, immediate, and spontaneous, rather than the 'genocidal massacres' and that in Queensland, more Aborigines were killed by other Aborigines, mainly by those in the Native Police Force than by colonists. Reynolds was also unwilling to classify the 'Stolen children' as victims of cultural or any other sort of genocide.

One of Reynolds' early objectives was to overthrow established views that there was little serious Aboriginal resistance to British colonization of Australia. He maintained that Aborigines were both highly belligerent; he set out to banish 'legends' that Australian history was 'uniquely peaceful' and Aborigines 'an inimitably mild race which abjectly acquiesced in British colonization.[235] Reynolds denied that 'blacks were helpless victims of white attack' or 'passive objects of European brutality'. He declared that they 'did not sit around their camp fires waiting to be massacred' but that, allowing for differences in firepower, they gave as much as they got.[23]

The greatest amount of detail he provided if found in the first Chapter of his 1987 Frontier. The Chapter is entitled 'Unrecorded Battlefields' and its sub-headings are 'Martyrs of their country', 'The enemy of everyday'. The guerrilla mode of warfare', 'Constant dread', 'The blacks are coming', 'From the barrel of the gun', 'Fear comes to town', 'Counting the Cost', 'Progress stalled' and 'The death toll'. For that last Reynolds estimated that Aborigines killed in Queensland alone between 1840 and 1897 between 900 and 1000 'Europeans and their "allies"—mainly Chinese miners and Aboriginal stockmen'. Reynolds considered that 'the most striking feature of frontier conflict' was that 'it continued for almost 150 years, spanning three quarters of the time of European occupation'.[237] What he did not add in that account was that nowhere did armed conflict last very long. Almost invariably Aboriginal tribes concluded after a few sharp encounters that their chances of defeating the intruders and sending them packing were very slight.

Robert Scott, a grazer prominent in the 'Black Association' formed in 1837 to protect the accused in the Myall Creek trial, held that history showed:

> Whenever any collision took place between them and the whites, the natives were led on by someone among themselves, best acquainted with the Europeans, and most civilized. Violence, however, ceases as they become better acquainted with our power to punish, and it is only in our first intercourse with the natives, that outrage is to be apprehended . . . Among themselves they have no governing principle but force; superior strength alone commands obedience; each person is free to do anything within his own daring; personal fear is his only control . . . Men so constituted, cannot be kept in check, except by force, and the certainty of instant retaliation.[3]

Reynolds does not argue against the thrust of Scott's assessment. Another problem Reynolds fails to confront adequately is what the British should have done, other than, as Professor Ann Curthoys advised, go back where they came from.

Reynolds' admiration for the martial spirit among Aborigines did not extend to the ANZAC spirit which Reynolds rejected as a species of militarism and male chauvinism. In What's Wrong With Anzac? Reynolds and Professor Marilyn Lake described the 'ANZAC Spirit as the vehicle by which the ideas of the Edwardian militarists are preserved and passed on to a new generation'. But, they objected, the ANZAC was not typical of the Australian people. The soldiers lived in all-male company for years on end and were governed by military laws which compelled obedience and severely punished mutiny or insubordination. They were men of their time and therefore convinced white supremacists. The dark side of such racial cockiness was the contemptuous treatment of non-Europeans and, in the Middle

East, of the Egyptians, Turks, Palestinians, and Bedouins. Some of the Australians behaved like overbearing bullies in their dealings with the people whose countries they were occupying; but 'the accompanying atrocities have been largely forgotten or repressed'.

Reynolds expressed great admiration for traditional Aboriginal culture. He attacked the 'unfavourable conception of the brutal and debased savage', which, he claimed, 'was still afloat in the parish ethnology of Britain'.[238] However, Reynolds' own sources cited in Chapter Three make it very understandable why such conceptions existed.[239]

When not extolling their belligerence, Reynolds often paid tribute to constructive usage many Aborigines made of white techniques and goods. He acknowledged that white settlements acted as a magnet to Aborigines. In some cases the only sources of food after white incursions disrupted traditional supplies were squatters' stations.

As well as depicting Aboriginal violence in detail, the early Reynolds also wished to show that Aborigines, far from being frozen in traditional practices, made substantial constructive accommodations to new ways. Contact with whites brought about massive and speedy changes on a scale totally unprecedented in the Aboriginal past. Many changes were involuntary and of a destructive character, but others were voluntary and potentially at least valuable and helpful to Aboriginal development.

Reynolds acknowledged that white settlements acted as a magnet to many Aborigines. In some cases the attraction was that only there was food was available after white incursions disrupted traditional food supplies, but the pull was frequently of a different kind. Reynolds described how 'all sorts of iron—shear blades, horse-shoes, nails—as well as glass, cloth and leather' were 'successfully incorporated into an increasingly modified traditional "tool-kit"'. He noted that the availability of food from the animals of the settlers made possible larger Aboriginal military formations and enabled them to stay together longer than in pre-contact times. He argued that Aborigines were quick and skillful in mastering new techniques introduced by whites, especially in the control of dogs and horses. He extended his admiration to systematic wounding of cattle and driving them over gullies and ravines so they could be killed finally in conditions of safety, and to judicious breaking of their legs to prevent sheep acquired from the whites from straying.[240]

Among examples of successful co-operation between black and white, Reynolds cited evidence from Normanton, and other Queensland towns, of Aborigines employed as houseboys, firewood cutters, stable hands, yard cleaners, nurse girls, washerwomen, charwomen and gardeners, some of whom could bargain for wages 'with all the shrewdness of a white man'. There was in addition much evidence of less constructive Aboriginal accommodations, such as prostitution, begging and pilfering. Sharing or prostitution of their women by Aboriginal males occurred almost as soon as whites appeared: Sturt reported that 'his camp was overwhelmed with offers of sexual accommodation'. Sometimes Aborigines expected such offers would strengthen amity and respect as well as elicit major material reciprocity, but the objective effect was to reduce respect for Aboriginal culture, even among those very willing to take advantage of the opportunities of sexual gratification thus made available. Reynolds criticized 'activists' who 'ignored and despised' Aborigines working with or assisting whites, or unfairly condemned black troopers, stock workers and servants 'either as collaborators and traitors to the Aboriginal cause or as people with wills so weak that they lacked minds of their own and became, as a result, willing tools of the whites'. Reynolds considered that Aboriginal co-operation, when it was forthcoming, was rational and productive. This was indeed very often the case, but by no means invariably.

Examples of possible benefits of the white presence then began to disappear from his works. He interpreted Aborigine opposition to education of their children by white people as resistance to 'assertive promotion of European culture and the continuous subversion of their children'. He claimed that 'many Aborigines have not wanted to emulate white Australians and have manifested a cultural resistance which is rooted in their ethnic history'.[241] Aboriginal men often prevented inter-racial co-operation. Reynolds noted that the 'array of methods' used to preserve their authority, especially over women, included 'threats, sorcery, ritual spearing, even execution'.[242]

LAND RIGHTS AND NATIVE TITLE

In 1987, Reynolds admitted that his interest in land rights questions was a 'very belated development' and he 'had gone on for years accepting at face value ideas and interpretations that were wrong'. Sometimes Reynolds agreed that in 1788 Britain gained sovereignty over Australia in terms fully acceptable in international law: 'The British claim of sovereignty over the whole of Australia was not surprising given the attitudes of European powers. It would have been unexceptional at any time in the nineteenth century.'[243] He wrote that in New South Wales 'the legal situation was clear from the beginning': namely, that it was 'a colony of settlement, not conquest. The common law arrived with the First Fleet; the Aborigines became instant subjects of the King, amenable to, and in theory protected by, the law. They could be murdered, outlawed or made subject to martial law but they could not be treated as enemies of the state'[244]. But he also argued that British sovereignty could only extend to the power of keeping out other European or 'civilized' powers and only then 'as far as the crest of the watershed flowing into the ocean on the line of the coast actually discovered'.

Reynolds argued, too, that the phrase 'desert and uncultivated' is 'ambiguous', since it might or might not mean 'uninhabited', and suggested that Blackstone really

203

meant uninhabited, or else he would have used the phrase 'desert or uncultivated', not 'desert and uncultivated'.[245] That was a meaningless quibble, since nobody ever seriously believed that the British government thought Australia uninhabited, given the testimony of Cook and Banks and several hundred other eye witnesses to their reality.

Reynolds claimed that 'over much of the continent the Aborigines clearly had possession of a character of which the land was capable', but except in the least fertile areas, this is not true and at best confuses actual and potential use.[246] No land in Australia before 1788 was used for purposes of agriculture, horticulture, or animal husbandry, but land was quickly put to these uses by the colonists. The argument that hunter-gatherers did not put land to the best uses of which it was capable was part of the ideological stock-in-trade of all the colonizing states. Vattel and Locke were often quoted on this matter. Earlier conquerors, it might be noted, felt no need to offer any justification for seizure and appropriation of territory.

The greatest confusion spread by Reynolds, however, concerned whether Native Title was ever acknowledged in any British, Colonial of Commonwealth Court before the Mabo adjudication of the 1990s. When writing as a scholar Reynolds had no doubts on the matter. His books are full of unequivocal judgments such as:

The official view is clear. The British claimed not only the sovereignty over New South Wales—then comprising the whole eastern half of Australia—but also the ownership of all the million and a half square miles contained therein.[247]

Mr Justice Isaacs declared, 'So we start with the unquestionable position that, when Governor Phillip received his first Commission from George III on 12 October 1786 The whole of the lands of Australia were already in law the property of the King of England.'

'The Act of the British Parliament in 1834 establishing South Australia gave no recognition to Aboriginal land rights.'

'Further research may eventually turn up a relevant case of two, but it is reasonable to assume that no colonial court ever defended the Aboriginal right of occupancy.'

'Aboriginal right of use and occupancy and the British recognition of native title were ignored, unenforced and apparently never tested in the colonial courts.'

The Crown regarded unalienated waste land as entirely its own to deal with as it pleased.

Usually accompanying such sober statements by Reynolds were his lamentations and/or denunciations that British and Australian judges, lawyers, politicians, and colonists unjustly refused to recognize any legally enforceable Aboriginal communal native title or land rights, Reynolds is also, of course, a committed activist in what he has conceived to be Aboriginal interests. When writing in that mode his object was to persuade opinion that some form of Aboriginal communal native title *ought* to have been mainstream opinion and *ought* to have been accepted by judges, lawyers, politicians, and colonists. However, as a scholar he had admitted that no such legal rights had existed.(My emphases)

Example of his wishful thinking about native title include:

In 1840 the Aborigines Protection Society argued that the rights of the original possessors were "not at all affected by Acts of Parliament or Commissioners' instructions; their right rests upon the principle of justice. It is impossible to deny the right which natives have to the land on which they were born, and which from age to age they have derived support and nourishment, and which has received their ashes".[248]

The fact that the black were the prior owners of Australia was accepted by many settlers and received official recognition in both Britain and the colonies in the 1830s'.[249]

The mainstream view has been that native title arose from the incontrovertible fact of occupation'.[250]

Leading English lawyers of the 1830s', such as James Stephen, Pemberton, Burge, Follet, and Lushington, were 'fully aware of native title and believed that it applied with equal force in Australia as in the other colonies of settlement'.

That last is, of course, a question-begging formulation, since those jurists followed Blackstone in holding that by definition all colonies of settlement adopted the common law, in so far as it could be transmitted, on coming under the sovereignty of the Crown.

Reynolds' claim that several eminent British lawyers held that Aborigines 'retained their rights based on prior occupation until the Crown exerted its exclusive rights of pre-emption' is quite accurate but again question begging, since the central question was whether Aboriginal rights were legal or moral and what they might comprise. Reynolds claimed that communal native title was accepted in London by the Colonial Office as 'an authoritative assessment of the law as it then stood'. This was not so: many British officials and politicians were sympathetic to the plight of Aborigines confronted by white tillage and pastoral squatting and by the entire paraphernalia of a new, different, and alien society, but they fully understood that the laws concerning land tenure were fatal to recognition of communal native title. That is why they concentrated their efforts on urging the Crown to exercise its legal power over all land titles in as solicitous a way as possible of Aboriginal interests.

The High Court of Australia in the Mabo case ignored or rejected what Reynolds, their main authority in these matters, had, together with virtually all previous scholars and lawyers, agreed upon: namely that no Native Title had ever been recognized. Instead they accepted Reynolds' condemnation of the law as wrong and in dire need of change. But in the standard interpretation of Westminster rules and conventions, it is not within the powers of the Courts of Law to make massive changes in the Law on the grounds that they find some laws obnoxious and contrary to natural justice. That is the province of elected legislatures. It was all very well for Reynolds to quip that 'the state of nature did not exist outside the European imagination', but neither did the Law of God exist outside human imagination. The truth or error of metaphysical suppositions is irrelevant to matters of civil and criminal law, as is whether 'many settlers' or even some of those who constituted 'official opinion' believed X or Y to be the case.

Reynolds underestimated the difficulties faced by British governments. It was difficult enough for politicians in Adelaide, Sydney, Hobart, Melbourne, Perth or Brisbane to exercise close control over distant frontiers and impossible from Westminster. Reynolds realized that.

> The settlers were transplanting a policy of possessive individualism, hierarchy, and inequality. Aboriginal society was reciprocal and materially egalitarian, although there were important political and religious inequalities based on age and sex. Two such diametrically opposed societies could not merge without conflict. One or the other had to prevail.[251]

He appeared to believe that the wrong one prevailed, but does not reveal what policies he thought the colonists should have adopted, other than evacuate from Australia. Morton's Fork is constantly at work: Government interventions are condemned as leading to cultural genocide, but lack of intervention is blamed for neglect, unfair discrimination, and failure to satisfy human rights. And even more pertinently Reynolds and those who think like him admire traditional life yet complain of injustice when entails far lower standards of education, health and life expectancy than the rest of the population.

Reynolds' career is not easy to appraise. His first aim, which he achieved, was to rebut impressions that Aborigines conceded possession of Australia without much of a struggle. However, the more details he offered of Aboriginal violence against colonists and other Aborigines, the more difficult it became to argue that frontier violence was almost entirely committed by the colonists. Reynolds seemed to have realized this and subsequently downplayed Aboriginal military prowess. Nevertheless, his dislike for martial fervour among his contemporaries contrasted sharply with his admiration for Aboriginal prowess in war. Reynolds has championed some sort of Aboriginal autonomy or sovereignty, but it is very difficult to discern what form he thinks it should take.

Highly relevant to a major theme in this book is the difference Professor Reynolds made to Australian society. He was an able but not an outstanding student; his first reputation as bard of Aboriginal resistance to white occupation faded as emphasis switched back to Indigenous inability to withstand superior weaponry. His discourses on land laws contained some contradictions. Yet it was Reynolds, directly and through his influence over his former student Eddy Mabo, who almost single-handedly overthrew what Judges Deane and Gaudron termed 'a basis of the real property law of this country for more than a hundred and fifty years'.[252] That this was accomplished by a historian and not a lawyer should surely feature prominently in the promotional literature of every history department in Australian universities.

On the negative side is the reluctance Reynolds shares with some of his progressive colleagues who, despite using the language of democratic equality frequently, are disposed to bandy words or enter into debate only with people within a charmed circle. Rosemary Neill was rightly disturbed when 66 academics from round the country wrote a Rentacrowd letter to The Australian which 'expressed their "outrage" and "dismay" at "the promotion and endorsement" of Partington's view'. Neill commented, " . . . these individuals did not simply dispute Partington's hymn to past, discredited polices. They argued that it was illegitimate for those 'other citizens who have for so long benefitted from the denial of basic citizens' rights to the indigenous people of this country to occupy the spaces from which indigenous voices may speak". In other words intellectuals from round the nation objected not just to what Partington had to say, but that he, as a non-Aboriginal and pro-assimilationist, had written about indigenous issues at all'.[253]

MARGARET SIMONS

Margaret Simons has been a freelance journalist and writer and also a senior lecturer and now professor at Swinburne University of Technology. She has written numerous books and essays, including *The Meeting of the Waters* about the Hindmarsh Island Bridge Affair. She was chosen by Malcolm Fraser to carry out research for his *Malcolm Fraser: Political Memoirs* and to co-write it with him. Simons might not seem at first sight a likely co-author with a former Liberal Prime Minister, but by and during the time of their collaboration, their outlooks were very similar. Simons would have found many passages in Fraser's 2002 *Common Ground* to be close to her own convictions, such as the following.

> One of the great dangers of today's world is that the world's one and only superpower has increasingly, over the last ten years, said that the determinations of the international bodies do not apply to them. That perhaps is the greatest single threat to world stability and progress.

> Australia is already a multicultural society that cannot be turned back. If it is a question of Islam and of Muslim fundamentalism, we need to remember that Christians through the ages and quite recently in the Balkans and also in Ireland have operated as terrorists. Muslims have no monopoly of violence.

> The greatest divide is between the haves and the have-nots. It is a divide infinitely more perilous than that of the Cold War.

> I recently reread a speech by Paul Hasluck given in Parliament in 1961 concerning the welfare of Aborigines. I contributed to the debate and supported the policies of the time, a time when assimilation represented the main thrust of government policy. I have no doubt that many of the people who pursued assimilation as an objective were sincere and well-meaning, but it was a policy that in the end would rob people of identity, of history, and of culture.

> The interface between white settlement pushing out and the Aboriginals was harsh and bloody . . . The works of Henry Reynolds have done much to describe the detail and the horror of what occurred.

> Nobody could doubt Paul Hasluck's sincerity in the fulfillment of his duties as Minister of the Territories, but the paternalism inherent in the policies and the attempt to blot out history, culture, and sense of origin from part-blood Aboriginals have had unfortunate and in its time possible unforeseeable consequences.

In the course of becoming a beloved figure at the ABC and in the Fairfax Press, Fraser expressed regret that as Federal Minister of Education and Prime Minister he had 'participated in policies which today we regard as outdated, barbarous, cruel and racist'. The arguments and policies he had advocated over many years apparently 'rested on a racist foundation. Aborigines or part-Aborigines were to be assimilated, mingled with whites, and "bred out". Today we find those policies abhorrent. They are totally outside our understanding and our belief in "human rights"'. It would be very difficult for a future historian who read any of Fraser's speeches in the twenty-first century to believe that it was the Liberal Party he had once led and a Liberal government over which he had presided.

Equally, if Fraser had read any of the works of Margaret Simons, he would have discerned talents likely to prove very helpful in their collaboration. Simons had the gift of passing on thoughts and conversations of which no direct evidence was available and from which she was far distant when they supposedly took place. For example:

> While Doug [Milera] got angry, Sarah became more, loving. She really thought she could help heal reconciliation.

> 'Sarah replied: "You can't leave. We'll send your bones back in a box." It was a joke, and Rose took it as a compliment.'

> '(Connie) Roberts looked intransigent. Immovable. She grumbled aloud that people shouldn't be talking about this sort of thing in public.'

Another useful gift was that of selective forgetfulness. For example, according to Simons, Doreen Kartinyeri was 'certain nobody would have mentioned a woman's privates in front of her and she would have smacked them in the mouth if they'd said that to me'. However, confidence in Kartinyeri's fastidiousness in language and in Simons' judgment of character is reduced when a few pages later Doreen Kartinyeri describes Colin James, a journalist who had bent over backwards to please the militant Aboriginal lobby, as a 'fucking white cunt' and advised him to 'fuck off and never come back.' Some of Simons' contributions to Aboriginal myth are discussed in Chapter 4. Colin James's acquiescence in the changing moods of Doreen Kartinyeri and the Affirmative women may have helped to secure his Award as a Journalist for his coverage of the Women's Business, whereas the less diplomatic Chris Kenny received no official praise recognition for what was at least as thorough and unbiased coverage as that of James.[254]

Margaret Simons became the fifteenth lead essayist in the *Quarterly Essay* series. Earlier essayists included Robert Manne, Guy Rundle, Don Watson, Mungo MacCallum, John Button, Tim Flannery, Germaine Greer, and Paul McGeough. Simons' subject was 'Latham's World: The New Politics of the Outsiders'.

Simons was favourably impressed by Mark Latham and remained so even after he had led the ALP to defeat. She saw Latham as a conviction politician who was 'one of the few thinkers to have achieved political leadership'. She praised him for his plain language. Simons recalled that she had once 'halted a political argument' at a dinner party simply by whipping out Latham's book From the Suburbs and reading out the first few pages. Evidently 'the silence afterwards lasted for minutes. It was both alarmed and impressed . . . "There are more ideas there than I have heard in politics or years"'. Simons recalled one person present then saying that she credited Latham of having the 'potential to lead us to a new understanding of poverty'.

Simons acknowledged that Latham had faults. For example, when he led the Liverpool Council he had been rude and cruel to members of the ALP faction he had displaced in municipal office. Although she proved herself to be above such personal discourtesies, she might well have borne a grudge against Latham, because, as Dennis Glover noted, despite her being a 'respected writer' and one of the few journalists who followed Latham's campaigning in the first months of 2004, Latham never accorded her an interview.'

Simons considered that Latham divided political ideas and policies into two parts: one about economic management and the other about the wider structure of society. She felt that he was redressing the balance but feared he had gone to the opposite position and had neglected some key financial issues.

Perhaps the most interesting responses to Simons' essay was that of John Button. He praised Simons for having 'investigated the gossip and allegations about Latham's past . . . and weighed up all the evidence she could assemble about her subject's character and personality. She observed him on television and, more importantly, at a community forum. And then she examined his ideas'. Button considered that 'intellectual rigeur of this kind is not part of the regular practice or culture of Australian political journalism, but held that Simons' effort is 'an encouraging sign that professionalism still exists, albeit out of the mainstream'. He assessed the essay as 'a lucid and interesting account of (Latham's) background and ideas, of paradigms of insiders and outsiders'.

Most of the invited respondents to Simons' essay praised it. David Burchell found the essay 'masterful'. He claimed that 'Australia's self-styled intelligentsia has almost entirely missed the point of Latham's "crazy-brave" assault on our inherited political verities from the 1980s and '90s and failed to offer the kind of moral support it required'. Annabel Crabb saw Simons as 'hungry for big, important ideas, and clearly relished the idea of a big, reformist Latham government'. Crabb thought too that Simons believed that Latham's reforms would 'include changes to our understanding of what it is to be poor and what it is to be privileged, and of what equality might entail'. Crabb considered that Simons had delivered an 'impressively curated highlights package of Mark Latham's policy back catalogue' and that her essay was 'an excellent read and a valuable job'. Crabb felt that Simons 'thrills to

Latham's work, especially his most central theme: that Australia is made up of insiders and outsiders, and that the insiders range across, rather than conforming to the old political axis of left and right'. Crabb judged that Simons perceived 'a vague messianic touch to what Latham was doing'. On the other hand, Irving Saulwick found Simons' summary of Latham's ideas 'rather frustrating. It was so dense, so abridged, that in many cases I found it hard to understand what Latham was saying'.

Simons admitted that she had thought 'Latham was doing better than the election results suggested'. She did not anticipate the swing against Labor, nor anticipate the Senate result. After the event, she surmised that Latham had underestimated the effect of the coalition's '"interest-rate campaign" and overestimated the effect of Labor's strong campaign on health, education and other issues.' She felt that 'most voters don't feel qualified in economics'. She was 'pretty sure that the voters who decided the election are no more qualified than I am on this topic'. She did not reflect that the electors are not expected to know, whereas she, as a purveyor of advice, is expected to know a bit more. She conceded that the election showed her that she was 'no longer sure what "left" and "right" mean in most contexts'.

Margaret Simons won new media interest in January 2009 with a hoax on *Quadrant*. Its editor, Keith Windschuttle, accepted a spoof article about biotechnology as genuine, submitted by one 'Sharon Gould', whose thoughts were rapidly relayed to the world by Simons. The article contained genuine information and defensible arguments interspersed with false claims with fraudulent references. According to Windschuttle, Simons contacted him and revealed detailed knowledge of the article's content. She promised to make a list that would separate the genuine from the fake references and would email it to Windschuttle. She was as good as her word, but the lengthy correspondence that followed wasted the time of all concerned. Simons seemed to take great pride in this infantile prank, but it earned her plaudits among most progressive commentators and may well have proved a plus in her journalism and academic engagements. It is hard, however, to conceive that it raised her in Malcolm Fraser's esteem.

Simons' partnership with one of the most important Australian leaders of our time also ended with whimpers rather than bangs. Few great issues were resolved, but there were many petty disagreements as to who told or failed to tell who, what, when, and where. There were no matters in contention that Simons could help to resolve, and in Gerard Henderson and others, she met minds of comparable tenacity to her own. After a time, only mild surprise continued to be expressed that so ardent an opponent of Fraser at the time of the Whitlam Dismissal could be so supportive of him in every disputed issue. A mysterious 'piece of paper' that may once have contained Fraser's note of an important conversation with Kerr evoked strange echoes of the 'sealed envelopes' of Hindmarsh Island.

Paul Kelly claimed that Fraser told him he had not kept that 'piece of paper' with notes of the most important phone exchanges on Dismissal Day. Clyde Cameron, in an interview recorded for the National Library of Australia, also stated that he did not keep his notes from the phone conversation. Henderson was not convincingly rebutted by Fraser or Simons, when he asserted that half of the disputed Fraser note had been written with a different pen from the time, date, and signature at the bottom of the same document. Still, it was hardly a hanging matter; one way or the other and Simons seemed to emerge still high in public opinions. She seemed more confident than ever to put the public right on the ethics of journalism in her capacity of Director of the Centre for Advanced Journalism in the University of Melbourne. Perhaps Malcolm Fraser would be invited to be Adjunct Professor? Their joint memoir certainly deserved to receive the Douglas Stewart Prize for non-fiction just as much as *The Meeting of the Waters* had merited its awards. Margaret Simons was awarded a literary award by the Premier of Queensland for The Meeting of the Waters, although there was surely some controversy as to whether it should have been included in the fiction or non-fiction sections. It must be conceded to most of our public intellectuals that they do support each other before the general public.

In 2011, Margaret Simons was appointed as adviser to an 'independent' media inquiry set up by the ALP Gillard government. She chose herself to be both a contributor to the hearings and a commentator on its findings. She also nominated journalist Denis Muller as a suitable candidate for evaluating submissions. Mr Muller has wide experience of newspapers her and in Britain, but, like Professor Simons he is well known as a critic of News Limited and Mr Rupert Murdoch, although by no means on the Simons' scale of ferocity. Predictably neither Simons nor Muller found any imperfection in the Finkelstein Report, which was sharply critical of News Corporation and several of its employees. Simons did not disclose publicly that she had been deeply involved in the structuring of the Finkelstein Inquiry. She maintained her consistency by denouncing the negative responses to the report by much of the Australian press. The Australian commented in its editorial:

> Professor Simons, who often rails against what she sees as poor journalism and undisclosed interests, never revealed, in her evidence at the inquiry or commentary about it, that she had been a party to some of its internal arrangements. Emails obtained under FOI show she had several conversations with inquiry organizers, offered to supply research services at a price and, in the end, recommended a third party to conduct that research for them. Christian Kerr accurately noted that Simons failed to demand the openness she demanded from others when conflicts of interest are possible, let alone very likely. Kerr observed en passant that Simons had been strangely silent about the passes granted by the University of

Canberra to overseas students who had been recommended for failure by their own tutor. The watch dogs have no teeth when the abuses are within the house, but outside the gates.

A. J. P. TAYLOR

Many historians have been gifted speakers, and some remain among us, but few, if any, can have equaled the impression on his listeners made by Professor Alan Taylor. No hesitations, frequent witticisms, logical order, and perfect timing, together with minimal reference to notes of any kind, had his audiences cheering and clapping as soon as his head finally fell forward and he became silent. Whether in a university lecture hall or a mass meeting organized by the Campaign for Nuclear Disarmament, Taylor was always the star of the show. As a television celebrity, he became the leading British public intellectual of his day.

Taylor was born into prosperous and sheltered circumstances in Birkdale on a pleasant stretch of Lancashire's coastline, before his family moved to Buxton Spa. He became aware of the ways of the world at an early age. Among the female servants, his special favourite was Jane, who took him for walks and bathed him. Jane gave Alan his 'first experience of sex: I sat in the bath and tickled her cunt, an activity that gave pleasure to both parties . . . the female anatomy had henceforward no mysteries for me'. His relationships with older women were not always to be as pleasurable.

Taylor had almost as early an initiation into international politics as into sex. His parents were bourgeois Bolsheviks and his uncle Harry solicitor to the British Communist Party. His mother, Constance, 'hankered to play a great revolutionary role'. Indeed, she became a British delegate to the Comintern, the then Communist International. She made large contributions to the Communist Party . . . but it was not her money. It was relayed to her from a Soviet bank in London, and he passed it on to the Communist Party. Sex and politics were closely associated, since Alan's mother and Henry Sara, another important link in the transmission of Moscow gold to the British comrades, were lovers for many years. Taylor's father was a compliant husband, as Alan himself became after marriage.

Alan fell in love at seventeen with a 'staggeringly beautiful' youth, but at Oxford he was 'straight', despite solicitations from Tom Driberg who, however, persuaded Taylor to join both the Labor Club and the Communist Party. During the 1920s and 1930s, Alan accompanied Mama and Henry Sara to the Soviet Union. They were treated just as ordinary tourists, except that they 'were given an interpreter and sometimes a car'. During their Potemkin travels, they found that 'the shops were stuffed with goods, everyone had plenty to eat. There were no restrictions. We could enter the Kremlin and wander about it whenever we felt like it'. A slight misunderstanding with the

213

police in Leningrad over taking photographs was resolved by no less a person than Kirov, then head of the entire party organizations in the region. Alas! Kirov was soon to be assassinated on the instructions of Comrade Stalin, who was jealous of Kirov's popularity, but that information was apparently too trifling for Alan to mention.

After graduation, Alan was appointed as a lecturer in history in Manchester University and soon afterwards a Fellow of Magdelen College, Oxford, where he remained for nearly forty years. Although his Communist Party membership apparently lapsed, Taylor continued to be a firm friend of the Soviet Union and as wrong on nearly every major issue as anyone could have been. He praised the five-year plans that 'were not run for the benefit of capitalists and landowners'; he was convinced that the British government 'were helping Nazi Germany to survive and even to rearm . . .' He believed that 'Communist victories [in Eastern Europe] would be an improvement on the existing regimes as in my opinion [in 1983] they have proved to be'; he believed that 'if Great Britain were involved in war it would be on Hitler's side against Russia'. In 1938, he judged that 'Chamberlain was so obviously working on Hitler's side'. Almost incredibly he was 'greatly cheered by the signing in 1939 of the Nazi–Soviet pact. This ruled out a German attack on Russia and therefore in my opinion the likelihood of any war'. Almost its equal was: 'The Russo-Finnish war put me in a great fright. I was convinced that Great Britain and France would aid Finland and use this as a cover to switch over to the German side. In this, too, I was not mistaken.' He also asserted in lectures that Franco would 'join the German side' soon in the war.

Taylor owed his later prestige largely to two aberrations from his normal lines of argument. The first was in May 1941 when he ended a public lecture with the words: 'Before we meet again Hitler will have attacked Russia'. The rapid fulfillment of this prophesy made him a national figure for the first time. The second came in September 1947 at a conference in Wroclaw (formerly Breslau). Taylor had been abjectly fellow-travelling since the war ended: He supported Soviet predominance in Eastern Europe and declared that the British 'became American satellites from the time we accepted the American loan in 1946'. However, at Wroclaw, he spoke boldly and eloquently against anti-Western diatribes, such as the claim by the Stalinist Soviet author Fadaev that 'if monkeys could type, they would produce poems like T. S. Eliot's'. Taylor became accepted as a principled defender of the best of the West overnight. This reputation lasted even after 1956, when he combined defense of the Soviet invasion of Hungary with denunciations of the British and French invasion of the Suez Canal zone.

Taylor's public combats and constant stream of historical works and contemporary commentary took place in conditions of domestic disharmony. His mother's lover had been a house-trained civilized lawyer. Taylor married three times, and his first wife,

214

Margaret Adams, who was frequently unfaithful to him, chose the bedroom-trashing Welsh poet Dylan Thomas. Taylor wrote of Thomas: 'He was cruel. He was a sponger even when he had money of his own. He went out of his way to hurt those who helped him . . . His greatest pleasure was to humiliate people.' Despite his accurate reading of Thomas's character, Taylor was foolish enough to lend and give him money: each donation supposedly the last one. Sometimes Taylor quoted Kipling, but evidently forgot: 'Once you pay the Danegeld, you'll never get rid of the Dane.' His second wife was Eve Crosland, with whom he had two children, but even after divorcing Margaret, Taylor continued to live with her, while maintaining a household with Eve. His third wife was the Hungarian historian Éva Haraszti, whom he married in 1976. There was considerable pressure on Taylor to write and lecture to keep his extended family in comfort.

Taylor's literary brilliance continued to be combined with strange judgments, such as that Hitler did little more than continue with the traditional foreign policy objectives of Bismarck and the Kaiser; yet he also perceived a symbiotic relationship between Hitler and the German people in a march towards their recognition as the true Herrenvolk: a vision not held by Bismarck or Wilhelm II. Taylor often preferred accident to intention as the cause of historical events: He argued that Hitler did not want or plan war in 1939. It began because of mistakes on everyone's part.

He was often equivocal as a spokesman for CND. He claimed it to be a campaign of the highest importance, yet he declared, 'No one cared whether Great Britain had the bomb or not.' He denounced newspaper proprietors in general as being among the greatest enemies of British democracy, but held that Lord Beaverbrook, who often featured Taylor in his newspapers, was 'the quickest intellect I ever encountered and his disposition in a curious way the kindest'.

Taylor was an enthusiast for ethnic cleansing, as indeed had been John Stuart Mill, who urged in less alarming language that in principle national boundaries should coincide with ethnic distributions. Taylor advised Beneš to expel the entire German population of Czechoslovakia after the war, which was carried out; whether because of or despite his advice. Taylor also proposed the expulsion of the entire Protestant Unionist population of Northern Ireland. He was more tender on individuals he considered had been persecuted, such as the art historian and Soviet spy, Anthony Blunt. Lenin, so admired by Taylor's mama, thought of people like Alan as 'useful idiots'. How should we regard him?

Chapter 9

CLASSROOM REVOLUTIONS

During the 1980s, a revolution in history teaching took place in much of the English-speaking world. It began in the United States and the United Kingdom, but entered Australian education largely through Australian teachers who undertook casual 'supply' teaching in Britain. In England, militant influence over history teaching in schools was obtained through the capture of the Historical Association and its journal *Teaching History* by Sallie Purgis, Carolyn Steedman, and their allies. They launched a series of attacks on school history as it had previously been taught and chose as a target the textbooks written by R. J. Unstead, which were among the most popular history textbooks and readers in the schools. According to Purkis, Unstead emphasizes the 'long-running, happy, and glorious success of the great (white) English people'
.

Unstead had revealed himself to be an utter racist, claimed Purkis, when he wrote:

> Our children are likely to grow up into the kind of race that in our better moments we know ourselves to be. If they have been made aware of the qualities of men and women whom successive generations have admired.

Purkis ridiculed those 'pious eugenic sentiments' and argued:

> His belief that one of the main reasons for teaching history was discredited in 1945 and 1956. His choice of material is out-of-date and insufficient for a world in which children see and sympathize with the Vietnamese boat people and become involved in schemes to buy mini-bikes for Tanzania.

The dates 1945 and 1956 were, one can be nearly certain, chosen for Hiroshima and Suez, not the defeat of Hitler and the Soviet invasion of Hungary. Were her students old by Purkis from what it was the Vietnamese were fleeing? H. E. H. Townsend and E. M. Britten were aghast in 1973 that 'Asian and West Indian children pupils n junior schools, even in highly illiterate areas, are more likely to learn about King Alfred and the cakes than about Africa and India'.[255] In fact there was very little in English history that they supposed was relevant to immigrant children, other than changes in immigration policies.

An especially annoying feature about Unstead's books to his critics was their readability and attractiveness to many children. Carolyn Steedman was dismayed:

> Unstead's chronology is also compelling and powerful, not in spite of its being racist and sexist and relentlessly Anglocentric, but because of the comforting simplicities of the drama it presents. The heroic view of history has not been foisted upon entirely unwilling eight year olds.[256]

had emigrated to Australia before this attack on Unstead. I wrote an article condemning the unjust treatment he had received and sent him a letter of sympathy. I received in return a letter that included:

> 'I must tell you that when I read aloud your letter to my wife at breakfast and came to the last paragraph in which you speak of what I have done for children, I could not go on, but had to go out into the garden and walk about and blow my nose, even perhaps wipe my eyes, for the attack by Sallie Purkis hurt beyond measure, because it was so vicious in tone and unscrupulous in misquoting things I had written (some of them a quarter of a century earlier) . . . Nor was I given any advance notice of her attack or offered even half a page to answer her criticism.'

Mr and Mrs Unstead invited me to visit them next time I was in England, but that was not to be

Birmingham University's Centre for Cultural Studies became a major source of reconstructionist educational thought in England. Among its ranks was Paul Willis, the main exponent of neo-Marxism revolutionary defeatism. Willis claimed that the prime importance of schools lies in 'social reproduction, or more exactly for their role in maintaining the conditions for continued material production in the capitalist mode', and in ensuring that the factories are filled on every Monday morning with workers displaying the necessary apparent gradations between mental and manual capacity and corresponding attitudes necessary to maximize profits'.

According to Willis, teachers help reproduce the capitalist order in three ways. Firstly, by feeding students with bourgeois ideology and its perverted version of knowledge,

217

teachers may help shape them into efficient learners and subsequently into efficient workers who make an especially high contribution to capitalist profits. Secondly teachers may, unconsciously, prepare young people for the soulless drudgery of mass production by boring them and thus rendering them listless and apathetic. Willis asserted:

> The 'transition' from school to work, for instance, of working class kids who had really absorbed the rubric of self-development, satisfaction and interest in work, would be a terrifying battle. Armies of kids equipped with their 'self-concepts' would be fighting to enter the few meaningful jobs available, and masses of employers would be struggling to press them into meaningless work.

Thirdly, teachers may provoke working class boys to 'resist the established values and relationships of the established school'. Willis noted, all too truly, that 'many aspects of the lads' culture, for instance, are "challenging and subversive and remain threatening"'. However, Willis warned that 'this oppositional informal culture . . may well actually help to accomplish the wider social reproduction which the official policy has been trying to defeat or change'.[257] He maintained that 'in contradictory and unintended ways the counter-school culture actually achieves for education one of its main though misrecognized objectives—the direction of a proportion of working kids "voluntarily" to skilled, semi-skilled and unskilled manual work'.[258]

It might be worthwhile to recall very briefly what the peoples of the British Isles had achieved between 1550 and 1900:
- produced arguably the world's greatest playwright;
- abolished slavery and the slave trade in its possessions;
- conquered territories over eighty times its own size.
- preserved and extended representative government to near manhood suffrage;
- significantly raised life expectancy;
- become the first country to carry out successively an 'industrial evolution and enable most of the world to be linked by steam ships, railways and paved roads'
- spread Christianity in almost all its tolerant forms throughout North America, the Pacific Isles, Australia and New Zealand, and much of Africa and Asia.

The children of many countries might well have taken legitimate pride in such achievements. However, according to Steedman, history Unstead-fashion was bad for them because 'conservative history (is) narratively bound to demonstrate the collective unimportance of most people's lives'.

218

Steedman's predecessors as editors of Teaching History, Martin and Killingray, gave four pages to A. G. Kiloskov of the USSR Academic Sciences, Moscow, who explained:

Training of Soviet schools children in history pre-supposed their study of K. Marx's, F. Engels' and VI Lenin's works, documents of the Communist Party of the USSR and the Soviet State and of the world communist and working class movement. History teachers study four cycles of subjects in teacher training institutes. The first cycle—social sciences—includes Marxist-Leninist philosophy, political economy, scientific communism, history of the USSR Communist Party, fundamentals of the Soviet State and law, ethics and aesthetics, and principles of scientific atheism.[259]

Oh! The ingratitude of the human race! The name of Comrade Stalin had been absent from the required readings for nearly twenty years and remained so in the USSR. Suitably mediated, however, it is available in plenty in Australia and Great Britain.

The Inner London Education Authority (ILEA) took the lead among local educational authorities in Britain. Around 110,000 copies of its *Race, Sex and Class* were distributed free to every teacher, teacher assistant, school governor or manager, and parent–teacher associations in the ILEA area. Its potted history included that the slave trade was 'basically an economic phenomenon that favoured European nations—no reference were made to the long centuries of Arab-Muslim slave-trading in the Mediterranean Africa and the Persian Gulf. Britain was accused of vile treatment of masses of immigrants, but very little information was provided about why those peoples fled their homelands, or why they wrote from Britain, Australia and comparable states to their relatives back home to come and join them'.[260]

So in many schools there was no more '1066 And All That'; not even '1917 and all that' Instead there were exposures of past evils of the industrial revolution, the patriarchal family and white racism and imperialism, together with as sweeteners projects on pop stars and the local football team. Yet, despite obstacles, many history teachers do a good job and inspire students still.

Chapter 10

SOME WOMEN IN HISTORY

OLD TESTAMENT WOMEN

The Tanakh (Christian Old Testament, OT) was compiled over several centuries, so it is not surprising that different judgments are made about women in its pages, starting with two conflicting Creation stories in its first two Chapters. In one version, man and woman are both created in the image of God at the same time; in the other, the male is created first and then the female from his rib, perhaps after God realized that he had forgotten to provide a mate for the male, whereas he had remembered to do so during his animal creation. The first version has gender equality, but the second deep inequality.

The second version places the main guilt for 'man's first disobedience' and the subsequent 'fall' on Eve. Her punishment is extended to all future women. Eve is told, 'In sorrow shall thou bring forth children; and thy desire shall be to thy husband, and he shall rule over thee.' So, Adam emerges relatively well and is given to believe, not quite accurately perhaps, that women will desire men even more than men will desire women. Eve is not even given some credit for wanting the fruit of the tree of knowledge more than Adam did.

Jewish law, more than almost every other code, has treated women as unclean after childbirth as well as during menstruation. Yet the OT often emphasizes the need for the women of Israel to go forth and multiply. 'Daughters of Israel' wanted children and feared childlessness. When Rachel saw that she could bear Jacob no children, Rachel envied her sister and said unto Jacob, 'Give me children, or else I die.' Like Sarah and Hagar two generations earlier, Rachel and Leah vied with each other in seeking pregnancy, through their handmaids as well as directly. When at last Rachel conceived and bore a child of her own and a boy at that, she said, 'God hath taken away my reproach.' She called the boy Joseph, meaning 'The Lord will add to me another son'.

After commanding Abraham to kill Isaac, his son, as a sacrifice, God relented at the last minute. God showed no such mercy to Jephthah's daughter. Jephthah, when in command of the Israelite army, vowed to God that if he defeated the Ammonites 'then it shall be, that whatsoever cometh forth of the doors of my house to meet me . . . shall surely be the Lord's and I will offer it up for a burnt offering'. When he returned home victorious, he met first his daughter, his only child. Jephthah stated that he would keep his vow, but allowed his daughter to go to the mountains to 'bewail her virginity'. This 'bewailing' became a festival for Jewish girls about to experience menarche. The mourning was probably for Jephthah's daughter's deprival of motherhood rather than of sexual intercourse.

David's first wife, Michal, daughter of Saul and sister of Jonathan, helped David escape from her father after they had quarreled and were at war. She 'let David down through a window . . . took an image, and laid it in the bed, and put a pillow of goats' hair for his bolster and covered it with a cloth'. Small gratitude did she receive. During his absence, David took many wives and concubines, many of whom give birth. When he returned to Jerusalem, he danced in the streets 'before the Lord with all his might . . . girded with a linen ephod'. The vigorous dancing in a scanty garment displayed David's genitals to the onlookers. Michal 'despised him in her heart' for this exhibitionism. She greeted David with sarcastic praise: 'How glorious was the king of Israel today, who uncovered himself today in the eyes of the handmaids of his servants, as one of the vain fellows uncovereth himself.' David would not accept her criticism and told her he would continue in his ways, but would never enter her again. 'Therefore Michal the daughter of Saul had no child until the day of her death.' And David had no heir who was of both the line of Saul and his own, which contributed to the succession crises that undermined his kingdom.

The OT frankly portrays both its patriarchs and matriarchs as willing to lie and deceive whenever convenient to do so. Travel was dangerous for attractive women, even when well veiled, and even more dangerous for male companions: The women could be raped, but the men murdered. When Abraham and Sarah were in Egypt, he was afraid that the Egyptians would not only seize his beautiful wife but also get rid of him at the same time. So he told them Sarah was his sister. Sarah must have been very desirable, since the Pharaoh himself added her to his harem. Abraham proved to be a successful pimp or at least a very compliant husband: After all, the Pharaoh and Sarah were unlikely to be just discussing race relations. Sarah so pleased the Pharaoh that he gave Abraham great possessions. It is suggested in extenuation that Abraham and Sarah were in fact half-siblings, but that might have been an attempt to fool the Lord God as well as the Pharaoh.

The Lord God, however, was angered by these goings-on and sent a great plague on Egypt. This seemed unfair on the Egyptian people as a whole, especially since Sarah and Abraham deceived the Pharaoh, not the other way round. The same sister–wife story is told twice more in Genesis: once with Abraham and Sarah fooling King Abimelech and once with Isaac and Rebekah deceiving a king of that name. Perhaps a single incident gave rise to different stories? Perhaps Abimelech was a ruling title like Pharaoh? The principal deceivers were the wives–sisters in their hours of intimacy with the deceived rulers.

Rebekah helped her favourite son Jacob to cheat his older twin Esau out of his Birthright and blessing. She suggested Jacob should impersonate his old blind father, Isaac . . . When Jacob wanted to marry Rachel, the younger daughter of his kinsman Laban, Laban struck a hard bargain and made Jacob work for him for seven years to get his girl. Then Jacob was given the elder daughter, Leah, not the one he fancied. A persistent man, Jacob put in another seven years' service to get Rachel as well. Laban then became the deceived, not the deceiver. Jacob cheated Laban out of his cattle, whilst Rachel stole her father's jewels and household gods. Rachel avoided detection by placing the stolen goods on her camel, sitting on them, and claiming she could not get up because she was menstruating.

Sarah, despite or perhaps because of her experiences of travelling, remained barren when old and post-menstrual: It had 'ceased to be with Sarah after the way of women'. Concerned that Abraham may have no heir, so that the Covenant with God could not be fulfilled, Sarah ordered her handmaid Hagar to give him, Abraham, a child but she became jealous and angry when Hagar became pregnant. Sarah told Abraham, 'When she saw that she had conceived, I was despised in her eyes: the Lord judge between me and thee.' Sarah forced the weak-minded Abraham to expel Hagar into the wilderness, but the Lord God intervened and Hagar returned to the camp of Abraham, where she gave birth to Ishmael.

Later, when Sarah heard three strange visitors tell Abraham that she would bear him a son, she 'laughed within herself, saying, "After I am waxed old shall I have pleasure, my lord being old also?"' The visitors were angels, one perhaps God himself, and the prediction proved true: Isaac, the child of promise, was born. Yet Sarah's jealousy increased, since she feared that Isaac, as the younger son, would only be co-heir at best to Abraham. Then in a much disputed verse, she saw Ishmael 'mocking' his young half-brother or 'playing with Isaac' or 'sporting with Isaac'. If Sarah had good grounds for suspecting Ishmael of sexually molesting Isaac, her renewed demand that Abraham should expel Hagar and Ishmael could be judged less harshly.

The story continues: 'Abraham rose early in the morning, and took bread, and a bottle of water, and gave it unto Hagar, putting it on her shoulder, and the child, and sent her away'. Hagar ran out of water after wandering in 'the wilderness of Beer-Sheba', cast the child 'under one of the shrubs', and walked far enough away so as not to see him die. Fortunately, God took mercy on her and provided a spring from which mother and son drank and survived. Neither Abraham nor Sarah came out well from the story. Abraham did not suffer from loneliness after the deaths of both Hagar and Sarah. At well over 100 years in age, he took another wife, Keturah, and some more concubines. He proved exceedingly fertile in extreme old age.

The OT is also inconsistent in its treatments of incest: Strict and elaborate regulations define relationships that prohibit marriage. On the other hand, massive breaches of the rules of consanguinity are related with little, if any, criticism of the acts. After the destruction of Sodom by Angels of the Lord and the loss of their mother who turned to salt, Lot's daughters found themselves living in a cave with their father. They supposedly thought Lot was the only man left alive, although they had recently been in the still inhabited small town of Zoar, which Lot had left 'for he feared to dwell in Zoar'. Perhaps Lot feared the men of Zoar might be similar to the men of Sodom?

Lot's daughters made him drunk on successive nights. First, the elder daughter had intercourse with him and next night the younger girl. Genesis gave no indication of how long Lot's daughters took before deciding to 'preserve seed' of him or whether they tried to confirm their fear that 'there is not a man in the earth to come into us after the manner of all the earth'. How did the two daughters get the wine or spirits needed to get Lot drunk? When they had intercourse with him, was their father really fast asleep? These are intriguing questions, but no major criticism is leveled against Lot or the daughters. A major reason for telling the story may have been to stigmatize the Israelites' enemies as progeny of incest, since the Moabites and Ammonites were alleged to be descendants of the father–daughters couplings in the cave.

In total contradiction to the tables of forbidden degrees, the Israelites had a custom known as the Levirate, which required the next brother to impregnate a childless brother's widow: Any offspring would be regarded as heir to the dead brother. Tamar, a Cushite woman, was married to Er, the eldest son of Judah, son of Jacob and Rachel after whom Judea was named. Just what Er got up to, we are not told, but he 'was wicked in the sight of the Lord; and the Lord slew him' (*Gen. 38: 7*). Er's next brother, Onan, was ordered by Judah to impregnate Tamar. Onan, fearing that her pregnancy might reduce his own inheritance from Er, prematurely withdrew during intercourse so that Tamar did not get 'seed from him'. Onan's ejaculation over the soil, the carpet, the bedding, or Tamar's stomach 'displeased the Lord; wherefore He slew him also' (*Gen. 38: 10*). It did not pay in those days to displease the Lord God.

As a childless widow not born an Israelite, Tamar would be cast out and impoverished, but she was a very smart woman. She obviously knew her father-in-law's habits

223

and routine thoroughly. She knew that Judah would go to the city markets, so she disguised herself as a harlot, covering her face but no doubt displaying other of her charms, and sat by the gate through which Judah would enter the city. Judah, feeling randy and failing to recognize his daughter-in-law, entered her before he entered the city and did not spill his seed.

Evidently, Judah did not have cash in hand; instead he promised the veiled harlot a lamb, but Tamar demanded a security and was given a signet, bracelets, and staff to be redeemed when the sheep was delivered. Tamar made herself scarce before the sheep could be delivered. Three months later, she was clearly pregnant and the double standard made a familiar appearance. Judah ordered that his immoral daughter-in-law should be burnt to death. Then Tamar displayed the signet, bracelet, and staff; she told Judah, 'By the man whose these are am I with child.' Tamar bore twins and became the ancestress of King David and subsequently of Joseph, husband of Mary, the mother of Jesus. Onan became part of history, too: His act became called Onanism.

Another Tamar, daughter of King David, was raped by her half-brother, Amnon. David himself put his Tamar into danger by ordering her to take food to Amnon, who raped her, then threw her out on to the street. David did not punish Amnon for either rape or incest. Revenge on Amnon taken by Tamar's full brother, Absolom, set in motion the struggles for the succession, in which Solomon proved to be trickier than his brethren.

Jewish law and custom strongly opposed mixed marriages, but there are several very notable exceptions, including even some marriages of Israelite women to non-Israelite men. In either case, any attempt to convert a spouse out of Judaism was punishable by death. In *Deuteronomy* 17: 2–6, the Lord commands, 'If any be found among you [that] hath gone and served other gods, and worshipped them, either the sun, or moon, of any of the host of heaven. Thou shalt bring forth that man or that woman . . . and shalt stone them with stones, till they die.'

A major difference between the two kinds of mixed marriage was that male circumcision was usually required before a Jewish woman wed a non-Jew, whereas there was no such demand in the reverse situation.

Male circumcision was practiced by several Middle Eastern peoples besides the Children of Israel, but its origin and purpose remain unclear. Some claimed a hygienic origin. Others suggested that it was a modified form of child sacrifice: the foreskin substituting for the whole body, analogous to the way animal sacrifice gradually replaced human sacrifice. The official Israelite view seemed based on more than hygienic considerations: 'And the uncircumcised male who is not circumcised in the flesh of his foreskin, that should shall be cut off from his people.'

Some outsiders, like the Edomites and Egyptians of 'the third generation', married into Israel; Ammonites and Moabites were permanently excluded. Yet Cushite Tamar, daughter-in-law of Judah, and Moabite Ruth became biblical heroines,

The Lord God forbid Abraham from taking a wife from the daughters of Canaan, and after Isaac and Rebekah married, they instructed Jacob not to marry a Canaanite. The reference to Rachel's father's household gods that she stole suggested that Jacob married into a tribe of polytheists, but Rachel proved an ardent convert. God's opposition to Moses' marriage outside the Daughters of Israel to the Cushite Zipporah may explain one of the most puzzling episodes in the OT:

> And it came to pass by the way in the inn, that the Lord met him [Moses] and tried to kill him. Then Zipporah took a sharp stone, and cut off the foreskin of her son, and cast it at his feet, and said, Surely a bloody husband art thou to me.

Perhaps God was angry that Moses was tardy in returning to Egypt to liberate the Israelites? More likely the implication was that God's wrath was caused by Moses' marriage to a non-Jewess, a black Cushite, and/or that their child, and Moses himself, had not been circumcised. Zipporah may have thought the son's lack of circumcision was the correct explanation. She acted quickly, and the Lord seemed to have been propitiated: 'So he let him go' is the sole comment. Perhaps we must assume it was God that let Moses go free. Some scholars suggest that God infected Miriam, Moses' sister, with leprosy, the 'white disease', because she had condemned Moses for his marriage to a black woman. Given the importance of Moses in Jewish and Christian scripture, it is strange that the courage and initiative of Zipporah in saving his life received no further mention.

Moses was very severe on Israelites who did as he had done. God told him to order that every Israelite in a relationship with a Midianite woman should be put to death. Moses passed the order along the line. When such a couple came into the Israelite camp and entered a tent together, Phineas, a grandson of Moses' brother Aaron, 'rose up among the congregation and took a javelin in his hand. And he went after the man of Israel into the tent and thrust both of them through, the man of Israel and the woman through her belly'. Phineas is not criticized for this act.

An ugly abuse of circumcision is found in the story of Dinah, daughter of Jacob and Leah. Dinah was raped or consensually seduced by Shechem, a Hivite (Canaanite) prince who loved her and wished an honourable marriage. Jacob was prepared to bargain about this. Shechem's father, Hamor, offered fair terms: intermarriage and life in the future as one people. Jacob agreed, but his sons Levi and Simeon were determined to take bloody revenge. As a condition of allowing the marriage, they

225

persuaded all the Hivite males to undergo circumcision. Once the Hivites were in a weakened condition, Levi and Simeon led the Israelites into the city to kill all the Hivites, including Hamor and Shechem, take the women and children captive, and steal all their goods. Jacob was alarmed that his sons may have given the family a bad name, but he showed no concern for Dinah, whose lover and his father had been murdered by her brothers.

Kings David and Solomon were renowned for the size and multinational variety of their harems of wives and concubines. So it was not surprising that commoners also disobeyed the mixed marriage bar when they could. The vast numbers in their harems did not reduce the royal appetite for more women. David encouraged Abigail to betray her husband, Nabal, persuade the Lord to smite Nabal dead, and then make Abigail another of his wives. David also seduced Beersheba, the wife of Uriah the Hittite, a soldier who had been utterly loyal to him. David then plotted Uriah's death. David retained the Lord's favour and died in his bed with a new female comforter by his side . . . There is seldom a hint in the OT that any of the women objected.

David was not homophobic and had energy left for a relationship with Jonathan, son of Saul. On Jonathan's death, for which David was in part responsible, David mourned, 'Very pleasant hath thou been unto me. Wonderful was thy love to me, passing the love of women.'

After the end of the Babylonian captivity, the returning leadership did not intend that there should be a return to the multicultural sexual policies of David and Solomon. Ezra demanded that descendants of Jews who had remained in Judea 'should not intermarry with non-Jews and that 'the wives and children of existing mixed marriages must be put away' (*Ezra* 10: 12) . . . . Ezra's command was not fully obeyed, so Nehemiah adopted sterner methods. Nehemiah 'contended with them, and cursed them, and plucked off their hair, and made them swear by God, saying, ye shall not give your daughters unto their sons, nor take their daughters for their sons, or for yourselves' (*Neh.* 13: 25).

Some OT stories have very little to do with religious affairs but are just the sort of 'human interest' stories that have fascinated our species since the first records of its existence. Illicit sex is usually at their centre. Such OT stories include those about Potiphar's wife and Joseph, Rahab, Ruth, Samson and Delilah, Deborah and Jael, Jezebel, and Esther.

The handsome and talented Joseph was propositioned by the wife of his Egyptian master, Potiphar: She cast her eyes upon Joseph, and she said, 'Lie with me.' Joseph rejected, 'This great wickedness.' A woman of great persistence, she 'spake to Joseph day by day, that he hearkened not to her, to lie by her or to be with her'. At last, when she got him on his own in the house, Potiphar's wife 'caught him by his garment, saying, "Lie with me", and he left his garment in her hand, and fled, and got him out'. She accused him of attempted rape and Joseph was sent to prison.

Prostitutes can be biblical heroines, provided they help the Israelites. In Jericho, Rahab the harlot sheltered two Israelite spies and enabled them to escape from the city. In return, she and her family were spared when the Israelites 'burnt the city with fire, and all that was therein', apart from silver, gold, and other valuables taken as loot. Would Rahab have been regarded as a heroine if she had helped two foreign spies in an Israelite city?

Many mothers-in-law oppose second marriages of their daughters-in-law, but Ruth, a Moabite widow, had a mother-in-law, Naomi, who planned a second marriage for her. Naomi must also have married 'out' and planned to return to Bethlehem, where she was born and had some wealthy distant relatives, the most prominent being Boaz. Naomi advised Ruth on how to catch him. Ruth was to go reaping on Boaz's land: This would show she was a hard worker and would enable her to contact Boaz without being accused of immoral conduct. After a successful introduction, Ruth gave Boaz food and drink in a barn and got him to 'lie down at the end of the heap of corn'. Then 'she came softly and uncovered his feet, and laid her down'. According to several scholars, 'uncovering the feet' was a euphemism for exposing the genitals.

When Boaz awoke at midnight, 'behold, a woman lay at his feet', who told him 'spread therefore thy skirt over thy handmaid'. We are not told what took place under Boaz's skirt, but 'spreading the skirt' was a euphemism for sexual intercourse. It cannot have been unpleasant to either party. Soon they married and were happy ever after. One of their grandsons was King David.

Against his parents' advice, Samson married a Philistine woman at a time when her people were in control of the Israelites. Samson had a wager with a group of her Philistine kinsmen that they could not solve a riddle he put to them. They tried hard but failed with only an hour or so left to get the answer. The Philistines threatened Samson's bride that they would burn her and her father, unless she got the secret from him. This she did, but she was seized by her family and married to a Philistine. In anger, Samson burnt the Philistines' crops and killed the soldiers they sent against him.

Samson did not learn from experience. He patronized a Philistine harlot in Gaza and was surrounded by their men, but he broke free of them. The Philistines found out that Samson had a fatal potential weakness, but they do not know what it was. They sent a beautiful woman, Delilah, to discover this secret, just as Samson's former wife had revealed the riddle to them. Three times Samson tricked her with false answers, retained his strength, and could not be taken by the Philistines. The fourth time proved fatal: Samson told Delilah the truth that he would lose his strength if his hair was shaved from this head. Delilah betrayed him and exited from the story. Samson was blinded and chained to the wall of the Philistine temple, where the Philistines could mock him. As his hair re-grew, Samson's strength returned and he pulled the temple down, killing himself and 3,000 Philistines. Delilah is a political seductress. She would probably have been portrayed as a great heroine if Samson had been a Philistine and she a daughter of Israel.

Deborah, the prophetess, was judge over Israel. When the Israelite men were fearful of battle, Deborah condemned Barak, the military commander of Israel's army, for his timidity and directed the army herself. After victory, another woman called Jael killed single-handedly the enemy Canaanite general, Sisera. Jael hammered a nail into Sisera's head as he lay fast asleep in her tent, presumably after sex as well as food and drink. Judges suggested that Sisera was struck at a moment of vulnerability: 'At her feet he bowed, he fell, he lay down: at her feet he bowed, he fell: where he bowed, there he fell down dead.' Jael may have been a prostitute. It seems otherwise unlikely that, even when fleeing from enemies, Sisera would enter her tent and ask for refreshments. Jael, like Rahab, is honoured for her action.

Jezebel was a Princess of Tyre married to King Ahab of Israel. Her murder is told with salacious pleasure (2 Kings 11: 3). Jezebel was condemned for persuading her husband to have Naboth stoned to death in order to acquire his vineyard. A wicked deed to be sure, but no worse than, say, David's plot to have the valiant Uriah killed so that he could seize his wife Bathsheba. The OT author hated Jezebel because as her name suggested, she worshipped Baal and not the Lord God of Israel. The prophet Elijah prophesied that 'the dogs shall eat Jezebel by the wall of Jezreel'. Jezebel became Queen-Mother on the death of Ahab, but her son, Joram, was overthrown by Jehu, outstandingly murderous among a very bloodthirsty crew. Jezebel showed courage: 'She painted her face, and (at) tired her head and looked out at a window', from which she defied Jehu. Jehu called on her attendants, eunuchs, to throw her out of the window. They obeyed. As Jezebel lay bleeding on the road, Jehu rode his horse over her and left her body to be eaten by dogs, so as to fulfill the prophecy of Elijah. After a series of massacres, the Lord God told Jehu: 'Because thou hast done well . . . and hast done unto the house of Ahab according to all that was in my heart, thy children of the fourth generation shall sit on the throne of Israel.' Not, perhaps, the most moral conclusion to that encounter.

BYZANTINE EMPRESSES

Over the centuries kings and their heirs have usually married on the basis of state or dynastic needs. Given their restricted marital options, they were rarely frowned upon if they took mistresses or concubines for sexual satisfaction. It was rare that a king rejected a bride chosen for political reasons simply because her appearance displeased him. One exception was Henry VIII, who took speedy steps to rid himself of Anne of Cleves, reputedly described by him as the Mare of Flanders, soon after he first set eyes upon her.

In the few surviving monarchies, kings and princes have had in recent years more latitude and some have chosen brides for their charms, although Edward VIII, had to renounce his throne in order to marry Mrs Simpson, perhaps mainly because he chose a woman already twice married and about to be divorced. The present Duke of York chose entirely for love, but experienced severe marital difficulties. It is very unlikely that Lady Diana Spencer would have become the beloved Princess Di, the People's Princess, if she had been frowsy-looking or disfigured, or that the heir to the Danish crown would have chosen Tasmanian Mary had she not been beautiful and charming, or that Kate Middleton would have become Duchess of Cambridge had she been as plain as a pikestaff.

Some queens and empresses regnant and royal heiresses presumptive have also been influenced by appearance as well as by diplomatic and dynastic concerns. Queen Victoria was captivated by Albert's good looks and Mary Queen of Scots by Boswell's strength and physique. When she was Princess Elizabeth, our Queen was not indifferent to the good looks of the suitor she chose.

Princesses Diana and Mary did not, however, catch their future husband's eye when parading before them, nor did the Duchess of Cambridge, but in the Byzantine (Eastern Roman) Empire a beauty competition was sometimes organized and the Emperor or his heir chose the woman he fancied most. A bit like Cinderella and her Prince Charming. That it was also a Jewish custom is shown by the story of Esther.

Shakespeare gave Henry IV the line, 'Uneasy lies the head that wears a crown. He could have added with equal truth that the heads of the wives of those that wear a crown are also very likely to lie uneasy, 'This was true for all of the Empresses considered here. Four held power as Empress Regents: Sophia, Irene of Athens, Zoe Carbonopsina and Theophano; three became Empress through specially arranged beauty competitions: Irene of Athens, the gorgeous aristocratic Paphlagonian Theodora, and Eudocia Balana.

We have already noted that the volume of interesting and valuable historical material available to us is so immense that far more must be completely omitted than can be included, even in outlines form. This seems to be true of the Byzantine or Eastern Roman Empire or Rum or whatever we term that state that endured in some form or another until 1453: a year in English history in which the factional disputes that became the Wars of the Roses became acute following the English expulsion from France and the end of the 'The Hundred Years War, although none could know this at the time.

Edward Gibbon was utterly contemptuous of the Byzantine record. He described it as 'without a single exception, the most thoroughly base and despicable form that civilization has yet assumed'. Protests against that harsh verdict have been made by Sir Steven Runciman and John Julius Norwich. Lord Norwich dismissed it as grotesque and drew attention to the 'deeply religious' character of Byzantine life, its high standards of learning and scholarship and its role in the preservation and transmission of the culture of the Roman Empire at its height. Norwich listed as its greatest Emperors the first Constantine its founder, Justinian, Heraclius, the two Basils and Alexius Comnenus. No woman's name appears there, but that of Zoe features among those Norwich concedes to have been "contemptible" the males he names are Phocas, Michael III and the Angeli. 'Scheming women' often play an important part in Norwich's accounts of Byzantine failures. Whatever our verdict may be it is all too true that even less is known by English and Australian children of a thousand years of Byzantium than are comparable periods of, say, Indian, Chinese or Scandinavian history.

I have included summaries of how Byzantine Emperors died, if only to remind us how uneasy it could be to wear a crown. They are not by a long chalk the group most prone to dangers that may beset a ruler. Even more striking, if we accept the theory of ancient kingship that Robert Graves supported after his lengthy studies of Greek myth, was that in matriarchies every King for many generations was ritually killed by his successor, after a year of kingship in which every pleasure he sought was satisfied, at least within the resources of the time. Readers of Homer and Greek myth in general may recall examples of kings who enjoy their positions to marriage to the queen, who is the legitimate heir and bequeather of rule. Penelope's suitors seek to marry her not only for her beauty and skill as a needlewoman, but because her husband will become King of Ithica. According to this theory Odysseus and his like were probably kings who refused to accept the fate for which they were destined under matriarchal and matrilineal laws presided over by a Mother Goddess.

Here we look briefly at the public careers of seven Byzantine Empresses. They might all have fallen into both categories and have won beauty competitions to become imperial brides and then be left as widows with political powers as regents, but only Irene appears on both lists. She was also the only one to be made a saint after death, although she certainly had not been one in life. Does my short account of these Byzantine empresses strengthen Gibbon's verdict or that of Lord Norwich?

SOPHIA: WIFE AND WIDOW OF JUSTIN II

In the reign of the Emperor Justinian (525-565) the power behind the throne until her death in 549 was his wife, the Empress Theodora.[261] Thus Byzantium had become accustomed to a woman in effective control. When Justinian died, his closest relatives were two nephews, both named Justin. It was believed that the two Justins agreed that whichever was chosen would make the other second in the state. However, when Justin, the son of Vigilantia, was chosen and became emperor, he arranged the murder of his cousin. The day after his inauguration, the successful Justin crowned as Augusta (Empress) his wife Sophia, a niece of Theodora. It was rumored that they sent for the head of the murdered Justin and kicked it around the palace. Sophia was the first empress to appear on coins together with the emperor.

Byzantium was then, as usual, wracked by theological disputes: at this time chiefly about the relationship between the three persons of the Trinity. Sophia had been openly Monophysite, regarded by the Greek Orthodox Church as one of many heresies, but she and Justin accepted Orthodox doctrine three years before Justinian's death, to improve their chances of succeeding him. The Monophysites believed that the Incarnate Christ had only one Nature and was not part Man and Part God. Divisions on this insoluble issue split Orthodox Christianity just as much as disputes over Icons had done. To this day the main Christian churches of Egypt (the Copts), of Syria (the Jacobites) and of Abyssinia and Armenia hold Monophysite doctrines.

In his last years Justinian bribed Avar tribes and the Persian Sassanids to keep the peace. Justin and Sophia thought this ignoble and a waste of money. However, when the Avars and Sassanids resumed their attacks they cost the Byzantine Empire much more than Justinian's subsidies had done. It was a case contrary to Rudyard Kipling's dictum: 'If once you pay the Danegeld, /You'll never get rid of the Danes.'

Defeats at the hands of the Persians drove Justin to madness and Sophia seized effective command. Sophia feared the people would not accept a woman as sole regent, so she persuaded the insane Justin to promote Tiberius, a capable although recently defeated general, as co-regent, with the rank of Caesar.

Sophia liked to throw her weight around and to humiliate possible rivals for power. She not only dismissed the most capable general, Narses, a eunuch, but sent him a spinning wheel with a message that he ought in future spend his time spinning wool with her women. In revenge Narses encouraged the Lombards to invade Italy, whilst the Byzantine armies on the eastern frontiers could hardly keep the Persians under check. Sophia played the woman card: when she reminded the Persian Shah Chosroes that once when he had fallen sick, she had sent her best doctors to treat him. Chosroes granted Sophia a truce, although for a considerable sum. Chosroes was not always sympathetic to women: he offered as a present to the Khan of the Turks 2,000 Christian maidens, many from within the Byzantine Empire. In a famous story all the virgins drowned themselves in a river rather than face a fate worse than death.

Sophia was forced to return to Justinian's policy of bribes for peace; her fiscal prudence, termed avarice by her enemies, built up a reserve that Tiberius quickly disposed of when he became emperor. By the time Justin died he demanded to be pushed around on a portable throne by his attendants. Only organ music soothed him. The childless Sophia may have hoped for a better husband once she was widowed and saw Tiberius as the answer. However, he would have to discard his wife Ino first. When Tiberius refused to divorce his wife and marry her, Sophia began to plot against him, but without success. Tiberius expelled her from the palace and placed her under close surveillance, but she was not physically harmed or forced into a convent.

Emperors from Justin II to Constantine VI

Justin II: died insane in 578

Tiberius II Constantine: poisoned in 582

Maurice: murdered in 602, together with his four sons

Phocas: blinded, murdered and chopped to pieces in 610

Heraclius: died of dropsy aided by poison in 641.

Constantine III: natural death in 541, and Heraclonas nose slit and exiled also in 641 (Joint Emperors);

Constans II 'Pogonatus': murdered in his bath in 668

Constantine IV: natural causes (dysentery) in 685

Leontius: beheaded in 698

Tiberius III: beheaded in 705.

Justinian II 'Rhinometus': beheaded and his severed head presented to his successor in 711

Philippicus Bardanes: blinded and murdered by his own soldiers in 715.

Anastasius II: clubbed to death by his own soldiers in 715.

Leo III: natural death in 741

Artabasdus: blinded publicly with his two sons and exiled in 742

Constantine V 'Copronymus:741-2 and 743-775 restored to throne in 742 died on campaign in 775.'

Leo IV: natural death (fever) in 780.

Constantine VI: blinding by mother led to death in 797

IRENE: WIFE AND WIDOW OF EMPEROR LEO IV

Irene Sarantapechaina, known as Irene of Athens, was empress consort between 775 and 780 and then empress mother. Byzantium still regarded itself, despite the loss of the western provinces, as legitimate ruler of the entire former Roman Empire. Its emperors fought to hold on to Italy and North Africa, but were faced with great and immediate threats from the Abbasid Muslim Caliphs in Anatolia and, in the Balkans, from the Bulgars. The Empire continued to be weakened by religious disputes, the main one in Irene's time being about the place of icons in worship. Icondules venerated icons, but Iconoclasts considered such veneration a breach of the Commandment not to bow down before idols.

Irene was apparently an orphan in an Athenian family of the minor nobility. She was brought to Constantinople by Emperor Constantine V in 769, and there married his son Leo. Irene was extremely beautiful and may have been selected in a bride-show: an up-market beauty competition, as at least three other imperial brides are known to have been. In 771 Irene gave birth to a son, the future Constantine VI. When Constantine V died in 775, Irene's husband became Leo IV at the age of twenty-five. Leo, an Iconoclast, pursued at first a policy of moderation towards Iconodules. However, after 780 he dismissed several courtiers for icon-veneration and promoted iconoclasts to leading positions in the Orthodox Church. Ever since the time of Constantine I, who first made Christianity the official religion of the Roman Empire, the Eastern Churches had been very much under imperial influence. Irene was a zealous iconodule, but managed to conceal her fervour, until Leo discovered icons concealed in her wardrobes; Leo was apparently so incensed that he refused to share the marriage bed with her again.

Leo died later in 780 and Irene proclaimed herself Regent on behalf of her nine-year old Constantine. Her first move was to grant toleration to both iconoclasts and iconodule, but, once iconodules had built up their strength, she launched a persecution of the iconoclasts. She was opposed by Iconoclastic mutineers who tried to rise to the throne Nicephorus, a half-brother of Leo IV. After suppressing the rebellion Irene had Nicephorus, his brothers and other conspirators tonsured and ordained as priests, normally a disqualification for imperial rule. Later she regretted her comparatively merciful policy.

Irene sought a closer relationship with the Carolingian dynasty that ruled the Franks and controlled he Popes in Rome. She hoped to reduce disputes between the Roman Curia and the Orthodox Patriarchs of Byzantium. Her crushing of Iconoclasm helped in this, but her diplomacy did not. She negotiated a marriage between her son and a daughter of Charlemagne, sent an official to instruct the princess in Greek, but then broke off the engagement, against her son's wishes.

After the election of one of her supporters, Tarasius, as Patriarch of Constantinople, Irene convened in 787 a Church Council at Nicaea, recognized by both Rome and Constantinople, which authorized the veneration of icons. Edward Gibbon noted that the secular sponsors of both famous Nicene Councils, Constantine the Great and Irene, each murdered one of their own children.

As Constantine the young Emperor approached maturity he resented his mother's control, especially after he married at eighteen the beautiful Mary of Amnia. Irene antagonized him by decreeing that her name should always precede his in ceremonies and on official documents. After crushing an attempt by Constantine to free himself from her grip, she ordained that the oath of fidelity, taken by soldiers and officials, should be made solely to her. This was met by mutiny and soldiers proclaimed Constantine sole ruler. Irene's chief official, Stauracius, was flogged, tonsured and exiled, and she was confined to her palace.

Irene had not been notably successful as commander-in-chief: she subdued a rebellion in Sicily but, after one of her generals defected, she was forced to agree to a huge annual tribute to the Arabs in exchange for a three year truce. Constantine, however, proved totally inept. He was defeated by the Caliph Harun al-Rashid, to whom he was forced to pay an even larger tribute. Then, in a rash moment of filial contrition, he restored his mother to her old position. This infuriated the iconoclasts who released Nicephorus from his monastery and proclaimed him Emperor. Constantine's troops defeated Nicephorus, who was blinded and had his tongue cut out by his nephew. Constantine soon alienated the Patriarch and the monastic party by divorcing Mary of Amnia, who had not provided a male heir, and then marrying one of the ladies of his divorced wife's court, Theodote, who gave birth to a son the following year.

Irene took advantage of clerical rage against her son and in 797, after Constantine failed to repulse another Arab invasion, she moved against him. Constantine fled but was captured by her agents. Irene decided she had been too merciful in the past to her disobedient son. He was carried back to Constantinople, where his eyes were gouged out in so savage a way that he died aged twenty-seven from his wounds. His baby son disappeared, very likely murdered. In those circumstances Irene became the first woman ever to reign in her own right exclusively, not as regent or conjointly, over the Byzantine Empire.

So, Irene finally held the position and status for which she had craved, but she was bitterly hated and had emptied the imperial treasury in bribes to gain support for her coup against her son. Her overthrow of Iconoclasm improved relations with the Papacy, but did not prevent war with the Franks, who seized Byzantine territories in Italy in 788. Irene faced a difficult problem in 800 when Pope Leo III crowned Charlemagne in Rome as Holy Roman Emperor. The Byzantine nobility, clergy and populace were united in opposing the establishment of a schismatic Roman Empire in the West. In her extremity Irene explored the possibility of marrying Charlemagne, at that moment a widower, in order to retain her power, refill the imperial treasury, and retain some sort of imperial unity.

News of her intention shocked her leading officials and generals, who considered that such a marriage would put Byzantium under the control of barbarian Franks.

Irene was deposed, arrested and sent to a convent. She died the following year. There was never again a unified Roman Empire. Despite the disasters of her rule and her mutilation and virtual murder of her son, Irene's restoration of icons and endowment of monasteries led to her sanctification by the Greek Orthodox Church as St Irene.

Theophano of Athens, Wife and Widow of Stauracius

In 811 Emperor Nicephorus assembled a range of beautiful girls who might be suitable brides for his teenage son Stauracius. Nicephorus acted as judge. He decided on gold, silver and bronze medalists, but kept the winner and runner-up for himself and gave third-placed Theophano of Athens to Stauracius as his bride. Perhaps his selfishness and lust brought down divine vengeance, because shortly afterwards Nicephorus was defeated in battle by the Bulgars and was beheaded by them. The Bulgar Khan, Krum, had Nicephorus's skull mounted in silver and used it as his drinking cup. The young Stauracius was deposed by a general, Michael Rhangabe, and lost his beautiful Theophano as well, when she was expelled to a monastery where he quickly died. So the three most beautiful young women of their time in the Byzantine Empire had no long-term gain from their triumphs. All three were sent off to convents and forced to take the veil.

EMPERORS FROM NICEPHORUS I TO LEO VI

Nicephorus I: killed in battle and beheaded by the Bulgars in 811
Stauracius: killed in the same battle as his father, Nicephorus.
Michael I Rhangabe: abdicated and died in a monastery in 813
Leo V: assassinated in a church in 820.
Michael II: died of kidney disease in 829
Theophilus: died of dysentery in 842
Michael III: assassinated in his own bedroom in 867.
Basil I: died whilst hunting in 886, perhaps by accident.
Leo VI: died of natural causes in 912.

THEODORA WIFE AND WIDOW OF THEOPHILUS

In 821 the seventeen year old Theophilus was crowned co-Emperor of Byzantium with his father Michael II, who had deposed young Stauracius. Almost immediately another beauty competition was arranged. Theophilus was allowed to choose for himself and picked a gorgeous aristocratic Paphlagonian named Theodora. For some years all went well, except that the couple, although they had five healthy daughters, had only one son who died in infancy. Then, after twenty years of marriage, Theodora gave birth to another boy who lived.

In 838 Theophilus, by then king, returned to Constantinople from victory over the Saracens, and was welcomed home by Theodora. Thousands of Muslim prisoners were paraded before them, but soon the fortunes of war changed: the Byzantines were defeated and Theophilus died. Theodora became Regent for her two-year-old son.

The Byzantine Empire had been wracked for years by religious disputes between Iconodules, who revered icons as symbols of Christ and His Holy Mother, and Iconoclasts, who regarded icons as objects of superstitious worship and destroyed them when they could. Theodora used her new power as Regent to support the Iconodules: she restored and added new icons in churches throughout the Empire. Then Theodora agreed to the persecution of the Paulician Christians, who were highly puritanical iconoclasts. The Paulicians were ordered to accept veneration of icons and other doctrines of the Greek Orthodox Church on pain of death. John Julius Norwich wrote that 100,000 were reported to have 'perished—by hanging, drowning, the sword, even by crucifixion.' Surviving Paulicians fled eastwards into the Saracen Emirate of Melitene. They became dedicated enemies of the Byzantine Empire.

Theodora fell from power through family quarrels. At fifteen her son Michael made Eudocia Ingerina, who was half-Swedish, his mistress and wanted to marry her. Theodora objected and pressured Michael into marrying another Eudocia, surnamed Decapolitana, for whom he felt no affection at all. In 855 a vengeful Michael plotted against his mother and banished her and his sisters to a convent where they were forced to take the veil. Twelve years later Michael III was himself murdered by a rival. Theodora and her daughters were allowed to return to Constantinople to mourn over Michael's mutilated body, but it was an unhappy ending.

EUDOCIA BAIANA: WIFE OF LEO VI

Emperor Leo VI ('The Wise') came to the imperial throne in 886. At sixteen he fell in love with the beautiful Zoe Zautsina, but, his father, Emperor Basil the Macedonian, was persuaded by his wife, Leo's stepmother Eudocia, to force Leo to marry instead one of her relatives, Theophano. Leo and Theophano produced a daughter, but he would not renounce Zoe Zautsina, even after she was married off to Theodore Gutzuniates. Leo was imprisoned for three months by his father, who contemplated having him blinded, so that he could not succeed to the throne. However, Leo was released and then within a few months Basil died whilst hunting, either by accident or murder. Leo then became Emperor.

Leo appointed Zoe Zautsina's father as his chief minister, but remained married to Theophano. Their daughter died in infancy and Theophano died in 897 still under thirty. Within a very short time Theodore Gutzuniates also died, so that Leo and Zoe

Zautsina could be united at last as man and wife. They had a daughter, too, but within two years Zoe Zautsina followed Theophano to the grave.

After he became a widower for the second time, Leo organized a bride show in which hundreds of the most beautiful girls in the Byzantine Empire competed. Leo chose Eudocia Baiana from Phrygia. Eudocia did her part and after nine months gave birth to a son. Unfortunately, she died in childbirth and the baby boy died a week later. Leo then took another beautiful Zoe, Zoe Carbonopsina, as his mistress, because Patriarch Nicholas Mysticus would not permit him a fourth marriage. The Patriarch also condemned Leo for living with Zoe Carbonopsina outside marriage and having two children, one a boy, out of wedlock. Leo and Zoe then married without the blessing of the Church, and Leo proclaimed Zoe Carbonopsina Empress.

ZOE CARBONOPSINA: WIFE AND WIDOW OF LEO VI

Leo ousted Nicholas from the Patriarchate and replaced him by the saintly but pliable Euthymius. Despite generations of opposition to Papal interference in the Orthodox Church, Euthymius and Leo placed the marriage issue before Pope Sergius III. A papal dispensation was granted, but the emperor was castigated as a penitent and forbidden to sit down during any church service. The key outcome for Leo was that his son, Constantine, was legitimized. When Leo died in 912 the boy was crowned as Constantine Porphyrogenitus (born in the purple').

Widowhood was disastrous for Zoe. Her dissolute brother-in-law Alexander set aside the boy as Emperor and expelled her and her friends from the imperial palace. She feared with good reason that Alexander would have the young Constantine castrated to debar him from the throne, but Alexander relented and just before his death named Constantine as his successor. However, the Council of Regency was dominated by Zoe's enemies and she was excluded from it. Nicholas Mysticus, restored as Patriarch, became First Regent, arrested Zoe and exiled her to a convent after her hair had been completely shorn. There she was known as Sister Anna.

After another two years Patriarch Nicholas was so unpopular that he was dismissed from the Regency Council; Sister Anna was recalled and became Empress Zoe and Regent again. Zoe's generals defeated Muslim armies in Armenia, Syria and Italy, and defended Adrianople successfully against a Bulgar army. She was immensely popular in 917. Then within months her generals quarreled and failed to support each other against fresh Bulgar attacks. The Byzantine navy and army were shattered and survivors tortured and massacred. Zoe became hated instead of praised. She decided her only hope of survival was to win the affection of one of the two generals who had let her down. She chose Leo Phocas, who accepted her offer and became her close adviser as well. Her enemies then appealed to the other failed general, Romanus

Lecapenus, to save Constantine, by then thirteen, from domination by Leo Phocas. Constantine was turned against his mother and personally announced that she was no longer Regent and would in future be confined to the women's quarter of the palace. Zoe was accused by Romanus Lecapenus of trying to poison him. Zoe was sent back with a shaven head to her convent and remained Sister Anna for the rest of her life. No sainthood was conferred upon her.

Emperors from Leo VI to Nicephorus Phocas

Alexander: died of a stroke in 913 after heavy drinking and drugs,

Constantine VII Porphyrogenitus: died in 959 of natural causes

Romanus I Lecapenus: deposed, exiled to a monastery died of natural causes in 944.

Romanus II: died in 963 probably of natural causes.

Nicephorus II Phocas: assassinated in his own bedroom in 969

THEOPHANO, WIFE AND WIDOW OF ROMANUS II

Romanus II became emperor in 959, a time of great success and prosperity in the Byzantine lands. Romanus was handsome, charming and clever in many ways, but he spurned royal princesses and married the beautiful daughter of a Peloponnesian innkeeper: Theophano. Although only eighteen, Theophano was already a powerful character and soon dominated her husband and the palace.

Theophano persuaded Romanus to dismiss from his presence his mother and five sisters, who had all previously been important influences upon him. The sisters all had their heads shaved, in Theophano's presence, by the patriarch Polyeuctus, and were packed off to five different convents. Theophano also purged Romanus's court, retaining as chief adviser the President of the Senate Basil Lecapenus, an illegitimate son of Emperor Romulus I.

Romulus died unexpectedly in 963. There was no evidence of any complicity by Theophano's in her husband's death, which left her and her four children in great danger, but there were rumors that she had poisoned him. Fearful of usurpers, Theophano looked around for a protector. She chose Nicephorus Phocas, ugly and violent but a very capable general. After a successful overseas campaign, Nicephorus returned to Constantinople to be proclaimed Co-emperor with Theophano's two sons. In what may have been a double bluff, Nicephorus banished Theophano to prison-like quarters, but then recalled her and married her. Perhaps he fell in love with her beauty or wanted continuity in government or both.

Polyeuctus declared the marriage illegal, because Nicephorus had been godfather to one of Theophano's children, but Nicephorus outmaneuvered him. Nicephorus was a man of his word and protected Theophano from her enemies, even though he claimed that they never had sexual intercourse, because each had been married previously.

After a few years, Theophano, still only 28, may have found Nicephorus increasingly repulsive compared with her first husband Romanus. She took as a lover a leading politician, a small but handsome Armenian John Tzimisces. Theophano and John plotted Nicephorus's death. Theophano ensured that her husband was alone and in his own bedroom, fast asleep. John sailed in a storm across the Bosphorus to join the conspirators. They inflicted multiple wounds on their former commander in battle. Then they proclaimed John Tzimisces Emperor.

Abetting her second husband's murder did Theophano no good. Patriarch Polyeuctus was firm and forbade John to marry her. John obeyed and banished her from court. Theophano was never seen again in Constantinople. The murderous John Tzimisces proved to be an outstanding Emperor and both of Theophano's sons lived safely under his protection. Theophano was perhaps more fortunate in her end than she deserved.

CONCLUSIONS

Sophia, Irene, Zoe and Theophano were very determined and unscrupulous women, but morally they were neither notably superior nor inferior to their husbands or to Byzantine rulers as a whole. They were handicapped because they were not themselves of royal lineage, because women were not expected to wield power, because they could neither control their generals nor lead the troops themselves, and because their sons resented control by mothers and stepfathers who were usurpers already or planned to be.

The empresses' careers give little support to claims that female rule is more peaceful at home or abroad than that of men. However, several of them demonstrated a capacity to survive difficult situations, before they were deposed from all power. Two died young in childbirth and five were locked up in convents and lived and died in obscurity but in relative comfort, whereas mutilation and assassination were the fates of many Byzantine Emperors. Reading Byzantine history may lead to agreement with Voltaire that 'History is just the portrayal of crimes and misfortunes' of mankind.'[262] On the other hand the survival of the Empire for a millennium until 1453 gives hope that our institutions may survive our own crimes and misfortunes.

Among many troublesome thoughts that arise from reading about the lives and times of rulers is that their downfalls may often be traced to their better deeds rather than to merciless actions. Machiavelli, of course, enlarged on this not very original proposition. Although she chose the path of personal power and was rarely restrained by excessive scruple, Sophia may well have looked back with regret to having spared the lives of Nicephorus, his brothers and other accomplices. She had injured them enough to ensure their permanent hostility, but could not be certain that she would always have the upper hand. Irene would not have been more execrated if she had seen to it that her son was murdered immediately once she had usurped his authority and incited his anger. Finally he suffered more than if she had ordered his death years earlier. She would still have been made a saint, one is forced with some regret to surmise. Theodora fell from power because of the minor peccadillo of putting pressure on her son Michael to marrying Eudocia Decapolitana, whom he did not love, but prayers were said for her after she ordered the persecution of the Paulicians. The most wicked act carried out by Theophano: her plotting of the murder of her second husband, Nicephorus, who had treated her and her children well, in order to marry and make emperor her lover, John Tzimisces, inaugurated one of the most successful reigns in Byzantine history

Chapter 11

TALES OF THE UNEXPECTED

CROESUS AND CYRUS

Croesus of Lydia and Cyrus of Persia provided Herodotus, 'The Father of History', with some of his best stories. As both an expert story-teller and an insightful historian, Herodotus provided us with many tales of the unexpected. Lydia was a kingdom which occupied the western half of Anatolia or Asia Minor, present-day Turkey. It was one of the wealthiest states of the ancient world because of its gold mines. Its capital city for several generations was Sardis, built by Gyges during the seventh century BC.

Lydia featured in several Greek myths: Tantalus was said to be their ruler and Niobe of the sorrows his daughter. After death, Tantalus was made to suffer for his sins by being given a dreadful thirst that he cannot satisfy from a pitcher of water that he cannot quite reach: so we get our English verb to 'tantalize.' His proud daughter Niobe boasts that her fourteen children prove her to be a superior mother to Leto, because the nymph has only the twins Apollo and Artemis. In spiteful revenge, Artemis and Apollo killed all fourteen of Niobe's children with poisoned arrows. Niobe is turned to stone and weeps forever as waters pour down her petrified cheeks. In Greek myth, Lydia was also the first home of the double axe, the labrys, and Omphale, daughter of the river Iardanos, was a queen for whom *Heracles* had to carry out one of his tasks and from whom he fathered two sons. A famous semi-mythical king was Midas of Phrygia, whose touch turned all, including his only daughter, to gold.

Croesus, like Midas, was famed for his wealth and admired for his generosity. He beautified Sardis and paid for the construction of the Temple of Artemis at Ephesus, which became one of the Seven Wonders of the Ancient World. Croesus often consulted the Oracle before taking any important decisions.

Croesus owed the throne to his great-grandfather, Gyges, who had assassinated hi friend and king for seventeen years, Candaules. The story was told that Candaule boasted to Gyges that the queen, his wife, was the most beautiful woman on earth To convince Gyges that he was not exaggerating, Candaules arranged for Gyges t be hidden behind curtains whilst the queen undressed so that he could see her in al her radiance. Gyges protested that such an act would be wicked and impious, bu Candaules insisted. The queen saw Gyges's shadow as he left the bedroom. Next day she sent for him and told him that she would never forget the insult. She gave Gyge a choice: Either he should kill Candaules, marry her, and seize the kingdom or h himself would be executed. Gyges chose life and the queen. The story and a paintin; of it play a key role in the tenth volume, called *Temporary Kings*. In the brilliar series of novels by Anthony Powell: *A Dance to the Music of Time*, Powell is th perfect novelist for historians.

In several versions of the myth, Gyges had a magical ring that conferred invisibilit on him. In all versions, civil war followed the assassination of Candaules, and it onl ended when the two sides agreed to abide by the verdict of the Delphic Oracle o Apollo. The Oracle decided in favour of Gyges, but warned him that his dynast would only last for five generations on the Lydian throne.

When Cyrus of Persia began to make great conquests on Croesus's eastern frontie Herodotus related that Croesus asked the Delphian Oracle whether or not he shoul challenge the Persian power before it became too great to oppose. The Oracle replie that if he made war on Cyrus Croesus would overthrow a great empire. Croesu declared war, but his own empire was overthrown. When Croesus's capital cit Sardis, was captured, Cyrus was placed on a funeral pyre, and as the flames reache him, he cried out, 'Solon! Solon! Would that I had listened to you.' Cyrus wanted t know what Croesus meant and damped the fire. Croesus explained that he had onc been visited by the great Greek sage, Solon, to whom he displayed his treasures an told of his wealth. Croesus then asked Solon who was the happiest man he had eve met and expected his own name to be the reply. Instead, Solon nominated an Athenia and two Argives. Solon said to Croesus, 'As relates to what you inquire of me, cannot say until I hear you have ended your life happily.' According to Herodotu Solon left Croesus with the words, 'Count no man happy until he is dead'. Anothe story Herodotus told of the seizure of the palace concerned the king's son, who ha been dumb since birth. The Oracle had told Croesus that the day the boy spoke woul be an unhappy one for his father. Croesus did not agree, since he hoped very muc for the boy to be able to speak. As Persian soldiers charged through the palace, on was about to strike Croesus dead, but the son spoke for the first time in his life to sa to the soldier, 'Pray do not kill the King, my father.' The soldier put away his swor and Croesus lived a few years longer

Then there was noise and tumult outside the palace. Croesus asked Cyrus what was taking place and was told that the Persian soldiers were sacking his city and plundering his riches. Croesus replied that the troops were sacking Cyrus's city and plundering his riches. Cyrus was so impressed that he had the fires put out and made Croesus his adviser.

According to Herodotus, Cyrus was the grandson of the Median king, Astyages, and was brought up by humble Persian herdsmen. Cyrus rose to power over the Persians, but they and he were under Median overlordship. Cyrus made the Persians the dominant ethnic groups, but won the allegiance and goodwill of the Medes as well. Cyrus respected the customs and religions of the lands he conquered. His mode of government came to be seen as a model for future rulers of many states to follow. His Edict of Restoration, which permitted peoples conquered by the Neo-Babylonian Empire to return to the native lands, made Cyrus the most venerated non-Jewish ruler in the Bible, in which he was described as 'the anointed of the Lord'.

Cyrus's early life as told by Herodotus was similar to that of other new rulers from afar, such as Oedipus. Many of these stories were set in matrilineal states, in which kingship was gained by marrying the daughter of the queen or the queen herself. The hero would appear to be only a peasant or woodcutter, but after valiant deeds and displays of wisdom, he would be revealed as the lost son or grandson of the last ruler of the true legitimate line. Typically, he would be the son of a queen or princess who was said to be destined to kill his father or grandfather. Orders would be given for him to be exposed and to eaten by wild animals, but the child would be spared by a farmer or woodcutter and brought up as his son, before he finally returned to his city of birth and became its king.

According to Herodotus, Cyrus was defeated and met his death because he ignored advice from Croesus. Cyrus had driven the Massagetae, whom he was fighting back, into the Asian steppes. Croesus told him that the Massagetae were poor and devoid of plunder so that Cyrus had much more to lose than he could possibly gain. Cyrus was determined to crush the Massagetae; however, on Croesus' advice, Cyrus first sent an offer of marriage to their queen, Tomyris, which she rejected. Tomyris challenged him to meet her forces in battle at a place in her country. Cyrus accepted her offer, but was told by Croesus that the Massagetae were unfamiliar with wine and its intoxicating effects. After setting up camp, he retreated, leaving behind large quantities of wine and only a small force. The Massagetian troops killed the group Cyrus had left there and soon became drunk, but Cyrus's main army attacked and destroyed them. Spargapises, their commander and a son of Tomyris, committed suicide once he was sober. Tomyris swore vengeance, leading a second wave of troops into a battle in which Cyrus was killed. Tomyris ordered the body of Cyrus brought to her, then decapitated him and dipped his head in a vessel of blood in a symbolic gesture of revenge for the death of her son. Death after defeat in battle, with his head soaked in a bucket of spirits and his body mutilated, was hardly a happy ending for Cyrus, but he may not have had time to recall the words of Solon to Croesus.

BAYEZIT AND TAMBURLAINE

On 15 June 1389, the Turkish Sultan Murad won a great victory at Kosovo. For the Serbs, it was the greatest defeat they had ever suffered. The victor, however, did not live to enjoy the spoils: Murad was stabbed to death in his tent, probably by a Serb, Milosh Obravich, who had pretended to desert to the Turks. Two of Murad's sons were close by: Each had distinguished himself in battle. The elder brother immediately ordered the execution of the younger brother, who was immediately garrotted with a bowstring. Thus Bayezit became a Turkish Sultan.

It became almost a Turkish tradition that before, during, or immediately after accession to the throne, one brother had some or all of his brethren murdered. Sometimes the operation was sexually non-discriminatory, and female relations and assorted wives and concubines were also disposed of. Strangulation was a popular method, but also favoured was the more expensive but crowd-pleasing device of placing the victims in a tower and then burning them alive.

Bayezit did not have an equable temperament. On occasion, he treated foreign embassies with courtesy and gifts; at other times, he gouged out their eyes or chopped off their hands. He was, however, industrious and persistent and determined to extend his conquests. Most of the Christian rulers of the Balkans were already his vassals, as had been the recently deceased Byzantine Emperor John VII Palaeologus. However, his successor Manuel II Palaeologus showed signs of independence. Bayezit was determined in the conquest of Constantinople.

The imperial city had withstood many sieges, including several from earlier Turkish and other Muslim leaders: Its excellent sea defenses were linked to the strongest walled defense in the world. Yet Byzantine power was much weakened, even though Manuel had the support of crusaders led by Sigismund of Hungary. Bayezit was ready for the crusaders and defeated them in 1396. He personally supervised the beheading of about 10,000 prisoners, although a few of the richest leaders were ransomed for huge sums. He was so confident that the city would surrender that he chose which palaces he would himself occupy and which churches should become mosques. By the summer of 1402, the failure of further Christian forces to come to their aid put the Byzantines on the brink of capitulation.

Then news came of Tamburlaine's invading Mongol armies in the East. Bayezit decided to take a few days off from the siege to crush the insolent intruders. It was

244

widely believed that the Byzantines promised to open their gates to Bayezit as soon as he returned from routing the Mongols. But it was the Ottoman army that was crushed, and Bayezit and his wife were captured.

Tamburlaine was also a man of moods. Apparently at first, he treated Bayezit as a fellow monarch in distress, but then changed his mind. The powerful tradition, adopted by Christopher Marlowe, is that Tamburlaine used Bayezit as a footstool, made public use of Bayezit's harem, and employed Bayezit's wife as a topless and bottomless waitress. Finally Tamburlaine is said to have imprisoned the couple in cages. In Marlowe's Tamburlaine, Bayezit committed suicide by dashing out his brains against the cage, and then the Sultana followed his example. What a fall in so short a time: from victor over the Christians of the Balkans and prospective first Muslim conqueror of Constantinople to a suicide in a cage.

The feeble Byzantine state was given a half century reprieve. Its rulers, apart from Constantine XI Dragases who died on the ramparts defending the city, did little to distinguish themselves during those decades, but when Constantinople finally fell to the Turks in 1453, their new ruler was a man of remarkable abilities. Whereas Bayezit would have been almost entirely a destroyer, Mehmet the conqueror proved to be a builder. After two days of dreadful massacres and plundering, Mehmet perhaps was struck by the advice Croesus had given to Cyrus two millennia earlier. He prohibited further destruction and went on to grant his Greek orthodox subjects religious freedom under the supervision of the patriarch Gennadius. Mehmet was wiser than Ferdinand of Aragon and Isabel of Castile, who expelled their Jewish and Moorish subjects to the great weakening of Spain. Many exiles from Spain fled to lands ruled by Mehmet. The patriarch ought to have ordered special prayers for the soul of Tamburlaine.

STALIN AND HITLER

During the late 1930s, there were few matters on which enlightened opinion on the Left and Right in Britain, France, the United States, and many other countries agreed, but one was that Marxism/Communism and Fascism/National Socialism were fundamentally opposed and in permanent conflict. Even those on the Left who were not advocates of a 'popular front against Fascism' thought of the polarization of Berlin and Moscow as one of the few international and ideological certainties. Conservatives from appeasers to Churchill also took that antagonism to be a permanent feature of the diplomatic landscape.

Stalin was convinced at the time that the Nazi–Soviet Pact of September 1939 was one of the cleverest moves of his career. When Churchill warned him in 1940 of the danger to the Soviet Union of German hegemony in Europe, Stalin replied that

Germany's military successes did not threaten the Soviet Union. Stalin got poor advice from his top military advisers: Most were party comrades and some had helped to purge the top Red Army talents between 1936 and 1938.

Stalin thought that he was utterly outmaneuvering Hitler. The Germans had made massive gains, but had lost many lives to get them. Stalin occupied Lithuania, Estonia, and Latvia without cost, even though Hitler, whilst agreeing that the Baltic States should be in the Soviet sphere of influence, had demanded they should not be incorporated into the Soviet Union. Stalin had also bullied Romania into surrendering Bessarabia and northern Bukovina to the Soviet Union. Hitler was furious at those Soviet moves, but his inability at that time to respond helped to blind Stalin from recognizing that once Hitler had no more battles in Western Europe the USSR might be dangerously vulnerable to German attack. Stalin was convinced that his clever diplomacy would ensure continued safety.

In a role reversal, Stalin made no response when Germany invaded first Yugoslavia and then Bulgaria, despite non-aggression pacts endorsed by the Soviet Union. He made no protest when German supplies promised to the USSR fell below the amounts promised, whereas Soviet exports to Germany increased in the spring of 1941. Even in April 1941 at a reception for Japanese and German diplomats, Stalin went out of his way to assure the Germans, 'We will stay friends with you whatever happens.' It was only in May that Stalin began to warn key cadres of imminent danger of war with Germany.

Even as reports flowed in from Sumner Welles, Churchill, and Cadogan (via Maisky) of German preparations for invasion, Stalin ordered Tass to denounce 'a clumsy propaganda maneuver of the forces arrayed against the Soviet Union and Germany, which are interested in a spread and an intensification of the war'. When Zhukov and Timoshenko pleaded with Stalin to put their troops on alert, he replied that Soviet mobilization would mean war which he intended to avoid. Molotov on his behalf told the generals, 'Only a fool would attack us.'

Soon the generals read out to Stalin an alert message that they proposed to send to all troops on the frontier; Stalin's answer was: 'It's much too soon to give a directive. Perhaps the questions may be settled peacefully. The troops must not be incited by any provocation.' At 4.30 a.m. on 22 June, as reports flooded in of German air attacks and tank movements, Stalin still argued that it must be a misunderstanding. When he finally accepted the truth, 'Stalin sank back in his chair and fell into deep thought'. By the time the German advance was halted, the Wehrmacht was at the gates of Moscow, Leningrad, and Stalingrad. The conceit of a leader had rarely been refuted so decisively and so swiftly. Finally both his state and Stalin himself survived, partly because Hitler's arrogance led to equally momentous errors.

Immediately after the German invasion of the Soviet Union, Adolph Hitler occupied a position of immense superiority. He then undermined that dominance and ruined his Third Reich by two unforced decisions. The first was to try to create a Europe Judenasrein: 'cleansed of Jews'. The second was declaration of war on the United States in December 1941, in the wake of Pearl Harbor. Hitler underestimated America as 'a society corrupted by Jews and niggers'. His anti-Semitism had already deprived Germany of the services of many scientists, engineers, and other creative minds. The Holocaust denied Germany the potential war effort of thousands more Jews; even their physical destruction took up time, effort, and manpower. Hitler's assaults on European Jews generated support for Roosevelt's peacetime aid to Britain and its allies and then for a massive war effort. Thus began a descent from a triumphal parade through Paris to ignominious death in a bunker in Berlin.

CHURCHILL AND THATCHER
WINSTON CHURCHILL

With the unconditional surrender of Germany in May 1945, Winston Churchill reached what proved to be the pinnacle of his success. He expected to continue as Prime Minister until the defeat of Japan and beyond. He thought the wartime coalition would continue, especially after Clement Attlee, Ernest Bevin, Herbert Morrison, and A V Alexander expressed the same sentiment on May 18. However, the Labor Party Conference at Blackpool voted to withdraw from the coalition and oppose him in the forthcoming general election: the first since 1935. Churchill offered his resignation to the King, but agreed to lead a 'caretaker' government until after a general election. Churchill made a fatal political error when during the campaign he suggested that a Socialist government in Britain 'would have to fall back on some sort of Gestapo, no doubt very humanely directed in the first instance. And this would nip opinion in the bud'. Coming after a tearful farewell to his Labor colleagues in the Wartime Cabinet just days before, this was unworthy and damaging . . . Even so, there seemed little reason to doubt that a grateful people would re-elect him.

With Attlee at his side, to guarantee continuity if all went wrong for him, Churchill headed off to Potsdam to confer with Stalin and the new United States President Harry S Truman. The tragedies of post-war Europe had already begun to take shape: Soviet police had arrested fourteen non-communist Polish leaders, most of whom had helped the allies during the war. Stalin seemed determined to shift Poland westwards by seizing its Byelorussian and Ukrainian majority provinces and compensating it with Silesia and Pomerania, from which Germans would be expelled. Better news for Churchill was that the United States had successfully exploded its first atomic bomb.

On 25 July at Potsdam, Churchill dined with Admiral Lord Louis Mountbatten and discussed strategic possibilities in the Far East. He invited Mountbatten to continue their talk in a few days' time in Downing Street. Then Churchill and Attlee returned to London for the general election results. Churchill had been advised by Anthony Eden to expect a majority of about seventy in the new House of Commons, so he expected to return to Potsdam within a week still as Prime Minister of Great Britain. When he landed in England, he was told that a lower, but still workable, Conservative majority of about thirty was likely. The next morning the news came of a Labor landslide. Churchill was in his bath when his aide, Captain Pim, told him the worst. David Margesson wrote six years later to Churchill, 'I shall never forget the courage and forbearance you showed at that most unhappy luncheon after defeat was known.' Churchill took defeat amazingly well. When his wife Clementine remarked, 'It may be a blessing in disguise', he replied, 'At the moment it seems quite effectively disguised', but he wept no tears . . .

Churchill wrote to Hugh Cecil, 'I must confess I found the event of Thursday rather odd and queer, especially after the wonderful welcomes I had from all classes . . . My faith in the flexibility of our Constitution and in the qualities of the British people remains unaltered.' He told Captain Pim, 'They are perfectly entitled to vote for whom they please. This is democracy. This is what we've been fighting for.' He promised Attlee his help in the continuing war with Japan and the difficult peace negotiations in Europe, and he kept that promise.

Churchill made errors during the war, but at the moments of highest trial, he was not found wanting. There was hardly a man or woman in Britain, of whatever political opinion, who thought the country could have had a better wartime leader. Yet he lost the election and his standing in 1945 was never restored. During his second period as Prime Minister he was enfeebled; it would have been better for his historical reputation and the national interest if he had never sought office again. In 1945, he still had much to give, and but for his 'Gestapo Speech' and undue confidence that he could hardly lose the election, he might have been able to give more very valuable service. By the time he returned to the premiership, he had lost his sharpness of thought and it would have been better for his own reputation and for the nation if he had resigned before the Conservative victory of 1951.

Margaret Thatcher

Early in 1990, Margaret Thatcher felt confident that her eleven and a half years as Prime Minister and leader of the Conservative Party would continue. Since 1965, there had been an established method of challenging for the party leadership; indeed, that was the procedure through which she had ousted Edward Heath. But Thatcher considered that there was an 'unwritten convention' that the opportunity to challenge was 'not intended for use when the Party was in office'. Although 'theoretically', as she put it, she had to be re-elected each year, no challenge to her had yet been made and she was confident one would not be made in the foreseeable future.

During 1989, some dissatisfaction had arisen with her leadership, partly over issues such as high interest rates, the poll tax, and her refusal to concede more authority to the European community and partly from disgruntled members dismissed from office or passed over. However, she thought these malcontents unimportant. In this, she was partly confirmed when Sir Anthony Meyer ran against her: He gained only 33 votes and she 314, with 27 abstentions or spoilt ballots.

Discontent among the parliamentary ranks increased during 1990, but the Conservative rank and file in the constituencies still overwhelmingly backed her. She was full of plans for the years beyond the next election, such as wider parental choice in education, greater help for the post-communist democracies in Central and Eastern Europe, and ridding Iraq of Saddam Hussein, even though she claimed later that she intended to resign from public life some two years after re-election.

Thatcher's chief foe still inside her cabinet was her longest-serving minister, Geoffrey Howe: He had never forgiven her for removing him from the Foreign Ministry, the office he had most relished. Howe was more pro-European than Thatcher but reluctant to spell out his own views, especially on the then vexed question of a single European currency. Howe resigned with a bitter farewell speech in the Commons that opened the door for the challenger in waiting, Michael Heseltine.

In November 1990 Thatcher remained confident of a substantial majority. Her campaign manager, Peter Morrison, estimated 220 votes for her, 110 against, and 40 abstentions. This would provide the necessary 15 per cent overall majority required until the new party rules to obviate a second ballot. On the day the results of the first ballot were issued, Thatcher was in Paris, heading a United Kingdom delegation. There she learnt that she had received 204 votes, Heseltine 152, with 16 abstentions. It was not enough to win on that first ballot, but she announced before she left for the ballet that she would face a second ballot.

Thatcher returned to London to sign the final European summit statement and to prepare for the next battle. Almost immediately Peter Lilley arrived, one of the younger men whom she had promoted. She had phoned him to help with her next speech, but he told her not to bother because she was finished as prime minister. She then consulted her husband Denis, to be told that she should not go on with the fight. Denis Thatcher would have been happy had she retired from public life much earlier and spared herself much strife and pain. Then another old supporter, John Wakeham, warned her that she faced possible humiliation if she contended again. Similar

249

messages came from John MacGregor and Tim Renton, from whom she had also expected encouragement, not advice to withdraw. Despite all the discouragement, Thatcher decided to fight on. She went to Buckingham Palace to inform the Queen of her decision.

Next came a round of one-to-one discussions with cabinet members and junior ministers. Nearly everyone told her the same story: Each strongly supported her, but was convinced she could not win. By the afternoon the main message was that if she stood again, she would be defeated by Michael Heseltine, who was strongly disliked by about a third of the party's parliamentarians. However, it was suggested that Heseltine might be defeated by John Major or Douglas Hurd. After a final word with her husband, Margaret Thatcher began to prepare her resignation speech.

One of her most hostile critics, Hugo Young wrote:

> On the upper scale, Maggie would order Europe, instruct Reagan, see off the Russians, and direct the Commonwealth. On the lower she took charge of problems large and small, from football hooliganism to the drugs crisis, from a detailed sub-clause in the Law of the Sea Treaty to the precise configuration of the Customs Hall at the British end of the Channel Tunnel.

It is a wonderful thing that liberal democracies can change their leadership peacefully, but leaders should never be complacent that those around them will support them in foul times as well as fair ones. Before the first ballot, Thatcher carried out no canvassing of her parliamentary party. She was adamant that her record as Prime Minister was sufficiently well known to every one of them to make such consultations unnecessary and demeaning. At the same time, the supporters of her opponent were assiduous in detailing her defects and making assurances about future prospects for his supporters. Whatever we term it, Thatcher's obstinacy, pride, or proper sense of what was due to her led to her failure to engage at the first possible moment in the rough-and-tumble of legitimate political contestation. A different decision might well have ensured the continuation of a remarkable career.

CHURCHILL AND ME

Winston Churchill was not admired by my parents. They were staunch Labor voters, and in particular, they associated him with Gallipoli, where one of my mother's brothers had been killed in 1915 on the first day of the British landings. In 1948, I was offered places in three university history departments. Ingrate that I was, I rejected Manchester University, because I would then have to live at home and travel into Manchester on two buses. This disappointed my parents very much. Of the other two, they warned that Durham was a cold place, even worse than York, Doncaster or Barnsley, which they had visited. So Bristol it was. Places south of Nottingham, where one of his sisters lived, were lumped together in my father's mind as 'down south': the part of England that spent the money earned for the country by the north of England, especially by Lancashire and most notably by the cotton spinning towns centred on Oldham.

Neither my parents nor I had any notion that Churchill, as well as being leader of the opposition, was Chancellor of Bristol University. None of us had any notion either that by Christmas, the end of my first term at university, I would have quitted the Baptist Church, into which I had been baptized only recently as an adult and had been a Sunday schoolteacher and an occasional preacher on 'Youth Sundays'. This *volte-face* was permanently associated in their minds with my choice of Bristol University, which they blamed for my folly.

Early in my third year at university, by which time I was well known, among Bristol University students that is, as a leading communist who sold *The Daily Worker* in the foyer of the Victoria Rooms, the main student Union building, Winston Churchill came to Bristol to present honorary degrees. There was a ballot among male undergraduates to form an escort party of six to accompany him up the long and steep stone staircase up to the Great Hall of the W. H. Wills Building (named after the philanthropic chairman of the great tobacco company). I put my name forward and was one of the six picked out from the hat. There was some hilarity, but no fears were expressed that I might prove a saboteur. The twenty or so members of the student branch of the Communist Party were non-violent in deeds if not in words.

As well as being Chancellor of Bristol University, Churchill was also Visitor to the Anglican Diocese of Bristol and combined his duties on this visit. Before arriving at the university, he had obviously lunched well and drunk even better with the Bishop of Bristol and the Lord Mayor. Until I took my place with the five other students, I had not realized how heavy and bloated he was—he must then have been over eighteen stone—and it was difficult to help him up the staircase without mishap. I was probably more fearful than the others, since I might be accused of plotting deliberate harm.

We finally made it to the platform and handed him over to the vice-chancellor, Sir Philip Morris. After words of welcome from Sir Philip, Churchill's oration began well, but after a few minutes, his speech became slurred and he began to sway. Sir Philip, who may have had earlier experience of such a situation, gently led him to a chair, where he soon fell asleep. Sir Philip then delivered the rest of Churchill's speech, which was rather a good one. No hint of the incident appeared in the Bristol and West Country newspapers. In subsequent discussion, the other students and I expressed surprise that the old man could still be leader of the Conservative Party.

We would have been even more surprised had we known he would return as Prime Minister in 1951 for a further four years. Yet we all, even I, looked on him as the 'Grand Old Man' who had won the war and was the main link in our public life with the last of Victorian Britain and the Edwardian reaction. What if I had slipped and Churchill had fallen down the stone staircase? Eden would have become Conservative leader and then Prime Minister; Eden would probably have done better as PM with an earlier start. Churchill's reputation would be significantly higher than it is today.

Sometime later, I related my experience to, as he was by then, Professor Charles Ross, a brilliant historian who wrote the standard accounts of the reigns of Edward IV and Richard III. Charles Ross told me that he was summoned late one evening by one of the pro-vice chancellors to Churchill's room at the Clifton Hotel, near the Clifton Suspension Bridge, after a dinner. Churchill was flat out on the bed, and Charles realized that his task was to undress the great man for his slumbers. Charles had just started to do this and was in the middle of easing off Churchill's elastic-sided boots when he opened his eyes wide and asked, 'Who the hell are you?' Charles replied that he was Ross, a lecturer in medieval history, to which Churchill exclaimed, 'But Morris takes my boots off in Bristol.'

Chapter 12

CROSSING PATHS

MALCOLM MUGGERIDGE AND WALTER CROCKER
BEFORE GENEVA

At first sight, there is little in common between Malcolm Muggeridge and Walter Crocker, but they were near contemporaries and spent some time in the same places. Muggeridge was born in 1902 in Croydon into a political family: His father became a Labor MP. Muggeridge married into a more illustrious political family: His wife, Katherine (Kitty), was a niece of Beatrice Webb. Muggeridge recalled how his father and his friends would plan together the downfall of the capitalist system and the replacement of it by one which was just and humane and egalitarian and peaceable, etc. I accepted completely the views of these good men that once they were able to shape the world as they wanted it to be they would create a perfect state of affairs in which 'peace would reign, prosperity would expand, men would be brotherly and considerate, and there would be no exploitation of man by man, nor any ruthless oppression of individuals'.[263]

Muggeridge attended Selhurst Grammar School and graduated from Selwyn College, Cambridge, with a pass degree in natural sciences, a field of knowledge in which he showed little subsequent interest. At Cambridge, he had 'a rather desolate time': 'I never much enjoyed being educated, and have continued to believe that education is a rather overrated experience.' As a boy from a government school, he felt an outsider among the public school boys. Yet he never showed any lack of self-confidence later in life.

Walter Crocker was born in 1901 in rural South Australia to a farming family whose forebears had been colonial pioneers in the 1840s. His parents, 'strongly British in sentiment' and self-styled 'English colonials', wished that South Australia had remained a province of Britain, but they strongly opposed the jingoism which succeeded in changing the name of Petersburg to Peterborough and obliterating other German names in 1914. Crocker always spoke glowingly about his education. His early schooling, both primary and in Peterborough High School, was described by him as 'of the excellent kind provided by the old un-Americanized South Australian Department of Education'. As a boy, like many young Australians, he read The Magnet and had Billy Bunter, Bob Cherry, and Greyfriars School as part of his cultural world. He went at fourteen to the Adelaide School of Mines and from there to the University of Adelaide. He was an excellent student and gained a scholarship to Balliol College, Oxford. He found that South Australian students had a high reputation in Oxford. Crocker enjoyed his Oxford years and felt great gratitude to Kenneth Bell, his tutor, and A. D. Lindsay, Master of Balliol. In his two years at Stanford, for which he gained a further scholarship, Crocker contrasted with its students: 'working their way through college' and eating in huge cafeterias where they were waited on by other students, with life in the Oxford colleges. He was struck by the intellectual energy of Stanford.[264]

After graduation, Muggeridge taught briefly in India and Egypt. He found teaching at a Syrian Christian College in a remote part of Travancore (now Kerala) very agreeable. Gandhi came to the college, and 'everybody got tremendously excited and shouted against Imperialism'. On the boat going to India, Muggeridge had been derided when he told other passengers that the British Raj had not long to survive, but his stay in Travancore convinced him he was right. Muggeridge wrote to Gandhi to advise him to drop the 'back-to-hand-spinning' policy and to support industrial development. Gandhi replied politely but took no notice. Neither did the authorities take any notice of Muggeridge's incitements to students to rise up and end the Raj. Muggeridge realized later that the police 'decided, quite rightly, that they were of no importance'.

As a lecturer in Cairo University, Muggeridge soon began writing articles about the wrongs of the Egyptian people and their passion for a democratic society, although he never actually heard any Egyptian make such a demand. He found that teaching at Cairo University was not very arduous: The students didn't understand English; they were nearly always on strike or otherwise engaged in political demonstrations, and many were drugged with hashish.

Whilst Muggeridge was teaching in Cairo, Arthur Ransome recommended him to the *Manchester Guardian,* and he was appointed in 1932 as its Moscow correspondent. Muggeridge and Kitty arrived in Moscow with strong Soviet sympathies: 'To my great delight Kitty was pregnant again, so our next child would be born a Soviet citizen. It all seemed wonderful.' Muggeridge was 'fully prepared to see in the Soviet regime the answer to all our troubles'. His explanation for his own credulity was that in 1932–33, especially in Lancashire, it 'seemed as though our whole way of life was cracking up'. The USSR seemed 'an alternative, some other way in which people could live'.[265]

But Kitty and he soon realized that 'what I had supposed to be the new brotherly way of life . . . was simply on examination an appalling tyranny, in which the only thing that mattered, the only reality, was power'. He was appalled by 'the extraordinary performance of the liberal intelligentsia, who, in those days, flocked to Moscow like pilgrims to Mecca'. Muggeridge wondered 'how people, in their own country ardent for equality, bitter opponents of capital punishment and all for more humane treatment of people in prison, supporters, in fact, of every good cause, should in the USSR prostrate themselves before a regime ruled over brutally and oppressively and arbitrarily by a privileged party oligarchy'.

Muggeridge became so contemptuous of the credulity of Western political pilgrims, among whom he had so recently been numbered, that he floated a spoof story that the huge queues outside food shops arose because Soviet workers were so ardent in building Socialism that the only way the government could get them to rest for even two or three hours was organizing a queue for them to stand in. Muggeridge's disillusionment with the Soviet Union occurred only a short time before the Webbs, Kitty's uncle and aunt, wrote their paean of praise: *Soviet Communism—A New Civilization.* Its first edition bore a question mark, but that was subsequently removed by Beatrice and Sydney.

Muggeridge investigated reports of famine in Ukraine and found them to be all too accurate, despite the denials of celebrated journalists such as Walter Duranty. Muggeridge did not last long with The *Manchester Guardian.* In November 2008, on the seventy-fifth anniversary of the Ukraine famine, Muggeridge was posthumously awarded the Ukrainian Order of Freedom to mark his exceptional services both to the country and its people.

After his Soviet experience, Muggeridge returned to India as assistant-editor of the Statesman in Calcutta. His year there was filled with self-pity, alleviated by heavy drinking and sexual encounters. He managed to complete a book on Samuel Butler (the author of *Erewhon* and *The Way of All Flesh*). Kitty paid him a short Christmas visit during which their marriage came close to breaking up: 'The immediate cause of strife was, inevitably, infidelities.' Muggeridge wondered, 'Can I really have been so obsessed by a relationship which made so little lasting impression that now I have difficulty in recalling the name of the person concerned?' However, his infidelities did not lessen until several years had passed.

Crocker went on from Stanford to Japan, where he finished a book on its demography. He returned to Britain via Russia, soon after Muggeridge was there.

Crocker found that 'hunger and dirt were the main trials', even for a traveller who had 'prudently taken with him a supply of dry biscuit, chocolate, cheese and raisins'. The trains were slow and frequently broke down. In Moscow, he did not see a single smiling face. In 1981, he considered that what had been achieved in the forty-five years since then, 'including industrialization and getting to the moon and standing up to the German invasion, which killed Russians by the millions and devastated whole regions, is one of the marvels of my life time', although 'the cost of the achievement is another matter—one of the horrors of the last couple of centuries'.[266]

Crocker joined the British Colonial Service in Northern Nigeria. He was based in Kano, the capital of the Hausa, whose language he speedily mastered. His extensive travel was all on horseback. He found the Hausa cheerful, good-natured, and tolerant and many of them adventurous and enterprising. Hausa women were rightly renowned for their looks and liveliness. Crocker also admired the British District and Assistant District Officers who formed the 'Native administration'. Although there were some 'ignoble careerists and back-biters', most were 'imbued with the best of the public-school spirit and sought to serve rather than line their own pockets' . . . . He considered that the system of 'indirect rule' developed by Lord Lugard worked much better than any regime West Africa had ever known before or has known since.

However, it was a hard life: Malaria, dysentery, and chronic malnutrition ensured that less than half of his colleagues lived to draw a pension. Hard drinking was the destructive solace of many. Although Crocker was resistant to that temptation, in 1934, after a severe bout of malaria, he resigned from the colonial service and took a post with the International Labor Office (ILO) in Geneva only a short time after Muggeridge had left.

GENEVA

After Moscow, Muggeridge secured a post in the International Labor Office (ILO), whose aim was 'to promote social justice, on the basis of fair wages and humane working conditions'. Muggeridge found that his section head, 'a tiny, pedantic Frenchman, M. Prosper', had very little interest in ILO's formal objectives. M. Prosper's concern was with 'the ILO's internal organizations; more particularly, promotions, salary scales and superannuation arrangements'. It soon struck Muggeridge that ILO's information 'came exclusively from government sources' and that it was unlikely that, for example, co-operative movements were more numerous and advanced in Cuba and Afghanistan than in France and Switzerland. However, M. Prosper told him that it was not their business to question the data provided by member states.

Muggeridge saw during their walks M. Briand, 'somnolent-eyed, heavily mustached, nicotine-stained', M. Laval, 'sallow complexion and white tie contrasting', 'fat little

Litvinov waddling along to propose once more the total disarmament of one and all, unconditionally and forever', and Sir John Simon, 'reptilian, a snake in snake's clothing'. Often the statesmen were pursued by 'innumerable campaigners of one sort or another, male and female, clerical and lay, young and old; all with some notion to publicize, some pet solution to offer. Their imprecations proved vain: 'Barely was the Palais des Nations completed and ready to be occupied than the Second World War was ready to begin.' As 'Hitler's panzers were actually roaring into Poland from the west, and Stalin's divisions lumbering to meet them from the east, the League was discussing—the codification of level-crossing signs'. Muggeridge did not then anticipate that 'another Tower of Babel' would 'spring up in Manhattan, to "outdo the League many times over in the irrelevancy of its proceedings, the ambiguity of its resolutions and the confusion of its purposes"'.

In the ILO, Crocker served under the American, John Winant, who had a striking patrician appearance, as indeed had Crocker. Winant had been elected three times as Governor of Vermont. He was an expert on the American Civil War and presented himself as a Lincoln for the twentieth century. He was considered by Republican leaders as a possible presidential challenger to Roosevelt. Winant was appointed to the ILO, Crocker suspected, as a lure to the United States to join the League of Nations.

As his *chef de cabinet,* Crocker found Winant ignorant of the work of the ILO and too idle to learn about it. Winant was rude and inconsiderate to subordinates and obsessive about espionage. He told Crocker that in America he curtained his windows to obstruct photographers in the pay of the Democrats or even of rival Republicans. Winant succeeded Joseph Kennedy as American Ambassador to London, but Harry Truman dismissed him. Soon afterwards, Winant shot himself.

Like Muggeridge, Crocker found Geneva full of self-seeking officials, but the permanent delegates usually even worse, although a few of the ILO representatives had genuine concern for the underdog. Among regular petitioners were two opposed groups of feminists: one demanding special protection laws for women, the other insisting that such laws were unfairly discriminatory against women.

Crocker believed that, if the League had focused on crises in Europe and if Britain and France had been firmer in 1936–7, war could have been avoided. In 1938, Crocker, his friends, 'and millions of others had come to hate Chamberlain'. He told me, 'Yes, nothing less than hate.' We held him largely responsible. Never did I feel such passion over public affairs as I did in 1936–9.

Moscow had inoculated Muggeridge against communism, but Crocker became a left-winger at ILO, partly in reaction against Anglo-French appeasement of Italy and Germany. His new friends included Balliol-educated Andrew Rothstein, then correspondent for the Moscow Tass and the sister of Britain's leading Marxist intellectual, Palme Dutt. In the winter of 1937–8, Crocker nearly joined the International Brigades in the Spanish Civil War. In later life, he wondered why he and many others had let themselves be blinded by intellectuals such as Gide, Wells, Romain, and Shaw to the evils of Soviet policy. Crocker believed that, if the League had focused on crises in Europe, and if Britain and France had been firmer in 1936–7, war could have been avoided, but he came to appreciate just how difficult the choices faced by Baldwin and Neville Chamberlain had been: 'How much I, and millions like me, were in the dark is now obvious. Chamberlain made mistakes but he was largely a prisoner of fate and was then turned into a national scapegoat'.

WORLD WAR II

Muggeridge enlisted and finally joined the Intelligence Corps. He was sent to Lourenço Marques as a vice-consul but really as a spy. Muggeridge claimed that he was so depressed at that time that he attempted suicide. Then he was posted to Algiers as a liaison officer with the French Sécurité Militaire. After the liberation of France, he was assigned to investigate Wodehouse's wartime broadcasts from Berlin. His reliability in counter-espionage may be gathered by his answer in 1979 to a question from Andrew Boyle about Donald MacLean.

There's no doubt that Maclean knew his stuff. I found him a dull, humourless, and rather pompous young man who tried a bit too hard to appear agreeable and relaxed. I can't say I ever warmed to Maclean. He was far too much of a cold fish beneath the polished surface charm. Nevertheless, during a bad period when the Americans were obviously determined to carry on in their own semi-isolationist way—Cold War or no Cold War—I couldn't but admire Maclean's astute appreciation of day-to-day diplomatic difficulties. He never struck a wrong note in public. He never lowered his guard.

Muggeridge was more perceptive, or so he claimed, about Guy Burgess: 'His very physical presence was, to me, malodourous and sinister . . . Etonian mudlark and sick toast of a sick society.' Muggeridge made MI6 sound farcical when he described Kim Philby: 'The prevailing impression I had was of a kind of boyishness, even naiveté', even though at that time Philby was an established Soviet agent. Philby's 'drinking, on any showing, was excessive and indiscriminate.

In 1939, Crocker was in Japan, trying unsuccessfully to persuade its government to pay its debts to the ILO. He returned to Geneva to complete his mission and then left to join the British army. He had not driven far when the Germans broke the French lines and huge numbers of refugees fled south and west. He managed to reach the coast at Bordeaux and board an already overfull boat which took him to Falmouth.

He was posted to West Africa, to work like Muggeridge in the murky world of intelligence. His team of spies had nearly as many problems with rival British and Free French, and later American, agencies as with Vichy and German intelligence. He was decorated with the Ordre du Lion by Belgium for his gallantry when a small plane in which he was flying over the equatorial forest caught fire. Later, he interpreted for De Gaulle both when the general was despised by most of his enemies and allies and three years later when he had become a major force. He also received the Croix de Guerre from France. Muggeridge and Crocker could easily have met in French stations.

Both Muggeridge and Crocker met General de Gaulle. Both were highly impressed by him. Crocker interpreted for de Gaulle in 1941 when the general was despised by most of his enemies and allies and three years later when he had become a major force. When Crocker first met him, he was seen by British generals as 'a recently promoted colonel who had not commanded troops, from an army that had been thoroughly defeated' and who had failed at Dakar in his first clash with the French Vichy forces. They 'treated him politely but coldly, as he treated them. They saw him as both useless and irritating, a token imposed on them by London', whereas de Gaulle saw himself as 'nothing less than France'. Crocker soon found that 'some at least of the Free French disliked their leader as much as the British generals did', but Crocker saw that de Gaulle was 'a leader all right'.

Muggeridge first met de Gaulle in London in 1942 at the general's request. During a difficult interview, Muggeridge was 'struck at one by the woebegoneness of his expression; but more like a clown's than a martyr's' In 1944, Muggeridge attended a Requiem Mass in Notre Dame for heroes of the Resistance. A pistol shot rang out, and everyone in the congregation seemed to have dropped to the floor, except for 'one solitary figure still standing, like a lonely giant'. Muggeridge was confident after that incident that de Gaulle 'must win, however strange and self-defeating his tactics at a particular moment might seem to be.' In a later interview, Muggeridge asked him about his future plans after his electoral defeat; the reply was 'J'attends', but that 'Ce n'etait pas l'heure'. Muggeridge wondered why de Gaulle had never taken trouble apparently to learn a single word of English when in London, but he thought his stubborn pride could be an advantage in French politics.

BRITISH POLITICIANS

Both Muggeridge and Crocker admired De Gaulle more than they did most British politicians. Muggeridge, like Crocker, had abiding contempt for Chamberlain. Listening to his speech announcing war with Germany, Muggeridge wrote, 'In my mind's eye I saw Chamberlain at the microphone, in black cutaway coat, with winged collar, and Adam's apple throbbing compulsively above it; as forlorn at this momen as he had been vainglorious in the corresponding moment of triumph, waving in the air his piece of paper signed by Hitler, and prattling of peace with honour Yet Muggeridge worried that the alternative to Hitler was Stalin so that 'all the evil things which, according to Chamberlain, we were to fight against—dictatorship, ba faith, intolerance, persecution of the weak, etc., etc.—must, whatever happened, get boost'. Chamberlain faced a comparable dilemma.

Muggeridge had little time for Ramsay MacDonald, even though his father had bee a Labor member of Parliament and had met MacDonald several times. They me again in Geneva when out walking. Muggeridge saw him as a character-actor, with his 'tweed knickerbocker suit, his grey curls I in the wind and a faraway look in hi eyes'. In the world of Muggeridge's father, MacDonald went from hero to villain with great speed when he deserted his own government in 1931 to head a coalition tha contained very few of his erstwhile comrades and was dominated by Stanley Baldwin and the Conservative Party.

At that time, according to Muggeridge, MacDonald was 'still relatively coherent but the verbal circumlocutions which was to make his last public utterances utterl incomprehensible had already begun to gain on him'. One of Muggeridge's mai complaints about MacDonald was that his appointments to offices in the Churc of England included Dr Barnes as Bishop of Birmingham and Dr Hewlett Johnso as Dean of Canterbury. Muggeridge feared that Barnes worshipped no god at al whilst Johnson 'preached Stalin and Him sanctified from the pulpit of the Anglica Church's senior cathedral'.

Crocker loathed the press lords, Beaverbrook and Rothermere, beneficiaries o peerages granted by another bête noire, Lloyd George. The 'Welsh Wizard' reminde Crocker of an Australian politician he despised: First World War Prime Minister Bill Hughes. The political fall of the British wartime prime minister was more permaner than that of the Australian: Hughes was a member of several governments afte 1922, but Lloyd George never returned to office. Muggeridge claimed that Lloy George's 'only asset was a political fund acquired by the sale of honours during hi premiership'. He became 'a ribald figure whose venerable white locks and black coa enclosed a goatish disposition'. It might be said of the ageing Muggeridge, of course that, despite his conversion to a brand of Evangelistic Roman Catholicism, he looke increasingly like a seedy music hall comedian.

Crocker considered Churchill ungrateful to Baldwin, who had rescued him fror the political wilderness in 1925 by appointing him Chancellor of the Excheque a position in which Churchill did not shine. Beaverbrook embodied much of wha Crocker most disliked. He read and believed that Beaverbrook, as Minister of Suppl in 1941, 'personally and specifically directed that Baldwin's elegant wrought-iron gates should be taken for scrap as a matter of priority'.

Muggeridge worked on the *Evening Standard* for Beaverbrook and regarded him, as did A. J. P. Taylor, with a mixture of dislike and awe. Beaverbrook, he wrote, 'never came to the office, but nevertheless managed to maintain from afar his chose control of how the paper was run, and of everything that went into it'.[267] Muggeridge asked Milton Shulman once 'what public he had in mind when he wrote his theatre and television criticism for the *Evening Standard*'. Shulman replied that he 'wrote with one little old reader in mind—Beaverbrook'. This was not easy because Beaverbrook, Muggeridge claimed, 'had no views at all, only prejudices, moods, sudden likes and dislikes . . . Overnight, he might reverse a previously held position as a result of a conversation, or of something he had read or heard'. One characteristic was that 'he read and believed his own papers, even thought they were fashioned to convey all his favourite fantasies. When they told him that there was not going to be a war, he having instructed them so to do, he felt assured . . . '

AFTER THE WAR

Muggeridge worked as a journalist again, gaining notoriety as a critic of the monarchy. He became a celebrated wit and television interviewer. Then his life was transformed. After years as an agnostic, roué, drinker, and womanizer, Muggeridge became an ardent Christian and a savage critic of promiscuity, drugs, and birth control pills. His new books had titles such as *Jesus Rediscovered, Jesus: The Man Who Lives, A Third Testament, and In the Footsteps of St. Paul*. In 1982, he and Kitty joined the Catholic Church, largely because of the influence of Mother Teresa.

Crocker accepted an invitation to become Chief of the Africa Section of the United Nations Secretariat, but he found that UNO had all the vices and weaknesses of the League of Nations but few of its virtues. It was 'a talking shop of unprecedented size and futility, spawning a huge, ill-disciplined, ever-growing and costly bureaucracy'. Trygve Lie proved an inept leader. Crocker found New York to be 'full of pollution, noise, tensions, hard-heartedness, crime, and living against nature'. He developed a 'plague on both your houses' view of the super powers: 'Neither America nor Russia is fit for the immense power they exercise.'

Crocker was very unhappy with the way in which the State of Israel was established. He considered that the situation of the UN in New York enabled massive pressure to be placed on delegates to support Jewish claims and ignore Palestinian concerns. This, he thought, 'produced a harvest of hate', which included branding critics of the settlement anti-Semitic and Holocaust deniers. He did not want to stay longer in New York and the UN than was necessary.

Crocker took a post as Foundation Professor of International Relations at the ANU in Canberra, but he was deeply disappointed. He found it, apart from the presence of Howard Florey and Mark Oliphant, remarkable only for the high salaries paid to generally mediocre academics. ANU had been publicized as a prestigious research university of the type of the Institute for Advanced Study at Princeton, but its library and research facilities were for many years very poor and its main distinction was the high salaries paid to a generally mediocre academic staff. One of his few retrospective satisfactions was that ANU would have been even worse had he not blocked some schemes then floated. Muggeridge's experiences in Cambridge as a student and Cairo as a lecturer had weaned him from any high expectations of universities of the sort Crocker still entertained.

When R. G. Casey first invited him to become the Australian High Commissioner in India, Crocker declined, because he felt he had given ANU too little service, but persistent renewal of the invitation and the failure of ANU to show improvement led him to accept in 1952. He served as Head of Mission in India, Nepal, Indonesia, Canada, Holland, Belgium, East Africa (including Ethiopia as well as Kenya and Uganda), and Italy. He felt fortunate to have met outstanding individuals, such as Canada's Lester Pearson and India's Rajagopalacharia, J. P. Narayan, and Krisnamurti, but he was disappointed by what he considered his own government's undue subservience to American policy. He soon realized that any hope he had entertained of influencing the Australian foreign policy had been naive. He opposed anti-Beijing policies and warned against support for authoritarian leaders simply because they seemed to be solidly anti-communist.

In post-colonial India, Crocker became increasingly nauseated by hypocritical official praise of a society full of colour and caste discrimination, subservience of women, shameless beggary, and deceit and corruption at nearly every level of life. Nearly twenty years on from Muggeridge's time in India, the Raj could not always be blamed. Crocker regarded his own main achievements as his contribution to the Colombo Plan and 'correcting prejudices and phobias behind the White Australia Policy, which was still Sacred Cow No. 1'. He cautioned the Australian government not to expect any gratitude or benefit for aid contributions, but backed an extensive educational programme. Crocker wrote in 1966 a biography of Nehru that received scholarly approval and sold well too.

On retirement at sixty-eight, Crocker accepted a knighthood and appointment as Lieutenant Governor of South Australia. He did not become hail-fellow-well-met in old age any more than in youth and thus stood in sharp contrast to the typical Australian public figure. His critics considered him aloof and over-fastidious. He regretted the way the ABC, following the BBC in Britain, suffered a sharp cultural decline. He deplored, too, the collapse in university standards, especially in the arts and social sciences. When on the Council of the University of Adelaide, he despaired of its declining intellectual level.

There was little likelihood that Crocker would take to religion as Muggeridge did. In Nigeria he had been impressed by the civilizing influence of Islam in keeping levels of drunkenness, murder and rape very low, but he worried that urbanization and more higher education seemed to exacerbate Islamic extremism, whereas modernity had rendered Christianity, broadly speaking, more tolerant and liberal, in some cases to excess. He had met admirable Christian missionaries, but he agreed with Lugard that Christian missions often caused needless strife. He applauded much of the Christian ethic and appreciated its generally positive effect on societies, but could not accept its theology and did not think that it would regain its former position. He strongly opposed several positions adopted by many Christians, such as condemnation of contraception; he championed voluntary euthanasia and was President of its organization in South Australia.

A major difference between Muggeridge and Crocker was in their sex lives. Crocker wrote his memoirs without any mention of his marriage, and during many conversations, the only allusion he made to me about his family, other than about his two sons of whom he was both fond and proud, was to his former brother-in-law, the historian Russel Ward, whom he detested.

When aged about sixty, Muggeridge arranged a spur-of-the-moment visit for Kingsley Amis and himself to George Orwell's widow, Sonia. According to Amis, Muggeridge went in first, but returned with the words: 'Afraid I couldn't manage anything in there. You go in and see what you can do.'[268] All Muggeridge's many affairs found forgiveness from Kitty, and their marriage lasted until death did them part.

Some repentance was no doubt due. Muggeridge's memoirs are full of praise for Kitty. She is his 'beloved Kitty' and 'somehow to me the shape and sense and sound of her existence in the universe would always be appreciable in every corner in it, and through all eternity'. However, Muggeridge admitted that their married life suffered from 'the strife of egotistic living, of spent appetites and surreptitious actual or envisaged infidelities, charging the atmosphere with currents of rage and mutual reproach and accusation'.

Crocker and Muggeridge worked in many countries, in very different physical, political, and cultural conditions. Both were excellent linguists and quick learners. They were both courageous physically and intellectually. Each was open to new ideas, including communism and internationalism, but quick to detect hypocrisy and deceit. Each was very conscious of not only the importance of the individual but also of general movements that affected everyone. The 'old' British Empire provided them with a structure in which men and women of high ability were able to make a significant mark in the world.

The contrasts are also clear: the polemical Muggeridge, the restrained Crocker; the promiscuous Muggeridge, the continent Crocker. Unlike Muggeridge, Crocker's pessimism about the world around him today was modified by his wonder at the advances made by the human race, especially medical advances that have greatly reduced the pains suffered in day-to-day life. Muggeridge became anguished at the prevalence of sins in which he had indulged more than average, whereas Crocker remained cool in religion. He would not have responded to Sister Teresa as did Muggeridge.

Sir Walter had a proper desire to influence public opinion on what he held to be the most important issues facing the world, but was quite indifferent to praise or censure. He lived to be 101 and was lucid and wise right to the end. Muggeridge was a very entertaining companion, but one would care little for his praise or blame. These two sketches illustrate how even brief biography can shed light on politics, war, and culture. Would they have got on well together? Crocker would probably have considered Muggeridge a cad and mountebank, whereas in Muggeridge's eyes Crocker might have appeared cold and aloof. I would like to have been a third at such a meeting.

Chapter 13

HENRY LAWSON AND JOSEPH FURPHY

Lawson and Furphy are not best known as historians, but both had keen historical interests, although Furphy was far more widely read and subtle I mind than Lawson. There were two contrasting kinds of Australian nationalism towards the end of the nineteenth century. One was anti-British, particularly anti-English, and emphasized everything that differentiated Australians from British antecedents. The other was British-Australian and emphasized continuities in values and ways of life of British emigrants. Even today this division survives: many non-British immigrants come to Australia because it is an open society with institutions derived from Britain; other immigrants firmly reject the idea that they are heirs and beneficiaries of British colonization.

HENRY LAWSON

Henry Lawson probably remains the most famous nineteenth century Australian short-story writer and balladeer. His political attitudes and the ways in which they changed help us to understand the roots of Australian republicanism and some of the reasons for its failure to date. Lawson's father was Swedish: Larsson modified to the English Lawson, but his radicalism was inherited from his mother, Louisa, a prolific writer, leading feminist and campaigning newspaper editor. Henry Lawson was an ardent republican and ferocious critic of Britain during his youth and middle age; and that is the picture of him held by most of those Australians who know anything at all of their political and literary history.

In 1888 Lawson wrote in an article in *The Republican,*

> Why on earth do we want closer connection with England? We have little
> in common with English people except our language. We are fast becoming

an entirely different people. We are more liberal, and, considering our age, more progressive than England is . . . The loyal talk of Patriotism, Old England, Mother Land, etc. Patriotism? After Egypt, Burmah, Soudan, etc. Bah! It sickens one. Go and read "His Natural Life", and other natural lives, by Marcus Clarke, and then talk of the dear old Mother Land that gave us birth.

The young Lawson believed that Australia's past had been full of oppression by the rich and misery for the poor. In his 1887 'Song of the Republic' he scorned 'old-world errors and wrongs and lies' and the 'Old Dead Tree' transplanted from Britain. In 'Wales the First', he described the Prince of Wales as 'a bloated prince of parasites—a libel on the past'. In 'When the Duke of Clarence Died' Lawson declared, 'Thrones of earth and earthly rulers soon shall be swept aside, / And 't'were better for his comfort that the Duke of Clarence died'. In 'The English Queen: A Birthday Ode' he lampooned Queen Victoria as 'that dull old woman, that cold and selfish woman, that dull and brainless woman, that fat and selfish person, that pure and selfish person, the dull, yet gilded dummy, that selfish, callous woman'. Lawson was strongly pro-Boer: in his 'Australia's Peril' he wrote of Australia's coming punishment for helping 'England, the hated of nations, whose existence depends on the sea . . . We must suffer, husband and father, we must suffer, daughter and son, / For the wrong we have taken part in and the wrong that we have done'.

Lawson condemned London long before he visited England. In 1888 he wrote 'I looked o'er London's miles of slums—I saw the horrors here, / And swore to die a soldier of the Army of the Rear'. His opinion was confirmed when he went to England in 1900 to try his fortune. He wrote, 'Englishmen know nothing beyond their own little selfish and paltry little commercial world', and that 'English women strike me as being, in nature and appearance, hard, unsympathetic, selfish and ungraceful'. Even St. Paul's was paltry in Lawson's eyes: 'Most of the statuary in St. Paul's is crude and—no, not theatrical—it doesn't even deserve that term. Reversing time, I would say that it belongs to the concert hall, living-picture school'.

Overall, the young Lawson found little in favour of preferential immigration from England, although he welcomed Irish Catholics. In his 1887 'Only a Sod', old Biddy brings out to Australia some of the soil of Ireland: 'It's only a sod, but it's parcel and part/ Of strugglin', sufferin' Erin'. The 1889 'To the Irish Delegates' called on a visiting group of Irish Nationalists to,

Tell Ireland—tell her in her desolation
That hearts within the south for her have bled—
That scalding tears of helpless indignation
By eyes that read her cruel wrongs are shed.

In 'Ireland Shall Rebel' Lawson deplored 'the tyrant's rod' and prophesied a new Irish rebellion. In 1891 in 'When the Irish Flag Went By', Lawson 'thought of ruined Ireland/ While crystals from the sky/ Fell like tears by angels shed, / As the Irish flag went by.'

During the years in which Lawson denounced Britain and its influence in Australia, he considered the Australian colonies safe from any danger from invasion. He feared no adverse consequences should Australia end its ties with Britain. He was convinced that Australians themselves could keep the Chinese out and attacked Joseph Chamberlain and other British politicians for their opposition to the White Australia policy.

Lawson was an internationalist of sorts, as well as a nationalist. He wrote in 1870 in the *Albany Observer,*

> Trades unionism is a new and grand religion; it recognizes no creed, sect, language or nationality; it is a universal religion—it spreads from the centres of European civilization to the youngest settlements on the most remote portions of the earth; it is open to all, and will include all—the Atheist, the Christian, the Agnostic, the Unitarian, the Socialist, the Conservative, the Royalist, the Republican, the black, and the white . . . There is something grand in the rise and progress of trades unionism; it is like a great vine growing steadily round the world and bearing fruit in all its branches.

Yet Lawson did not consider all peoples equally qualified to join together in universal brotherhood. He added,

> Of course, we all know that there is one great flaw in the theory of universal brotherhood. It is where the Chinaman comes in. There will no difficulty in including the progressive 'Jap' in the scheme, and the American Negro is already a man and brother. The American Indian, the African and South Sea savage, and the aboriginals of Australia will soon in the course of civilization become extinct, and so relieve the preachers of universal brotherhood of all anxiety on their account. The Chinaman remains to be dealt with. For my part I think a time is coming when the Chinaman will have to be either killed or cured—probably the former—but it would be advisable for the world to wait further (Chinese) developments before taking decisive action in the matter . . . I think the European nations should have left the Chinaman alone in the first place.

A semi-facetious tone alternated with shrill hostility in Lawson's references to the Chinese in Australia. In the 1887 'Flag of the Southern Cross' 'the yellow men next to her lust for [Australia)'. In 1892 he warned Western Australians against 'the reeking crowds of Chinamen and their wretched European women'. In 1895 in 'Years After the War in Australia' an Aussie battler reminds his mate of 'the night when the traps got me for stousing a bleeding Chow'. His 1899 'The Songs They Used To Sing' endorses the misquoted verse,

> Rule Britannia! Britannia rules the waves!
> No more Chinamen will enter New South Wales!

Lawson's thinking changed with the rapid rise of Japanese power, especially at sea and after the triumph of Japan over Russia in 1904-5. The 'progressive Jap' presented a far greater national and racial menace to Lawson than the Chinese, so much less progressive in either military or industrial strength. Lawson came to share Alfred Deakin's fear of the Japanese, with their 'inexhaustible energy, their power of applying themselves to new tasks, their endurance', a people 'separated from us by a gulf which we cannot bridge to the advantage of either.'

The emergence of this new enemy changed all Lawson's perspectives. Once he had denounced Russia as the jailor of Poland but now he saw the Russians as the main bulwark of the west against the hordes of Asia: 'Every hour he holds Port Arthur/ May postpone the White Man's doom'. In 1905 Lawson proclaimed that his 'hope's in IVAN yet', since 'across the path from Asia run the Russian trenches still' and 'the vanguard of the White Man is the vanguard of the Russ!'

Lawson now condemned Britain for having supported the Ottoman Empire against the Czars in 1854 and 1878. He praised Nicholas II for refusing to 'take advantage' of Britain's difficulties during the South African War. Searching farther back in the Russian past Lawson found that Peter the Great had heroic qualities: Peter had arrived on the scene 'when Russia was pent and helpless, and barred by every State. The Turk was mighty, and Sweden held the way to the sea'. Given Lawson's Scandinavian ancestry, it might have been supposed that Russia's victory over Sweden might have been a matter of regret rather than of satisfaction. Instead the Swedes, like the Poles, were now cast as the enemies of the enemy of his new enemy.

Even more spectacular was Lawson's reversal of attitudes towards England. Instead of the old vituperation, he called Australians 'The youngest and strongest of England's brood' and celebrated 'The spirit of a single race, / From London round to Bourke'. By the time he wrote in 1917 'England Yet', Lawson could outdo Kipling in John Bullism. He wrote poems that extolled crusaders, courageous old Dame Ruths, and redeemed outlaws. He praised Alfred the Great as the ancestor most to be emulated: Alfred had, saved 'the Saxon tongue', the English language, and 'He fought with arm and heart and brain. / And fought and fought and fought again'

Like many radical anti-British nationalists the young Lawson never shown much interest in parliamentary institutions or the Common Law, but once the Yellow Peril became his greatest fear, he urged Britain to increase its military power. He tried to revive a martial spirit among the British as well as among Australians. He wrote poems on medieval themes that extolled crusaders, courageous old Dame Ruths, and redeemed outlaws. He praised Alfred the Great as the ancestor the new monarchs ought most to emulate, partly because he, above all others, saved 'the Saxon tongue', the English language, but mainly because 'He fought with arm and heart and brain. / And fought and fought and fought again'.

In 'The Song of the Heathen' he had once identified himself with the Cavaliers as convivial drinkers, but now the stern Oliver Cromwell became the historical figure he admired most. Lawson urged that England should be grateful that Cromwell 'thrashed her enemies at home/ And crushed her foes abroad'. With the help of Robert Blake, another hero of the later Lawson, Cromwell 'soon lowered the Dutchman's tone', rescued 'each captured Englishman' from 'pirate ports in Africa', and used his military power to secure toleration for 'the Protestants of Southern lands'. In sum: 'Englishmen were Englishmen, / While Cromwell carved the roast'. In a disturbing expression of totalitarian populism, Lawson called for an Australian Cromwell,

> If you find him stern, unyielding, where his living task is set,
> I have told you that a tyrant should uplift the nation yet;
> He will place his country's welfare over all and everything,
> Shall the King of our Republic, and the man that we call King.

Lawson's rapid change of heart when confronted with Japanese power is a good example of how in many people a wide range of opinions is erected on only one or two beliefs, so that, if one of these changes, so does more or less the entire mind set

Some may think that Lawson's political trajectory vindicates Hilaire Belloc's words in *Jim*: 'And always keep a hold of Nurse/For fear of finding something worse'.

JOSEPH FURPHY

Australian intellectuals of the Left especially esteemed Furphy, the bullocky who became a frequent contributor to *The Bulletin* under the pen-names of Warrigal Jack and, more famously, Tom Collins. Miles Franklin and Kate Baker wrote in 1944, 'By his feeling for it [Such is Life], any literary Australian betrays whether he lives in a state of Australian grace or in one of mere mental colonialism.'[269] Miles Franklin described his best work, Such Is Life, as 'so much more than a novel: it is our *Don Quixote*, our *Les Miserables*, our *Moby Dick*, our *Vanity Fair*'. Franklin and Baker praised Furphy because in his novels 'the doctrine of State Socialism and the importance of the common man are forcefully promulgated' and enthused that Furphy's 'creed was the brotherhood of men, as taught by Christ, and to be put into effect by State Socialism'.[270] Vance Palmer praised Furphy's 'robust egalitarianism', radical populism, and anti-authoritarianism, finding in Furphy's bullockies 'a passion for social equality' among 'the men who pioneered unionism'.[271] Lloyd Ross, son of the proprietor of the Broken Hill *Barrier Truth* who first published Furphy's *Rigby's Romance,* thought its strength was that 'the ethical case for socialism is blended with the rich deep humour of an open-air Australian': it was 'propaganda for socialism woven into a series of short stories'[272] Ian Turner praised Furphy for his dedication to the revolutionary proletariat and the socialist future, and his belief that 'the individual is powerless to determine his own destiny', since 'collective humanity holds the key to the kingdom of God on earth'.[273] J.K. Ewers commended Furphy, not only as a socialist and a republican, but as an advocate of 'the 'common humanity of the Slav and the Mongol'.[274]

When *Meanjin* first appeared in 1940, it regularly featured 'Letters to Tom Collins'. Contributors included Kate Baker, Nettie Palmer, Kylie Tennant, Jim Devaney, James Duhig, John McKellar and Manning Clark. Clark praised Furphy because he and Henry Lawson had 'almost canonized the word "mate"'.[275] When *Overland* appeared in 1954, it took, and retains, as its motto Furphy's self-description: 'temper democratic, bias Australian'

In an early 1955 *Overland* number the radical literary critic, A.A. Phillips, claimed that 'no richer, more vigorous novel than *Such is Life* came from any English or American publishing-house during the period' of its writing. Ian Milner wrote a 'Letter to Tom Collins' in 1957 from exile in Prague, to commend Furphy's 'invincible conviction that the coming New Order of socialism was destined to fulfill the moral purposes of man', although, unfortunately, Australia had fallen behind Czechoslovakia and the other 'People's Democracies' in that onward march.

Furphy, however, as we saw when examining the White Australia Policy, feared that substantial immigration of peoples subservient to arbitrary authority would undermine Australian democracy. His concerns about immigration policy did not centre on the prospect of lower wage levels or reduced working conditions, important as those were to him. His basic political idea was of a socialist republic of 'mates' who shared common values and would back each other up in times of trouble, but who were autonomous individuals. He appreciated that most Chinese in Australia were industrious, a quality he admired. He also expressed sympathy for Chinese in the treaty ports and attacked British and other European interventionists there, but this virtue was insufficient to endear them to him, because there seemed to him no way in which they could share Australian 'mateship'.[276]

n his *Rigby's Romance* Joseph Furphy ('Tom Collins'), drover Tom asks socialist intellectual Rigby, 'Are we to understand that you State Socialists would concede freedom of entry and terms of equality to the few million coloured brothers named Sling Cat and Jamsetjee Ramchunder, who would promptly avail themselves of your system?' Seeking to reconcile his socialist egalitarianism with 'White Australia' policies', Rigby replies, 'we would welcome either Chow or Baboo, provided that he left himself behind. We draw no colour line, no educational line, but we fix a very distinct standard of progress potency.'[277]

Furphy remained a committed 'White-Australian' right to the end. Close to death, he recalled 'the long, lean, sunburnt comrades I left among the mulga—with a subtle undercurrent of homage to the Ideal that is always with me, namely the White Australia. There is nothing else I am so thankful for as for the White Australia.'[278] One of his last published poems, 'A Psalm of Counsel', urges that as well as keeping up 'an Asiatic boundary fence', Australians must be 'White in every sense'.[279]

Furphy considered the best prospect for Aborigines was for them to become absorbed into a wider Australian 'mateship', but he did not underestimate the difficulties on both sides of achieving that goal Furphy, born in 1843 in rural Victoria, knew many Aborigines well as a boy and later as a bullocky, Furphy held that 'from the first contact of black and white races on the Yarra a mutual good-feeling prevailed', largely because of changes in white opinion brought about by the abolition of slavery. He wrote that:

'The movement had been of slow growth, definitely affecting popular thought in the direction of sympathy with dark-skinned races in general. Hence the moral atmosphere at that time was tinged by a theoretical recognition of common manhood, irrespective of colour. This was manifested in the attitude of the Port Phillip squatters and their employees towards the local blacks, as well as in strongly worded official charges from the Colonial Office. Owing to this wave of popular sentiment, the blacks were not only better treated than defenceless natives usually are, but were better understood. Happily, no rash act of hostility on either side precipitated a collision; and the cordial relations of the two races remained unbroken to the last . . . The last days were already in sight. No benevolence could have preserved the indigenous race. Born into a narrow horizon of life, their fatal contentment had paralyzed initiative so effectually that all individual potencies of innovation—never lacking where man is found—died with each brain so endowed. Apart from social disposition, their idea of personal excellence implied nothing beyond a superior dexterity in the construction and use of their anomalous weapons . . . the supernatural element-also inseparable from human nature-found exercise in a far-reaching cult of sorcery.'

He admired virtues he discerned in traditional tribal life and wrote that the Aborigines of the Upper Yarra, 'disturbed by no aspirations, and governed by tradition alone', had 'undisputed possession of a tribal heritage unsurpassed in all resources tha conduce to physical welfare' and a moral temperament which was 'genial, generou and magnanimous.' Physically they were 'athletes incredibly expert in bush craft; and the women were comely'. He held that all people who were born in Australia and who were determined that it should always be their home were 'indigenous'. Furphy frequently saw Aborigines in his youth, recalling later in *The Bulletin* how the women burnt feathers and skin to procure rain (12 September, 1896) and carried lighted bark when travelling (6 October, 1900). Furphy attributed to Aborigines 'undeniable brain-power' that had enabled pre-historic Aborigines to reach 'a degree beyond tha of our own lineal forefathers' and recalled the great prowess with spears of Aborigina men he had known on the Upper Yarra in his boyhood.[280]

In *Such Is Life* there is a 'lost child' episode of the type common in nineteentl century Australian fiction, and real life as well, and it is an elderly Aboriginal womar who comes closest to finding the missing girl. Had her help been sought earlier the girl might well have been found alive. At Runnymede Station, the Aborigina stockman, Toby, is presented as a very positive figure. Toby has racial pride and claims 'Why, properly speaking, I own this here (adj.) country as fur as the eye car reach'. Yet Toby also identifies with much of White Australia, including a loyalty to New South Wales in sporting contest with upstart Port Phillipers. Toby also show: himself a true mate by his fondness for Collins' kangaroo dog Pup.[281]

However, Furphy feared that their lack of adaptability to modernity and thei attachment to magic and superstition would lead to the extinction of 'full-blooded stocks. He was frank and objective about the shadow side of tribal life, as well a about its admirable qualities. One of the Aboriginal friends of his boyhood wa: killed by an enemy, who tore out his kidney fat while he was still alive, althougl badly injured. His death was the basis for the incident in Furphy's 'A Vignette o Port Phillip', in which the one armed Baradyuk is killed because he is suspected o bringing about by sorcery the death of a child of the Gippsland tribe. [282] Eating the kidney fat of defeated enemies was a motif in many 'Dreamtime' stories that sorel troubled many missionaries and anthropologists who first heard them.

In the encounter of Lillian Falkland-Pritchard and Barefooted Bob *in The Buln-Buln and the Brolga,* Mrs. Falkland-Pritchard, a precursor of twentieth century progressivism who reveres all Aboriginal customs, argues that 'in spite of the paramount significance of local designations—or, perhaps because of it—the map o this young land is already defaced by ugly and incongruous names, transplanted from the other side of the world'. White deeds have been worse than white names in her view. She asks Bob, 'aren't the poor creatures often treated cruelly by new settlers? and suggests, 'we boast of our civilization but the trail of the serpent is over it all'.[28] Bob, who has lived many years among Aborigines, explains:

I never studied blackfellers. In fact, missus, to tell you the truth, they don't bother much about manners and customs, so there ain't much to study. Anyway, they're dyin' out by degrees, so the time ain't fur off when it won't matter sixpence what their manners and customs was like.[284]

When invited by Mrs. Pritchard for further details of their way of life, Bob replies, 'they smoke when they can git tobacker; an' they booze when they can git grog; an' they got no shame in regard o' cadgin, an' very little shame any other way'. Bob praises Aboriginal women because 'they won't part with their kids at no price', but condemns many of the men for being willing to sell their womenfolk for 'thirty bob cash an' a couple of notes in second-hand truck'.[285] Furphy's authorial sympathies are clearly with Bob rather than Lillian.

The process of evolution, seen as a form of progress politically as well as genetically, will bring about the replacement of 'Jacky XLVIII'; 'the Evolution of Intelligence has stripped him of former prerogatives'[286]

In a disquisition on heredity and environment, Rigby denies Lushington's claim that 'dipsomania is a transmitted weakness, or, at least, that heredity is a very powerful factor here' by asserting that 'Noah's unfortunate propensity [was] latent for-let's see-take Ussher's chronology—latent for, say a hundred and thirty generations', before reappearing in the Australian Aborigines, 'a race as susceptible to the temptation of drink as any on earth'.[287]

Aborigines are however conceded certain qualities: after the failure to find the lost child in time to save her life, Thompson remarks 'You see, we were nowhere beside Bob, and Bob nowhere beside the old lubra', whose aid had not been sought[288]. A Vignette of Port Phillip includes both a sympathetic description of a 'noble savage' Aboriginal past and profound pessimism for the Aboriginal future.[289]

Furphy sometimes expresses the anti-Semitism common strong among *fin-de-siècle* radicals and socialists, who disliked the role of Jews in high finance and commercial speculation but ignored the equal prominence of Jewish intellectuals on the left. Dixon, after getting a Bible in a swop for an Ouida novel, wonders whether it is simply a good yarn or literally true and provides a ribald and hostile version of *Exodus.*[290]

Fact, I got no pity for anybody that crawls after Jews. Bad eggs, the Jews. When them temporizers was commanded to do anythin' good they used to forgit, or buck, or dodge out of it some (adj.) road; but when they was commanded to stone anybody—whoop! they was there quick an' lively. My (adj.) oath.

273

A second key question for Furphy concerned the value of the English past. His attitude here was also ambivalent. Little good is said about past or present aspects of English life. The Wentworth St. John Frenches the supercilious Folkestone, the inept squatter Smythe, the amiable but feckless Willoughby, and the slow-moving Sollicker, thick in body and mind, are the main representatives of the English in the novel[291]. The 'so-called Anglo-Saxons are 'a people unpleasantly apt in drawing a limitline to aggression on its pocket' and were 'the most contumacious brood at that time in Western Europe'. In a discussion on 'the secret of England's greatness', the principle of the division of labor advanced by Adam Smith is held by Willoughby to be less important than 'her dependencies'. The text implies that this is so, but only because imperial power is gained at the expense of colonies such as Australia. [292]

Lushington's Burkean claim that, 'and yet our British freedom has broadened down from precedent to precedent' is simply the occasion for Rigby to maintain that on the contrary, 'the freedom to oppress is the only growth of socio-political organizations which, in any race, or any times or under any form of government, has of its own accord broadened down from precedent to precedent.'[293]

Particularly odious to Furphy was Orangism, even though earlier generation of Furphys in both County Armagh and Shepperton had been members of Orange Lodges. Furphy held that Orangism was deliberately introduced into Ireland with the aim of disrupting the Irish radical and nationalist movements by sectarian discord, and its importation into Australian was an even greater 'criminal folly' than that of sorrel, cockspur, Scotch thistle, foxes, rabbits and sparrows, and comparable only with the deliberately introduction of hydrophobia or glanders. [294] Yet Mary O'Halloran, the lost child in the bush, is the 'perfect Australian' who embodies the best characteristics of the ancient Brito-Irish race which, Furphy believed, pre-dated the Celts in Ireland, as well as of the new Australia.

In his discussion of a century of White Australia Collins is clearer about his dislikes than his likes. Indignation is expressed about the dogmatizing on 'the Coming Australian' indulged in by Marcus Clarke, Trollope, Froude and Francis Adams, but, after disclaiming any special authority himself on the subject, Collins considers the matter at some length. The bush is for Collins the authentic Australia. The true laconic Australian has been formed by a man's life in the bush:[295]

> It is not in our cities or townships, it is not in our agricultural or mining areas, that the Australian attains full consciousness of his own nationality; it is in places like this, and as clearly here as at the heart of the continent. [296]

> No young fellow in that great rendezvous dared to embellish his narrative in the slightest degree, on pain of being posted as a double-adjective

blatherskite; for his audience was sure to include a couple of critical, iron-grey cyclopedias of everything Australian—everything at least untainted by the spurious and blue-moulded civilization of the littoral.[297]

A theme which fascinated Furphy was the effect of life in Australia on the original stocks from the British Isles. Collins tackles the question of degeneration in typically facetious vein, but with a bite behind the humour. Furphy believed exposure to Australian conditions had increased masculine tendencies in women: Jemima (Jim) is an androgynous figure, while both Mrs. Sollicker and Molly Cooper are described as having strong growths on their upper lips.

Furphy's strong pro-Boer feelings arose as much from his White Australianism as antagonism to Great Britain. In the course of discussing some poems Furphy wrote in 1911 in old age in Western Australia, which refer to a 'slant-eyed menace' and the need for an 'Asiatic boundary fence', John Barnes (suggests that 'the Christian Socialist idealism of *Such Is Life* had degenerated into a hearty patriotism based on an ideal of racial purity', but all Furphy's novels contain this belief, no less if no more.[298]

Furphy, as a radical nationalist, sought the political independence of Australia from Britain, and was in consequence in matters of day-by-day political disputes generally antagonistic to British institutions and policies. Like other radical nationalists however his arguments for radicalism, socialism or nationalism did not originate in Australia, but chiefly in Britain itself

This uneasy co-existence between anti-British political and pro-British racial and cultural attitudes was made even more precarious for Furphy through his deep affection for English literature. In a 1890 essay on World Federation of a generally utopian and naive character, Furphy argued that it was English literature had more relevance to the world than British power: 'it is only because our English is the most widespread and powerful of literature, and not by any means owing to superior adaptability or enthusiasm in the type Englishman, that Anglo-Saxon communities may lead the way.

Another contradiction was between Furphy's overt and explicit rejection of the political structures and traditions derived from Britain, particularly England, and his admiration not only for the literature and cultural values so closely linked to them, but also for the political virtues of liberty and equality before the law which, however imperfectly represented in English life, were more fully developed there than anywhere else. At the heart of White Australian radicalism was a tension between the need to define a distinctive national ethos with 'temper democratic; bias offensively Australian', by emphasizing the differences between Australia and England, and the desire to develop political institutions which were essentially an extension of English political traditions and not a repudiation of them. Furphy did not find in any contemporary or past states that were superior models to follow to the radical strand inherent in the English traditions he so sharply criticized.

Chapter 14

AN AUSTRALIAN REPUBLIC?

Paul Keating targeted Robert Menzies for liking Britain too much and alleged that Menzies' 'endless and almost endlessly regressive era sunk a generation of Australians in Anglophilia and torpor'.[299] Keating claimed that this pro-British attitude 'has long been, and remains debilitating to our national culture, our economic future, our destiny as a nation in Asia and the Pacific'. Keating specifically linked his republican and Asian pushes, declaring, 'I am pleased, though not surprised, by the positive reaction in South-East Asia to the recent surge of independent and republican thinking in Australia.'[300] Keating insisted that 'Geophysically speaking this continent is old Asia'.[301] He always had kind words for the liberators of Tibet and declared, 'If anything is inevitable about the twenty-first century, it is the growing weight and influence of China in the region and the world.' He added with incredible optimism 'Australia has nothing to fear from this'.[302]

Malcolm Booker, a former Australian diplomat and later an enthusiastic republican, followed the Keating line and claimed:

> The Union Jack is a symbol of imperial rule and oppression, especially among people in our own Asia-Pacific region. The present flag gives this symbol pride of place, and it cannot be expected to win the devotion of all those people and their descendants who have come to this country to find freedom from domination and exploitation.[303]

On the contrary, tens of thousands of people defied their own governments, pirates, and sharks in and out of the water to get away from their 'own Asia-Pacific region' and to reach lands where the Union Jack was part of the national flag.

New migrant groups, in their turn, from the Baltic countries and Eastern Europe, northern Europe, Mediterranean, and finally Asian countries, were highly vocal that they simply wanted to be able to share fully in Australia's way of life. They came in the full knowledge that Australia was an English-speaking country and had a legal system and constitution derived from Great Britain. That was one of Australia's chief attractions to potential migrants. If any group had stated then that everything that had previously happened in Australia was irrelevant to them and that Australia ought to change its way of life in order to become more like the countries they had left, the numbers of legal immigration would have plummeted immediately.

Now, however, republicans often claim that Australia's constitutional monarchy, its flag, and its post-1788 history are alien and irrelevant to ethnic groups of non-British origins and must therefore be repudiated. Paul Keating argued that 'the people of modern Australia are drawn from virtually every country in the world. It is no reflection on the loyalty of a great many of them to say that the British monarchy is a remote and inadequate symbol of their affections for Australia'.[304] Of course, if Australians were to be persuaded that our constitutional monarchy is irrelevant, the next demand would be that the Union Flag is removed from the flag of Australia. Then soon afterwards Iranian, Chinese, Vietnamese, and Timorese migrants and refugees will be asked by our republicans how they feel about Australian states and cities being named after dead foreign queens, as are Queensland, Victoria, Adelaide, and Elizabeth, or that city streets are named after dead Englishmen, as are King William, Wakefield, Gouger, and Grote streets and a thousand more. Once a retreat begins, there will be great difficulty in regrouping to stop all the attacks to come.

Perhaps one should take Keating's opinions with a pinch of salt. He and Bob Hawke, despite their later conflict, shared some valuable political skills. Each had pro-market economic ideas that were hated by many on the ALP Left. In order to protect themselves from too much antagonism among the rank and file, both became more vitriolic in matters that concerned them less than the economy but on which their stances would draw cheers from many ALP activists. Republicanism and Aboriginal Rights were very valuable cards to supplement an ever sharper invective.

Paul Keating was in one sense right when he claimed that 'the fact is that if the plans for our nationhood were being drawn up now, by this generation of Australians and not those of a century ago, it is beyond question that we would make our Head of State an Australian'.[305] So was Malcolm Turnbull right when he maintained that 'Her Majesty is Queen of Australia simply because at the time our Constitution was enacted Australia was a colony of Great Britain'.[306] Who can doubt that that if the colonies which formed the Commonwealth of Australia had not been British the Queen of England would not be Head of State in Australia today? Nor would English be Australia's national language, nor would Australia enjoy the rule of law, parliamentary government, and freedom of speech and association inherited from Britain, nor would Australians engage in the sports in which they are so often world leaders. But Australia has had the history it has had. There is no justification for ignoring or rejecting that history, especially since it is not one of shame, but one of the most successful stories of national advancement ever known. That Australia is an offspring of Britain is the main single fact in Australian history, and our constitutional monarchy and other major institutions should be no less valued by Australians because of their British origins.

Paul Keating was absolutely right when he noted that Australians 'are not as we once were, in a parent–child relationship'.[307] Yet Paul Keating, surely, must acknowledge that when children achieve full independence of their parents, as all sensible parents hope they will, they are still the offspring of their parents and filial obligations and ties remain which are of a different order from those of even the closest friendship. To acknowledge and value those ties is not to kowtow to a foreign power.

Chapter 15

THE 2006 CANBERRA HISTORY SUMMIT

In 2006 Julie Bishop, then Minister for Education in the Howard Coalition government, convened a national 'summit' conference on the teaching of Australian History in the nation's schools, across states and types of schools. This seemed a sensible move, since 'History Wars' had been raging for a decade or more and the tone of debate had become increasingly bitter.

Perhaps a less sensible move on the part of the minister was to exclude from the summit certain persons, unnamed by her, on the grounds that they had 'extreme views. She described the twenty-three invited as the 'Sensible Centre'. This interdict meant that the generals of the History Wars were absent from the summit. Absent were Henry Reynolds, Stuart Macintyre, and Robert Manne on the radical side and Patrick McGuinness and Keith Windschuttle among the liberal-conservatives. That being said, none could accuse Julie Bishop of partisanship in her selection of historians to write preparatory documents for the summit. A survey of history teaching across the nation was entrusted to two entrenched radicals in Dr Anna Clark, a granddaughter of Manning Clark, and Associate Professor Tony Taylor. An established historian of moderate conservative views, Associate Professor Gregory Melluish, was commissioned to prepare a specimen or model syllabus for Australian history in the schools.

Melluish, although doubtless well aware of the perennial problem in teaching history of the opposing claims of depth and breadth, to my mind was inclined too far towards breadth. What he had prepared was certainly scholarly enough, but would have better suited a second year university course.

As might have been expected, there were two sorts of response to the Melluish presentation. There seemed to be no demands that any person or event or movement

MAKING SENSE OF HISTORY

n the Melluish syllabus be rejected, but several favourite items were proposed as additions, thus presenting even greater overload. The other reaction, expressed mainly by Professor John Hirst and me, was that the starting point should be to formulate the most important questions that school students might get round to answer within the time available in the school year. I had circulated in advance what I thought were questions that would not only provide structure but also enable the teacher in the classroom to choose some people, places, and proceedings in enough depth to be three-dimensional.

I found myself under attack from the Right. Greg Melluish noted, correctly, that Prime Minister John Howard had specifically urged teachers to offer coherent narratives. I am no foe to narrative coherence, but that emerges only in response to pertinent questions. My questions on pre-contact indigenous history were:

How long have Aboriginal peoples lived in what is now Australia? Did they migrate from elsewhere, perhaps when there was a land bridge between Australia and South-East Asia?

What were their means of livelihood? Did these differ in various parts of Australia? Did these change over the generations? If not, why not?

What were their family and group structures? Did these change over the generations? What evidence is available to us?

What did they believe about the origins of life and its meaning? Did these beliefs change over the generations?

Why did contacts over generations across the Torres Strait remain very limited and have little apparent affect upon Aboriginal life?

Why were peoples of Western Europe able from the sixteenth century onwards to navigate the South Pacific and to make landfalls on Australia?

What did Cook, Banks, and their companions conclude about Australia and possible British colonisation?

In a chapter in *The Howard Era,* edited by Keith Windschuttle, David Martin-Jones and Ray Evans, Gregory Melluish derided 'two members of the Summit [who] had submitted written documents to the members of the Summit. They were Peter Stanley and Geoffrey Partington . . . Just why they felt the need to do so is unclear'. My purpose was certainly unclear to Melluish.

Dr Kevin Donnelly described the Melluish paper as 'a clear, succinct and convincing outline of what constitutes essential learning in Australian history'. Donnelly was disappointed that 'instead of detailing essential, understanding and skills that all students should be taught in relation to Australian history, the majority of the participants agreed to define the curriculum by a series of open-ended questions'. Dr Mark Lopez claimed that the meeting had been hijacked by the 'Left establishment view' of history teaching. Keith Windschuttle praised Melluish's paper as 'a perfectly accurate and eminently teachable model, but a caucus at the summit successfully dumped it in favour of a curriculum based not on narrative and politics but on 'issues and questions'. Windschuttle regretted that the majority at the summit 'agreed to define the curriculum by a series of open-ended questions', such as 'How did convict society change into a free society?' and 'What were the relationships between settlers and Aborigines?' Richard Allsop of the Institute of Public Affairs commented that 'in rejecting the narrative approach of the Melluish paper in favour of a question-based model proposed by Professor John Hirst, the participants demonstrated that they were largely content to see the collectivist assumptions behind much of what is taught in our schools remain unaddressed'. Greg Melluish expressed his disappointment at the outcome of the 'summit' in *The Australian*:

> To me the questions approach is just another version of the issues and themes approach that the summit was meant to remedy. It is the lowest common denominator form of history. My paper, it is claimed, is too advanced and sophisticated. Does this mean that we have to move to a boneheaded approach to the study of Australian history?

Melluish wrote that 'Geoffrey Partington complained that the real problem was that we were deciding what students had to learn rather than letting them discover things for themselves. What he was saying was that the Summit should not be engaged in what it had been summoned to do'. He must have heard a different contribution from the one I made. The debate fairly accurately reflected the balance of opinion among history teachers in schools and higher education in Australia. That balance is to me a matter of regret and something I have tried as hard as most to change, but no conspiracy theory was needed to explain the situation.

Do my questions imply a collectivist outlook or bone-headedness? It is strange that some of our most able liberal-conservative historians should press for detailed central prescription of the content of school history syllabuses. Of course, 'bottom-up' reform is slow and unspectacular, but 'top-down' policies are likely further to strengthen political activism. The Left is much more adept at caucusing than the Right.

Melluish also gratuitously sneered at John Hirst: 'For some reason John Hirst had been made chair . . .' of one of the sessions. I don't think I had met Hirst, one of he most gifted Australian historians of his generation, before that conference but, vhatever qualifications he brought with him as a chairman, he dealt capably with debate that lacked direction other than which he provided. In a later article on he summit Hirst generously wrote about the escape from the bog into which Greg Melluish had led us, 'The clue came from Geoffrey Partington, an old campaigner gainst the excesses of progressive education, but unlike many of that ilk an ducationalist himself.' I do not always take it as a compliment to be called an ducationist, but I accept that Hirst's intent was kindly. I can understand that Gregory Melluish felt some resentment at the lack of enthusiasm at the summit for a document o which he must have devoted considerable time and energy, but his reaction to riticism from people who esteem him as an author and historian was excessive and nprovoked.

n contrast I was praised too highly by Jenny Gregory, then Associate Professor f History at the University of Western Australia and previously Director of UWA 'ress and UWA's Centre for Western Australian History. She agreed with me that most believed that the proposed syllabus was pitched at too complex a level for 'ears 9 and 10'. Like some others who recognised excess of content, Jenny Gregory onetheless felt that even more should be included, since 'there was 'inadequate ttention to Aboriginal history, social history in general and multiculturalism in articular, no recognition of regional differences, nothing on the environment, and he recommended detail was too extensive to fit the limited number of hours available 90 to 100 hours per year at secondary level)'. I began to wonder whether all other ubjects other than History, perhaps only Australian History, were to be omitted in 'ears 9 AND 10.

t that stage, Jenny Gregory feared the summit was at a stalemate. However, a knight n shining armour saved the day. She wrote,

> 'There had been a tantalizing suggestion during earlier debate when Geoffrey Partington argued that in teaching the place to begin is with questions. And so the final session, chaired by Bob Carr, was devoted to the development of a series of open-ended questions that could be linked with the chronology to guide the development of a Year 9 and 10 curriculum and could be used by teachers and students. The idea struck a chord with participants. The ideas bubbled and the adrenaline surged as we rushed headlong towards the end of the summit. We decided that students should deal with three or four questions in the course of a year and should apply these questions over a chronological time scale of a century or more. Eleven questions were developed in this final session, which was lively, argumentative, stimulating and positive.'

Appendix A

MERLIN DONALD ON THE DEVELOPMENT OF MIND

For human evolution I have relied largely on the Canadian Professor of Psychology Dr Merlin Donald. Donald devised a sequence in cultural evolution from the 'episodic' through the 'mimetic' and 'mythic' to the 'theoretic'. He saw the episodic phase as characteristic of primate cognition—largely reactive to stimulus, but requiring considerable social intelligence to facilitate group cooperation; the mimetic as the phase in which early hominids developed non-verbal skills in gesture and vocal variation and mastered simple tool production that could be transmitted through imitation; the mythic as the achievement by *homo sapiens* during the late Palaeolithic period of complex language skills, narrative thought, and a wide range of skill needed for successful hunter-gathering.

Donald's final theoretic stage is characterized by 'institutionalized paradigmatic thought' accompanied by, or made possible by, 'massive external memory stores' he called exograms, in contrast to engrams: the internal brain storage which had been adequate for all earlier human activities. Once literacy is achieved, external memory becomes necessary and storage devices, such as books, are developed to contain and extend abstract or theoretical knowledge that is rarely derivable from everyday experience.[308] Possession of external memory to extend biological memory appears to be an important requirement for achieving the theoretic level. Australian Aborigines had not yet entered the material symbolic or theoretic modes of thought before 1788. Initially very gradual, the gap between peoples with and without external memory soon widened very rapidly.

Persuaded by Leslie White, Donald interpolated after the mythic a 'material symbolic' phase that began about the time of the Childe's Neolithic revolution and the beginning of settled life. It includes the building of monuments, usually

284

for non-utilitarian purposes, and the growing use of material symbols of rank and authority in hierarchical societies.

In general, tribal peoples were skilled in narrative, but their culture had little or no place for features of this second mode of thinking, such as formal arguments, systematic taxonomies, deduction, verification, differentiation, quantification, idealization, and formal methods of measurement, culminating in formal theory. A contrast is often made between the collective natures of traditional tribal thought and the individualistic nature of modern Western thought; yet in one important respect, the contrast is the other way round. Each initiated tribal man and woman has a sufficient stock of lore and skills to perform adequately all that life required, whereas to cope in modern societies access is necessary to many repositories of information and knowledge that no single individual possesses. It was in response to the development of such theoretical knowledge, in areas such as astronomy, mathematics, and engineering, as well as to the demands of commerce and administration in increasingly complex societies that the institution we call the school first emerged in Egypt, Sumeria, and China.

Donald's approach is confirmed by the work of American psychologist Jerome Bruner who identified two major forms of thinking: the narrative and the paradigmatic (or analytical or logico-scientific). The first is concerned to tell a story, the second to analyses experience through empirical induction or deductive logic. The first emerged historically long before the second, just as it precedes it in the individual development of each child. The first is universal, although it may wither or degenerate in some conditions, but the second is relatively rare and recent. Story telling is adequate in societies with little or no division of labor but not in organized states.[309] Bruner's model supplements that of Donald's by demonstrating the importance in very early years of access to external memory and immersion in analytical and deductive thought.

Failure of the Aborigines to acquire external memories or theoretic modes of thought was not, so far as can be determined, the result of some innate inadequacy. Donald put it this way:

> Although the brains of the very young are sufficiently adaptable to develop in many ways, only potentialities actually utilized are likely to mature: 'Cultures restructure the mind, not only in terms of its specific contents, which are obviously culture-bound, but also in terms of its fundamental neurological organizations.'[310]

There is ongoing dispute about the rival influences of nature and nurture, but it is certain that human beings are not born with, say, the ability to read and write and would never learn to do so in a bookless and illiterate world. Such potentialities need favourable conditions that were not available for Indigenous Australians. A key passage of Donald's is: 'Without deep enculturation, we are relatively helpless to exploit the potential latent in our enormous brains because the specifics of our modern cognitive structure are not built in.'[311] If you don't use it, you lose it, and quite quickly, too; if you don't use it early enough, you are unlikely ever to develop it at all! Just what Sir Paul Hasluck believed.

Donald emphasizes that new sources of information and ideas often profoundly disturb traditional beliefs and practices. He suggested that 'the first step in any new area of theory development is always anti-mythic: things and events must be stripped of their previous mythic significance before they can be subjected to what we call "objective theoretical analysis"'. He added:

> Nothing illustrates the transition from mythic to theoretic culture better than this agonizing process of demythologization, which is still going on, thousands of years after it began. The switch from a predominantly narrative mode of thought to a predominantly analytic or theoretic mode apparently requires a wrenching cultural transformation.[312]

Donald noted that 'the first step in any new area of theory development is always anti-mythic: things and events must be stripped of their previous mythic significance before they can be subjected to what we call "objective" theoretical analysis. In fact, the meaning of "objectivity" is precisely this: a process of demythologization'. The period of transformation was often traumatic for those who sought to undertake it, but refusal to try to undertake it was and is tantamount to accepting a position of inferiority in relation to people who had mastered such theoretic modes.

Even optimum learning conditions may come too late because modes of thought incompatible with the new ideas are too firmly set in place. The brains of the very young are sufficiently adaptable to develop in many ways, but within a specific culture, only those potentialities actually utilized have the opportunity of realization. Experiences in the most formative years may well reconfigure the sensory cortexes of individuals and enhance certain capacities. There is unlikely to be direct inheritability of such specific adaptations, although natural selection may favour some developments in fairly long-term stable situations, but groups with well-nigh uniform experiences may develop common belief systems which are highly resistant to the new ideas and concepts.

Donald argued that 'cultures restructure the mind, not only in terms of its specific contents, which are obviously culture-bound, but also in terms of its fundamental neurological organizations'. It was with glimmers of this argument in their minds hat many Western missionaries or administrators thought the best possibility of educating native peoples was 'to catch them early', to remove some of them from their customary surroundings, and to place them with foster-parents or in boarding schools so that they could acquire Western knowledge and culture, and then act as cultural heralds between the two ways of life.

APPENDIX B

REVIEW OF IS HISTORY FICTION? BY ANN CURTHOYS AND JOHN DOCKER

Review of Ann Curthoys & John Docker: *Is History Fiction?*, 2006, NSW University Press, pp. 296

Professors Curthoys and Docker chose as the title of this book a question that they never answer satisfactorily. One quite sees their problem: hunting with the hounds and running with the deer is never easy. In early life both read Marx and Engels and accepted elements at least of their 'Materialist Concept of History', the epistemology of which is starkly objectivist. Classical Marxism had great confidence that diligent research and reading can produce unassailable facts and truths. Then the Krushchev Revelations and the end of Stalinism and overall disappointment with the traditional Marxist agenda led in academia in the west to the virtual replacement of 'Old Left' ideology and tactics by a New Left' which was 'Neo-Marxist' and in epistemology owed more to Idealism, in its philosophical sense, than to Materialism.

I share the objections of Curthoys and Docker to attempts to make historical understanding cognate with physical sciences or mathematics, but one should avoid throwing out the baby with the bath water. They really should consider seriously the merits of variations of conditional relativism, or conditional absolutism as these positions might also be termed. In short they accept a number of first-order goods, such as the superiority of freedom to slavery, of prosperity rather than poverty, or knowledge rather than ignorance, security rather than continual fear of violence and so on; but they also recognised that specific historical conditions assist or threaten advances on one or more fronts, and understand that there are permanent tensions between first-order goods, such as that between freedom and safety which creates the Paradox of Freedom: each of us wishes greater personal freedom of action but fears

he consequences if others are have like freedom and are unrestrained by law, custom
or morality.

An 'overview' by Greg Clarke written for the Evatt Foundation quoted Curthoys and
Docker with approval for the following:

> We think, however, that the temptation to declare that the historian can
> objectively establish the truth about the past is to be resisted There has
> always to be a question mark hovering above the claim to having attained
> an objective, let alone scientific, status for one's own findings.

Once again the very real obstacles to establishing truth are too quickly taken as
grounds for rejecting the very possibility of objectivity, yet each of us knows full
well that at the very minimum we can differentiate between the greater and lesser
bias or distortion, and detect bad arguments when they come from 'our' side' and
acknowledge some occasional merit in arguments advanced by those we consider
our foes. If Greg Clarke is right, there is a good case for closing down history
departments in our universities or merging them with Literature Departments.
Fortunately, he is wrong.

Docker and Curthoys are rather thin on their classical historiography, with only
Herodotus and Thucydides getting adequate attention and Polybius, as Alan Barcan
noted, virtually ignored. Tacitus and his preference for the noble savage over the
degenerate city-dwellers dependent upon the bread and circuses or as, we would say,
on Centrelink and TV, might well have been of interest to them. However, Tacitus
gets only passing mention as a one of a group thought by Bury to have been good
historians because they were 'partial and biased' (p. 89)

I lost some confidence in Curthoys and Docker early in the piece when they asserted
that Herodotus regarded Croesus of Lydia as a foolish ruler, because he completely
misinterpreted the reply of the Delphic Oracle to his fatal question: 'Shall I attack
the rising power of Cyrus of Persia? 'In general Herodotus seems to me to have been
highly respectful of both of them.

Curthoys and Docker leap from the ancient world to the nineteenth century, with
Walter Scott and Leopold (von) Ranke as another pair to compare and contrast Since
the two were not playing the same game, a final score cannot emerge. However,
Sir Walter, who attracted far more people to historical reading than did the learned
German, would have had no doubt that History and Fiction are very different kettles
of fish, as several of his Prefaces to his novels illustrate in detail.

Curthoys and Docker were perhaps a little unfair to choose Scott's *Quentin Durward* and criticisms of its historical inaccuracies by Von Ranke to illustrate their general argument. In *Quentin Durward* Scott was writing very much at second hand, but he was an outstanding historian of Scotland as well as its greatest novelist. His capacity to 'get to the inside', in Collingwood's sense, of people, high and low, with conflicting interests and contrary beliefs, has rarely been equaled and perhaps never surpassed. Here we face once more the breadth-depth dilemma. Scott often lacked depth and the telling detail when writing on events outside Britain and even outside Scotland, but he consistently grasped the essence of life and death, and of reasons for action and the consequences as well, in the land of his birth during the two centuries before his birth.

It is regrettable that Curthoys and Docker did not introduce readers to Procopius, Augustine, Bede, Ibn Khaldun, Francis Bacon and Hume, to name no more. Even Vico only gained a mention because Croche rented his house generations after his death. They have a case for including, Nietzsche, Lord Acton, Bury, Croche, Herbert Butterfield and E.H. Carr. And not much remains to be said about Historical Materialism: debates about the priority of the chicken and the egg seem to have become exhausted. Yet David Hume was eminent both as historian and philosopher. Perhaps Curthoys and Docker may find in Hume further clues helpful to solving the problems of causation that are at the heart of the philosophy of history.

Curthoys and Docker gave space, and their own time and effort, to a large number of men who had not contributed much to the philosophy of history, including Foucault, Derrida, Benjamin, Barthes and, Lemkin, although the Index is not troubled by the names of Karl Popper, Ernst Gellner, William Dray, G. Kitson Clark, Maurice Mandelbaum, W.H. Walsh, R.F Atkinson or Lewis Namier Numerous women, such as Joan Zemon Davies, Susan Magarey, Jill Matthews, Susan Macintyre and Kate Millett, gain mention as contributors to philosophy of history, but not Rebecca West or C.V. Wedgwood.

The number of important and informative books competing for our attention is far greater than we can ever read, and criteria of selection are contestable, but it is difficult to work out which criteria they applied. Worrying, too, are their comments on 'war-hungry demagogues like Cleon', who gratuitously spread death and destruction. Clearly an analogy is intended with the United States; a comparison strengthened by almost immediate reference to 'the 'atrocities . . . in regard to Hiroshima'. Why no reference to the atrocities of Mao that killed more Chinese than the Japanese did, or of the party, police and prison departments of Stalin's regime in Ukraine and other parts of the former Soviet Union? What about ongoing killings in Africa? Double standards and special pleading undermine efforts to expose wickedness among one's foes.

Could either Curthoys or Docker have envisaged in, say 1963, that half a century on they would write a book on history and fiction in which Lenin and Mao did not appear at all, and Stalin in a single reference to a 'resurgence of European nationalism in its ugliest and most murderous form. Mussolini's Fascism, Hitler's Nazism, Stalin's Communism, a second global war, the Holocaust . . . .' (p.116). Curthoys and Docker suggested that it is only recently that History has 'become a source of public debate and anxiety in many societies'. Well, it depends on your time scale It existed when I was a little boy.

Also widely challenged is their claim that it is 'conservative historians; whom we find 'fiercely critiquing historical narratives that suggest, for example, that European settler societies were founded in violence, dispossession, cruelty and trauma for the indigenous inhabitants'. All historians are surely aware that nearly every kingdom or empire was created on the basis of the defeat and suppression of other peoples?. How do they think that Neanderthals became extinct?

Part of the answer to the central question of 'Can historians tell the truth about the past'? must surely be that we can come very close to it if we try hard enough to do so. Our main lack is not so much in relevant data, even though only a fragment of the past survives to satisfy our inquiries, but that we are often tempted to distort an account in the interest of what seems to us a noble cause. Once we try to protect people from distress or loss of self-esteem or pride in country, religion or party, or put loyalty before evidence, we find ourselves on the slippery slope: *Facilis descensus Averno.*

With the now customary genuflection to Indigenous historical insights, Adrian Jones of Latrobe University praised Curthoys and Docker for understanding early on in the piece the 'need "to go native", so to speak, and to escape English' The Second Edition of Is *History Fiction?* received a highly supportive review from Paul Kiem on behalf of the New South Wales History Teachers Association. As an aside, he explained that history had become important in schools because: 'there is great concern for the environment, there has been a loss of faith in the western progress narrative and there is a search for a global perspective'. Kiem has a point or two there. It would help any children who lie awake at night worrying about global warming to study the history of climate and discover that Ice Ages and periods of rapid heating took place with very little influence by *homo sapiens*. Then they could sleep in peace. However but that is unlikely, since that is not what children are taught in our schools. As for 'Progress' Kiem should ask his students to 'compare and contrast', as the old exam formula had it, the numbers of Australians and other 'westerners' seeking to migrate to 'non-western' parts of the world with the numbers from such countries seeking by hook or by crook, mainly the latter, to enter Australia and other 'western' countries. His faith in the 'western progress narrative' might recover after that.

Yet, *Is History Fiction?* bears witness to wide reading and keen analytical minds; and it could very well be read in conjunction with Keith *Windschuttle's The Killing of History*. Each is both scholarly and combative and together they offer valuable insights into the thinking of Foucault, Derrida, Barthes and contemporary and recent epistemology and literary, linguistic and historical theory as a whole. Windschuttle emphasizes the destructive and negative dangers presented by challenges to the concept of a canon, which, though its precise content is contestable, is the prime justification for humanistic studies. Curthoys and Docker are sympathetic to much of the thinking behind challenges to the canon, and in the course of their critiques they reveal some insights within the doctrinaire jargon of which readers like myself were unaware.

It would be futile to wish for consensus rather than contention in the interpretation of history and literature or in what we judge to be progress or decay in cultures, but we ought to be able to conduct disputes with less rancor and animosity. In particular we could make a start by assuming good faith behind arguments we reject as deeply mistaken, unless there is solid evidence to believe otherwise. It is the imputation of *quo bono* rather than of intellectual mediocrity that most prevents civil discourse on contested issues such as sexual morality, the role of punishment in deterrence of crime, global warming, and distributions of power and affluence in different societies etc.

It is often claimed that a major justification for generous public funding of universities is that they provide, as well as skills required by societies and enhanced public appreciation of much of the best in the arts, a forum for informed and mannerly discussion of great issues of the day. At the present time in Australia universities are not very successful in providing such a forum. Historians, despite our claims about the uplifting and insightful qualities we attribute to our studies, can hardly assert higher merit in this respect than scientists or engineers and physicians, nor do those of our number feted as Public Intellectuals offer a standard for us lesser lights to emulate. We should be grateful that we live in an open, constitutional realm, under the rule of law, in which governments can be changed without fighting on the streets or military coups. That they can be changed without a verdict of the electorate is perhaps a more disputable feature of our public life, but those of us who are historians should surely regard it as one of our public duties to enable whatever we most value in the Past to elevate the quality of thought and life in our own day.

Also by Geoffrey Partington

Publications since Arrival in Australia, 1976
Books

Women Teachers in England and Wales, in the Twentieth Century (1976). London: National Foundation for Educational Research Publishing Company, p. 107.

The Idea of an Historical Education (1980). London: National Foundation for Educational Research Publishing Company, p. 247.

Parents Who Change Schools (1985). Bedford Park, South Australia: Flinders University of South Australia Press, p. 119.

The Treatment of Sex in South Australian Education (1983). Adelaide: Malvern Press, p. 39.

What Do Our Children Know? A Study of Educational Standards (1988). Perth: Australian Institute for Public Policy, p. 79.

The Australian Nation: Its British and Irish Roots (1994). Melbourne: Australian Scholarly Publishing, p. 347 (American Edition (1996). New Brunswick, NJ: Transaction Press).

The Australian History of Henry Reynolds (1994). Perth: Australian Mining and Exploration Council, p. 53.

Social Studies in the New Zealand Curriculum (1995). Wellington: Education Forum, p. 71.

Hasluck versus Coombs: White Politics and Australia's Aborigines (1996). Sydney: Quaker Hill Press, p. 156.

The Origins of the Bennelong Society (2001). Melbourne: The Bennelong Society, p. 25.

Chapters in Books

'Social Studies in South Australian Primary Schools' (1982) in A. Barcan (ed.). *The Quality of the Curriculum.* Sydney: Australian Council of Educational Standards, pp. 41–49.

'The Keeves Report and Control of the Curriculum' (1982) in C.N. Power (ed.). *The Illusion of Progress: The Keeves Report and the Future of Education.* Bedford Park, SA: Flinders University of South Australia Press.

'Que Historia Deboriamos Ensenar?' ('What History Should We Teach?') (1982) in M. Peyreyra (ed.). *La Historia En El Ayla.* Tenerife: University of De La Laguna Press, pp. 229–26.

'History: Rewritten to Ideological Fashion' (1986) in D. O'Keeffe (ed.). *The Wayward Curriculum.* London: Social Affairs Unit, pp. 63–81.

'Educational Reform in Britain' (1990) in Dame Leonie Kramer (ed.). *Education Examined: Curriculum and Assessment in the 1990s.* Sydney: IPA Education Policy Unit, pp. 10–12.

'Conceptions of Quality in Education' (1991) in Judith Chapman et al. (eds.). *Improving the Quality of Australian Schools.* Hawthorn, Vic.: Australian Council for Educational Research, pp. 140–46.

'Moral Education in Some English-Speaking Countries: Antinomian and Fundamentalist Challenges' (1991) in G.L. Anderson and M.A. Kaplan (eds.). *Morality and Religion.* New York: Paragon House, pp. 273–88.

'Preparing Teachers for the Realities of the Classroom' (1991) in Dame Leonie Kramer (ed.). *Educating the Educators: New Directions in the Recruitment and Training of Teachers.* Sydney: Institute of Public Affairs, pp. 16–21 (reprinted with permission in *Scholastic Times*, 2 (4), pp. 19–22, May 1992).

'The Aetiology of Mabo' in Samuel Griffiths Society (1994). *Proceedings of the Fourth Conference of the Samuel Griffith Society*, Brisbane, pp. 1–13.

'Trade Unions and the New Protection' (1994) in From Industrial Relations to Personal Relations: The Coercion of Society. *Proceedings of the XVIth Conference of the H.R. Nicholls Society.* Melbourne: H.R. Nicholls Society.

Families and Education' (1995) in A.N. Barcan and P. O'Flaherty (eds.). *Family, Education and Society: The Australian Perspective.* Canberra: Academic Press, pp. 9–28.

Historical Origins of Australia's Values' (1995) in *A Stitch in Time: Repairing the Social Fabric.* Melbourne: Institute of Public Affairs, pp. 19–32.

Educational Contestability and the Role of the State' (1995) in J.D. Turner (ed.). *The State and the School: An International Perspective.* Brighton: Falmer Press, pp. 37–54.

'The Kindness that Kills' (1997) in *Wrong Way – Go Back: Proceedings of the XVIIIth Conference of the H.R. Nicholls Society,* Brighton Savoy Convention Centre, Victoria, 5–6 September 1977.

'What is Left in Education?' (1997) in *Old Boundaries and New Frontiers in Histories of Education.* Australia and New Zealand History of Education Society, pp. 476–92.

'Social Studies in the New Zealand Curriculum' (1998) in Pamela Benson and Roger Openshaw (eds.). *New Horizons for New Zealand Social Studies.* Massey University: ERDC Press, pp. 83–102.

'The National Identity of Australia' (1999) in R. Brown (ed.). *The No Case Papers.* Sydney: Standard Publishing House.

'The Universal and the Particular in Education' (1999) in *International Journal of Social Education,* 14 (2), pp. 72–86.

'Republicanism and the Repudiation of post-1788 Australia' in Samuel Griffiths Society (1999). *Proceedings of the Tenth Conference of the Samuel Griffith Society,* Brisbane, pp. 187–228.

'A Short Critique of Indigenous Education' (2013) in Rhonda Craven, Anthony Dillon, and Nigel Parbury (eds.). *In Black and White: Australians All at the Crossroads.* Melbourne: Connor Court, pp. 229–47.

Guest Editorship

International Journal of Social Education (1994), 9 (1), p. 104. Special number on 'Cultural Literacy' with 'Guest Editor's Introduction', pp. vii–ix.

International Journal of Social Education (1999), 14 (2), p. 100. Special number on 'Universal Significance and Local Relevance' with 'Guest Editor's Introduction', pp. vii–ix.

Commissioned Reports and Assessments

The Education of Females in South Australia (1980). Commissioned Assessmen of Submissions Received by the Inquiry into Teacher Education in South Australi (Gilding Committee).

Ethnicity and Education: The Significance and Relevance of the Past: Aspirations o Some Ethnic Groups in Australia concerning the Cultural Content of the Curriculum of Schools (1981). Canberra: Educational Research and Development Committee.

The Draft Social Studies Syllabus in the New Zealand Curriculum: A Submission on the Draft (1995). Wellington: Education Forum, pp. 71.

Social Studies in the New Zealand Curriculum: A Submission on the Revised Draf (1996). Wellington, pp.62:

Teacher Education and Training in New Zealand (1997). Wellington: Educatior Forum, pp. 262.

Teacher Education in England and Wales (1999). London: Institute of Economic Affairs, p. 163.

Articles

'School-Based In-Service Training' (1976) in *British Journal of In-Service Education,* 3 (1), pp. 21–29.

'Community Schools and Community Education' (1976) in *Forum for the Advancement of State Education*, 18 (3), pp. 11–18.

'Foundations of Historical Education' (1977) in *Tradition* (History Teachers Association of South Australia), No. 17.

'SEMP Material' (1978) in *SAIT Teachers Journal*, 13 September.

'Relativism, Objectivity and Moral Judgment' (1979) in *British Journal of Educational Studies*, 28 (2), pp. 125–39.

'M.A.C.O.S., S.E.M.P. and the Study of Society in Schools' (1979) in *ACES Review*, 6 (2), pp. 3–7.

A Guide to a Process of Curriculum Development: The Blind Lead the Blind in South Australia' (1979) in *Pivot*, 6 (1), pp. 25–28.

Curriculum Decisions: School Based and Centrally Determined' (1979) in *Pivot*, 6 2), pp 25-27

Why Teach History' (1979) in *Bulletin of Australian Historians Association*, 19, pp. 21–28.

Social Studies in South Australian Primary Schools' (1979) in *ACES Review*, 6 (1), p. 10–14 and 7 (1), pp. 5–8.

Historical Generalization' (1980) in *The History Teacher*, 2, pp. 385–400.

Social Studies in South Australian High Schools' (1980) in *ACES Review*, 7 (3), pp. 5–10.

Teaching Time: Children's Understanding of Time' (1980) in *Teaching History* Historical Association, Great Britain) (27), pp. 31–35.

What History Should We Teach?' (1980) in *Oxford Review of Education*, 6 (2), pp. 157–76.

The Mathematical Education of Girls: Some Feminist Misconceptions' (1980) in *Unicorn (Journal of the Australian College of Education)*, 6 (4), pp. 401–07.

Is the Core Sound?' (1980) in *Quadrant*, November, pp. 14–18.

Attitudes to Ethnic Groups: Reasonable Expectations and Unreasonable Prejudices' 1981) in *Quadrant*, January–February, pp. 10–14.

Morton's Fork, or Having It Both Ways' (1981) in *Quadrant*, April, pp. 10–17.

Gender and Promotion among South Australian Teachers 1950–1979' (1981) in *South Australian Journal of Educational Research*, 1 (3), pp. 44–57.

Curricular Incoherence' (1981) in *ACES Review*, 8 (2), pp. 1–4.

Heritage and Identity' (1981) in *Quadrant*, September, pp. 25–30.

Ethnicity and the Cultural Curriculum of Australian Schools' (1981) in *The Australian History Teacher*, (8), pp. 17–33.

Gramsci and Education' (1981) in *Educational Theory and Philosophy*, 13 (2), pp. 31–42.

'Sexuality and Schools' (1981) in *Australian Family*, 2 (3), pp. 14–21.

'Sexist Stereotypes and School Studies' (1981) in *ACES Review*, 8 (5), pp. 1–5.

'Race Riots in England' (1981) in *Quadrant*, December, pp. 43–51 (reprinted with permission a 'Who Taught the Rioters?' in *Police* (*Monthly Journal of the Police Federation*, UK), July, 1992, pp. 32–37).

'Education for a Multicultural Society: A Policy Statement and a Critique' (1981) in *Australian Quarterly*, Summer, 53 (4), pp. 467–75.

'Discrimination against Women Teachers: Does It Persist?' (1982) in *Australian Journal of Social Issues*, 17 (1), 12–29.

'Parents, Ethnicity and History' (1982) in *Bulletin of Australian Historians Association*, 30, pp. 18–28.

'Mediterranean Studies in History Courses: Some Suggestions' (1982) in *Teaching History*, 16 (1), pp. 55–70.

'Cultural Relativism and Education' (1982) in *ACES Review*, 9 (2), pp. 9–12.

'The Keeves Report's Analysis of South Australian Education' (1982) in *ACES Review*, 9 (4), pp. 5–11 and 9 (5), pp. 7–12.

'The Limits of Curriculum: Reflections on Keeves and into the Eighties' (1982) in *Pivot*, 9 (5), pp. 23–29.

'*Per ardua ad* Nowhere' (1982) in *Quadrant*, May, pp. 95–97.

'Caesar or the Superpowers?' (1982) in *Education News*, 17 (11), pp. 35–39.

'Our Ailing Schools' (1982) in *Bulletin of the National Council for Educational Standards*, (6), pp. 25–30 (reprinted with permission in *Quadrant*, August, pp. 32–37).

'The Unexamined Life' (1982) in *Quadrant*, November, pp. 47–51.

'Australia in 2000' (1982) in *Quadrant*, December, pp. 54–57.

'The Classification of History Syllabuses' (1983) in *Teaching History*, 17 (2), pp. 46–54.

'Clarifying Students' Values' (1983) in *Unicorn*, 9 (1), pp. 34–38.

'Clarifying a New Orthodoxy' (1983) in *Education News*, 18 (5), pp. 42–45.

'Ethnicity and Curriculum Content: The Case of Mediterranean Studies' (1983) in *Curriculum Perspectives*, 3 (1), pp. 7–12.

'(Im)moral Education in South Australia' (1984) in *Journal of Moral Education*, 13(2), pp. 90–100.

'How Can Curricula Be Analyzed? The Case of History Syllabuses' (1984) in *Australian Journal of Education*, 28 (2), 202–11.

'Two Marxisms and the History of Education' (1984) in *History of Education*, 13 (4), pp. 251–70.

'Means and Ends in Education' (1984) in *Canadian Journal of Education*, 9 (1), pp. 66–69.

'Gender, Class and Education' (1984) in *Canadian Journal of Education*, 9 (2), pp. 111–15.

'Liberal Education and Its Enemies' (1984) in *Canadian Journal of Education*, 9(4), pp. 395–411.

'Women in Australian Universities' (1984) in *Quadrant*, January–February, pp. 127–30.

'An Herodotus for Our Time' (1984) in *Quadrant*, March, pp. 80–83.

'Race, Sex and Class in Inner London' (1984) in *The Salisbury Review*, Spring, pp. 33–37.

'Radical Feminism and the Curriculum' (1984) in *The Salisbury Review*, Summer, pp. 4–9.

'Problems Afflicting State Schools' (1984) in *ACES Review*, 11 (4), pp. 1–5.

'Opportunities More Equal than Others' (1984) in *The Bulletin*, 30 October, pp. 64–6.

'How to Guard Children against AIDS' (1984) in *The Bulletin*, 18 December, pp. 36–39.

'Multiculturalism and the Common Curriculum Debate' (1985) in *British Journal of Educational Studies*, xxxiii (1), pp. 35–56.

'The Australian Aborigines and the Human Past' (1985) in *Mankind*, 15 (1), pp. 26–40.

'After the Sheridan Affair: The State of Australian Education' (1985) in *Quadrant*, June, pp. 48–54.

'Blacks, Sport and Schools' (1985) in *The ACHPER National Journal*, June, pp. 18–21

'The Same or Different? Curricular Implications of Feminism and Multiculturalism (1985) in *Journal of Curriculum Studies*, 17 (3), pp. 275–92 (reprinted by permission in *Paspoort Onderwijspraktijk* 1987, 3 (pp. 637–67) under the title of 'Hetzelfde of anders?').

'Down the Multicultural Memory Hole: Ukrainian History in Australian Schools (1985) in *Quadrant*, September, 1985, pp. 23–28.

'Feminism and Co-Education (1985) in *Educational Research and Perspectives*, 12 (2), pp. 55–60.

'The Peace Educators' (1986) in *Quadrant*, January–February, pp. 58–66.

'At the Interface' (1986) in *Times Educational Supplement*, 10 January, p. 22.

'Peace and Education' (1986) in *ACES Review*, 13 (1), pp. 1–6.

'Nazis and the ABC' (1986) in *Quadrant*, June, pp. 31–33.

'The Peace Educators: A Reply to Andrew Mack' (1986) in *Quadrant*, July–August, pp. 19–24.

'Some Problems Concerning Peace Studies' (1986) in *Curriculum Perspectives*, 5 (2), pp. 45–49.

'School Children Fodder in a Feminist War' (1986) in *The Bulletin*, 3 June.

'Feminist Ironies' (1986) in *Times Educational Supplement*, 6 June.

'Discrimination and Women Teachers' (1986) in *The Bulletin*, 15 July.

'It Depends What You Mean by Equal?' (1986) in *Times Educational Supplement*, 22 August.

'Playing at Ideological Two-Up' (1987) in *The Bulletin*, 3 February.

'The Excessive Protests of Andrew Mack' (1987) in *Quadrant*, June, pp. 68–72.

'The Disorientation of Western Education: When Progress Means Regress' (1987) in *Encounter*, 68 (11), pp. 5–15.

Technology and Our Schools: Recent Thinking in South Australia' (1987) in *ACES Review*, 13 (4), pp. 12–15.

The Concept of Progress in Educational Thought: Instrumentalist Theories Considered' (1987) in *Oxford Review of Education*, 13 (2), pp. 141–49.

The Moral Revolution in Our Schools' (1987) in *IPA Review*, 41 (1), pp. 31–34.

The Compassionate Society' (1987) in *Quadrant*, August, pp. 60–64 (reprinted with permission as 'The Social Philosophy of the Compassionate Society' (1987) in *The Salisbury Review*, September, pp. 4–8 (awarded 1987 George Watson prize for best political essay published in Australia)).

Peace Education in South Australia' (1987) in *Quadrant*, October, pp. 57–62.

History Teaching in Bicentennial Australia' (1987) in *History Forum*, December, pp. 17–32.

The Concept of Progress in Marxist Educational Theories' (1988) in *Comparative Education*, 24 (1), pp. 75–89.

Education: Where Do They Go?' in *Quadrant*, April, 1988.

Whither Higher Education?' in *Quadrant*, May, 1988.

Sex Education in Australia Today' (1988) in *ACES Review*, 14 (4), pp. 8–12.

Education for Citizenship in Bicentennial Australia' (1988) in *Quadrant*, August, pp. 29–35.

Education: Which Way Forward' in *Quadrant*, September, 1988

Roll Changes in Australian Schools' (1988) in *Australian Quarterly*, 60 (2), pp. 216–19.

Schools and Child Abuse' (1988) in *Australian Quarterly*, 60 (3), pp. 347–59.

Schools and Child Abuse' in *The Australian Family*, June, pp. 6–25.

Playgrounds for Reform' (1988) in *The Australian*, 6 April.

Reading a Text: The First Book of Samuel' (1989) in *Religious Education*, 84 (3), p. 411–17.

'Schools and Child Abuse: Some Recent Findings' (1989) in *Australian Quarterly* 61 (2), pp. 276–81.

'Parental Changes of School in South Australia' (1989) in *Australian Educational Researcher*, 16 (4), pp. 27–44.

'Enrolments in Australian Schools: An Update' (1989) in *Australian Quarterly*, 6 (4), pp. 498–500.

'Catherine Helen Spence and the Wonderful Century' (1990) in *Quadrant* January–February, pp. 63–67.

'Why Parents are Choosing Independent Schools' (1990) in *Education Monitor*, (3), pp. 23–29.

'The Legacy of a "Racist Murder": Death in the Playground' (1990) in *Encounter* June, pp. 56–62.

'History for Nineteenth Century Australians' (1990) in *History Forum*, August, pp. 25–29.

'The Consequences of State Aid' (1990) in *Education Monitor*, 2 (1), pp. 5–9.

'Moral Education in Some English-Speaking Countries: Antinomian an Fundamentalist Challenges' (1990) in *Journal of Moral Education*, 19 (2), pp. 182–91

'Quality and Schools' (1990) in *Educational Research and Perspectives*, 17 (2), pp. 83–97

'Marcus Clarke and the Significant Past' (1990) in *Victorian Historical Journal*, 6 (4), pp. 270–78.

'Changing Patterns of School Enrolment in Australia' (1990) in *Australian Educational Researcher*, 17 (3), pp. 65–84.

'Educating for a More Law-Abiding Society' (1991) in *Australian Quarterly*, 62 (4 pp. 346–60 (awarded George Watson Essay Prize, 1991).

'Education and the Transmission of Values' (1991) in *Australian Family*, 12 (1), pp. 3–18

'Morals and Education' (1991) in *Quadrant*, April, pp. 54–60.

'Daniel Deniehy and the Significant Past' (1992) in *Journal of the Royal Historical Society of Australia*, 77 (4), April, pp. 40–49.

The Politics of Educational Research' (1992) in *Education Monitor*, Autumn, pp. 32–35.

Rocky Road to the Republic' (1992) in *The Bulletin*, 2 June, pp. 40–42.

The Republic: Why Kenneally Is Wrong' (1992) in *News Weekly*, 31 July, pp. 20–21.

'Alfred Deakin and the Significant Past' (1992) in *Journal of the Royal Australian Historical Society*, 78 (3 and 4), December.

'Obstacles to Liberal Education in Australia' (1993) in *Comparative Education*, 29 (1), pp. 93–105.

'Political Correctness South Australian Style' (1993) in *Education Monitor*, 4 (1), pp. 19–23.

'Science in the Clever Country' (1993) in *Independence (Journal of the Association of Heads of the Independent Schools of Australia)*, 18 (2). pp. 35–39.

'Cricket and the "Crimson Thread of Kinship"' (1993) in *Quadrant*, December, pp. 9–14.

The State and Education' (1994) in *Australian Quarterly*, 66 (1), pp. 58–73.

'Family Influence' (1994) in *Education Monitor*, 5 (2), pp. 3–7.

'Families and Educational Achievement' (1994) in *Independence*, 19 (2), pp. 13–17.

'Historical Literacy' (1994) in *International Journal of Social Education*, 9 (1), pp. 41–54.

'Determining Sacred Sites: The Case of the Hindmarsh Island Bridge' (1995) in *Current Affairs Bulletin*, 71 (5), pp. 4–13.

'An Australian Republic? Light from Fiji' (1995) in *Australia and World Affairs*, (26), Spring, pp. 16–27.

'Families and Education: Reform from Above or Below' (1995) in *International Journal of World Peace*, xii (3), pp. 49–70.

'"Women's Business" at Hindmarsh Island' (1996) in *Australia and World Affairs*, (28), Autumn, pp. 33–43.

'Henry Reynolds and the Mabo Judgment' (1996) in *Australia and World Affairs*, (30), pp. 23–32.

'One Nation for All People' (1996) in *The Australian*, 17 June.

'The Interpretation of Aboriginal Policies: A Riposte to Tim Rouse' (1997) in *Meanjin*, 56 (2), 439–46.

'Problems Afflicting New Zealand Teacher Education' (1997) in *Education Research and Perspectives*, 24 (2), December, pp. 107–139.

'Cultural Variance and the Denial of Moral Regression: A Critique of Piaget and Kohlberg' (1997) in *International Journal of Social Education*, 11 (2), pp. 105–19.

'Saying "Sorry!" about Aboriginal Children' (1998) in *Australia and World Affairs*, 37, pp. 14–23.

'One Nation's Furphy' (1998) in *Journal of Australian Studies*, 57, pp. 23–31.

'Culture in an Iron Lung: Maori Rights and Wrong' (1998) in *Codex*, 5, pp. 18–23.

'The Left and Education' (1998) in *Codex*, 6, pp. 10–29.

'The Continuing Struggle for Educational Ascendancy' (1999) in *Quadrant*, September, pp. 25–32.

'Political Correctness Reconsidered' (2000) in *Quadrant*, June, pp. 29–34.

'"Empowered" But Impoverished: Multiculturalism and Aboriginal Education' (2000) in *Quadrant*, October, pp. 33–43.

'Political Correctness Today' (2000) in *National Observer*, Spring, pp. 33–41.

'Non-Indigenous Australians and Indigenous Autonomy' in *The Australian Journal of Indigenous Education*, 28 (2), pp. 15–19.

'Manning Clark and White Australia' (2001) in *Quadrant*, July–August, pp. 15–21.

'Current Orthodoxy in Aboriginal Education' (2001) in *National Observer*, 50, pp. 20–29.

'Gallipoli – The Facts behind the Myths' (2001–2) in *Endeavour*, pp. 2–3.

'Educational Contestability' (2001) in *Oxford Review of Education*, 27 (3).

'Christmas in Australia' (2001) in *Amity*, 1 (3), pp. 31–33.

'Identifying the Enemy' (2002) in *National Observer*, Winter, pp. 17–25.

'Joseph Furphy and the Aims of Education' (2001) in *Educational Research and Perspectives*, 28 (2), pp. 83–102.

'Sir Walter Crocker at One Hundred' (2002) in *National Observer*, Spring, 54, pp. 45–59.

'Knowledge and Innovation in Education' (2002) in *Quadrant*, March, pp. 60–66.

'Child Sexual Abuse, Real and Unreal' (2002) in *Quadrant*, November, pp. 30–34.

'Aboriginal Children and Mathematics' in *Quadrant*, November, pp. 56–61.

'The Future of Teacher Education' (2004) in *Quadrant*, April, pp. 41–47.

'Legacies of an Historian' (2001) in *Quadrant*, November, pp. 78–82.

'Communist Teachers within the NUT: The Case of "Middlesex Secondary"' (2004) in *History of Education Researcher*, 73, May, pp. 34–43.

'What History Should We Teach?' (2005) in *Quadrant*, January–February, pp. 68–71.

'Twenty-One Reasons to Vote against John Howard' (2007) in *Quadrant*, April, pp. 58–59.

'Cannibalism: A White Colonist Fiction?' (2008) in *Quadrant*, May, pp. 87–90.

'On the Reading of Books' (2008) in *Quadrant*, December, pp. 90–95.

'The Incivility of Marcia Langton' (2010) in *Quadrant*, April, pp. 69–82.

Lukács and Gramsci, 'Curiously Conservative Radicals' (2011) in *Quarterly Review*, 5 (1), Spring, pp. 12–22.

'The Universal Class' and unintended consequences(2011) in *Quarterly Review*, 5 (3), Autumn., pp. 20-31.

'The Emperor Needs a Wife' (2011) in *Quadrant*, May, pp. 74–76.

'Pride and Self-Esteem' (2011) in *Journal of Religious Education*, 59 (4), pp. 59-62.

Reviews

'What Should We Conserve? A Review of *New Conservatism in Australia,* edited by Robert Manne (1983) in *Quadrant,* May, pp. 63–68.

'What a Dilemma!' (1983) in *Quadrant,* December, pp. 92–95 (essay-review of B. Grant: *The Australian Dilemma: A New Kind of Western Society*).

'Antony Flew on Social Thinking' (1986) in *Quadrant,* September, pp. 76–79.

'Groucho Marx and the Girls of Adelaide' (1985) in *ACES Review,* 12 (1), pp. 18–19 (review of Mackinnon, A. *One Foot on the Ladder)*

'A Nation Apart' (1984) in *Quadrant,* January–February, pp. 140–42 (essay-review of J. McLaren: *Essays in Honour of Andrew Fabinyi*), 8.

'Medieval Mysteries' (1985) in *Quadrant,* January, pp. 141–43.

'Above the Ruck: A Review of D. A. Low (ed.). Keith Hancock: The Legacies of an Historian' (2001) in *Quadrant,* November, pp. 78–82.

'Review of Miller, P. "Long Division"' (1987) in *ACES Review,* 14 (1), pp. 14–15.

'Review of Sharp. Rachel 'Capitalist crisis and schooling' (1988) in *Education Research and Perspectives,* 14 (2), pp. 124-125.

'The Rocky Horror Shore: A Reappraisal of Robert Hughes' (1988) in *Quadrant,* April, pp. 35–37.

'All Those Peaceful, Happy Natives' (a review of *The Culture Cult* by Roger Sandall) (2001) in *Quadrant,* December, pp. 104–06.

'Pyrrhic Victory' (2004). Review of *Victory* (2004) in *Quadrant,* June, pp. 68–70.

Endnotes

1   See Allport, G.W. (1946) *The Nature of Prejudice*. Cambridge Mass, Addison-Wesley, pp. VI-VII

2   Collingwood, R. G. (1962). *The Idea of History*. Oxford: Oxford University Press, p. 199.

3   Elton, Geoffrey (1967). *The Practice of History*. Sydney: Sydney University Press, p. 13.

4   Quoted by C.V. Wedgwood (1960) in *Truth and Opinion*: London: Collins, p. 27. Original source: Leopold Von Ranke, 1854, *On the Epochs of Modern History*, Berlin, p. 22.

5   Wedgwood,1960, p,27, citing Von Ranke, L. (1854)

6   Simpson, K. (1982) 'The Identity of Educational Theories' in *Educational Philosophy and Theory*, 14 (2), pp. 51-59.

7   Roberts, A. (2009). *Masters and Commanders*. New York: HarperCollins, p. 118.

8   Thucydides, *The Histories*, 1, 23.

9   Thucydides, 3, 10.

10 Thucydides, 4, 14.

11 Ignatieff, M. (1998). *A Life of Isaiah Berlin*. New York: Metropolitan Books, p. 202 ff.

12 Hume, David (1778). *The History of England*, Ch. LIII.

13 Marx, Karl (1909). *Preface to a Contribution to the Critique of Political Economy* (trans. N. I. Stone). London.

14 Engels, F. (1942). Letter to J. Bloch, September 21, 1890, in Torr, Dona (ed. and trans.). *Marx and Engels: Selected Correspondence, 1846–1895*. New York: International Publishers.

15 Muggeridge, M. (1972).*Chronicles of Wasted Time: The Green Stick*. London: Collins, p. 15.

16 *Ecclesiastes* 1: 5–9.

17 Cited by Leff, G. (1962). *Medieval Thought: St Augustine to Ockham*. Harmondsworth: Penguin Books, p. 135.

18   Coulton, G.G. (1930) *Ten Medieval Studies*, London: Beacon Press, p. 37.

19 Cited in Trethewey, A.R. (1968) 'The Rise and Fall of History in the Victorian State Primary School: a Study of Response to Changing Social Purposes' in *Australian Journal of Education*, XII (3), 266

20 *Australasian*, 18 May 1872.

21 For fuller discussion see Barcan, A.(1977). 'A History of History Teaching' in N. Littl and J. Mackinolty (Eds). *A New Look at History Teaching.* Sydney: History Teacher Association of New South Wales.

22 Engels, F. (1942). 'Letter to Karl Marx, 23 May 1851', in *Marxist Library.* New York International Publishers, p. 37.

23 Vansittart, R. (1941). *Black Record: Germans Past and Present.* London: Loder, p. 41.

24 The passages from Michelet, Michiewitz, Fichte, and Mazzini are cited in Namier, Sir L (1962). *Lost Supremacies.* New York: Penguin Books, pp. 57–62.

25 Michelet, J. (1898). *Histoire de France au Moyen Age: Jeanne d'Arc. Paris,* p. 269. Cited by Clark, G. Kitson (1967). *The Critical Historian.* London: Methuen, p. ix.

26 Butterfield, Herbert (1931). *Whig Interpretations of History.* London: Bell, p. 108.

27 Oakeshott, Michael (1962). *Rationalism in Politics and Other* Essays. London: Methuen p. 165.

28 Stove, David (1993). *Cricket and Republicanism and Other Essays.* Sydney: Quakers Hill Press, Ch. 13.

29 Cited in Ferguson, N. (1997). 'Introduction' to *His Virtual History: Alternatives and Counterfactuals.* London: Picador, p. 34.

30 Hempel, Carl (1959). 'The Function of General Laws in History' in Gardiner, P. (ed.), *Theories of History.* New York: Free Press.

31 Namier, Lewis (1962). *Vanished Supremacies.* Harmondsworth: Penguin Books, p. 203.

32 Greater knowledge of other peoples does not always leads to good will and toleration of differences. Mutual dislike between neighboring peoples is common.

33 Acton, Lord (1904). *Life and Letters of Mandell Creighton,* Vol. 1. London: Longmans, Green, p. 372.

34 Popper, K. (1957). *The Poverty of Historicism.* London: Routledge, p.v.

35 Flew, A. (1990) 'Popper and Historical Necessity' in *Philosophy,* January, Vol 65 (no. 251). Pp. 54-60.

36 Carr, E.H. (1961) *What Is History?.* London: Macmillan, pp. 87-88

37 The title of Elector was given to the holders of the seven offices that chose the Holy Roman Emperor of the German People. By the sixteenth century there were seven Electors, four were lay: the Dukes of Saxony and Brandenburg, the King of Bohemia and the Prince Palatine of the Rhine; the other three were Princes of the Church: the Archbishops of Mainz, Cologne and Triers.,

38 His fame was such that the well-known tune to which we sing the words 'For he's a jolly good fellow' was sung in French as Malbrouk s'en va en guerre

39 Clark, M. C. H, (1968). *A History of Australia,* Vol. 1. Melbourne: University of Melbourne Press, p. 3.

40 Clark, 1968, p. 4.

41 Howells, W. (1954). *Man in the Beginning.* London: Bell, p. 315.

42 Childe, V. G. (1958). *The Prehistory of European Society.* Harmondsworth: Penguin Books, p. 34.

43 Maddock, K. (1995). 'Prehistory, Power and Pessimism' in P. Gathercole et al. (eds.). *Childe and Australia*. St. Lucia: University of Queensland Press, p. 112.

44 Berndt, R.M. and Berndt, C.H. (1964). *The World of the First Australians*. Sydney: Ure Smith, p.422-3.

45 Cited in D. J. Mulvaney, 'The Australian Aborigines, 1606–1929: Opinion and Fieldwork, 1859–1929' in *Historical Studies*, 8 (1971), 295.

46 Banks, Sir J. (1962). *The Endeavour Journals of Joseph Banks, 1769–1771* (ed. J. Beaglehole). 2 vols. Sydney: Trustees of the Public Library of New South Wales in association with Angus & Robertson, Vol. 1, p. 305.

47 Cook, J. (1955). *The Journals of Captain James Cook: The Voyage of the Endeavour, 1768–1771*, Vol. 1. (ed. J. Beaglehole). Cambridge: Hakluyt Society, pp. xxi–xxii.

48 Locke, J. (1965). *The Treatises on Government* (ed. P. Laslett). New York: New American Library, pp. 321 and 341.

49 .*Sydney Herald*, 7 November 1838.

50 Cited in Russell, P. (2010). *Savage or Civilised? Manners in Colonial Australia*. Sydney: University of New South Wales Press, p. 31

51 Reynolds, H. (1981). *The Other Side of the Frontier: An Interpretation of the Aboriginal Response to the Invasion and Settlement of Australia*. Townsville: James Cook University, pp. 56-7.

52 Eliade, M. (1960). *Birth, Dreams and Mysteries*. London: Harvill Press.

53 Thompson, D. F. (1949). *Economic Structure and the Ceremonial Exchange*. Melbourne: University of Melbourne Press.

54 Berndt, R. M. & C. M. (1970). *Man, Land and Myth in North Australia: the Gunwinggu People*. Sydney: Ure Smith, pp. 5; 17.

55 Maddock, K. (1988). 'Myth, history and a sense of oneself' in J.R. Beckett (ed) . . . *Past and Present: The Construction of Aboriginality*. Canberra: Aboriginal Studies Press.

56 Reynolds, H., 1981, pp. 39-41.

57 Stanner, W.E.H., 'Continuity and Change among the Aborigines' in *Australian Journal of Science*, XXI (1958–9), 100–2; (1979). *White Man Got No Dreaming: Essays 1938–1973*. Canberra: Australian National University Press, pp. 42–5.

58 R. Keynes (ed.). (1988). *Charles Darwin's Beagle Diary*. Cambridge: Cambridge University Press, p. 399.

59 Grey, G. (2003). 'Report Upon the Best Means of Promoting the Civilisation of the Aboriginal Inhabitants of Australia' enclosed in *Russell to Hobson, 9 December 1840, GBPP, 1841/311*, pp. 43–4, cited in Ward, No. 37.

60 Earl Grey, (2003). *Minute on Robe to Colonial Office, 10 July 1845, CO/59*, cited in Ward, No. 73.

61 Hutt to Russell, (2003). 10 July 1841, CO 18/28, ff. 53–4, cited in Ward,

62 Stephen to Colonial Secretary, (2003). 1 July 1845, CO/209/35, cited in Ward, No. 75.

63 Reynolds, H. (1993). 'Native Title and Pastoral Leases' in A. Stephenson and S.Ratnapala (Eds). *Mabo: A Judicial Revolution*. St. Lucia: University of Queensland Press, p. 125.

64 Reynolds, 1993, p. 127.

65   ALR, (1992). p. 105.

66   A.L.R.(1992), p. 111.

67   Clark, 1968. pp. 109–10.

68   Stanley to Fitzroy, 13 August 1844, GBPP, 1845/1.1, cited in D Ward (2003) 'Savage customs' and 'civilized laws': British attitudes to legal pluralism in Australasia, c. 1830–48, *London Papers in Australian Studies*, no. 21.

69   Russell to Hobson, (2003). 9 December 1840, GBPP, 1841/311, p. 27, cited in Ward, No. 22.

70   Clark, C. M. H. (1973). *A History of Australia III: The Beginning of an Australian Civilisation, 1824–1851*. Melbourne: Melbourne University Press, p. III.

71   See. Reynolds, H. (1972). *Aborigines and Settlers: The Australian Experience, 1788–1939*. Stanmore: Cassell Australia, pp. 109–10.

72   Cited in Yarwood, A. T. and Knowling, M. J. (1982). *Race Relations in Australia: A History*. Sydney: Methuen, p. 66.

73   Reynolds, H. (1978). *Race Relations in North Queensland*. Townsville: James Cook University, p. 110.

74   Mulvaney, 1971, pp. 1–2, 38, and 45.

75   *The West Australian*, 10 March 1928.

76   Letter of William Cooper, Honorary Secretary, Australian Aborigines League, to Minister for the Interior, 22 February 1936, cited in R. McGregor, 'Protest and Progress: Aboriginal Activism in the 1930s' in *Australian Historical Studies*, 101 (October 1993), 556.

77   McGregor, 1993, p. 568.

78   Berndt, R. M. and Berndt, C. H. with Stanton, J. E. (1993). *The World That Was: The Yaraldi of the Murray River and the Lakes, South Australia*. Melbourne: Melbourne University Press at the Miegunyah Press, p. 13.

79   Saunders, C. (1994). *Report to the Minister for Aboriginal and Torres Strait Islander Affairs on the Significant Aboriginal Area in the Vicinity of Goolwa and Hindmarsh (Kumarangk) Island*. Melbourne: Centre for Comparative Constitutional Studies, University of Melbourne, p. 37.

80   Report of the Hindmarsh Island Bridge Royal Commission (RC) (1995). Adelaide: South Australian Government Printer, pp. 103–5 and 292.

81   L. O'Brien and G. Williams (April 1992). 'The Cultural Significance of the Onkaparinga River' in *Kaurna Higher Education Journal*, 2, 67–70.

82   RC, pp. 107–8 and 292.

83   Saunders, 1994, p. 31.

84   *RC* pp. 111–13.

85   RC, p. 293.

86   RC, pp. 156–7.

87   Lucas, R. (1996) 'The Failure of Anthropology' in *Journal of Australian Studies*, 48, 45.

88   Lucas, 1996, p. 46.

89   RC, pp. 123–30 and 294.

[90]   RC, p. 295.
[91]   RC, pp. 134–6 and 295.
[92]   Saunders, (1994). p. 23.
[93]   Saunders, p. 24.
[94]   RC, p. 65.
[95]   RC, p. 296.
[96]   RC, p. 160.
[97]   RC, pp. 145–7.
[98]   Saunders, (1994). p. 26.
[99]   Saunders, (1994) p. 31.
[100] RC, p. 161.
[101] RC, pp. 168–74.
[102] RC, pp. 175–7.
[103] RC, pp. 183–5.
[104] RC, p. 161.
[105] RC, p. 234.
[106] RC, p. 292.
[107] Fergie, D., (1996). 'Secret Envelopes and Inferential Tautologies' in *Journal of Australian Studies*, 48, 13.
[108] Fergie, 1996. p. 23.
[109] Wilson, D., (1996). 'Telling the Truth: A Dissident Aboriginal Voice' in *IPA Review*, 49 (1), 43.
[110] *Adelaide Review*, January 1996.
[111] Clarke, B. A. and Sumner, K. (1997). *Kumarangk—Hindmarsh Island: Whose Truth?* Adelaide: Uniting Church of South Australia, p. 38.
[112] *Uniting Church Newspaper New Times*, July 1995.
[113] RC, pp. 179–82.
[114] Saunders, (1994). p. 41.
[115] Saunders, (1994). p. 42.
[116] RC, pp. 243–50.
[117] Lucas, (1996). p. 48.
[118] Bell, D. (1998). *Ngarrindjeri Wurruwarrin: A World At Is, Was, and Will Be.* North Melbourne: Spinifex, p. 259.
[119] Bell, (1998). p. 268.
[120] Bell, (1998). p. 256.
[121] Bell, (1998). p. 270.
[122] Bell, (1998). p. 267.
[123] Bell, (1998). pp. 57–8.
[124] Bell, (1998). p. 296.
[125] Bell, (1998). p. 309.
[126] Bell, (1998). p. 310.
[127] Bell, (1998). p. 318.

128 Bell, (1998). p. 332.

129 Bell, (1998). pp. 561–2.

130 SA Department of Education (1990). *The Ngarrindjeri People: Aboriginal People of the River Murray, Lakes and Coorong.* Adelaide: Department of Education, p. 51.

131 Butlin, N, (1985) 'Reply to Charles Wilson and Hugh Morgan' in *Quadrant*, June, pp 30-33, Professor Butlin's arguments are set out fully in 'Macassans and Aboriginal Smallpox: the "1789" and "1929" epidemics' in *Historical Studies,* 21, April, 1985, pp 315-335,

132 Tatz, C. (1999). *Genocide in Australia.* Canberra: Aboriginal Studies Press.

133 Clendinnen, 2001: 26 (Cited in Windschuttle, Keith (2006) 'The Return of Postmodernism in Aboriginal History' in *Quadran*t, April, p. 11..

134 Attwood, B. (2005). Telling the Truth about Aboriginal History'. Crow's Nest: Allen and Unwin, pp. 88-89.

135 Neville A.O. (1937). In conference transcript, *Aboriginal Welfare: Initial Conference of Commonwealth and State Aboriginal Authorities* held at Canberra, 21–23 April, Government Printer, Canberra, p. 11 (cited in Windschuttle, 2006, p..

136 *Aboriginal Welfare, (*1937), cited in Windschuttle.

137 *C. E. Cook to Administrator of the Northern Territory, 7 February 1933,* National Archives of Australia, Commonwealth Records Series, Department of the Interior file A659/1; 1940/1/408, cited in Windschuttle.

138 Levi-Strauss, C. (1974). *Tristes Topiques.* New York: Athenaeum, p. 89.

139 Todorov, T. (1984). *The Conquest of America.* New York: Harper & Row, p. 5.

140 Frederickson, G. (2002). *Racism: A Short History.* Princeton, NJ: Princeton University Press.

141 Snow, P. (1988). *The Star Raft: China's Encounter with Africa.* Ithaca, NY: Cornell University Press, 3–4, 14, 33, 189, cited in D'Souza, D. (1995). *The End of Racism.* New York: Free Press, p. 47.

142 Moses, A.D. (2001). 'Coming to Terms with Genocidal Pasts in a Comparative Perspective' in *Aboriginal History*, 25, 104.

143 Moses, A.D. (2000). *Journal of Genocide Research*, 93. Cited in Windschuttle, 2006, p. 9.

144 Moses, 2001, 102 (cited in Windschuttle, 2006, p, 9.

145 Curthoys, A. and Docker, J. (2001) *'Introduction' to Aboriginal History*, Special Issue on Genocide edited by them (cited in Windschuttle, 2006, p. 12)

146 The recorded conversation was organised in 2002 by the *Australian Humanities Review.*

147 Docker, 2008, p. 18.

148 Macintyre, S. (1991). *A Colonial Liberalism.* Melbourne: Melbourne University Press, pp. 211–12.

149 Ryan, L. (1996) *The Original Tasmanians.* Sydney: Allen and Unwin, second edition, p.255. (cited in Windschuttle, 2006, p. 13)

150 Cited in Windschuttle, 2006, p. 9.

151 See D'Souza,1995 . . . p. 118 et seq.

152 S. Parkinson, (1773). *A Journal of a Voyage to the South Seas*, 23.

153   J. Banks, *Endeavour Journal*, II: 30.

154   Powelson, J.P. (1994). *Centuries of Economic Endeavour*. Ann Arbor: University of Michigan Press (cited in R. Sandall, 2001, *The Culture Cult*. Boulder: Westfield Press, P. 172).

155   Cited in Yarwood, A.T. (1972) *Attitudes to Non-European Immigration*. Melbourne: Cassell, p. 32.

156   Intercolonial Trades and Labor Unions Congress of Australasia: *Official Report of Third Congress*. (1885), p. 97.

157   Intercolonial Trades and Labor Unions Congress of Australasia: *Official Report of First Congress*. (1879), pp. xi–xii.

158   Cited in Curthoys, A. (1973) *Race and Ethnicity*: PhD Thesis, Macquarie University and A.T. Yarwood & M.J. Knowling, 1982, *Race Relations in Australia: A History*. Melbourne: Methuen, p. 174.

159   Curthoys, A. (2003) 'Liberalism and Exclusionism, A Pre-History of the White Australia Policy' in L Jayasuriya et al. (Eds). *Legacies of White Australia*. University of Western Australia Press, pp. 16–7.

160   Cited in C. Pearl (1972). *Brilliant Dan Deniehy*. Melbourne: Nelson, P. 73.

161   *Ibid*.

162   *Albany Observer*, (1890) cited in *Henry Lawson: Autobiographical and Other Writings 1887–1922* (ed. Colin Roderick), Sydney, 1972, pp. 16–7.

163   *The Bulletin*, 8 December, 1900.

164   Pearson, C.H. (1891) *National Life and Character*, in Turner (ed.), 1968, pp. 164–5.

165   Baldwin Spencer in D.J. Mulvaney and J.H. Calaby, 'So Much That *Is* New: Baldwin Spencer 1860–1929, a biography', Melbourne University Press, 1985, p. 281.

166   Yarwood (1972) pp. 25–6.

167   *Sydney Morning Herald*, 4 June 1888 (cited in W. Phillips: *James Jefferis: Prophet of Federation*. 1993: Australian Scholarly Publishing, p. 175).

168   Markey, R. (1978) in A. Curthoys and A. Markus, (Eds). *Who are our Enemies? Racism and the Working Class in Australia*. Sydney: Hale and Ironmonger, p. 69.

169   Palmer, Vance (1962) *National Portraits*. Melbourne University Press p.124/

170   Tennant, K. (1953) *Australia: Her Story*. London: Macmillan, pp. 119; 205–6; 209.

171   Ward. R. (1967) *Australia*. Sydney: Ure Smith. pp. 159–61; 73.

172   Curthoys (1978) p. 55,

173   *The Boomerang*, 7 March 1888.

174   Hirst, J. (1988) *The Strange Birth of Colonial Democracy*. Sydney: Allen & Unwin, p. 159.

175   Burgmann, V. (1978) 'Responses to Immigration in the Nineteenth Century' in Curthoys and Markus, (Eds).

176   Evans, R. (1999) *Fighting Words: Writing About Race*. St Lucia: University of Queensland Press, p.79.

177   Reynolds, H. (2003) *North of Capricorn: The Untold Story of Australia's North*. Sydney: Allen & Unwin. (Cited in Windschuttle, K. (2004) *The White Australia Policy*. Sydney: Macleay Press, p. 7.)

178 Willard M. (1923) *History of the White Australia Policy*. Melbourne University Press, p 191.

179 Windschuttle (2004) pp. 76–82.

180 Nile, R. and Walker, D. (1988) 'Marketing the Literary Imagination: Production o Australian Literature, 1915–1965' in L. Hergenham (Ed.) *New Literary History o Australia*. Ringwood: Penguin, p.296.

181 Windschuttle (2004) p. 59.

182 Windschuttle (2004,) p. 91.

183 Commonwealth Parliamentary Debates, Volume IV, pp. 5168, 5812.

184 Meaney, N. (1999) *Towards a New Vision: Australia and Japan through 100 years* Sydney: Kangaroo Press, p. 18 (cited in Windschuttle, 2004, p.287).

185 Walker, D, 'Race Building and Discipline of White Australia' in Jayasuriya *et al*. (Eds), p. 34 (Cited in Windschuttle, 2004, p. 287.)

186 Windschuttle (2004) pp. 287, 289.

187 Sherington, G. (1980) *Australia's Immigrants*. Sydney: Allen & Unwin, p. 91.

188 Windschuttle (2004) p. 8.

189 *CPD*, Volume IV, pp.4638–9.

190 *CPD,* Volume IV, p. 4633.

191 Private communication. I am grateful to Dr Sammut for helpful suggestions about this paper.

192 *CPD*, Volume I., p. 4631.

193 *CPD*, Volume IV, p. 7246.

194 *CPD,* Volume IV, pp. 4839–40.

195 *CPD*, Volume IV, p. 5153.

196 *CPD,* Volume IV, p. 7235.

197 *CPD,* Volume IV, p. 4832.

198 *CPD,* Volume VI, p. 7174.

199 *CPD*, Volume IV, p. 4804–6; 4811.

200 Cited in Souter, G. (1976). *Lion and Kangaroo: The Initiation of Australia*. William Collins, pp. 86; 88.

201 Cited in Gascoigne, J. (2002). *The Enlightenment and the Origins of European Australia,* Cambridge University Press, p.164.

202 *Personal communication.*

203 *NSW Parliamentary Debates,* 21 March, 1899, p. 751.

204 *Daily Telegraph*, 30 October 1909, (cited in M. Booker (1980). *The Great Professional: A Study of W.M. Hughes.* Sydney: McGraw-Hill, p. 165.

205 *Imperial War Cabinet Minutes,* 26 November 1918, p. 5 (cited in Booker), 1980, pp. 258–9.

206 Moses, D. (2005) 'Windschuttle, History Warriors and Real Historians' in *Online Opinion,* 11 April.

207 Kendall, T. (2007) *Federation and the Geographies of Whiteness:* Presented to Australian Parliamentary Fellowship Work-in-Progress Seminar, 19 September.

208 Sammut, J. (2005) 'The Long Slow Demise of the White Australia Policy' in *Quadrant*, November, p. 42.

209 Windschuttle (2004) p. 9.

210 *Westralian Worker*, 9 November, 1923.

211 *Westralian Worker*, 18 January 1924.

212 McGregor, R. 'Whiteness in the Tropics' in *A Queensland Historical Atlas*.

213 *Advertiser*, 5 June 1875 (cited in Phillips, 1993, p.176.).

214 Biber, K. (2005) 'Cannibals and Colonialism'. *Sydney Law Review*, 27 (4). p, 629/

215 Lestringant, F. (1997) *Cannibals: The Discovery and Representation of the Cannibal from Columbus to Jules Verne*. Trans. Rosemary Morris. Berkeley: University of California Press, p. 7

216 Several citations are taken from contributions made on an Internet Website under the heading of 'Cannibalism in Australia', on which there was lively but brief interest.

217 Roth, W. E. (1897). *Ethnological studies among the north-west central* Queensland Aborigines. Brisbane: Government Printer, p. 166

218 Roth, W. E. (1907*) Burial ceremonies and disposal of the dead*. Sydney: Records of the Australian Museum, VI (5)m pp. 398-401/.

219 Howitt, A. W. (1904). *The native tribes of South-East Australia*. London: Macmillan.

220 Spencer, B. (1928). *Wanderings in Wild Australia*. 2 vols. London: Macmillan Vol.1, p. 203.

221 McConnel, U. (1937). 'Mourning Ritual among the tribes of Cape York Peninsula' in *Oceania*, VII (3)., pp. 364-8

222 Elkin, A. P. (1937). 'Beliefs and practices connected with death in north-eastern and western South Australia' in *Oceania*, VII (3), p.283-5; Elkin, A. P. (1954) *The Australian Aborigines: how to understand them*. Sydney: Angus & Robertson., p 317.

223 Berndt, R.M. and Berndt, C.H. (1964). *The World of the First Australians*. Sydney: Ure Smith. Republished in 1999 by Aboriginal Studies Press. (1999. pp. 467-470).

224 Clark, C.M.H. (1973) *A History of Australia III: The Beginning of an Australian Civilization 1824-1851*. Melbourne University Press, p.170;

225 Clark, C.M.H. (1978) *A History of Australia IV: The Earth Abideth For Ever 1851-1888*. Melbourne University Press. pp. 350-3.

226 Crikey, 16 November 2009

227 Crikey, 22 October 2009

228 Crikey, 10 June 2010

229 Crikey, 28 June 2010

230 Crikey, 28 January 2010

231 See Warin, Jenness (with James Franklin). (2007*) Remote Aboriginal Communities: Why the trade in girls and other human rights abuses remain hidden*. The Bennelong Society; and Jarrett, Stephanie (2013*) Liberating Aboriginal People from Violence*. Melbourne: Connor Court.

232 *Live Chat Programme*, September 6.

233 Langton, M. et al., '*Too Much Sorry Business: Report of the Aboriginal Issues Unit of the Northern Territory'*. S, Canberra.

234   Langton, (2008), M. The End of Big Men Politics' in *Griffith Review*, 19.'

235   Reynolds,1981., p. 23.

236   Reynolds, 1981, p. 40

237   Reynolds, H. (1987a). *Frontier: Aborigines, Settlers and Land.* Sydney: Allen & Unwin, p. 30. See Chapter 3 above.

238   Reynolds, 1987a,. p 108.

239   See Chapter 3.

240   Reynolds, 1981, pp. 39-41.

241   Reynolds, H. (1972) *Aborigines and Settlers. The Australian Experience 1788-1939.* Cassell Australia, p. 4; Reynolds, 1972, p. 57.

242   Reynolds, 1982, p. 133.

243   Reynolds, H. (1987b). *The Law of the Land.* Melbourne: Penguin Books Australia, pp. 12–13.

244   Reynolds. 1987a, p. 4

245   Reynolds, 1987b, p. 33.

246   Reynolds, 1987b, p. 22.

247   Reynolds, 1987a, p. 3

For these and similar statements as to the absence of Native Title see Reynolds, H, (1987b) *The Law of the Land,* pp. 3; 7, 8, 17; 19; 27; Reynolds, H. (1987a*). Frontier: Aborigines, Settlers and Land,* Allen & Unwin, pp. 144, 156; Reynolds, H, (1992), *Law of the Land.* Penguin: Ringwood, Victoria, 2nd Edition, pp. 8; 9; Reynolds, H (1993). 'Native Title and Pastoral Leases' in A, Stephenson & S, Ratnapala (Eds) *Mabo: A Judicial Revolution.* St Lucia; University of Queensland Press, pp. 128; 129.

248   Reynolds, 1987b, p. 144.

249   Reynolds, 1981, p. 168.

250   Reynolds,1987a, pp. 158-9.

251   Reynolds, 1982, pp. 69–70.

252   107 A.L.R. 1 (1992), p. 82.

253   Neill, Rosemary (2020) *White Out: How politics is killing black Australia.* Allen & Unwin, pp. 44-5

254   Kenny, Chris (1996). *Women's Business: The story behind the Hindmarsh Island affair,* Sydney: *Duffy & Snellgrove*

255   Townsend, H. E. H. and Britten, E. M. (1973). *Multicultural Education: Need and Invention.* London: Evans/Methuen Educational, p. 7.

256   C. Steedman, (1984). 'Battlegrounds: History in Primary Schools' in *History Workshop Journal,* 17, 109.

257   Willis, P. (1977). *Learning to Labour.* Farnborough: Saxon House, p. 175.

258   Willis, 1977, p. 178.

259   A. G. Kiloskov, (1983). 'Teaching History on the Soviet Secondary General Education School' in *Teaching History,* 37, 12–16.

260   ILEA (1983). *Race, Sex and Class*, p. 8.

61 I had intended to portray the greatest Empress, Theodora, wife of Justinian, using the two conflicting versions of her life written by Procopius, but my resolution failed me. Interested readers should read Robert Graves' novels that centre on Belisarius and, if still strong in the stomach, proceed to *The Secret History* by Procopius.

62 Voltaire. *The Age of Louis XIV and other Selected Writings* (trans. and Ed. J.H. Brumfitt) New York, p. 261

63 Muggeridge, M. (1972).*Chronicles of Wasted Time: The Green* Stick. London: Collins, pp. 46-7.

264 Crocker, Sir Walter (1981. *Travelling Back: The Memoirs of Sir Walter Cocker.* Melbourne: Macmillan

265 Muggeridge, 1972, pp.205 ff.

266 Crocker, 1981, p. 70.

267 Muggeridge, M. (1973) *Chronicles of Wasted Time: The Infernal Grove,* London: Purnell, p. 50.

268 Amis, Kingsley (1991) *Memoirs,* London: Hutchinson, p. 231.

269 Miles Franklin (in association with Kate Baker), *Joseph Furphy: The Legend of a Man and his Book*, Sydney, 1944, p. 3.

270 Franklin, 1944, pp. 164; 127.

271 Vance Palmer, *Preface to Tom Collins' Such is Life,* third edition (abridged), London, 1937.

272 Lloyd Ross, 'Socialist Ideals: Comments on *Rigby's Romance'*, *Meanjin Papers*, 1947, 6 (1), p. 40.

273 Ian Turner (1954) *Communist Review,* June, p. 7.

274 J K Ewers, *Tell the People: An examination of the little-known writings of Joseph Furphy (Tom Collins) in the light of their value or Australia today,* Sydney, 1943, p.12.

275 C M H Clark, 'Letter to Tom Collins', *Meanjin Papers*, 1943, II (3), pp. 40-1.

276 Furphy, J, (1948) *The Buln-Buln and the Brolga and Other Stories* (Sydney: Angus & Robertson, pp. 163 ff. (from now BB)

277 'Tom Collins' (Joseph. Furphy) *Rigby's Romance,* Adelaide, 1971, p. 212.(RR)

278 *Letter from Joseph Furphy to Kate Baker, 24 October* 11910, NLA MSS 2022.

279 *The Bulletin,* 23 Feb 1911.

280 J Barnes (ed), *Portable Australian Authors: Joseph Furphy,* St. Lucia, Queensland, 1981, pp. 377-8.

281 Furphy, J (1903) *Such Is Life,* Sydney: *The Bulletin Publishing Company*, pp. 292; 226.

282 Barnes, 1981, pp. 379-81.

283 Furphy, 1981, p, 91.

284 Furphy, 1981 p. 132.

285 Furphy, 1981, p. 88.

286 Furphy, 1903, p. 142

287 RR, p. 132

288 x, p.241.

289 BB, pp.179 ff.

290   RR. pp. 37ff

291   Furphy, p.5.

292   Furphy, 1903, p.71

293   RR, p. 95

294   Furphy, 1903. P. 87.

295   Furphy, 1903, p. 207.

296   Furphy, 1903, pp. 180; 81.

297   Furphy, 1903, p.207:

298   Barnes, J. p. 376.

299   Keating, P. (1995a). *The Speeches of Paul Keating, Prime Minister* (selected and edited by Mark Ryan). Sydney: Big Picture Publications, p. 189.

300   Keating, (1995a). p. 188.

301   Keating, (1995a). p. 190.

302   Keating, (1995a). p. 210.

303   Booker, (1992). p. ix.

304   Keating, P. J. (1995b) *An Australian Republic: The Way Forward*, Speech of 7 June 1995 (Australian Government Publishing Service), p. 3.

305   Keating, (1995b). p. 2.

306   Turnbull, (1993). p. 13.

307   Keating, 1995a. p.

308   Donald, M. (1993) *Origins of the Modern Mind: Three States in the Evolution of Culture and Cognition.* Cambridge, MA: Harvard University Press, p. 273.

309   Bruner, J. (1986). *Actual Minds, Possible Worlds.* Cambridge, MA: Harvard University Press.

310   Donald, 1991, p. 14.

311   Donald, M. (2001). *A Mind So Rare: The Evolution of Human Consciousness.* New York: W. W. Norton, pp. 10–12.

312   Donald, 1991, p. 275.

Index

X

www.ingramcontent.com/pod-product-compliance
Lightning Source LLC
LaVergne TN
LVHW090158280325
807142LV00008B/43